The Hidde
EAST ANGLIA

including Essex, Suffolk, Norfolk and Cambridgeshire

By
Barbara Vesey

© Travel Publishing Ltd.

Published by:
Travel Publishing Ltd
7a Apollo House, Calleva Park
Aldermaston, Berks, RG7 8TN

ISBN 1-902-00752-2
© Travel Publishing Ltd

First Published:	*1989*	*Fourth Edition:*	*1996*
Second Edition:	*1993*	*Fifth Edition:*	*1999*
Third Edition:	*1994*	*Sixth Edition:*	*2001*

HIDDEN PLACES REGIONAL TITLES

Cambs & Lincolnshire	Chilterns
Cornwall	Derbyshire
Devon	Dorset, Hants & Isle of Wight
East Anglia	Gloucestershire & Wiltshire
Heart of England	Hereford, Worcs & Shropshire
Highlands & Islands	Kent
Lake District & Cumbria	Lancashire & Cheshire
Lincolnshire	Northumberland & Durham
Somerset	Sussex
Thames Valley	Yorkshire

HIDDEN PLACES NATIONAL TITLES

England	Ireland
Scotland	Wales

Printing by: Scotprint, Haddington
Maps by: © Maps in Minutes ™ (2000)
Editor: Barbara Vesey
Cover Design: Lines & Words, Aldermaston
Cover Photographs: Windmill by the River, Hunsett Mill, Norfolk; Thatched Cottage, Arkesden, Essex; Water Splash, Kersey, Suffolk - courtesy of © Britain on View/Stockwave

Foreword

The Hidden Places is a collection of easy to use travel guides taking you, in this instance, on a relaxed but informative tour of East Anglia. The East Anglian counties offer plenty for the visitor to explore in real *Hidden Places* country. **Norfolk** is famous for the Norfolk Broads but has a rich and interesting past, gentle hills as well as expansive horizons, delightful pastoral scenes, a beautiful coastline rich in wildlife and many interesting hidden places to visit. **Suffolk** was made famous by the brush of John Constable and is blessed with incomparable rural beauty which encompasses wide open spaces broken by gentle hills and tidal rivers meandering from a coastline teeming with birdlife. **Essex** contains England's oldest recorded town (Colchester), has a strong maritime tradition, pretty villages, a coastline with attractive estuaries and a rich history going back to Roman times. **Cambridgeshire** is famous for its ancient university and being the birthplace of Oliver Cromwell and Samuel Pepys but offers a wealth of peaceful and attractive countryside with many towns and villages steeped in history which are truly "hidden places".

This edition of *The Hidden Places of East Anglia* is the third title to be published *in full colour*. All *Hidden Places* titles will now be published in colour which will ensure that readers can properly appreciate the attractive scenery and impressive places of interest in Norfolk, Suffolk, Essex and Cambridgeshire and, of course, in the rest of the British Isles. We do hope that you like the new format.

Our books contain a wealth of interesting information on the history, the countryside, the towns and villages and the more established places of interest in the county. But they also promote the more secluded and little known visitor attractions and places to stay, eat and drink many of which are easy to miss unless you know exactly where you are going.

We include hotels, inns, restaurants, public houses, teashops, various types of accommodation, historic houses, museums, gardens, garden centres, craft centres and many other attractions throughout East Anglia, all of which are comprehensively indexed. Most places are accompanied by an attractive photograph and are easily located by using the map at the beginning of each chapter. We do not award merit marks or rankings but concentrate on describing the more interesting, unusual or unique features of each place with the aim of making the reader's stay in the local area an enjoyable and stimulating experience.

Whether you are visiting the area for business or pleasure or in fact are living in the county we do hope that you enjoy reading and using this book. We are always interested in what readers think of places covered (or not covered) in our guides so please do not hesitate to use the reader reaction forms provided to give us your considered comments. We also welcome any general comments which will help us improve the guides themselves. Finally if you are planning to visit any other corner of the British Isles we would like to refer you to the list of other *Hidden Places* titles to be found at the rear of the book and to the Travel Publishing website at www.travelpublishing.co.uk.

Travel Publishing

Regional Map

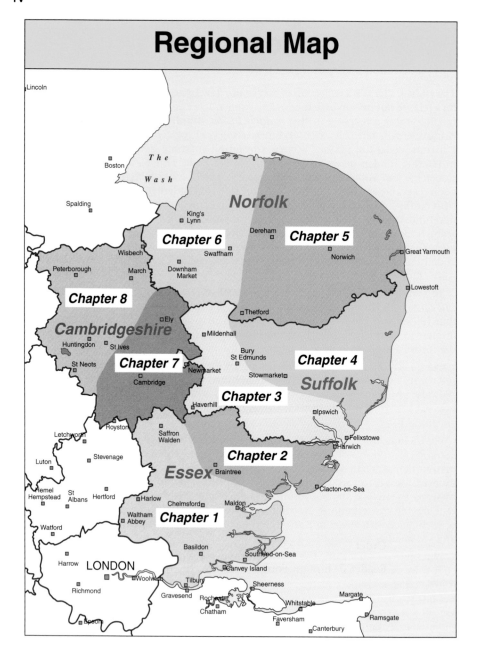

Contents

1 South and West Essex

The small northwest Essex towns of Saffron Walden, Thaxted, Great Dunmow and Stansted Mountfichet are some of the most beautiful and interesting in the country. This area is also home to a wealth of picturesque villages boasting weatherboarded houses and pargetting. The quiet country lanes are perfect for walking, cycling or just exploring. This area also retains three beautiful and historic windmills, at Stansted Mountfichet, Aythorpe Roding and Thaxted.

Visitors to southwest Essex and the Epping Forest may associate it solely with its larger towns, some of the most populous in the county, including Harlow and Brentwood.

All offer excellent shopping and a variety of very good entertainment venues, but focusing on these towns is to overlook the region's wealth of woodland, nature reserves, superb gardens and rural delights.

The Epping Forest dominates much of the far western corner, but all of this part of Essex is rich in countryside, forests and parks, including the magnificent Lee Valley Regional Park, Thorndon Country Park at Brentwood, and Weald Country Park at South Weald. Many of these parks arrange special events during the year. Southwest Essex is also home to the famous Waltham Abbey.

Hunting Lodge, Epping Forest

Bordering the north bank of the Thames, the southern Essex borough of Thurrock also boasts a good number of fine towns and villages, with attractions ranging from superb heritage sites and museums to family-run specialist shops as these communities continue to go from strength to strength. Henry VIII built riverside Block Houses at East and West Tilbury, which later became Coalhouse Fort and Tilbury Fort. It was at West Tilbury that Queen Elizabeth I gave her famous speech to her troops, gathered to meet the Spanish Armada threat. Both forts played an important defence role during the two World Wars. At the extreme southeast of the county, Southend is a popular and friendly seaside resort with a wealth of sites and amenities. There are also smaller seaside communities which repay a visit.

The area surrounding the Blackwater and Crouch estuaries boasts one of the county's principal towns, Chelmsford, and a wealth of ancient woodland and other natural beauties, particularly along the estuaries and the Chelmer and Blackwater Canal. This corner of Essex is ideal for those who enjoy any kind of watersports activities. The island of Northey near Maldon is owned by the National Trust and is a haven for wildlife.

This is also the region of Essex dominated by hundreds of acres of ancient woodland, much of it coppiced, the traditional woodland management technique which encourages a vast array of natural flora and fauna.

Audley End House & Gardens

SOUTH AND WEST ESSEX

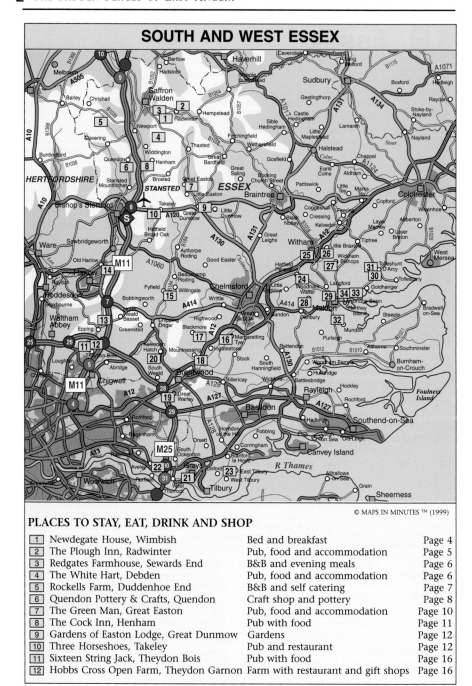

© MAPS IN MINUTES ™ (1999)

PLACES TO STAY, EAT, DRINK AND SHOP

SAFFRON WALDEN

Named after the Saffron crocus, which was grown in the area to make dyestuffs and fulfil a variety of other uses in the Middle Ages, a great deal of Saffron Walden's street plan survives, as do hundreds of fine buildings, many timbered with overhanging upper floors and decorative plastering (also known as pargetting). Gog and Magog (or in some versions folk-hero Tom Hickathrift and the Wisbech Giant) battle forever in plaster on the gable of the **Old Sun Inn**, where, legend

Saffron Walden

has it, Oliver Cromwell and General Fairfax both lodged during the Civil War. A typical market town, Saffron Walden's centrepiece is its magnificent church.

At the **Saffron Walden Museum**, as well as the gloves worn by Mary Queen of Scots on the day she died, is a piece of human skin which once coated the church door at Hadstock. The museum first opened to the public at its present location in 1835, and was founded 'to gratify the inclination of all who value natural history'. It remains faithful to this credo, while widening the museum's scope. The museum has won numerous awards, including joint winner of the Museum of the Year Award for best museum of Industrial or Social History in 1997. At this friendly, family-sized museum visitors can try their hand at corn grinding with a Romano-British quern, see how a medieval timber house would have been built, admire the displays of Native American and West African embroidery and come face to face with Wallace the Lion, the museum's faithful guardian. Over two floors, exhibits focus on town and country (with a wealth of wooden plough and other agricultural artefacts), furniture and woodwork, costumes, ancient Egyptian and Roman artefacts, geology and ceramics and glass. In the 'ages of man' gallery, the history of northwest Essex is traced from the Ice Age to the Middle Ages. The ruins of historic Walden Castle are also on-site.

On the local **Common**, once Castle Green, is the largest surviving Turf Maze in England. Only eight ancient turf mazes survive in England: though there were many more in the Middle Ages, if they are not looked after they soon become overgrown and are lost. This one is believed to be some 800 years old.

Though many miles from the sea, Henry Winstanley, inventor, engineer and engraver, and designer of the first Eddystone Lighthouse at Plymouth, was born here in 1644. He is said to have held 'lighthouse trials' with a wooden lantern in the lavishly decorated 15th to 16th century church. The Lighthouse, and Winstanley with it, were swept away in a fierce storm in 1703.

The town was also famous for its resident Cockatrice, which was hatched from a cock's egg by a toad or serpent and could, it was said, kill its victims with a glance. The Cockatrice was blamed for any inexplicable disaster in the town. Like Perseus and Medusa the Gorgon, a Cockatrice could be destroyed

Saffron Walden Parish Church

by making it see its own reflection, thereby turning it to stone. The Saffron Walden Cockatrice's slayer was said to be a knight in a coat of *'cristal glass'*.

To the north of the town is **Bridge End Gardens**, a wonderfully preserved example of an early Victorian garden, complete with the unique Hedge Maze, which is open only by appointment (which can be made at the TIC). Next to the gardens is the **Fry Art Gallery**,

NEWDEGATE HOUSE

Howlett End, Wimbish, Saffron Walden, Essex CB10 2XW
Tel: 01799 599748

Owners Jacky and John bring a wealth of experience to **Newdegate House**, which offers bed and breakfast accommodation. They proffer warm hospitality and a high standard of service and quality to all their guests. The house is a haven of comfort, modern, airy and cosy. There are two guest bedrooms (one double, one twin). Both rooms are very tastefully furnished and decorated, and offer full facilities. The house is set in nearly two acres of gardens, which guests are welcome to enjoy. Boules or croquet equipment is available, and the attractive paved patio and conservatory are also open to guests. In the lovely dining room, guests take the excellent English breakfast. In the evenings a tray snack menu is available until 8 p.m., with a choice of supper including toasted sandwiches and jacket potatoes. Just 10 miles from Stansted, and near many of the county's best sights and attractions, this fine B&B makes a perfect base from which to explore the area. ETC 4 Diamonds/Silver Award. No which has a unique collection of work by artists and designers, such as Edward Bawden, Eric Ravilious, John Aldridge and Sheila Robinson, who have lived in and around the town, as members of the famous artistic community which flourished in and around Great Bardfield between 1930 and 1970. It also exhibits work by many notable 20th century artists who lived and worked in the area before and after the Second World War, as well as contemporary artists working in Essex today. The gallery was purpose designed and opened in 1856 to house the collection of Francis Gibson. The gallery also houses the Lewis George Fry RBA, RWA (1860-1933) Collection, which is exhibited each summer, along with works by Robert Fry (1866-1934) and Anthony Fry.

Close to Bridge End is the Anglo-American War Memorial dedicated by Field Marshal the Viscount Montgomery of Alamein in 1953 to the memory of all the American flyers of the 65th Fighter Wing who lost their lives in the Second World War.

Audley End House was, at one time, home of the first Earl of Suffolk, and at one time home of Charles II. The original 17th century

house, with its two large courtyards, had a magnificence claimed to match that of Hampton Court. Unfortunately the subsequent earls lacked their forebear's financial acumen, and much of the house was demolished as it fell into disrepair. Nevertheless it remains today one of England's most impressive Jacobean mansions; its distinguished stone facade set off perfectly by Capability Brown's lake. The remaining state rooms retain their palatial magnificence and the exquisite state bed in the Neville Room is hung with the original embroidered drapes. The silver, the Doll's House, the Jacobean Screen and Robert Adam's painted Drawing Room are just among the many sights to marvel at. The natural history collection features more than 1,000 stuffed animals and birds. To complement this, there are paintings by Holbein, Lely and Canaletto. Fascinating introductory talks help visitors get the most from any visit to this, one of the most magnificent houses in England. This jewel also has beautiful gardens landscaped by Capability Brown, including the 'Temple of Concord' which Brown dedicated to George

THE PLOUGH INN

Sampford Road, Radwinter, Saffron Walden, Essex CB10 2TL
Tel: 01799 599222 Fax: 01799 599161

The Plough Inn at Radwinter stands at the crossroads created by the B1053/B1054, just east of the unspoilt village of Radwinter. The pub stands astride the top of a hill overlooking open farmland to the west. this welcoming pub and restaurant, which also offers accommodation, is set in a handsome 17th century Grade II listed building with a wealth of old beams and studding, brasses, old photographs and memorabilia adding to the warm and friendly atmosphere.

There's ample seating both on the lawn and on the clematis-covered patio - the ideal place for a summer lunch or al fresco evening meal - as well as within, surrounded by traditional comforts. The

menu and specials board offers a range of delicious meals at lunchtime and evening. Fine real ales on hand include Greene King IPA, while the locally brewed Nethergate beers have proved particularly popular. The small select wine list emphasises the best of French and New World vintages. Booking is advised for Friday and Saturday evenings and Sunday lunch.

The three self-contained ensuite rooms (one twin, two doubles) adjoining the main building are very attractive and comfortable.

REDGATES FARMHOUSE

Redgates Lane, Sewards End, Saffron Walden,
Essex CB10 2LP
Tel: 01799 516166

At **Redgates Farmhouse** guests can enjoy all the comforts of home in a peaceful and very relaxed setting. Owner Alison Colbert offers bed and breakfast accommodation at this lovely property, parts of which date back to the 16th century. This smallholding is set in 10 acres of grassland, commanding lovely views in every direction. There are two cosy and comfortable guest bedrooms, tastefully furnished and decorated and with a truly homely feel. In these charming surroundings guests can enjoy country walks after starting the day with one of Mrs Colbert's outstanding breakfasts (she is, after all, a former Cordon Bleu chef).

Delicious evening meals are also available by prior arrangement. The decor and ambience of this attractive B&B are very traditional, from the handsome hallway and elegant breakfast room to the lovely guests' sitting room. Mrs Colbert offers the very best in hospitality and service to all her guests. A pet-owner herself, with three cats and three dogs - five-year-old German shepherd "Minnie", two-year-old black spaniel "Molly", and four-year-old "Storm", a flat-coated retriever - she is happy to welcome guests with dogs. This delightful establishment is open all year round.

THE WHITE HART

High Street, Debden,
Essex CB11 3LE
Tel: 01799 541109

The White Hart in Debden is a friendly and pristine public house dating back to the 17th century, with many later additions.

Completely refurbished inside and out in 2000, it offers the best in modern comforts within a traditional setting. Set near the 13th-century parish church of St Mary the Virgin and All Saints, it occupies a peaceful place at the centre of this lovely village.

Real ales at this Free House include Abbot ale, Greene King IPA and regularly changing guest ales. The menu is varied and innovative, with a range of traditional English dishes and Continental, Russian and Ukrainian specialities - owner Didenko Valeriy was born and bred in the Ukraine, and has lived in Britain since 1995, buying this fine pub in 1998. Tempting delicacies such as genuine Chicken Kiev, borscht, *shashleak* (a type of kebab), *varenikea* (ravioli with meat or cream cheese; can also be served with fruit as a dessert) and *liha* (a succulent fish soup) are well worth sampling. Accommodation is available, too, in either the former barn which has been tastefully converted to offer self-catering accommodation, or in the four comfortable and cosy guest bedrooms (three doubles and one single) within the main pub building.

III. There is a lovely parterre, lake and Pond Garden. Circular walks help visitors make the most of all there is to see. The organic kitchen garden was recently opened to the public for the first time in 250 years. The gardens are managed by the Henry Doubleday Research Association, who grow and sell a wide range of organic produce in the shop, which also features a restaurant. The Audley End Miniature Railway (separate admission charge) is 1.5 miles long and takes visitors along Lord Braybrooke's private 10¼ inch gauge railway through the beautiful private woods of the house.

Within the rolling parkland of the grounds there are several elegant outbuildings, some of which were designed by Robert Adam. Among these are an icehouse, a circular temple and a Springwood Column.

AROUND SAFFRON WALDEN

RADWINTER
4 miles E of Saffron Walden off the B1053

Radwinter boasts a fine church, which was largely renovated and rebuilt in the 19th century by architect Eden Nesfield and has a fine 14th century porch. The village also has cottages and almshouses designed by Nesfield.

HEMPSTEAD
5 miles E of Saffron Walden off the B1054

The highwayman, Dick Turpin, was born here in 1705. His parents kept the Bell Inn, later renamed the Rose and Crown and more recently known by the sobriquet 'Turpin's Tavern'. Gilt letters announce that *'It is the Landlord's great desire that no one stands before the fire'* over the wide hearth where logs still burn; pictures all around celebrate the infamy of the former innkeeper's son.

Inside the 14th to 15th century village church, an impressively life-like bust carved by Edward Marshall recalls the town's rather worthier son, William Harvey (1578-1657). Harvey was chief physician to Charles I and the discoverer of the circulation of blood, as recorded in his De Motu Cordis of 1628. Like many other villages, Hempstead once boasted a village cockpit; its faint outline can still be traced, though the steep banks are now crowned with trees.

WIDDINGTON
4 miles S of Saffron Walden off the B1383

Covering nearly 25 acres, **Mole Hall Wildlife Park** offers visitors the chance to come close to a range of wild and domesticated animals. With the private fully moated 13th century manor house as a backdrop, the wide variety of animals in this excellent park include South American llamas, flamingos, Formosa Sika deer (which are extinct in the wild), chimpanzees, muntjac, Arctic fox, wallabies,

ROCKELLS FARM

Duddenhoe End, Saffron Walden, Essex CB11 4UY
Tel: 01763 838053 Fax: 01763 837001

Rockells Farm is a lovely Georgian house set on an arable farm with a large garden and a three-acre lake. Here in this peaceful rural environment, guests are welcome to enjoy excellent bed and breakfast accommodation in one of three comfortable and attractive ensuite guest bedrooms (a single, a twin and a family room - the family room occupies the ground floor and is accessible to wheelchairs). There is also a charming guests' lounge. All rooms have full facilities. Eggs fresh from the farm are used in the delicious cooked breakfasts. In addition, the farm boasts superb self-catering accommodation in the carefully converted former stables. Welcoming and equipped with every modern amenity, washing machine and drying facilities are made available to guests. The lake is stocked with tench and carp, while chub, rudd and roach make interesting winter fishing. Platforms provide excellent coarse fishing facilities. For a true country retreat, look no further.

red squirrels and much more. Mole Hall is also home to two species of North American otter: Short-clawed and North American. Domesticated animals such as guinea pigs, rabbits, goats, pigs and sheep can also be seen. The Butterfly Pavilion offers a tropical experience where brilliantly coloured butterflies flit about freely. Within the tropical pavilion you can also find lovebirds and small monkeys, along with a variety of snakes, spiders and insects (safe behind glass). The pools are home to goldfish, toads and terrapins.

Widdington is also home to **Priors Hall Barn**, one of the finest medieval barns in all of southeast England, and owned by English Heritage.

STANSTED MOUNTFICHET
8 miles SW of Saffron Walden off the B1383

Though rather close to Stansted Airport, there are plenty of reasons to visit this village. Certainly pilots approaching the airport may be surprised at the sight of a **Norman Village**, complete with domestic animals and the reconstructed motte and bailey

Thatched Cottage, Arkesden

Mountfichet Castle, standing just two miles from the end of the runway. The original castle was built after 1066 by the Duke of Boulogne, a cousin of the Conqueror. Siege weapons on show include two giant catapults. Visitors can take a trip to the top of the siege tower and tiptoe into the baron's bed chamber while he sleeps! Next door to

QUENDON POTTERY & CRAFTS

Cambridge Road (B1383), Quendon, nr Saffron Walden, Essex CB11 3XQ
Tel/Fax: 01799 543439

A wide range of unique and top-quality British hand-made crafts are to be found at **Quendon Pottery & Crafts**. Opened in 1978, it is owned by Russ and Brenda Smith, a potter himself, who together have made this lovely shop a thriving concern. Anyone looking for unusual and distinctive gifts - for themselves or someone else! - will find many attractive and well-crafted items here, from ceramics, paintings, prints, basketwork, ironwork, woodwork, glass and more. There's also a large selection of lighting, iron-framed mirrors, aromatic candles, cards, soft and wooden toys, and bronze miniatures, celebrating the finest in English arts and crafts.

This large and airy shop occupies an attractive building which dates back some 200 years. Once the village store, it has been carefully renovated to accommodate the craft shop. There's a welcoming and relaxed atmosphere, conducive to leisurely browsing. Russ and Brenda are happy to advise on choosing the perfect gift or objet d'art to suit every taste and pocket. The old bakery to the rear is now Russ' pottery. Open: Wednesday to Sunday and Bank Holidays, 10 am - 5.30 pm.

the castle is **The House on the Hill Toy Museum**, where children of every age are treated to a unique and nostalgic trip back to their childhood. There is every toy imaginable here, many of them now highly prized collectors' items. There is a shop selling new toys and a collectors' shop with many old toys and books to choose from.

Stansted Windmill is one of the best preserved tower mills in the country. Dating back to 1787 and in use until 1910, most of the original machinery has survived. It is open on the first Sunday of each month from April to October; every Sunday in August and on Bank Holiday Mondays.

HADSTOCK
4 miles N of Saffron Walden off the B1052

As well as claiming to have the oldest church door in England, at the parish **Church of St Botolph**, Hadstock also has a macabre tale to tell. The church's north door was once covered with a piece of human skin, now to be seen in Saffron Walden Museum. Local legend says it is a 'Daneskin', from a Viking flayed alive.

Lining doors with animal leather was common in the Middle Ages and many so-called 'Daneskins' are just that. However, the skins at Hadstock and at Copford, in northeast Essex, are almost certainly human, the poor wretch at Hadstock undoubtedly having his hide nailed there as a warning to others. The door itself is Saxon, as are the 11th century carvings, windows and arches, rare survivors that predate the Norman Conquest.

Linton Zoo near the village is a privately owned collection of wild animals set in 10½ acres of gardens. There is a free car park, children's play area, picnic areas and a cafe on site.

BARTLOW
5 miles NE of Saffron Walden off the B1052

Bartlow Hills are reputed to be the largest burial mounds in Europe dating from Roman times. Fifteen metres high, they date back to the 2nd century.

THAXTED
7 miles SE of Saffron Walden on the B184

This small country town has a recorded history which dates back to before the Domesday book. Originally a Saxon settlement, it developed around a Roman road. Yet, although the town is full of beautiful old buildings, it has a special character all its own. To its credit Thaxted has no need of artificial tourist attractions and is today what is has been for the last ten centuries: a thriving and beautiful town.

Thaxted has numerous attractively pargetted and timber-framed houses, and a magnificent **Guildhall**, built as a meeting-place for cutlers around 1390. The demise of the cutlery industry in this part of Essex in the 1500s led it to becoming the administrative centre of the town. Restored in

Thaxted Village

Georgian times it became the town's Grammar School, as well as remaining a centre of administration. Once more restored in 1975, today the Parish council still meet here.

The town's famous **Tower Windmill** was built in 1804 by John Webb. In working order until 1907, it fell into disuse and disrepair but has now been returned to full working order.

It contains a rural life museum, well worth a visit. Close to the windmill are the town's **Almshouses**, which provided homes for the elderly even 250 years after they were built for that very purpose.

Thaxted Church stands on a hill and soars cathedral-like over the town's streets. It has been described as the finest Parish church in the country and, though many towns may protest long and loud at this claim, it certainly is magnificent. It was also the somewhat unlikely setting for a pitched battle in 1921. The rather colourful vicar and secretary of the Church Socialist League, one Conrad Noel, hoisted the red flag of communism and the Sinn Fein flag in the church. Incensed Cambridge students tore them down and put up the Union Jack; Noel in turn ripped that down and, with his friends, slashed the tyres of the students' cars and motorbikes. A fine bronze in the church celebrates this adventurous man of the cloth.

Conrad Noel's wife is remembered for encouraging Morris dancing in the town. Today, the famous Morris Ring is held annually (usually on the Spring Bank Holiday), attracting over 300 dancers from all over the country who dance through the streets. Dancing can also be seen around the town on most Bank Holiday Mondays, usually in the vicinity of a pub!

Gustav Holst, composer of, amongst other pieces, the renowned 'Planets' Suite, lived in Thaxted from 1914-1925, and often played the church organ. To celebrate his connection with the town, there is a month-long music festival in late June/early July which attracts performers of international repute.

In Park Street, at Aldborough Lodge, the Thaxted Garden for Butterflies is an ordinary garden which has been developed with a view to pleasing birds, butterflies and other wildlife species - including humans. Displays depict the 22 native wild butterfly species which have visited the garden since its inception in 1988.

GREAT EASTON
3 miles S of Thaxted off the B184

Great Easton boasts a wealth of cottages and farmhouses with ornamental plasterwork,

THE GREEN MAN

Mill End Green, Great Easton, Dunmow, Essex CM6 2DN
Tel/Fax: 01371 870286

The Green Man public house in Great Easton occupies a handsome building dating back to the 15th century. It is traditional in decor and furnishings, with a comfortable, homely feel.

One unusual feature is the central fire with its original locally-made hood which can be lowered or raised as necessary. Proprietor Steve Cooper is a former chef who took

over at this popular pub in August 2000, bringing his wealth of experience as a trained chef with Trust House Forte and other notable country hotels. His menu changes daily and features traditional English cooking freshly prepared and beautifully presented. Make sure to leave room for the delicious home-made desserts! Lunch is served everyday; evening meals Monday-Saturday. Booking is advised for the deservedly popular three-course Sunday lunch.

Real ales on tap include Ridleys IPA, Greene King IPA and Adnams, plus a good selection of lagers, cider, wines, spirits and soft drinks. There is a lovely patio - a real suntrap - as well as extensive and well-tended gardens and a tennis court. The excellent accommodation comprises a self-contained flat with two bedrooms (one twin, one single); continental breakfast is included in the tariff.

clustered Tudor chimneys and half-timbering. Great Easton's well-known and very popular Green Man pub occupies a handsome building dating back to the 15th century.

LITTLE EASTON
5 miles S of Thaxted off the B184

The charming 12th century **church** in this small village is rich in historic features. Its Maynard Chapel features some outstanding marble monuments of the family as well as some famous brasses. The church's oldest treasures are, however, a well-preserved and priceless 12th century wall painting and several 15th century frescoes. Two recent additions, two stained glass windows, were unveiled in 1990. The Window of the Crusaders and the Window of Friendship and Peace are a lasting memorial to the American 386th Bomb Group. Known as 'The Marauders', they were stationed nearby for 13 months and lost over 200 of their number in that short time.

The Barn Theatre at Little Easton Manor is one of the finest and oldest tithe barns in the country, with magnificent oak timbers and ancient tiled roof. Host to performances by many of the most distinguished actors over the years - including Ellen Terry, Hermione Baddeley, Charlie Chaplin, George Formby and many others - the sympathetic restoration of the facilities has meant it can continue to be used for a host of special events.

BROXTED
3 miles SW of Thaxted off the B1051

The parish **Church of St Mary the Virgin** here in the handsome village of Broxted has two remarkably lovely stained glass windows commemorating the captivity and release of John McCarthy and the other Beirut hostages, dedicated in January 1993. Though just a few minutes drive from Stansted Airport off the M11, it is a welcoming haven of rural tranquillity.

Church Hall Farm Antique and Craft Centre in Broxted is housed in a magnificent Grade II listed barn flanked by a willow-lined pond with its own resident ducks! The building itself is a miracle of medieval craftsmanship, located just a few yards from Broxted parish church.

HENHAM
4 miles SW of Thaxted off the B1051

This picturesque village boasts pretty greens and ponds. The parish church dates from the 13th century.

GREAT DUNMOW
13 miles SE of Saffron WAlden on the A120

The town is famous for the 'Flitch of Bacon', an ancient ceremony which dates back as far as the early 12th century. A prize of a flitch, or side, of bacon was awarded to the local man who, in the words of then-Lord Mayor

THE COCK INN

Church End, Henham, Bishops Stortford, Essex CM22 6AL
Tel: 01279 850347 Fax: 01279 816676

The Cock Inn is at the heart of Henham village life, set opposite the parish church of St Mary. The building is over 300 years old, as attested to by the wealth of black beams exposed along the ceiling and uprights. Other traditional features include the enormous inglenook fireplace and pew-style upholstered seating along the walls. Fans of the television series Lovejoy may have a strange sense of déjà vu here: many scenes were filmed in the bar. Photos of days gone by adorn the walls, and the dining area is intimate and comfortable. Cask ales include a regularly changing guest ale. The superior home-cooked food is worth seeking this pub out for. There's an excellent wine list. Although it is just three miles from Stansted Airport it is not on the flight path, so noisy planes do not intrude on the rural delights of this small village (population 1,000) nor on those of this convivial and welcoming public house.

Robert Fitzwalter, *'does not repent of his marriage nor quarrel, differ or dispute with his wife within a year and a day after the marriage'*. Amidst great ceremony the couple would be seated and presented with their prize. The custom lapsed on the dissolution of the monasteries, was briefly revived in the 18th century and became established again after 1885. 'Trials' to test the truth are all in good fun, and carried out every leap year. The successful couple are carried through the streets on chairs and then presented with the Flitch. The 'bacon chair' can be seen in Little Dunmow parish church.

THE GARDENS OF EASTON LODGE

Easton Lodge, Great Dunmow, Essex CM6 2BB
Tel/Fax: 01371 876979
website: www.eastonlodge.co.uk
email: enquiries@eastonlodge.co.uk

The Gardens of Easton Lodge were originally the creation of the famous landscape designer Harold Peto, commissioned by the Countess of Warwick in 1902 to construct extensive, varied and spectacular gardens in the grounds of the 16th-century Easton Lodge. After falling into disuse, in the 1970s Brian Creasey and his family arrived and began the careful and sensitive restoration, so that the gardens are again a feast of sights and rural splendour, with features such as an Italian garden and an impressive glade. The garden is open for its main season Easter - 31st October, Friday - Sunday and Bank Holiday Mondays, midday - 6 p.m.; it is also open when the snowdrops are in bloom in February and March, Fridays - Sundays, midday - dusk. For current fees and information about groups and appointments at other times of the year, please telephone.

THREE HORSESHOES

Mole Hill Green, Takeley, Bishops Stortford, Essex CM22 6PQ
Tel: 01279 870313

Three Horseshoes in Takeley is a charming and delightful pub. The exterior alone is worth the journey: approximately 500 years old, this Grade II listed building has pristine white walls outlined in black, casement windows, crowned by a handsome thatched roof and unusual rounded chimney.

But much more awaits guests inside: excellent food, great drink and a wonderful, traditional English interior, with low heavily beamed ceilings and walls and large inglenook fireplace. The horseshoe-shaped bar leads on one side to the gracious and handsome dining area. Real ales on tap include Greene King IPA, Abbot, Courage and Directors. There's also a good range of lagers, wines and spirits.

Lunch is served 12-2.30 Monday to Saturday; Sundays 12.30 to 3.30. Evening meals are from 7 - 9 every day. There's a comprehensive menu ranging from snacks and sandwiches to traditional roasts, home-made pies, steaks with the excellent chef's special sauces, fish and vegetarian dishes and more, all freshly prepared and cooked to order. On Sundays there is a choice of two roasts.

Hosts Trevor and Sophie are friendly and welcoming. Both locally born, their experience in the licenced trade shows in the high standard of service they offer all their guests.

Other places of historical interest include the parish church of St Mary at Church End, Great Dunmow, dating back to 1322. The Clock House, a private residence built in 15896, was the home of St Anne Line, martyred for sheltering a Jesuit priest. The Great Dunmow Maltings, opened to the public in 2000, is a focal point for local history. H G Wells lived at Brick House in Great Dunmow, overlooking the Doctor's Pond, where in 1784 Lionel Lukin is reputed to have tested the first unsinkable lifeboat.

The Flitch Way is a 15 mile country walk along the former Bishop's Stortford to Braintree railway, taking in Victorian stations, impressive views, and a wealth of woodland wildlife.

Lych-gate, Aythorpe Roding Church

TAKELEY
4 miles W of Great Dunmow off the A120

The village is built on the line of the old Roman **Stane Street**. There are plenty of pretty 17th century timbered houses and barns to be seen in the village, and the church still has many of its original Norman features along with some Roman masonry. Rather unusually it has a modern font that is surrounded by a six-foot high medieval cover.

HATFIELD BROAD OAK
3 miles SW of Great Dunmow off the B184

This very pretty village has many notable buildings for the visitor to enjoy, including a church dating from Norman times, some delightful 18th century almshouses and several distinctive Georgian houses.

Nearby **Hatfield Forest** to the extreme west of the county was once a Royal hunting forest; many of the features of a medieval forest can still be seen today, including deer, cattle, coppice, pollards, grasslands and rabbit warrens. Once covering a great deal more land, the remaining 400 hectares are now protected by the National Trust and offer

splendid woodland walks along with good chases and rides.

AYTHORPE RODING
4 miles SW of Great Dunmow off the B184

Aythorpe Roding Windmill is the largest remaining post mill in Essex. Built around 1760, it remained in use up until 1935. It was fitted in the 1800s with a fantail which kept the sails pointing into the wind. It is open to the public on the last Sunday of each month from May to September, 2-5 p.m.

SAWBRIDGEWORTH
6 miles SW of Great Dunmow off the A1184

Quite a number of fine old buildings survive in this small town, many of which are Georgian. To the south is **Pishiobury**, a fine house built by James Wyatt in 1782, now a school. In St Mary's church are 15 wonderful ancient and beautifully preserved brasses.

WALTHAM ABBEY

The town of Waltham began as a small Roman settlement on the site of the present-day Market Square. The early Saxon kings maintained a hunting lodge here; a town formed round this, and the first church was built in the 6th century. By the 8th, during the reign of Cnut, the town had a stone minster church with a great stone crucifix

Waltham Abbey

The town became known for the Abbey, which was one of the largest in the country and the last to be the victim of Henry VIII's dissolution of the monasteries, in 1540.

The Abbey's Crypt Centre houses an interesting exhibition explaining the history of both the Abbey and the town, highlighting the religious significance of the site. Some visible remains of the Augustinian Abbey include the chapter house and precinct walls, cloister entry and gateway in the surrounding Abbey Gardens. The Abbey Gardens are also host to a Sensory Trail exploring the highlights of hundreds of years of the site's history; there's also a delightful Rose Garden.

that had been brought from Somerset, were it had been found buried in land owned by Tovi, a trusted servant of the king. This cross became the focus of pilgrims seeking healing. One of those cured of a serious illness, Harold Godwinsson, built a new church, the third on the site, which was dedicated in 1060 - and it was this self-same Harold who became king and was killed in the battle of Hastings six years on. Harold's body was brought back to Waltham to be buried in his church. The church that exists today was built in the first quarter of the 12th century. It was once three times its present length, and incorporated an Augustinian Abbey, built in 1177 by Henry II.

Along the Cornhill Stream, crossed by the impressive stone bridge, the town's **Dragonfly Sanctuary** is home to over half the native British species of dragonflies and damselflies. It is noted as the best single site for seeing these species in Greater London, Essex and Hertfordshire.

A Tudor timber-framed house forms part of the **Epping Forest District Museum** in Sun Street. The wide range of displays includes exhibits covering the history of the Epping Forest District from the Stone Age to the 20th century. Tudor and Victorian times are particularly well represented, with some magnificent oak panelling dating from the reign of Henry VIII, and re-creations of Victorian rooms and shops. There is also an archaeological display and temporary exhibitions covering such subjects as contemporary arts and crafts. The museum has several hands-on displays which help to bring history to life, and features special events and adult workshops throughout the year.

Sun Street is the town's main thoroughfare, and it is pedestrianised. It contains many buildings from the 16th century onwards. The Greenwich Meridian (0 degrees longitude) runs through the street, marked out on the pavement and through the Abbey Gardens.

The Denny Tomb, Waltham Abbey

In spite of its proximity to London and more recent development, the town retains a peaceful, traditional character, with its timber-framed buildings and small traditional market which has been held here since the early 12th century (now every Tuesday and Saturday). The whole of the town centre has been designated a conservation area. The Market Square boasts many fine and interesting buildings such as the Lych-gate and The Welsh Harp, dating from the 17th and 16th centuries respectively.

The **Town Hall** offers a fine example of Art Nouveau design, and houses the Waltham Abbey Information Office.

To the west of town, the **Lee Navigation Canal** offers opportunities for anglers, walkers, birdwatching and pleasure craft. Once used for transporting corn and other commercial goods to the growing City of London, and having associations with the town's important gunpowder industry for centuries, the canal remains a vital part of town life.

Gunpowder production became established in Waltham as early as the 1660s; by the 19th century the **Royal Gunpowder Mills** employed 500 workers, and production did not cease until 1943, after which time the factory became a research facility. In the spring of 2000, however, all this is set to change, and the site will be opened to the public for the first time. Of the 175 acres the site occupies, approximately 80 have been designated a Site of Special Scientific Interest, and the ecology of the site will offer a rare opportunity for study. With two-thirds of the site a Scheduled Ancient Monument, there are some 21 listed buildings to be found here, some of which date from the Napoleonic Wars. The site also contains some of the finest examples of industrial archaeology in the world. Up until 2000 there are free site tours being held on special National Heritage Open Days, giving visitors the opportunity to experience the Royal Gunpowder Mills prior to its development as a nationally recognised Heritage attraction.

Lee Valley Regional Park is a leisure area stretching for 23 miles along the River Lea (sometimes also spelled Lee) from East London to Herfordshire. The Lee Valley is an important area of high biodiversity, sustaining a large range of wildlife and birds. Two hundred species of birds, including internationally important populations of Gadwall and Shoveler ducks, can be seen each year on the wetlands and water bodies along the Lea. The Information Centre in the Abbey Gardens provides displays and information on a range of countryside pursuits and interests, sport, leisure and heritage facilities and special events. Of national importance for overwintering waterbirds including rare species of bittern and smew, this fine park makes an ideal place for a picnic. Guided tours by appointment.

At the southern end of Lee Valley Park, **The House Mill**, one of two tidal mills still standing at this site, has been restored by the River Lea Tidal Mill Trust. It was built in 1776 in the Dutch style, and was used to grind grain for gin distilling.

Lee Valley Park Farms, along Stubbins Hall Lane, boasts two farms on site: **Hayes Hill Farm**, where visitors can interact with the animals and enjoy a picnic or the children's adventure playground. This traditional farm also boasts old-fashioned tools and equipment, an exhibition in the medieval barn and occasional craft demonstrations. The entry fee to Hayes Hill Farm also covers a visit to **Holyfield Hall Farm**, a working farm and dairy where visitors can see milking and learn about modern farming methods. Seasonal events such as sheep-shearing and harvesting are held, and there's an attractive farm tea room and a toy shop. Recently a farm trail has been added to this site's attractions, offering wonderful views of the Lee Valley, an expanse of open countryside dotted with lakes and wildflower meadows, attracting a wide range of wildlife including otters, bats, dragonfly, kingfisher, great crested grebe and little ringed plover. The area is ideal for walking or fishing and the bird hides are open to all at weekends; permits available for daily access. Guided tours by arrangement.

Myddleton House Gardens within Lee Valley Park is the place to see the work of the famous plantsman who created them - E.A. Bowles, the greatest amateur gardener of his time. Breathtaking colours and interesting plantings - such as the National Collection of award-winning bearded iris, the Tulip Terrace and the Lunatic Asylum (home to unusual plants) - are offset by a beautiful carp lake, two conservatories and a rock garden.

AROUND WALTHAM ABBEY

EPPING
4 miles E of Waltham Abbey off the B182

Just off the B1391, on the outskirts of Epping town centre towards Waltham Abbey, this town's handsome St John's Church was designed over 100 years ago by G F Bodley.

LOUGHTON
5 miles SE of Waltham Abbey off the A121

Corbett Theatre in Rectory Lane in Loughton is a beautiful Grade I listed converted medieval tithe barn, where classical, modern and musical theatre

Epping Forest

productions are performed. The theatre is set in a five-acre site with lovely gardens.

Loughton borders **Epping Forest**, a magnificent and expansive tract of ancient hornbeam coppice, mainly tucked between the M25 and London. There are miles of leafy walks and rides (horse can be hired locally), with some rough grazing and occasional distant views.

Sixteen String Jack

Coppice Row, Theydon Bois, Essex CM16 7DS
Tel: 01992 813182

The **Sixteen String Jack** pub took its unusual name from highwayman Jack Rann, known for the sixteen string laces he wore from his breeches to his knees. A dandy despite his profession, he was hanged in 1774 at the age of 24, having already been tried for and acquitted of highway robbery on six previous occasions. The pub dates back to Jack's day, as can be seen from the elegant Georgian exterior. The interior is handsome and comfortable. A full account of Jack and his exploits, including poems of the day written to laud him, are mounted and displayed in the lounge bar. Here guests can enjoy a range of real ales including McMullens Country and A.K., plus draught stout, ciders and lagers. Great food is available Monday to Saturday and Sunday lunchtime. Guests choose from over 20 daily blackboard specials and a good variety of snacks and sandwiches.

Hobbs Cross Open Farm

Hobbs Cross Road,
Theydon Garnon,
Epping, Essex CM16 7NY
Tel: 01992 814764

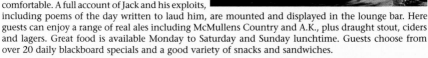

Hobbs Cross Open Farm makes learning about farming fun. One of the few working livestock farms with the M25, it offers plenty to see and do. There's also a fine licensed restaurant, excellent farm shop, giftshop and a programme of entertainment - such as live jazz every Thursday - throughout the year. Open: 9.00 am to 5.00 pm, summer; 9.00 am to dusk, winter.

THE CARPENTERS ARMS

The High Road, Thornwood Common, Epping,
Essex CM16 6LS
Tel: 01992 574208

Adjacent to the B1393 in Thornwood Common, the impressive **Carpenters Arms** is situated within the boundaries of Epping Forest. Formerly cottages that date back to the late 17th century, it has been an ale house since 1741. Open Monday to Thursday 11 a.m. - 3 p.m. and 6 - 11 p.m., Friday and Saturday 11 a.m. - 11 p.m. and Sunday midday - 10.30 p.m., there are always at least four real ales on tap including McMullens A.K., Crouch Vale Best and Adnams Broadside, together with a good range of draught lagers, stout, cider, and some good wines and spirits. Food is available every lunchtime, from the set menu or range of at least three daily specials. Voted Essex Pub of the Year by CAMRA in 1998, there is music at weekends and a relaxed and informal atmosphere every night of the week. The top bar is nicknamed the Hurricane Bar, as it is adorned with photographs and memorabilia of pilots and planes used at nearby North Weald Aerodrome in both World Wars.

ABRIDGE
7 miles SE of Waltham Abbey off the A113

The **BBC Essex Garden** at Crowther Nurseries, Ongar Road, is a working garden consisting of a vegetable plot, two small greenhouses, and herbaceous and shrub borders. Sheila Love works in the BBC garden on Sundays. Sheila Chapman, clematis expert, is also on site, as the garden boasts over 400 varieties of clematis. The garden is also home to a range of farmyard animals which visitors are welcome to see and interact with, and there's a delightful tea shop filled with homemade cakes.

CHIGWELL
8 miles SE of Waltham Abbey off the A113

Hainault Forest Country Park is an ancient woodland managed by the Woodland Trust on behalf of Essex County Council. Here visitors will also find a handsome lake and a rare breeds farm, managed by the London borough of Redbridge.

CHINGFORD
6 miles S of Waltham Abbey off the A11

Queen Elizabeth Hunting Lodge in Ranger's Road, Chingford, is a timber-framed hunting grandstand first built for Henry VIII. This unique Tudor-era survivor boasts exceptional carpentry, and is situated in a beautiful part of Epping Forest with ancient oaks and fine views. The Visitor Centre can be found at High Beach, Epping.

BROXBOURNE
5 miles NW of Waltham Abbey off the A10

At **Broxbourne Old Mill and Millpool**, the remains of the old watermill can be seen, the waterwheel of which has been restored to working order.

HODDESDON
6 miles NW of Waltham Abbey off the A10

Rye House Gatehouse in Rye Road was built by Sir Andre Ogard, a Danish nobleman, in 1443. It is a moated building and a fine example of early English brickwork. Now restored, visitors can climb up to the battlements. A permanent exhibition covers the architecture and history of the Rye House Plot of 1683. Guided tours by prior arrangement. The building lies adjacent to a Royal Society for the Protection of Birds reserve. Other features include an information centre, shop, and circular walks around the site.

HARLOW
10 miles NE of Waltham Abbey on the A414

The 'New Town' of Harlow sometimes gets short shrift, but it is in fact a lively and vibrant town with a great deal more than excellent shopping facilities. There are some very good museums and several sites of historic interest. The **Gibberd Collection** in Harlow Town Hall in The High offers a delightful collection of British water-colours, featuring works by Blackadder, Sutherland,

Frink, Nash and Sir Frederick Gibberd, Harlow's master planner and the founder of the collection.

Harlow Museum in Passmores House, Third Avenue, occupies a Georgian manor house set in picturesque gardens which includes a lovely pond and is home to several species of butterfly. The museum has extensive and important Roman, post-medieval and early 20th century collections, as well as a full programme of temporary exhibitions.

Mark Hall Cycle Museum and Gardens in Muskham Road offers a unique collection of cycles and cycling accessories illustrating the history of the bicycle from 1818 to the present day, including one made of plastic, one that folds, and one where the seat tips forward and throws its rider over the handlebars if the brakes are applied too hard. The museum is housed in a converted stable block within Mark Hall manor. Adjacent to the museum are three period walled gardens.

Gibberd Gardens, on the eastern outskirts of Harlow in Marsh Lane, Gilden Way, is worth a visit, reflecting as it does the taste of Sir Frederick Gibberd, the famous architect. This 7-acre garden was designed this century by Sir Frederick on the side of a small valley, with terraces, wild garden, landscaped vistas, pools and streams and some 80 sculptures.

Harlow Study and Visitors Centre in Netteswellbury Farm is set in a medieval tithe barn and 13th century church. The site has displays outlining the story of Harlow New Town.

Parndon Wood Nature Reserve, Parndon Wood Road, is an ancient woodland with a fine variety of birds, mammals, and insects. Facilities include two nature trails with hides for observing wildlife, and a study centre.

OLD HARLOW
1 mile E of Harlow off the A414

Facing the village green in the tranquil and picturesque village of Old Harlow,

With Stansted Airport just a few miles north, and close to many areas of scenic beauty and interest, the hotel makes a good base from which to explore this part of Essex and environs.

ROYDON
3 miles W of Harlow off the A414

Preserved in this handsome village are the old parish cage, stocks and a whipping post. Just about 1 mile southwest of Roydon are the ruins of Tudor **Nether Hall**, a manor house that once belonged to the Coates family. Here Thomas More came to woo and win the elder daughter of John Coates.

CHIPPING ONGAR
8 miles SE of Harlow on the A414

Today firmly gripped in the commuter belt of London, Chipping Ongar began as a Saxon market town protected beneath the walls of a Norman castle. The motte and bailey were built by Richard de Lucy in 1155. Indeed, the town's name comes from 'cheaping',

THE GABLES RESTAURANT

1 Fore Street, Old Harlow, Essex CM17 0AA
Tel: 01279 427108
website: www.gables-restaurant.co.uk

Parts of the distinguished and justly well-known **Gables Restaurant** date back some 500 years. Built as an open hall house, the front door is on the site of the original medieval entrance. Over the years various additions and extensions were made to the original building, to create the impressive structure that stands today. There has been a restaurant on the premises since the 1930s. Owners Stephen and Anne-Marie Taylor have been here since 1991, offering a high standard of service, comfort and quality to all their guests. Open midday to 2 p.m. for lunch and 7 to 9 p.m. for evening meals, this fine restaurant offers an extensive menu of traditional and more innovative dishes. The decor and furnishings match the understated elegance and classic presentation of the many tempting dishes. Closed Saturday lunch, Sunday evening, Monday lunch and Bank Holidays. Booking advised at all times.

meaning market. Only the mound and moat of the castle remain, but the contemporary **Church of St Martin of Tours** still stands. Built in 1080, it has fine Norman flint walls and an anchorite's recess.

There are several other interesting buildings in the town, some dating from Elizabethan times.

Explorer David Livingstone was a pupil pastor of the town's 19th century United Reform Church, and lived in Livingstone Cottages before his missionary work in Africa began.

BOBBINGWORTH
2 miles NW of Chipping Ongar off the A414

Blake Hall Gardens at Bobbingworth near Chipping Ongar incorporates a Tropical House, an Ice House, water garden, wild gardens, herbaceous borders, rose garden, sunken garden, duck pond and an ornamental wood. There is also an 'Airscene Aviation' Museum run by local RAF enthusiasts.

WILLINGALE
3 miles NE of Chipping Ongar off the B184

St Christopher's and **St Andrew's**, churches of the respective parishes of Willingale Doe and Willingale Spain, stand side by side in the same churchyard in the heart of this lovely village. St Andrew's is the older, dating back to the 12th century; it is protected by the Churches Conservation Trust.

FYFIELD
2 miles N of Chipping Ongar off the B184

The name 'Fyfield' means five river meadows. Originally a Saxon enclave, the village church of St Nicholas is Norman. There's a beautiful mill house with flood gates in village. Fyfield Hall, opposite the church, is said to be the oldest inhabited timber frame building in England (870 AD).

BEAUCHAMP RODING
3 miles NE of Chipping Ongar off the B184

One of the eight Rodings, it was at Beauchamp Roding that a local farm labourer, Isaac Mead, worked and saved enough to

THE QUEENS HEAD FYFIELD

Queens Street, Fyfield, Essex CM5 0RY
Tel: 01277 899231

The Queens Head Fyfield is approximately 500 years old, and has probably always been an ale house. Traditional features inside and out add to the pub's charm and comfort. The interior features low heavily beamed ceilings and upright beams, wood floors and bar, and a log-burning stove within the attractive brick fireplace. Totally unspoilt, this wonderful old English Free House is well worth a visit, not least for its great range of real ales, including Adnams Broadside and changing guest ales including Castle Eden, Camerons Strong Arm, and those from local breweries like the one at Crouch

End. The menu is yet another attraction of this superior pub, with a menu boasting tempting and expertly prepared dishes such as pan-fired veal, steaks, duck, pork fillet or sirloin steak. Fish is a speciality; a typical menu offers four different fruits of the sea including red mullet, Dover sole, halibut, skate, cod, red snapper, and king prawns with mussels. Food is served at lunch and evenings, from midday to 2 p.m. and 7.30 to 10 p.m. The service is courteous, friendly and efficient.

THE WHITE HART

Swan Lane, Margaretting Tye,
Ingatestone, Essex CM4 9JX
Tel: 01277 840478 Fax: 01277 841178
email: @thewhitehart.uk.com
website: www.thewhitehart.uk.com

An excellent public house serving great food, **The White Hart** in Margaretting Tye is well worth seeking out. Fresh home-cooked food awaits all guests at this popular pub, which dates back in parts to the 1600s. Swan Lane is a Grade II listed street, and the snug bar is over 200 years old. The heavily beamed vaulted ceiling and open fires add to the traditional feel of this cosy pub.

Classic favourites abound, such as liver and bacon, Sunday roasts, steak and ale pie, gammon, and spotted dick for pudding, but there are also more innovative dishes including lemon Sole filled

with crab and seafood sauce, and Cajun chicken curry. There are also special children's, vegetarian, and "evening snacks" menus. Owners Jim and Jan offer all their guests a warm welcome, and the atmosphere in this superior pub is always friendly and comfortable.

Real ale enthusiasts will find at least four permanent ales on tap - including Adnams and Greene King IPA - along with up to two regularly changing guest ales from local breweries and those further afield.

Two fine walks start at the pub - the Margaretting Tye walk and the Fristling walk - which makes it a popular rest stop

with walkers, ramblers and cyclists. The pub is also home to the village darts and golf society, cribbage league, and car clubs such as the Panther club and Rovers club (new members always welcome). Traditional games played here include shove ha'penny. Very much at the heart of village life, this great pub hosts regular theme nights, such as curry or pasta nights, once a month.

Jim and Jan's future plans include a new conservatory dining area, and two letting rooms in the lovely thatched barn adjacent to the pub. More delights await the visitor outside, with a safe children's play area with bouncy castle, interesting pets corner with goats and other farm animals, Arthur's Aviary, and large duck pond with waterfall.

The pub is open: Monday to Saturday 11.30 - 3 p.m. and 6 - 11 p.m.; Sunday midday - 10.30 p.m. Lunch is served every day from midday to 2 p.m.; dinners Monday to Thursday 6.30 - 9 p.m., Friday and Saturday 6 - 9.30 p.m. For more information on the menus and special events, please do visit this pub's very helpful website.

become a farmer himself in 1882. To show his gratitude to the land that made him his fortune, he had a corner of the field consecrated as an eternal resting place for himself and his family. Their graves can still be seen in the undergrowth.

Beauchamp's **Church of St Botolph** stands alone in the fields, marked by a tall 15th century tower and reached by a track off the B184. Inside, the raised pews at the west end have clever space-saving wooden steps, pulled out of slots by means of iron rings.

GOOD EASTER
5 miles NE of Chipping Ongar off the B184

A quiet farming village, now in the commuter belt for London, Good Easter's claim to fame is the making of a world-record daisy chain (6,980 ft 7 inches) in 1985. The village's interesting name is probably derived from 'Easter', the Old English for 'sheepfolds' and 'Good' from a Saxon lady named Godiva.

Close to Good Easter and thus named because it stands on higher ground than its neighbour, **High Easter** is a quiet and very picturesque village not far from the impressive **Aythorpe Post Mill**.

BLACKMORE
3 miles N of Chipping Ongar off the A414

The plague almost totally destroyed the village of Blackmore. Red Rose Lane was so-named because a red rose had to be given at the toll to indicate clear health from the dreaded disease. Henry VIII's mistress Bessie Blount lived in Jericho Priory in the village. Her son by Henry, the Earl of Rochford, also made his home here.

INGATESTONE
6 miles E of Chipping Ongar off the B1002

Ingatestone Hall on Hall Lane is a 16th century mansion set in 11 acres of grounds. It was built by Sir William Petre, Secretary of State to four Monarchs, whose family continue to reside here. The Hall contains family portraits, furniture and memorabilia accumulated over the centuries. Guided tours by prior arrangement.

MARGARETTING TYE
6 miles E of Chipping Ongar off the A12/B1007

The nickname of the town is Tigers Island. In bygone days it would flood all round the village and legend has it that on Fridays bare knuckle fights took place called *Tigers*.

THE BULL

Church Street, Blackmore,
Essex CM4 0RN
Tel: 01277821208 Fax: 01277824966
e-mail: bullblackmore@freenetname.co.uk
www.bullblackmore.co.uk.

The Bull dates back to 1387. Today it boasts a good selection of real ales and guest beers and has gained a reputation for excellent home-made food and a friendly ambience. It opens daily, for lunch and dinner.

Situated in the lovely village of Blackmore, along the St. Peter's Way Walk, The Bull is popular with a varied clientele including young and old, walkers, cyclists, locals and visitors alike.

Susan and Victor Moor, the proprietors, are welcoming hosts and they and their staff work hard to ensure a high quality of service. The daily specials board offers a large selection of home-made curries, pasta or game dishes and traditional English fayre together with a vegetarian option and a mouth-watering choice of sweets, Reservations are advisable. For details of their special culinary evenings telephone or view the website. The traditional decor of the Pub helps create a relaxed and cosy atmosphere. In the summer the garden, overlooking the village green, is open to guests and their children. The "Bicycle Shop" is a non-smoking, intimate eating area off the main bar, ideal for private parties up to 14 people and also available for meetings and lunches.

Susan and Victor look forward to welcoming you to The Bull.

THE PLOUGH

169 Roman Road, Mountnessing, Brentwood, Essex CM15 0UG
Tel: 01277 352026

The outstanding **Plough** public house stands in the picturesque village of Mountnessing, found on the B1002 old Roman road between Brentwood and Chelmsford. Large and welcoming, it is set back from the road behind an attractive white picket fence. Owners Steve and Carol took over back in November 1999; the pub is well recommended both locally and in the outlying villages. Carol and Steve have many years'
experience in the trade,
and it shows: the service
and hospitalilty are second
to none.

Parts of the building
date back to the 18th
century, with additions
over time. The interior is
a real eye-opener: tasteful
and traditional, with
brasses, photographs and
a wealth of memorabilia
adorning the exposed
beamwork and walls. The
ambience is always warm
and inviting.

Open all day every day
for quality ales, there are
always at least four real
ales on tap at this fine Free
House, including Courage Best and Crouch Vale Best, together with two regularly changing, selected for their quality, guest ales from all round the country. Carol buys direct from brewers. There's also a smooth ale, plus draught lager, cider and stout. The wine list offers a range of fine vintages. Excellent meals are available at every session bar Sunday evening, with lunch served between midday and 3

p.m. and dinner from 6 to
9.30/10 p.m. Steve prepares
all the dishes, and is an
accomplished cook, creating
the many hot and cold
home-made dishes on the
extensive menu, listed on the
blackboard. Regular changes
are made to the menu all the
time to accommodate the
changing seasons and
availability of the freshest
local ingredients. Special
individual requests for
particular dishes can even be
catered for, with two days'
notice. Booking is essential
on Fridays, Saturdays and
Sundays at this popular and
friendly establishment. The
Sunday lunch is particularly renowned, with three - sometimes four - roast meats on offer. The seating is very comfortable, the staff attentive, helpful and amiable.

Outside there is seating at the front of the pub and to the rear, in the lovely beer garden equipped with swings and slides for the children. This top-of-the-range pub is well worth seeking out.

MOUNTNESSING
6 miles SE of Chipping Ongar off the A12

This village has a beautifully restored early 19th century windmill as its main landmark, though the isolated church also has a massive beamed belfry. **Mountnessing Post Mill** in Roman Road is open to the public. This traditional weatherboarded post mill was built in 1807 and restored to working order in 1983. Visitors can see the huge wooden and iron gears; one pair of stones have been opened up for viewing.

KELVEDON HATCH
4 miles S of Chipping Ongar off the A128

A simple bungalow in the rural Essex village of Kelvedon Hatch is the deceptively simple exterior for the **Kelvedon Secret Nuclear Bunker**. Built in 1952, 40,000 tons of concrete were used to create a base for up to 600 top Government and civilian personnel in the event of nuclear war. Visitors can explore room after room to see communications equipment, a BBC studio, sick bay, massive kitchens and dormitories, power and filtration plant, government administration room and the scientists' room, where nuclear fall-out patterns would have been measured.

GREENSTED
1½ miles SW of Chipping Ongar off the A414

St Andrew's in Greensted is the country's oldest wooden church, dating from the 9th-11th centuries, with a later Tudor chancel. It is famous as the only surviving example of a Saxon log church extant in the world, built from split oak logs held together with dowells. Over the centuries the church has been enlarged and restored; later additions include the simple weatherboarded tower, Norman flint walls, the Tudor tiled roof, Victorian stone coping, porch and stained glass windows. The body of King Edmund is known to have been rested here in 1013.

The village also has associations with the Tolpuddle 'martyrs', six Dorset farm labourers who were taken to court on a legal technicality because they agitated for better conditions and wages, and formed a Trade Union. After their conviction in 1834 they were condemned to transportation to Australia for seven years. There was a public outcry for their release, and their sentences were commuted in 1837. Unable to return to Dorset, they were granted tenancies in Greensted and High Laver. One of the martyrs, James Brine, of New House Farm (now Tudor Cottage, on Greensted Green), married Elizabeth Standfield, daughter of one of his fellow victims - the record of their marriage in 1839 can be seen in the parish register.

NORTH WEALD
3 miles W of Chipping Ongar off the A414

North Weald Airfield Museum at Ad Astra House, Hurricane Way, North Weald Bassett is a small, meticulously detailed museum displaying the history of North Weald from 1916 to the present. Collections of photos and artefacts such as uniforms and the detailed records of all flying operations are on display. There is also a video exhibit recounting a day to day account of North Weald history. Guided tours of the airfield can be arranged for large groups.

BRENTWOOD

Brentwood is a very pleasant shopping and entertainment centre, with quite a distinguished past. The town was on the old pilgrim and coaching routes to and from London. Mainly post-war in character, the town is the headquarters of Ford Motors.

Brentwood Cathedral on Ingrave Road was built in 1991. This classically-styled church incorporates the original Victorian church that stood on this spot. It was designed by the much-admired architect Quinlan Terry, with roundels by Rapael Maklouf (who also created the relief of the Queen's head used on current coins).

Brentwood Centre on Doddinghurst Road is one of the top entertainment venues in the UK, with an extensive programme of concerts, shows, bands and top comedy names. Sport and fitness facilities include pool, health suite, sunbeds, jacuzzi, and sauna.

Brentwood Museum at Cemetery Lode in Lorne Road, in the Warley Hill area of

Brentwood, is a small and picturesque cottage museum concentrating on local and social interests during the late 19th and early 20th centuries. It is set in an attractive disused cemetery, which is in itself of unique interest.

Thorndon Country Park and Hartswood, boast historic parkland, lakes and woods. The site, formerly a Royal deer park, also features a wildlife exhibition and attractive gift shop.

Another good day out in the open air can be had at Old Macdonald's Farm Park, where visitors can see the largest selection of pure bred British farm animals and poultry in the southeast of England.

AROUND BRENTWOOD

STOCK
6 miles NE of Brentwood off the B1007

Stock boasts a fine old 19th century tower windmill on five floors, with superb 19th century machinery which has been restored to working order. Stock's delightful church

has a traditional Essex-style wooden belfry and spire, lending character to this pleasant village of well-kept houses.

BILLERICAY
6 miles E of Brentwood off the A129

There was a settlement here as far back as the Bronze Age, though there is no conclusive explanation of Billericay's name. There is no question about the attraction of the High Street, though, with its timber weather-boarding and Georgian brick. **The Chantry House**, built in 1510, was the home of Christopher Martin, treasurer to the Pilgrim Fathers.

The Peasants' Revolt of 1381 saw the massacre of hundreds of rebels just northeast of the town at **Norsey Wood**. Today this area of ancient woodland is a country park, managed by coppicing (the traditional way of ensuring the timber supply), which also encourages plant- and birdlife.

Barleylands Farm Museum features a glass-blowing studio and has one of the largest collections of vintage farm machinery in the country.

THE THATCHERS ARMS

Warley Road, Great Warley, Brentwood, Essex CM13 3HU
Tel: 01277 233535
email: JimSarah@supernet.co.uk

The Thatchers Arms is a large and handsome public house believed to date back to the 16th century. Adjoining Warley Place Nature Reserve, it attracts many walkers and other visitors to this beautiful part of the county. Though just a mile and a half from Brentwood, it is a haven of peace and relaxation surrounded by lovely countryside. The interior is old-fashioned in the best sense of the word, with comfortable seating and lovely panelling. Real ales include Courage Best and Directors Plus, as well as a changing guest ale. Owners Jim and Sarah are well experienced in the licenced trade and came here to The Thatchers Arms in January 2000.

In the separate (no smoking) dining area, Jim's excellent lunch and dinner menus offer a range of traditional main courses and light snacks at lunchtime (served between midday and 3 p.m.) and hearty and delicious evening meals (6 to 9.30 p.m./10 p.m. at weekends), including braised lamb, breast of duck, scampi, trout and sirloin steaks. There are also daily specials. Booking is essential for the justly popular Sunday roast. An attractive decked patio area adjoins the dining room.

THE GREEN MAN PUB AND RESTAURANT

Navestock Side, Brentwood, Essex CM14 5SD
Tel: 01277 372231

The **Green Man Pub and Restaurant** in Navestock Side, near Brentwood, is a hospitable and friendly pub with an excellent menu of traditional favourites and a good range of beers, wines and spirits. Londoners Bob and Janet came here in April of 1994, and offer all their guests a warm and friendly welcome. Previously a hunting lodge for the Dubbrook Estate (the "big house" is only a mile away, though now operates as a nursing home), the very attractive building has been a pub since 1620. The exterior is pristine, with whitewashed stonework and elegant red shutters over the traditional casement windows. The interior boasts three separate bars, with high ceilings and a feeling of spaciousness. real ales include Tetleys, Friary and Courage. Booking is advised for the popular Sunday roast. The menu offers a variety of delicious meals, expertly prepared and presented. Fish is particularly popular - guests have a choice of halibut, dover sole and swordfish, to name but three.

GREAT WARLEY
1 mile S of Brentwood on the B186

Warley Place was formerly home to one of the most famous women gardeners, Ellen Willmott, who died in 1934. She introduced to Warley - and to Britain - many exotic plants. A trail takes visitors through what is now Warley Place Nature Reserve, with 16 acres of what was once domesticated garden but has now reverted to woodland. A fascinating selection of trees, shrubs and wildlife make this well worth a visit.

SOUTH WEALD
2 miles W of Brentwood off the A12

This very attractive village has at its outskirts, **Weald Country Park**, a former estate with medieval deer park, partially landscaped in the 1700s. Featuring lake and woodland, visitors' centre, landscapes exhbition and gift shop, with facilities for fishing and horse-riding, there are guided events and activities programmes held throughout the year.

Old Macdonalds Educational Farm Park in Weald Road is a centre specialising in British farm livestock, with nine breeds of pig, 23 of sheep, six of cattle, 30 of poultry and 30 of rabbit to see and learn about. There are also Shire horses, owls, deer and lots more - in short, the largest selection of farm animals and birds in Essex. Guided tours by appointment. The farm holds daily demonstrations and craft displays; the site

also boasts nature trails, an attractive gift shop, playground, classroom facilities and café.

THE NORTH THAMES CORRIDOR

Bordering the north bank of the Thames, the borough of Thurrock has long been a gateway to London but also affords easy access to southwest Essex and to Kent. This thriving borough encompasses huge swathes of green belt country, and along its 18 miles of Thames frontage there are many important marshland wildlife habitats. This stretch of Essex affords some marvellous walking, cycling, birdwatching and other nature pursuits. The area has many bridleways, footpaths and country parks, including Davy Down within the Mardyke Valley. The river's flood plain is a broad tract of grassland which is an important feature of the landscape of the area.

GRAYS
12 miles S of Brentwood on the A1089

Thurrock Museum is in the Thameside Complex in Grays. It collects, conserves and displays items of archaeology and local history from prehistoric times to the end of the 20th century. The archaeological items include flint and metal tools of people who

The Theobald Arms

Kings Walk, Grays, Essex RM17 6HR
Tel: 01375 372253

By far the smartest and most loved public house in Grays, **The Theobald Arms** is situated opposite the once thriving Grays dockyard. There has been an alehouse alongside the docks for hundreds of years. Once known as The Hoy, in 1816 the pub changed its name to honour the lord of the manor. Leaseholder Maureen Smith and her son Roy are friendly and hospitable hosts. Locals and visitors mix happily in this cosy milieu. Open every session weekdays and all day Friday to Sunday, there are always four real ales on tap, including Courage Best and changing ales from all over the nation. Over 500 ales have been on offer over the years. the varied pump clips are proudly displayed above the bar and on the exposed beamwork. Food is available at lunchtime from Monday to Friday, with a range of home-made dishes. The pub holds a popular beer festival every summer - please ring for details.

lived in prehistoric Thurrock and pottery, jewellery and coins from the Roman and Saxon period.

Thameside Theatre in Grays town centre offers a good range of productions throughout the year, with a popular pantomime now 24 years strong.

WEST THURROCK
1½ miles SW of Grays off the A13

Immortalised by the film *Four Weddings and a Funeral*, little **St Clement's church** occupies a striking location and is one of a number of picturesque ancient churches in the borough. Although this 12th century church is now deconsecrated, it was in its day a stopping point for pilgrims; visitors can see the remains of its original round tower.

Arena Essex is the chief venue for motorsports in the area. Regular 'banger racing' takes place at the track in West Thurrock, near **Lakeside Shopping Centre** and Retail Park. The Centre attracts around 22 million visitors a year, and boasts over 300 shops, a children's indoor adventure centre, food court and multiplex cinema. The Retail Park features more shops as well as restaurants, a cinema, a leisure bingo complex and a watersports centre at the lake.

PURFLEET
3 miles W of Grays off the M25

Fans of Bram Stoker's novel *Dracula* will know that in this book the famous vampire

buys a house called 'Carfax' in Purfleet. The town's esteemed **Royal Hotel** is said to have played host to Edward VII, while still Prince of Wales in the 1880s and 1890s, at which time the hotel was called Wingrove's.

The **Purfleet Heritage and Military Centre** is a heritage and military museum featuring displays of many items of interest and memorabilia in the setting of the No 5 Gunpowder Magazine on Centurion Way. This remaining magazine was built in the 1770s for testing and issuing gun powder to the army and navy.

Purfleet Conservation Area includes several buildings which were part of a planned village built by the one-time owners of the chalk quarry, the Whitbread family.

AVELEY
3 miles NW of Grays off the M25

Mardyke Valley is an important wildlife corridor running from Ship Lane in Aveley to Orsett Fen. Many pleasant views can be had along the seven-mile stretch along footpaths and bridleways. Davy Down within Mardyke Valley is a public centre of leisure and learning. The Visitors' Centre in the gatehouse leads to a well-preserved water pumping station, which is open on the first Sunday of each month.

Aveley's 12th century **St Michael's Church** features many Flemish brasses and other items of historical interest.

THE PARK TAVERN

Romford Road, Aveley, South Ockenden, Essex RM15 4PH
Tel: 01708 863798

The Park Tavern is a friendly family-run public house which is run by Peter and Jackie, assisted by their children Peter, Paul and Paige. Since their arrival in 1999 they have given a new lease of life to this excellent inn. Prior to this, Peter worked as host to celebrities performing at the well-known Circus Tavern in Purfleet, as attested to by the numerous photos of Peter and famous faces which are

displayed above and around the bar area. The range of bitters, lagers, cider and stout is truly impressive, including Worthington, Toby, Caffreys and Scrumpy Jack, and the atmosphere always welcoming in this superb pub. There's live entertainment Friday and Saturday nights, and a lovely beer garden. Great food is available midday to 5 p.m., with a varied menu of dishes made from the freshest ingredients. The Sunday roast is particularly popular, and rightly so.

SOUTH OCKENDEN
3 miles N of Grays off the A13

Belhus Woods Country Park covers approximately 180 acres and contains an interesting variety of habitats, including woodland, two lakes and the remains of a pond designed by 'Capability' Brown. The Visitors' Centre to this superb park can be found at the main entrance off Romford Road. Belhus Park Golf Course is a well-established 18 hole course set within this beautiful parkland.

Grangewaters Country Park, also in South Ockenden, has two lakes. Managed by Thurrock Environmental and Outdoor Centre, it offers watersports such as water-skiing, windsurfing, sailing and canoeing, as well as mountain biking, climbing and other outdoor pursuits. **Brannetts Wood** is one of the oldest recorded ancient woodlands in South Essex. It can be reached from the Mardyke Way, or from Stifford Road here in South Ockendon.

The village **Church of St Nicholas** has one of only six round church towers in Essex. This one was built in the 13th century and used to have a spire, which was sadly destroyed by lightning in the 17th century.

ORSETT
4 miles NE of Grays off the A13

This village was the original seat of local government for the area, and in medieval times the site of one of the palaces of the Bishop of London. The village animal pound and lock-up, the latter last used as a prison in 1848, still exist.

Thurrock Aerodrome, located between Orsett and Bulphan on the A128, hosts the Orsett Air Fete every year in early August.

HORNDON-ON-THE-HILL
6 miles NE of Grays off the B1007

Listed in the Domesday Book as *Horninduna*, a name which also appears on a Saxon coin of Edward the Confessor (1042-1066), it is said to have once been the site of a Royal Anglo-Saxon mint. The town's 16th century **Woolmarket** indicates the importance of the wool trade to the region, and is one of the area's historical treasures. The upper room served as Horndon's manor courtroom, while the lower, open area was used for trading in woollen cloth.

The main entrance and Visitors' Centre for **Langdon Hills Conservation Centre and Nature Reserve** are located off the Lower Dunton Road north of Horndon-on-the-Hill. A bridleway and footpaths lead visitors to meadows, a pond and outstanding ancient woods. Also within the reserve is the **Plotlands Museum**, housed in an original 1930s plotland bungalow known as the Haven.

CORRINGHAM
7 miles NE of Grays off the A1014

Corringham has a picturesque cluster of timber-framed houses in the old village, leading up to its medieval church, which retains some Saxon and Norman features. **Langdon Hills Country Park** north of Corringdon is 400 acres of ancient woodland and meadows. It has many rare trees and spectacular views of the Essex countryside.

FOBBING
8 miles NE of Grays off the A1014

Fobbing is known for its association with the Peasants' Revolt of 1381. On the outside of the village's White Lion public house there is a plaque from 1981 commemorating the 600th anniversary of this people's rebellion.

LINGFORD
3 miles NE of Grays off the A13

Walton Hall Farm Museum on Walton Hall Road has a large collection of historic farm machinery in a 17th century barn. It afford visitors the opportunity to watch traditional craftsmen, such as a blacksmith, saddlemaker, printer and wheelwright.

STANFORD-LE-HOPE
4 miles NE of Grays off the A1014

Stanford Marshes is an area to the south of Stanford-le-Hope, next to the Thames. The Marshes are home to a variety of wildlife and are an ideal location for birdwatching. **Grove House Wood** in Stanford-le-Hope is a nature reserve managed by Essex Wildlife Trust and the local Girl Guides. A footpath here leads to reed beds, a pond and a brook as well as an area of woodland.

The graveyard of St Margaret's Church has an unusual half-barrelled tomb decorated with a gruesome stone-carved symbol of death.

CANVEY ISLAND
10 miles NE of Grays off the A130

Canvey Island is a peaceful and picturesque stretch of land overlooking the Thames estuary with views to neighbouring Kent.

The island boasts two unusual museums: **Dutch Cottage Museum** is an early 17th century eight-sided cottage built by Dutch workmen for Dutch workmen and boasting many traditional Flemish features. **Castle Point Transport Museum** is housed in a 1930s bus garage. It houses a fascinating collection of historic and modern buses and coaches, mainly of East Anglian origin.

WEST TILBURY
3 miles E of Grays off the AA1089

West Tilbury was the site chosen for the Camp Royal in 1588, to prepare for the threatened Spanish invasion. Queen Elizabeth I visited the army here, and made her famous speech,

'I know I have the body but of a weak and feeble woman: but I have the heart and stomach of a king, and a king of England too.'

Hidden away in rural tranquillity overlooking the Thames estuary, West Tilbury remains unspoilt in spite of its proximity to

THE SHIP

Princess Margaret Road, East Tilbury Village, Essex, RM18 8PB
Tel: 01375 843041

Well known for its excellent ales and food, **The Ship** is a fine Free House open all day every day. There are always four real ales to choose from at this comfortable and friendly pub, including Greene King Abbot and Tetley Cask Conditioned as well as two regularly changing guest ales. Food is available from midday to 2 p.m. and 6 to 9.30 p.m. The owners, David and Lesley Burrough share cooking duties, preparing a tempting range of menu dishes and daily specials such as home-made steak and kidney pie. The pub is spacious and welcoming, with a warm and inviting interior decor and furnishings; outside there's a large beer garden with safe children's play area. While visiting Coalhouse Fort and the other attractions of East Tilbury, this is the perfect place to enjoy a relaxing drink or meal.

busy, industrial Tilbury. The former local church (now a private dwelling) in this quaint little village is a nautical landmark used for navigation. The list of Rectors of the church, dating from 1279-1978, when the church was disestablished, can be seen in The Kings Head Pub.

EAST TILBURY
5 miles E of Grays off the A13

Coalhouse Fort is considered to be one of the best surviving examples of a Victorian Casement fortress in the country. As such it is a protected Scheduled Ancient Monument. Built between 1861 and 1874 as a first line of defence for the Thames area to protect the Thames area against invasion, it stands on the site of other defensive works and fortifications dating back to around 1400. Even before the Middle Ages, this was an important site.

Part of the construction work on the Fort was overseen by Gordon of Khartoum. It was constructed to be a dedicated Artillery casement fortress, which means that the guns were housed in large vaulted rooms with armour-plated frontages. Beneath these rooms lies an extensive magazine tunnel system to service the artillery.

Over the years many alterations were made to the Fort to accommodate new artillery. The Fort was manned during both World Wars, and is now owned by Thurrock Borough Council and administered by The Coalhouse Fort Project, a registered charity manned entirely by volunteers. Open to the public, it contains reconstructions of period guns and other displays, and also houses the **Thameside Aviation Museum**, with a large collection of local finds and other aviation material. In the two parade grounds visitors will find various artillery pieces and military vehicles. One recent addition to the many pieces of historical military equipment is a Bofor Anti-Aircraft Gun of the Second World War. The site also offers visitors the chance to handle period equipment or try on a period uniform.

During the year the Fort hosts a range of shows, including an historic artillery rally when various big guns are fired by crews in the uniforms of the period, including a Second World War crew firing a 1940 25pdr

field gun. A guided tour (included in the price of admission) allows visitors to see the magazine tunnels beneath the gun casements and offer a feel for the work and conditions of a Victorian gunner. The tour also takes in the roof of the Fort, from which you will be able to judge for yourself the value of a fortification at this point along the Thames. The view from here is outstanding, taking in the two sister forts in Kent and, on a clear day, Southend.

The Fort is set in a lovely riverside park with walks and a children's play area, as well as other items of military history including a Quick Fire Battery and Minefield Control box. You can also follow the old railway tracks, from the Fort to the side of the old jetty, where many of the armaments and supplies for the fort were shipped in.

It is possible that East Tilbury's St Catherine's church occupies the site of one of the first Christian monasteries in the 7th century. Its half-built tower was constructed by the First World War Garrison of Coalhouse Fort.

The Bata Estate is a conservation area of architectural and historical interest. Established in 1933, the British Bata Shoe Company was the creation of Czech-born Thomas Bata, who also developed a housing estate for his workforce. This range of uniform flat-roofed houses can still be seen on site.

TILBURY
3 miles SE of Grays off the A1089

Tilbury Fort is a well-preserved and unusual 17th century structure with double moat. The fort affords tremendous views of the Thames estuary. The most violent episode in the fort's history occurred in 1776, during a particularly vociferous cricket match which left three people dead. For a small fee visitors to the fort can fire a 1943 3.7 anti-aircraft gun - a prospect most children and many adults find irresistible!. Owned by English heritage, the site was used for a military Block House during the reign of Henry VIII and was rebuilt in the 17th century. It remains one of Britain's finest examples of a star-shaped bastion fortress. Extensions were made in the 18th and 19th centuries, and the Fort was still being used in the Second World War.

Tilbury Festival is held every year in July in the field near the fort, and features arena events, craft and food stalls and re-enactments. **Tilbury Energy and Environment Centre** at Tilbury Power Station provides a nature reserve and study centre for schools and community education. There is a flat two-mile nature trail leading to and from the Centre.

SOUTHEND-ON-SEA
22 miles E of Grays on the A127

Beside the seaside in Southend-on-Sea there is always plenty to do and see, and many events throughout the year to ensure its interest and popularity. The town is one of the best loved and most friendly resorts in Britain, featuring the very best ingredients for a break at the seaside. With seven miles of beaches and the only European Blue Flag award in Essex, this treasure trove boasts **Adventure Island** theme park, **Cliffs Bandstand, Cliffs Pavilion**, a distinguished art gallery and several interesting museums.

Southend Pier and Museum brings to life the fascinating past of the longest Pleasure Pier in the world. The Pier itself is 1.3 miles long; visitors can either take a leisurely walk along its length or take advantage of the regular train service that plies up and down the pier.

Central Museum and Planetarium on Victoria Avenue is the only planetarium in the southeast outside London, and also features local history exhibits. **Beecroft Art Gallery** boasts the work of four centuries of artistic endeavour.

The Sealife Centre employs the most advanced technology to bring you incredibly close to the wonders of British marine life. The Centre offers fun ways of exploring life under the waves, with concave bubble windows helping to make it seem you're actually part of the sea creatures' environment. Another exhibit features a

walk-through tunnel along a reconstructed seabed. The Shark Exhibition is not to be missed.

A floral trail guided tour around the parks and gardens will reveal why Southend has won the Britain in Bloom Awards every year since 1993, as well as medals at the Chelsea Flower Show.

The Kursaal is a new indoor entertainment complex, one of the largest in the country, with indoor bowling, synthetic ice and roller rink, a fun casino, children' play area, snooker and pool, arts and crafts, retail units and theme restaurants.

Boat trips in summer include occasional

Southend Beach

outings on a vintage paddle steamer. Ferry trips to Felixstowe are also available from Southend.

The **Southchurch Hall Museum** in Park Lane is a delightful 13th to 14th century timber-framed manor house with various displays and landscaped gardens. Period room settings are among this museums many delights.

Prittlewell Priory Museum, slightly north of Southend town centre in Priory Park, is a

Prittlewell Priory Park

well-preserved 12th century Cluniac Priory set in lovely grounds and housing collections of the Priory's history, natural history and the Caten collection of radios and communications.

OLD LEIGH
½ mile W of Southend off the A13

The unspoilt fishing village of Old Leigh has a long and distinguished history. It is picturesque, with seafront houses and narrow winding alleys. It has also earned its place in history: The pilgrim ship The Mayflower restocked here enroute to the New World of America back in the mid-17th century, and the Dunkirk rescue embarked from here, as commemorated in a framed poem on the wall of the local pub, The Crooked Billet.

LEIGH-ON-SEA
2 miles W of Southend off the A13

Leigh-on-Sea has quite a distinct character to Southend, being more intimate and serene, with wood-clad buildings and shrimp boats in the working harbour. The shellfish stall on the harbourside is justly famous. The **Leigh Heritage Centre**, housed in a former ancient blacksmith's, now houses historical artefacts.

HADLEIGH
5 miles NW of Southend off the A13

Hadleigh Castle, built originally for Edward III, is owned by English Heritage and once belonged to Anne of Cleves, Catherine of

Aragon and Katherine Parr. The ruins were also immortalised in a painting by Constable. The remains of this once impressive castle can still be seen.

Hadleigh Castle Country Park offers a variety of woodland and coastal walks.

HULLBRIDGE
8 miles NW of Southend off the A132

Jakapeni Rare Breed Farm at Burlington Gardens in Hullbridge is a pleasant small holding set in 30 acres of rolling countryside. Specialising in sheep and pigs, with other pets and wildlife, there's also a fishing lake, country walk and pets corner. Snacks and light refreshments are available from the café, and there's an attractive shop.

HOCKLEY
6 miles NW of Southend off the A129

Hockley Woods is a 280 acre ancient woodland, managed for the benefit of wildlife and the public. Traditional coppice management encourages a diverse array of flora and fauna, including the nationally rare Heath Fritillary butterfly.

Volpaia in Woodlands Road is a lily specialist's small but beautiful woodside garden, with rare collected species and own-bred hybrid lilies, shade-loving shrubs and plants for sale.

RAYLEIGH
6 miles NW of Southend off the A1016

Dutch Cottage at Crown Hill in Rayleigh is a traditional Flemish eight-sided cottage based on a 17th century design created by Dutch settlers.

Rayleigh Mount is a prominent landmark in this part of the county. Once a motte and bailey castle built in the 11th century, it was abandoned some 200 years later. Rayleigh Windmill, in Bellingham Lane close to Rayleigh Mount, was built circa 1798; the tower mill houses a fascinating collection of bygones mostly used in and around Rayleigh.

ROCHFORD
3 miles N of Southend off the B1013

The Old House, at 17 South Street, is an elegant lovingly restored house originally built in 1270. The twisting corridors and handsome rooms of this fine structure offer a glimpse into the past; the building now houses some District Council offices, and is said to be haunted.

CHELMSFORD

Roman workmen cutting their great road linking London with Colchester built a fort at what is today called Chelmsford. Then called *Caesaromagus*, it stands at the confluence of the Rivers Chelmer and Can. The town has always been an important market centre and is now the bustling county town of Essex. It is also directly descended from a new town planned by the Bishop of London in 1199. At its centre are the principal inn, the **Royal Saracen's Head**, and the elegant **Shire Hall** of 1791. Three plaques situated high up on the eastern face of the Hall overlooking the High Street represent Wisdom, Justice and Mercy. The building now houses the town magistrates court.

Christianity came to Essex with the Romans and again, later, by St Cedd (AD 654); in 1914 the diocese of Chelmsford was created. **Chelmsford Cathedral** in New Street dates from the 15th century and is built on the site of a church constructed 800 years ago. The cathedral is noted for the harmony and unity of its perpendicular architecture. It was John Johnson, the distinguished local architect who designed both the Shire Hall and the 18th century **Stone Bridge** over the River Can, who also rebuilt the Parish Church of St Mary when most of its 15th century tower fell down. The church became a cathedral when the new diocese of Chelmsford was created. Since then it has been enlarged and re-organised inside. The cathedral boasts memorial windows dedicated to the USAAF airmen who were based in Essex from 1942-5.

The Marconi Company, pioneers in the manufacture of wireless equipment, set up the first radio company in the world here in Chelmsford in 1899. Exhibits of those pioneering days of wireless can be seen in the **Chelmsford and Essex Museum** in Oaklands Park, as can interesting displays of Roman remains and local history.

The **Essex Regiment Museum** is also situated in Oaklands Park. Together these two fine museums exhibit temporary and permanent displays exploring local and social history from prehistoric times up until the present. The history of the distinguished Essex Regiment, a wealth of fine and decorative arts (including costume, ceramics and glass), coins, natural history displays recounting the geology and wildlife of the region (including a live beehive) and changing special exhibitions add to the interest and informative power of these two Chelmsford landmarks.

Also in the town, at Parkway, is **Moulsham Mill**, an early 18th century water mill that has been renovated and now houses a variety of craft workshops and businesses. Crafts featured include jewellery, pottery, flowers, lace-making, dolls houses and bears, and decoupage work. There is a charming picnic area nearby, and a good café.

Three modern technologies - electrical engineering, radio, and ball and roller bearings - began in Chelmsford. At the Engine House Project at Sandford Mill Waterworks, museum collections from the town's unique industrial story provide a fun and fascinating insight into the science of everyday things.

AROUND CHELMSFORD

GREAT BADDOW
1 mile S of Chelmsford off the A130

Baddow Antiques Centre at the Bringy, Church Street, is one of the leading antiques centres in Essex. Here, 20 dealers offer a wide selection of silver, porcelain, glass, furniture, paintings and collectibles. There is also a collection of 300 Victorian brass and iron bedsteads on display.

SANDON
2 miles SE of Chelmsford off the A414

The village green here in Sandon has produced a notable Spanish oak tree, the biggest in the country, planted in the centre of the village green. This oak tree is remarkable not so much for its height as for the tremendous horizontal spread of its branches. Around the green are a fine church and a number of attractive old houses, some dating back to the 16th century when Henry VIII's Lord Chancellor, Cardinal Wolsey, was Lord of the Manor of Sandon.

SOUTH HANNINGFIELD
6 miles S of Chelmsford off the A130

The placid waters of nearby **Hanningfield Reservoir** were created by damming Sandford Brook, and transformed the scattered rural settlement of Hanningfield into a lakeside village. Now on the shores of the lake, the 12th century village church's belfry has been a local landmark in the flat Essex countryside for centuries. Some of the timbers in the belfry are said to have come from Spanish galleons, wrecked in the aftermath of Sir Francis Drake's defeat of the Armada.

HIGHWOOD
3 miles SW of Chelmsford off the A414

Hylands House was built in 1728 and is slowly being restored. It is set in beautiful parkland and hosts many outdoor events, including the annual 'V' concerts (V98 was a great success) and the Chelmsford Spectacular. The more than 500 acres of beautiful parkland feature lawns and formal gardens. Closed for restoration in 1998, the House is now again open to the public.

WRITTLE
2 miles W of Chelmsford off the A414

From a tucked-away corner of St John's Green in this village came Britain's first regular broadcasting service; an experimental 15 minute programme beamed out nightly by Marconi's engineers. Opposite the Green, the Cock and Bell is reputed to be haunted by a young woman who committed suicide on the

Writtle

railway. Further along this street is the Wheatsheaf, one of the smallest pubs in the country. Writtle's parish church of St John features a cross of charred timbers, a reminder of the fire which gutted the chancel in 1974. Ducks swim on the pond of the larger and quite idyllic main village green, which is surrounded by lovely Tudor and Georgian houses.

GREAT LEIGHS
4 miles N of Chelmsford off the A131

The Great Leighs Great Maze is one of the most challenging in the world. Set in 8.5 acres of lovely North Essex countryside, it is open every summer. The year 2000 brought further innovations, with extra twists and turns to make this wonderful maze even more of a brain teaser. Ten per cent of all profits go to the Essex Air Ambulance service.

HATFIELD PEVERAL
5 miles NE of Chelmsford off the B1137

Located between Chelmsford and Maldon, this quiet rural village offers bucolic scenes, a handsome village green and some charming architecture.

THE WHEATSHEAF
Malden Road, Hatfield Peveral, Chelmsford, Essex CM3 2JF
Tel: 01245 380330

The Wheatsheaf is an attractive and welcoming pub with a large beer garden and aviary with over 100 birds including cockatiels and quail. The interior features low beamed ceilings, large open fire, brickbuilt bar and original "off sales" (or "bottle and jug") window. Commended (1998 and 1999) in Ridleys Best Kept Cellar Competition, the cask ales are complemented by a good range of lagers, wines and spirits. Diners choose from a range of tempting home-cooked and home-prepared dishes.

WITHAM
6 miles NE of Chelmsford off the A12/B1018

The River Brain flows through this delightful town; a continuous walk has been created along its length for a distance of about three miles. The settlement dates back to at least the 10th century; remains of a Roman temple have been found at Ivy Chimneys, off

Hatfield Road. Blackwater Lane leads to Whetmead, a nature reserve of 25 acres between the rivers Blackwater and Brain.

LITTLE BRAXTED
6 miles NE of Chelmsford off the A12/B1018

Little Braxted has been voted the best kept village on a regular basis since 1973. St

THE SPREAD EAGLE HOTEL

Newland Street, Witham, Essex CM8 2BD
Tel: 01376 512131 Fax: 01376 502458

The Spread Eagle Hotel in Witham is a charming coaching inn dating back to the 13th century. Impressive outside and in - from the whitewashed gabled exterior to the comfortable interior which retains many original features - this characterful inn is just the place to enjoy real ales, excellent food and the relaxed and welcoming ambience. The oldest building in Witham, it occupies a place at the heart of the town. Tastefully furnished and decorated throughout, the accommodation comprises 13 cosy and comfortable guest bedrooms, 12 of which are ensuite. The food alone makes a visit here worthwhile, with a menu
boasting a range of delicious
traditional favourites such as
roast beef, braised liver and
onions, home-made flans, hot
pot and salads and sandwiches.
There are also changing daily
specials

And to drink? There's
Greene King IPA and changing
guest ales, as well as a good
variety of lagers, stout, wines
and spirits. Open seven days a
week, food is served every lunch
and evening. Booking is advised
for the tempting and popular
three-course Sunday lunch.

THE GREEN MAN

Kelvedon Road, Little Braxted, Essex CM8 3LB
Tel: 01621 891659

The Green Man is a relaxing and peaceful country pub.
This charming pub upholds the long fine traditional
of English public houses - it is quiet, comfortable and
serves great food and drink. Originally a farmhouse
and some 500 years old, it has been a pub since the
mid-19th century. There's an attractive tree-fringed
garden with flowerbeds, nice lawn, picnic tables and

pretty pond. Inside, a plethora of memorabilia adorns the walls, in the shape of carpenters' tools, horse brasses and Royal Marines artefacts. The public bar contains old photos of the pub over the years and a collection of miniature cars in glass cases. The pumps in both bars are Bofor gun shells. Winner of the Best Kept Cellar award in 1998, 1999 and 2000, real ales include Ridleys IPA, Ridleys Rumpus and Ridleys Monthly Events. Everything on the excellent menu is home-cooked and freshly prepared - worth special mention are the hot French bread snacks and locally produced sausages with a choice of delicious gravies. The food has merited a place in the Egon Ronay guide.

St Nicholas Church, Little Braxted

Mary's chapel was built in 1888, and can only accommodate 12 people at a time. Services are held every Wednesday. The village church of St Nicholas is mentioned in the Domesday Book, and is famous for its murals.

WICKHAM BISHOPS
6 miles NE of Chelmsford off the A12/B1018

This charming village has two handsome local chapels dating back to the 17th century.

LITTLE BADDOW
5 miles E of Chelmsford off the A414

Blakes Wood is a designated Site of Special Scientific Interest, an ancient woodland of hornbeam and sweet chestnut renowned for its bluebells. There is a good circular way-marked one-and-a-half mile walk.

Cruising along the **Chelmer and Blackwater Canal** provides the visitor with a unique view of this part of rural Essex. Chelmer Cruises at Paper Mill Lock in Little Baddow offers the barge Victoria for group hire. Individual day trips at weekends and bank holidays can also be arranged.

DANBURY
5 miles E of Chelmsford off the A414

This village is said to take its name from the Danes who invaded this part of the country in the Dark Ages. In the fine church, under a rare 13th century carved effigy, a crusader knight was found perfectly preserved, when the tomb was opened in 1779, in the pickle which filled his coffin. Fine carving is also a feature of the bench ends; the oldest among them have inspired modern craftsmen to continue the same style of carving on all the pews. In 1402, *'the devil appeared in the likeness of Firor Minor, who entered the church,*

THE CHEQUERS
32 The Street, Wickham Bishops, Essex CM8 3NN
Tel: 01621 891320

The Chequers public house is a friendly inn run by Caroline and Jeff Lasslett, welcoming hosts who make every effort to ensure that all their guests enjoy their unique brand of hospitality. Believed to be the oldest pub in Wickham Bishops, its origins have been traced back to the early 1600s. Occupying a handsome Grade II listed building, the interior is large but also remains cosy , with the original upright beams and wattle and daub walls. Here in the open-plan bar area visitors can enjoy a range of real ales including Greene King IPA and changing guest ales. One step down in the attractive dining area, food is served lunchtime and evenings Monday to Saturday and all day Sunday. The menu offers a good selection, particularly of fish including trout, salmon, haddock, plaice and cod, fresh from Billingsgate. Booking is essential for the justly popular Sunday lunch, which features shoulder of lamb or roast beef. The excellent desserts on offer include a tempting home-made cherry pie. There are also special children's and over-55s menus.

raged insolently to the great terror of the parishioners ... the top of the steeple was broken down and half the chancel scattered abroad.' And, in 1941, another harbinger of disaster, a 500lb German bomb, reduced the east end to ruins.

At **Danbury Common**, acres of gorse flower in a blaze of golden colour for much of the year. To the west, **Danbury Country Park** offers another pleasant stretch of open country boasting woodland, a lake and ornamental gardens. Guide available by appointment. Along with Lingwood Common, Danbury Common is at the highest point of the gravel ridge between Maldon and Chelmsford. There is evidence here of Napoleonic defences and old reservoirs. Circular nature trails make exploring the area easily accessible.

WOODHAM WALTER
6 miles E of Chelmsford off the B1010

Woodham Walter is a small village which lies two and a half miles west of the ancient market town and coastal port of Maldon. It is rumoured that Henry VIII hunted in Woodham Walter during his reign. During the troubled times after his death Mary Tudor was concealed in Woodham Walter Hall, from whence she was planning to escape from England in 1550. The church in Woodham, **St Michael's**, was constructed in April 1564 and is said to be one of the oldest still standing in the world.

MALDON
10 miles E of Chelmsford on the A414

The steep winding streets of Maldon are full of intriguing shops and welcoming inns. The town's High Street, of which the **Moot Hall** is a distinctive feature, runs right down to the River Blackwater estuary. Filled with craft of all shapes and sizes, the quayside is overlooked by the Queen's Head pub, which organises an annual mud race across the river at low tide.

Part of the old Moot Hall is used to display the arresting and ambitious tapestry commemorating the 1,000th anniversary of the crucial Battle of Maldon. The rest of the hall can only be seen by prior arrangement. Built in the 15th century for the D'Arcy

Queen Victoria
The Street, Woodham Walter, Maldon, Essex CM9 6RF
Tel: 01245 222176

The Queen Victoria is a charming and welcoming public house dating back to the 18th century and located down a quiet country lane at a T-junction in the handsome village of Woodham Walter. There are two very comfortable bars and a small garden in which to enjoy a pint of real ale from among the range available, or a sandwich or other snack, or a hot meal (the traditional steak and ale pie is just one speciality). Owners Linda and Ken Brewer - born to be publicans, perhaps, with a surname like theirs? - are amiable and warm hosts, eager to ensure that guests have the best in service and personal attention. The pub's walls are adorned with memorabilia from Ken's 31 years of service with the London Fire Brigade, such as fire helmets, old axes, numerous commendations and the smart chrome axe he was presented with on his retirement.

The atmosphere is always convivial. The clientele is a range of loyal locals and holidaymakers from the Chelmer and Blackwater Canals. The pub is happy to host local dominoes, darts and pool teams. Real ales on tap at this traditional English pub include Green King IPA and a changing guest ale. Linda is in charge of the cooking, and presents a range of delicious home-cooked and freshly prepared meals, snacks and daily specials.

family, the original spiral brick staircase and 18th century court room are of particular interest.

Just outside the town lies the spot where this decisive battle of England's early history took place. At the Battle of Maldon in 991, the English leader, Byrthnoth, was killed by the invading Danes after a fierce three-day battle. As a result of this defeat the English king, Ethelred the Unready, was obliged to pay an annual tribute to his conquerors. The Danes soon tired of this arrangement, however, and overthrew Ethelred, putting Cnut on the throne. Maldon is also famous for its sea salt, produced for generations in the traditional manner of letting sea water evaporate naturally, leaving just the mineral-rich salt behind.

Maldon's **Millenium Gardens** are also named in commemoration of the Battle of Maldon, and re-create what a garden would have looked like at the time of this famed event.

Maldon District Museum at 47 Mill Road is a handsome and traditional museum with a range of changing exhibits showcasing a selection of objects associated with the area and the people of the Maldon District. The museum stands adjacent to **Promenade Park**, stretching into nearby Hythe Quay. This Edwardian park boasts magnificent river walks and views. The park comprises a marine lake, amusement centre, mini-golf, boat hire and numerous year-round events. There's also an interesting museum.

At the top of this waterside town, a narrow staircase in the church tower leads to the wonderful **Plume Library**, which is still much as it was when the founder, Dr Plume, died in 1704. He built it as a home for the 6,000 books he had collected and then gave it to the town. The Maldon Public Library is below.

Above the town stand the ruins of **St Giles the Leper Hospital**, founded by King Henry II in the 12th century. As with all monastic buildings, it fell into disuse after Henry VIII's dissolution of the monasteries, though it retained its roof and was used as a barn until the late 19th century.

LANGFORD
2 miles NW of Maldon off the B1019

The **Museum of Power** at Steam Pumping Station, Hatfield Road, Langford, is an ex-waterworks pumping station which houses a large T. E. steam engine and pumps. Many other engines and other interesting artefacts are also on display.

NORTHEY ISLAND
1 mile E of Maldon off the B1026

This small island in the Blackwater Estuary has a large area of undisturbed salt marsh. There are pleasant circular walks along the uneven sea wall. The site is open by appointment with the Warden, who, due to tides which regularly cover the causeway, requires at least 24 hours' notice.

THE QUEEN'S HEAD INN

The Hythe, Maldon, Essex CM9 5HN
Tel: 01621 859154 (restaurant)
Tel: 01621 854112 (pub)

The Queen's Head Inn has been here at the water's edge on The Hythe for some 500 years. This impressive public house overlooking the Blackwater Estuary features a large riverside patio with seating for up to 400 people. There's a nautical feel throughout this welcoming pub. Real ales on tap include Greene King, Abbot and Shepherd Neame's Spitfire, as well as winter guest ales. Caribbean rums are also available, together with a good range of
other spirits, wines and hot and cold beverages. The pub's new waterside restaurant was built in 1999 - comfortable and attractive, the large windows command excellent views. The lunch and evening menus boast a variety of tempting dishes, all home cooked and freshly prepared, using fresh local ingredients. Dishes sea bass, sirloin steak, minted lamb and mushroom stroganoff are just a few of the delicious choices on offer. Breakfast is also served, all day from 10.30 a.m.

THE THATCHERS ARMS

1 North Street, Tolleshunt D'Arcy,
Maldon, Essex CM9 8TF
Tel: 01621 860655
website: www.thethatchersarms.co.uk

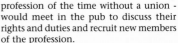

The **Thatchers Arms** is a friendly
traditional public house dating back to the
mid-18th century. Hosts Jim and Angie
Errington have been running this
welcoming pub since 1995. They have
worked in the licensing trade for 26 years,
and are members of the British Institute
of Innkeepers. Born in Leicestershire, Jim
spent many years working in London and
is an ardent Arsenal supporter. Angie is a
Londoner by birth. Together they have a wealth of experience in providing excellent service and
warm hospitality to all their guests. The clientele is a good mix of faithful locals and visitors to the
area, as well as those tempted by the pub's excellent reputation for its food - this is a destination pub.

Live music adds to the lively atmosphere on certain nights. Jim runs an entertainment agency,
with a recording studio, singing tuition and management and publicity help for artistes, so he can
always book the finest singers and bands. This fine pub earned its name because thatchers - the only
profession of the time without a union -
would meet in the pub to discuss their
rights and duties and recruit new members
of the profession.

Outside there's a charming white picket
fence around the pub, and to the rear
there's a large lawned and tree-lined secure
garden with barbecue area, picnic tables
and children's safe play area. Inside, the
pub boasts an attractive open plan design
around the L-shaped bar, with a separate
dining area. The walls are lined with an
impressive array of sports trophies, won by
the pub's various competitive teams. The
ceiling is festooned with china jugs. The
atmosphere is classically traditional, with
features such as open fires in the bar and
dining area, and old photos of the village adorning the walls, but the pub has also kept up to date
with modern additions like the wide screen TV.

The menu is full and very varied, with up to 60 different dishes available. There are also changing
daily specials. Jim and Angie take joint
responsibility for the delicious dishes,
which offer the finest in freshly
prepared and home-cooked favourites
and innovative meals and snacks. Fish
is just one of the specialities: a typical
day sees no fewer than three different
fruits of the sea on the menu, including
Dover sole, sea bass and rainbow trout.
Just as tempting are the steaks, curries,
lamb and poultry dishes. The excellent
food is matched by the fine selection
of real ales, wines, spirits and other hot
and cold beverages. The wine list is
particularly impressive.

GOLDHANGER
4 miles NE of Maldon off the B1026

Maldon District Agricultural & Domestic Museum, at 47 Church Street in Goldhanger, features a large collection of vintage farm tools and machinery manufactured locally, as well as printing machinery and domestic artefacts.

TOLLESBURY
6 miles NE of Maldon off the B1026

Located at the mouth of the River Blackwater, **Tollesbury Marina** has been designed as a leisure centre with a range of on-site activities including two tennis courts, a heated covered swimming pool, a welcoming bar and a handsome restaurant. The marina is ideally

located for exploring the rivers and creeks of the coast - the River Crouch lies south, while the West Mersea and the Rivers Colne, Orwell and Deben are to the North.

TOLLESHUNT D'ARCY
7 miles NE of Maldon off the B1026

The author of *101 Dalmations*, Dodie Smith, was born in this modest but pictureque and quiet village.

MUNDON
3 miles S of Maldon off the B1010

Mundon and the surrounding area boast some excellent walking. The St Peter's Way passes through village on way from Purleigh to Maylandsea. This quiet and unassuming

THE RED LION
9 South Street, Tolleshunt D'Arcy,
Essex CM9 8TR
Tel: 01621 860238 Fax: 01621 858253
The Red Lion is a large and impressive public house offering a good range of real ales and meals. This Free House serves up Ridleys, Greene King and Adnams ales, as well as regularly changing guest ales. Traditional bar snacks and tempting main courses such as steaks, salmon, seafood tagliatelle and the old favourite bangers and mash in white onion sauce are on the menu, which is supplemented by changing daily specials. All the food is home-cooked and makes use of the freshest ingredients. One unusual feature is the 'Golfing Breakfast', a delicious and hearty repast served from 6 a.m. every Saturday. There's a good wine list including some fine house wines. Hosts Deborah and Ray have many years' experience in the licenced trade, and their high standard of service and warm hospitality attract a good variety of locals and visitors to the area.

THE WHITE HORSE INN
Main Road, Mundon, Maldon, Essex CM9 6PB
Tel: 01621 740276
The White Horse Inn is the perfect place to enjoy a relaxing drink and some great food in convivial and picturesque surroundings. Landlord John Vincent has been here since 1988. A member of the British Institute of Innkeepers, he brings experience and expertise to offering all his guests a high standard of service and warm hospitality. Very much at the heart of the community, guests are also made most welcome. Approximately 400

years old, it is thought that the pub was once two back-to-back cottages, which would explain the back-to-back fireplaces inside. Over the bar of this fine traditional inn there's a large collection of caps and hats. The low ceilings and exposed black beamwork add to the cosy and traditional ambience. Appearing in the millennium edition of the CAMRA guide, there's a good range of real ales. Renowned for its Sunday lunches, the pub offers exceptionally good food all week long.

THE BENBRIDGE HOTEL

The Square, Heybridge, Maldon, Essex CM9 4LT
Tel: 01621 857666 Fax: 01621 841966

The Benbridge Hotel in Heybridge is a gracious and elegant Georgian house, cosy and welcoming and enjoying an enviable reputation for quality, excellent hospitality, and good food and wine. Manager Helen Jury recently took the helm. She brings a great deal of experience and enthusiasm, having worked in the management team of a large and distinguished London hotel.

The surrounding area of canal and countryside is perfect for walking, cycling, and taking part in the many sporting and leisure facilities nearby including sea, coarse and fly fishing, sailing, canal

cruising, golf, riding, and hot air ballooning. Bird watchers will also delight in the opportunities for spotting ospreys and other feathered friends along the sea wall and elsewhere - Northey Island RSPB Reserve is nearby. The village of Heybridge is on the edge of the historic port of Maldon, and just a few miles from the county town of Chelmsford. The hotel has its own canal wharf, with regular launch services on the Chelmer and Blackwater Navigation. Within minutes guests can be amid rolling, open countryside.

The hotel was built as a fine family residence in the 1700s. During the Industrial Revolution it was part of William Bentall's engineering empire, being used as offices and accommodation for the firm's apprentices. Now restored to its 18th century glory, and boasts 14 superior and elegant ensuite guest bedrooms (single, double, twin and family accommodation). The generous proportions of the drawing room encapsulate the graciousness of this

fine establishment, its rich decor reflecting the regal pomp of the period. Throughout the hotel there is a wealth of natural timber, many of the guest bedrooms having exposed beams. Comfortable and attractive furnishings and fabrics add to guests' comfort and sense of enjoying authentic Georgian surroundings. Guests never fail to appreciate the thoughtful little touches that make the Benbridge such a memorable place to stay. The Special Suite boasts a luxurious bathroom and four-poster bed.

The hotel bar offers a range of real ales and a good list of fine wines. Old Scottish malts are a speciality. Also in the bar guests can enjoy tempting snacks and meals. The handsome dining room features a menu of delicious traditional English fare and Continental cuisine, all home-cooked and using fresh local fish and farm produce wherever possible.

Thames Barges at Maldon

THE OLD SHIP

Lock Hill, Heybridge Basin, Maldon, Essex CM9 4RX
Tel: 01621 854150

For over 200 years, **The Old Ship** in Heybridge Basin has served both the village and waterfront, built primarily for the 'navvies' who were cutting the canal, and later a haven for the seamen and bargees who traded in the Basin. This traditional waterfront pub remains an excellent place for fine ales and good food. While enjoying the delights of this coastal port - tranquil and charming, where up to 200 traditional fishing and pleasure craft can be moored - what better way to relax than with a quiet drink or tasty meal.

The canalside community of Heybridge Basin was founded to man the boats and local waterways. The area surrounding the canal is rich in wildlife, flora and fauna. Seals are seen regularly, and it is a paradise for bird-watchers. Anglers, walkers on the canal towpath and Estuary seawalls, artists and the boating fraternity also frequent this peaceful setting, which has been referred to as the jewel in the Essex countryside.

The pace of life is gentle here. The pub occupies a site right on the lockside where the Chelmer and Blackwater canal meets salt water. The view that greets visitors from the pub is over Northey and Osea islands, with the tideway twisting between them. The pub is renowned for its well-kept ales, which include Kentish beers such as Shepherd Neame, together with carefully selected wines from around the world. The interior is homely and welcoming, with a wealth of natural timber. Downstairs is the cosy and characterful bar; upstairs is a recently refurbished wardroom and restaurant.

The menu offers an imaginative a la carte selection, expertly prepared by chef Mark Killick. Dishes range from simple snacks to full feasts, all home-cooked and using local produce when possible. Sketches of local maritime characters adorn the walls. Picnic tables line the lockside - just the place to enjoy a drink or bar snack on fine days.

Managers David and Jan Allsop and their capable, friendly staff offer all their guests a genuine welcome. David and Jan have been here since 2000, and bring a wealth of experience to running this vibrant pub. Worth seeking out, the pub can be found by taking the B1026 from Heybridge village towards Goldhanger. After about a mile, turn right towards Heybridge Basin. The pub is along the canal bank. Visitors mooring in Heybridge Basin are given discount vouchers for beer.

village was home to Tolstoy at one point, and here he wrote a chapter of his mammoth *War and Peace*. The disused parish church of St Mary dates back to the 14th century and is maintained by volunteers and open to the public.

HEYBRIDGE BASIN
1 mile E of Maldon off the B1019

The lively boat and barge quay at Heybridge Basin just outside the town offers visitors the best chance to see one of the classic Thames barges with their ox-blood sails in action.

ALTHORNE
6 miles SE of Maldon off the B1010

The church of **St Andrew's**, over 500 years old, has a fine flint and stone tower, built in the perpendicular style. Inside the church there's an octagonal font dating from around 1400 which retains its original carvings of saints and angels. A brass plate dated 1508 records that William Hyklott 'Paide for the werkemanship of the wall'; an inscription over the west door remembers John Wilson and John Hill, who probably paid for the tower.

To the south, where Station Road meets Burnham Road, stands the villagers' own **War Memorial**. This solid structure of beams and tiles lends dignity and honour to the tragic roll call of names listed on it. To the north of the village is the golden-thatched, white-walled Huntsman and Hounds, which dates partly from the 14th century.

STEEPLE
4 miles SE of Maldon off the B1021

This small community of thatched and weatherboarded cottages stands on the south bank of the Blackwater Estuary, where the dazzling white yachts with multi-coloured sails and the occasional stately sailing barge can be seen. The countryside around the village is a rich green land of fertile meadows, patterned by lanes bordered with banks of trees.

BURNHAM-ON-CROUCH
9 miles SW of Maldon on the B1012

Burnham-on-Crouch is an attractively old-fashioned yachting station, lively in summer, packed around August Bank Holiday Monday for its regatta, and very nice wintertime too, with the yachts left to ride at anchor offshore gently rolling, their rigging clacking forlornly.

From the gaily coloured cottages along the quay, the town climbs away from the seashore, its streets lined with a delightful assortment of old cottages and Georgian and Victorian houses and shops. This is the yachting centre of Essex. In Tudor times sailing barges thronged the estuary, where now yachts ply to and fro. Seafarers still come ashore to buy provisions, following a tradition that goes right back to medieval times when Burnham was the market centre for the isolated inhabitants of Wallasea and Foulness Islands, out in the estuary, who travelled in by ferry. The whole area was, and still is, famous for its oyster beds.

Burnham-on-Crouch & District Museum at The Quay features agricultural and maritime exhibits relating to the whole of the historic Dengie Hundred. Social history is revealed here too, as well as a good archaeological collection.

The Limes in Southminster Road is a decent farm shop with nature trails and pick your own fruit available.

Mangapps Farm Railway Museum, also in Southminster Road, offers an extensive collection of railway relics of all kinds, including steam and diesel locomotives, carriages and wagons, historic buildings and one of the largest collections of signalling equipment open to the public.

St Mary's Church, on the outskirts of town, is constructed of Kentish ragstone which was transported to Burnham by sea. Construction began in the 12th century and was completed in the 14th. The arches and pillars are particularly fine examples of medieval craftmanship.

SOUTHMINSTER
3 miles NE of Burnham off the B1021

The old market town of Southminster rises dramatically from the flat and often desolate expanse of the surrounding landscape.

The **Rural Discovery Church of St Lawrence** in Southminster is situated on a hill overlooking the River Blackwater. Exhibitions are held during the summer months, featuring themes with strong local connections.

BRADWELL-ON-SEA
6 miles NE of Burnham off the B1021

The village of Bradwell-on-Sea, the name of which is derived from the Saxon words *brad pall*, meaning 'broad wall', is home to the famous St Peter's on the Wall church, the oldest church in England. It is also the site of Bradwell Bay Secret Airfield, used during the Second World War for aircraft which were unable to return to their original base.

A visit to Bradwell-on-Sea is well worth the long drive for the sense of being right out on the edge of things - the timeless emptiness is if anything exaggerated by the distant views of the vast industrial installations nearby. The walk eastwards down the old Roman road across the marshes takes you to a little restored Saxon chapel right on the sea wall, the scene of an annual pilgrimage every July.

The first regular inhabitants of this little community at the head of the Dengie Peninsula were the Romans, who built a huge fort here. Little remains of the fort today, as in around AD 650 the Saxons used its bricks, stones and tiles to build the tiny chapel of **St-Peters-on-the-Wall**. In the 14th century the chapel was abandoned and forgotten for 600 years, except by farmers who used it as a barn. Now restored and re-consecrated, it is well worth the half-mile walk from the car park to reach it. This 7th century Celtic chapel was built by St Cedd and his followers.

Erskine Childers, who fought for the Irish Republican Army and was shot by the Irish Free State in the 1920s, wrote the wartime thriller *The Riddle of the Sands* at **Bradwell Lodge**, an attractive and part-Tudor former rectory

To the south lie the vast and remote marshes of the **Dengie Peninsula**. The salty tang of sea air here, brought inland by the east coast winds, gives an exhilarating flavour to the marshlands. Like the Cambridge and Lincolnshire fens, this once-waterlogged corner of Essex was reclaimed from the sea by 17th century Dutch engineers. The views across the marshes take in great sweeps of countryside, inhabited only by wildfowl, seabirds and cattle grazing on the saltings.

St Peter On the Wall, Bradwell-on-Sea

To the north, Bradwell's vast nuclear power station looms over a nature reserve. **Bradwell-on-Sea Power Station** has a high-tech Visitors' Centre which takes visitors through a tour of the history of generating electricity through the ages. The Centre also includes exhibitions, nature trails and audio-visual displays.

PURLEIGH
3 miles SW of Maldon off the B1010

The first recorded vineyard in Purleigh was planted in the early 12th century, only 400 yards from the site of New Hall Vineyards in Chelmsford Road. It covered three acres of land next to Purleigh Church, where first US president George Washington's great-great-grandfather was the rector - until the time he was removed from this office for sampling too much of the local brew! Purleigh Vineyard became Crown property in 1163; subsequently the wines produced were taken each year to London to be presented to the King.

SOUTH WOODHAM FERRERS
5 miles SW of Maldon off the B1012

The empty marshland of the Crouch estuary, a yachtsman's paradise, was chosen by Essex County Council as the site for one of its most attractive new towns schemes. At its centre, this successful 20th century new town boasts a traditional market square surrounded by pleasant arcades and terraces built in the old Essex style with brick, tile and weatherboard.

Marsh Farm Country Park in Marsh Farm Road, South Woodham Ferrers, is a working farm and country park adjoining the River Crouch. Sheep, pigs, cattle and hens roam; visitors can also partake of the adventure play area, farm trail, Visitors' Centre, gift shop and tea rooms. Guided tours are available by prior arrangement. Special events are held throughout the year.

RETTENDON
6 miles SW of Maldon off the A130

The **Royal Horticultural Society Garden** at Hyde Hall comprises eight acres of year-round hillside colour, with a woodland garden, large rose garden, ornamental ponds with lilies and fish, herbaceous borders, shrubs, trees, and national collections of malus and viburnum. Meals and snacks are available in the attractive thatched barn; there is also a plant centre. Fine views can be had from this attractively landscaped hilltop garden.

BATTLESBRIDGE
7 miles SW of Maldon off the A132

Battlesbridge Antiques Centre at Hawk Hill in Battlesbridge is the largest in Essex. Housed in five period buildings, more than 80 dealers display and sell their wares. The heart of the Centre is Cromwell House, its ground floor dedicated to specialist dealers with individual units. They will advise, value and give an expert opinion free of charge. They offer a wide variety of old and interesting pieces and collectibles.

The Centres' Haybarn Cottages were constructed as dwellings, while, alongside, The Bridgebarn began life as a barn with thatched roof and dates from the 19th century, at which time there were lime kilns nearby. It was converted to its present tiled roof in the 1930s. The building retains some fine oak beamwork, and houses a small 'Penny arcade' with working model roundabout, fortune teller, and 'What the Butler Saw' as well as a large collection of antiques for sale.

The Old Granary is nestled on the riverbank and houses five floors of dealers selling collectibles, reproductions, antiques and crafts, including specialists in old phones, clocks, furniture, cigarette cards, jewellery, fireplaces, interior design, dried flowers and much more. There are superb views from the top floor of the River Crouch and surrounding area, to be enjoyed as you take tea in the top-floor coffee shop.

This superb location is also the site of a Motorcycle Museum, with displays evoking the history of motorcycling through the ages with some interesting memorabilia. Three classic vehicle events are held annually.

2 Colchester and North East Essex

Northeast Essex has the true feel of East Anglia, particularly around the outstanding villages of the Stour Valley - which has come to be known as Constable Country, shared with its near neighbour Suffolk. The inland villages and small towns here are notably historic and picturesque, offering very good touring and walking opportunities. A plethora of half-timbered medieval buildings, farms and churches mark this region out as of particular historical interest. Monuments to engineering feats past and present include Hedingham Castle, Chappel Viaduct and the postmill at Bocking Church Street. Truly lovely villages such as Finchingfield abound, rewarding any journey to this part of the county. There are also many lovely gardens to visit, and this region's principal town, Colchester, is a mine of interesting sights and experiences.

The north Essex coastal region is redolent with distinguished history and a strong maritime heritage, as exemplified in towns like Harwich, Manningtree and Mistley. Further examples are the fine Martello Towers - circular brick edifices built to provide a coastal defence against Napoleon's armies - along the Tendring coast at Walton and Clacton. Dating from 1808 to 1812, each is mounted with a gun on the roof.

Ramsey Mill

The Tendring Peninsula, which takes its name from the old Tendring Hundred (a name coming from the county divisions of Saxon times, of which Tendring was a centre), has a rich and varied heritage ranging from prehistoric remains to medieval churches and elegant Victorian villas. It was settled by successive waves of invading Romans, Angles, Saxons and Vikings. Place names include the Danish ending 'by', meaning a settlement, and the Old English 'ea' and 'ey' for an island. Among the many attractive villages in the district are Thorpe-le-Soken, Kirby-le-Soken and Great Bentley - the last reputed to have the largest village green in England. The Tendring Coast contains an interesting mix of extensive tidal inlets, sandy beaches and low cliffs, and the Tendring District Council publishes a series of ``Tendring Trails'' beginning at Mistley, Manningtree, Dedham, Ardleigh and other points around the North Essex Coast.

The Stour Estuary, Hamford Water and Colne Estuary are all renowned for seabirds and other wildlife. Many areas are protected nature reserves. The Manningtree-to-Ramsey road passes through some of the best coastal scenery in Essex, with some outstanding views of the Suffolk shore.

This is of course also the part of the county known as 'the sunshine holiday coast'. Resorts, both boisterous and more placid, dot the coastline here: Clacton-on-Sea, Frinton-on-Sea and Walton-on-the-Naze to name but three - and offer many opportunities for relaxation and recreation.

COLCHESTER AND NORTH EAST ESSEX

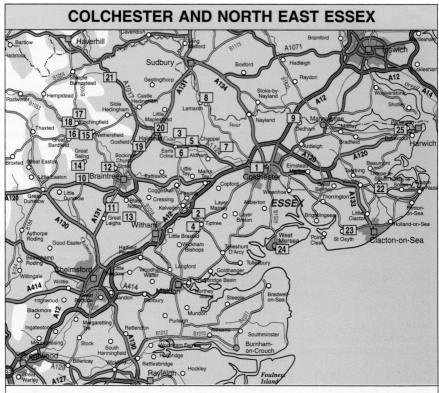

© MAPS IN MINUTES ™ (1999)

PLACES TO STAY, EAT, DRINK AND SHOP

COLCHESTER

This ancient market town and garrison stands in the midst of rolling East Anglian countryside. England's oldest recorded town, it has over 2,000 years of history to discover. First established during the 7th century BC, west of town there are the remains of the massive earthworks built to protect Colchester in pre-Roman times. During the 1st century, its prime location made it an obvious target for invading Romans. The Roman Emperor Claudius took the surrender of 11 British Kings in Colchester. In AD 60 Queen Boudicca helped to establish her place in history by taking revenge on the Romans and burning the town to the ground, before going on to destroy London and St Albans. Here in this town that was once capital of Roman Britain, Roman walls - the oldest in Britain - still surround the oldest part of town. Balkerne Gate, west gate of the original Roman town, is the largest surviving Roman gateway in the country and remains magnificent to this day.

Today the town is presided over by its lofty town hall and enormous Victorian water tower, nicknamed 'Jumbo' after London Zoo's first African elephant, controversially sold to P T Barnum in 1882. The tower has four massive pillars of one and a quarter million bricks, 369 tons of stone and 142 tons of iron, which work to support the 230,000 gallon tank.

The town affords plenty to see and explore. There are many guided town walks available, as well as bus tours. The local Tourist Information Centre on Queen Street has details of the many places to visit. Market days in this thriving town are Friday and Saturday. A good place to start is **Colchester Castle** itself and its museum. When the Normans arrived, Colchester (a name given the town by the Saxons) was an important borough. The Normans built their castle on the foundations of the Roman temple of Claudius. Having used many of the Roman bricks in its construction, it boasts the largest Norman keep ever built in Europe - the only part still left standing. The keep houses the Castle Museum, one of the most exciting hands-on historical attractions in the country. Among its fascinating collection of Iron Age, Roman and medieval relics there are tombstones carved in intricate detail and exquisite examples of Roman glass and jewellery. Visitors can try on Roman togas and helmets, touch some of the 2,000-year-old pottery unearthed nearby, and experience the town's murkier past by visiting the Castle

ATHELSTON HOUSE

201 Maldon Road, Colchester, Essex CO3 3BQ
Tel: 01206 548652
e-mail: mackman@mcmail.com

Athelston House in Maldon Road, Colchester offers excellent bed and breakfast accommodation. Owner Virginia Mackman and her husband are friendly and outgoing, with a conscientious, helpful concern for all their guests. A real home from home, this comfortable home is a peaceful haven yet close to all of the sights and attractions of Colchester, Dedham, and the surrounding area in the

picturesque and historic part of Essex. There are three attractive and welcoming guest bedrooms, all decorated and furnished to a high standard of comfort and quality with pine furniture and the original cast-iron fireplaces. Lovely touches like the wealth of pictures, books, photographs and Art Nouveau objets d'art add to the warm and homely ambience. The guests' dining room is spacious and cheerful, with an imposing fireplace and French windows leading out to the pretty garden. No smoking.

prisons, where witches were interrogated by the notorious Witchfinder General Matthew Hopkins.

Hollytrees Museum in the High Street is located in a fine Georgian home dating back to 1718. This museum on the edge of Castle Park houses a wonderful collection of toys, costumes, curios and antiquities from the last two centuries. Purchased for the town by Viscount Cowdray it first opened as a museum in 1920. Also nearby, housed in the former All Saints' Church, is the **Natural History Museum**, with exhibits and many hands-on displays illustrating the natural history of Essex from the Ice Age right up to the present day. Around the corner on Trinity Street, another former church, Holy Trinity - the only Saxon building left in Colchester - is home to the Museum of Social History, containing displays of rural crafts and country life. An arch opposite this museum leads to **Tymperleys Clock Museum**, the 15th century timber-framed home of William Gilberd, who entertained Elizabeth I with experiments in electricity. Today this fine example of architectural splendour houses a magnificent collection of 18th and 19th century Colchester-made clocks. The **Colchester Arts Centre**, not far from Balkerne Gate, features a regular programme of visual arts, drama, music, poetry and dance; the **Mercury Theatre** is the town's premiere site for stage dramas, comedies and musical theatre.

Dutch Protestants arrived in Colchester in the 16th century, fleeing Spanish rule in the Netherlands, and revitalised the local cloth industry. The houses of these Flemish weavers in the **Dutch Quarter** to the west of the castle, and the Civil War scars on the walls of Siege House in East Street, bear testimony to their place in the town's history. The Dutch Quarter west of the castle remains a charming and relatively quiet corner of this bustling town. Close to the railway station are the ruins of **St Botolph's Priory**, the oldest Augustinian priory in the country. Victim of the long siege of Colchester during the Civil War, when the Royalists, who held out for 11 weeks, were finally starved into submission, its remains are a potent reminder of the bitterness of those times.

On Bourne Road, south of the town centre just off the B1025, there's a striking stepped and curved gabled building known as **Bourne**

Mill. Built in 1591 from stone taken from the nearby St John's Abbeygate, this delightful restored building near a lovely millpond was originally a fishing lodge, later converted (in the 19th century) into a mill - and still in working order.

Colchester Zoo, just off the A12 outside the town, stands in the 40-acre park of Stanway Hall, with its 16th century mansion and church dating from the 14th century. Founded in 1963, the zoo has a wide and exciting variety of attractions. The zoo has gained a well-deserved reputation as one of the best in Europe. Its award-winning enclosures allow visitors closer to the animals and provide naturalistic environments for the 170 species. There are 15 unique daily displays including opportunities to feed an African elephant, bear, chimp or alligator, stroke a snake and watch a penguin parade.

Colchester has been famous in its time for both oysters and roses. This legacy is remembered in the annual Oyster Feast and Colchester Rose Show. Colchester oysters are still cultivated on beds in the lower reaches of the River Colne, which skirts the northern edge of town. A visit to the **Oyster Fisheries** is a fascinating experience, and the tour includes complimentary fresh oysters and glass of wine.

Just north of the centre of town, **High Woods Country Park** offers 330 acres of woodland, grassland, scrub and farmland. A central lake is fed by a small tributary of the River Colne. The land originated as three ancient farms, and forms part of a Royal hunting forest. Large numbers of musket balls dating from the Civil War period have been unearthed, indicating that the woods served as a base for the Roundheads.

AROUND COLCHESTER

ABBERTON
3 miles S of Colchester off the B1026

Two natural beauties are within reach of this village. **Abberton Reservoir** is a 1,200 acre reservoir and wildlife centre, ideal for birdwatching. The site features a conservation room, shop, toilets and hides. Four miles further east, **Fingringhoe Wick Nature**

Reserve offers visitors 125 acres of woodland and lakes by the Colne estuary.

COPFORD GREEN & COPFORD
3½ miles SW of Colchester off the B1022

Copford is home to the wonderful Norman church of **St Michael's and All Angels**, with its magnificent, well-restored medieval wall paintings whilst Copford Green, a lovely and peaceful village, is home to **Springfields at Copford** with 17 acres of gardens and parkland. Here visitors will find old established south gardens with roses and shrubbery, as well as a parterre planted in 1997 with 330 rose bushes. Other attractions include a rare Maidenhair Gingko tree, ancient mulberry, woodland walks spring-fed water gardens and lake, and croquet and putting greens. The church of **St Mary the Virgin** is also worth a visit.

LAYER BRETON
5½ miles SW of Colchester off the B1026

On the right side of Layer Breton Heath there's **Stamps and Crows**, a must for gardening enthusiasts. Two and a half acres of moated garden surrounding a 15th century farmhouse (not open to the public) boast herbaceous borders, mixed shrubs, old roses and good ground cover. There is also a recently created bog garden and dovecote.

LAYER MARNEY
6 miles SW of Colchester off the B1022

The mansion, which was planned to rival Hampton Court, was never completed, but its massive 8-storey Tudor gatehouse, known as **Layer Marney Tower**, is very impressive. Built between 1515 and 1525, it is one of the most striking examples of 16th century architecture in Britain. Its magnificent four red brick towers, covered in 16th century Italianate design, were built by Lord Marney, Henry VIII's Lord Privy Seal. As well as spectacular views from the top of the towers, they are surrounded by formal gardens designed at the turn of the century, with lovely roses, yew hedges and herbaceous borders. There is also on site a rare breeds farm, farm shop and tea room.

THE PRINCE OF WALES

Inworth, Colchester,
Essex CO5 9SP
Tel: 01376 570813
Fax: 01376 573479

The Prince of Wales is a superb public house owned and personally run by Paul and Sharon Allen, who offer a warm welcome to locals and visitors alike. After many years as stewards at golf clubs throughout Britain, the Allens bought these premises in 1995 and have slowly refurbished and improved them. Dating back in some parts to the 15th century, with additions made during the 19th, part of the downstairs area of this former cottage was once used as a chapel of rest; this area has recently been renovated and now houses a very cosy and intimate dining area. Among the many original features are the floor-to-ceiling beams and open fires.

Full of charm and character, this homely pub boasts an extensive menu of excellent home-cooked food. The variety and choice are outstanding, with traditional and more innovative meals and hot and cold snacks, including many daily specials. Only British meat is used, as well as free-range eggs and freshly picked vegetables. This Free House features a good range of ales, including guest ales. Paul and Sharon, themselves proud owners of dogs Chloe and Libby, welcome guests' dogs with a free biscuit. Adjacent to the pub is The Inworth Barn, where garden and conservatory furniture and accessories are sold at very competitive prices. The beer garden is another new feature, comprising a grass and patio area to the front of the pub.

The Five Bells

7 Mill Lane, Colne Engaine, Colchester, Essex CO6 2HY
Tel: 01787 224166

Here in the picturesque village of Colne Engaine, secluded and peaceful, **The Five Bells inn** is worth seeking out. This top-of-the-range inn boasts an extremely handsome interior, with many original features and an air of real luxury and comfort. The elegance and grace of a gentler age is captured in this superior inn. Everything to be seen is to be admired, and visitors will be struck by the character, style and charm of the place. Much bigger inside than first impressions of the exterior might bode,

the building dates back over 500 years. A record of the inn's landlords going back to 1579 is proudly displayed in the bar area. Owners Tim and Sheila Borley are happy to uphold the inn's long and fine tradition of hospitality, quality and service, and have been here since 1986. Tim is a local man born and bred, affable and welcoming.

Open every session weekdays and all day Saturday and Sunday, there are three real ales available which include Greeene King IPA along with two changing guest ales. Also on hand are John Smiths Smooth, four draught lagers, Guinness, Strongbow and a good range of wines and spirits. Tim is the cook, preparing a superb range of excellent dishes which include specialities such as fish dishes, steaks, lasagna, pasta dishes, and venison in

season. All dishes are home-cooked, freshly prepared and expertly presented. Guests choose from the blackboard menu to sample the range of delicious favourites and more innovative dishes on offer. Food is available between midday and 2.15 and 7 and 9.15 p.m. There are two separate dining areas, with seating for 80 downstairs and 30 upstairs, along with room for 20 more in the saloon bar. Booking is advised at weekends to avoid disappointment. The downstairs restaurant is no-smoking.

This wonderful inn also offers three fine guest bedrooms, all doubles and all ensuite. Comfortable and cosy, they make for the perfect base from which to explore the delights of the village and the surrounding region. For a real taste of old world charm, great food and drink and genuine hospitality, look no further.

TIPTREE
7 miles SW of Colchester on the B1023

As all true jam-lovers will know, Tiptree is famed as the home of the **Wilkin & Sons jam factory**, a Victorian establishment which now boasts a fascinating visitors' centre in the grounds of the original factory (see panel below).

ALDHAM
4 miles W of Colchester off the A604

This picturesque village was, for a time, home to the famous Essex historian Philip Morant, who held the post of vicar here. He is buried in the local churchyard. **Old Hill House** in Aldham is a one-acre garden with mixed shrubs, herbaceous borders and formal herb garden for year-round interest.

CHAPPEL
5 miles W of Colchester off the A604

Here, on a 4 acre site beside Chappel and Wakes Colne Station, is the **East Anglian Railway Museum**, a comprehensive

TIPTREE JAM SHOP, TEA ROOM AND MUSEUM,
Wilkin & Sons Ltd, Tiptree, Colchester, Essex CO5 0RF
Tel: 01621 815407 Fax: 01621 814555 email: tiptree@tiptree.com

The famous Wilkin & Sons' Tiptree jam business dates back to 1885. Today, the **Tiptree Jam Shop, Tea Room and Museum** is a charming family-run establishment located on the former Trewlands Farm - the surrounding land is still farmed. The shop opened in 1991, the tea room and museum in 1995 - all housed in the former stable block and farm store. The splendid museum depicts the changing times of the business, from its inception to the present day. There's a wealth of interesting memorabilia, including pictures, letters, photographs, jam-making machinery, and an area detailing the visit from HRH Princess Alexandra in 1985. The machinery on display in this truly special museum includes jam-filler, a mechanical cherry-stoner, labelling machine, marmalade peel-cutter and much more. A

video accompanies any tour of the museum, outlining the work involved and the factory's output over the course of the four seasons of every year.

The shop is stocked with hundreds of jams, marmalades, jellies, mustards, honeys, pickles, chutneys, and teas, as well as handsome craftware (pottery, stationery, souvenirs), gift ideas and more. The tea room is stylish and smart, serving a variety of delicious home-made cakes. Try the speciality: a cream tea with Little Scarlet Strawberry Conserve. Open: Monday to Saturday 10 a.m. - 5 p.m.; Sundays (June - August) midday - 5 p.m.

EAST ANGLIAN RAILWAY MUSEUM
Chappel Station, nr Colchester, Essex CO6 2DS Tel/Fax: 01206 242524

The **East Anglian Railway Museum** is a fascinating and comprehensive collection of period railway architecture, engineering and memorabilia housed in beautifully restored station buildings. A grand day out for railway buffs young and old, this is the place to try your hand at being a signalman and to admire the handsome engines and carriages. There is also a delightful miniature railway. Special steam days and events are held throughout the year.

THE LION

11 High Street, Earls Colne,
Colchester,
Essex CO6 2PA
Tel: 01787 224120
e-mail: vandapeter@hotmail.com

Situated on the main street in Earls Colne, **The Lion** is a friendly and attractive public house. The premises date back to the late 13th century, when they were occupied by one Thomas Segg, a priest of the parish.

The interior is warm and welcoming, with tasteful traditional furnishings and decor. There are always three real ales on tap including Greene King IPA and Speckled Hen plus a changing guest ale. A good range of lagers, stout, cider, wines and spirits can also be found at this convivial pub. Excellent hot and cold food is available from 11.30 to 2.30 and 6.30 to 9.30 p.m. every day. Booking is advised for Friday and Saturday evenings and Sunday lunch. Diners choose from a comprehensive menu of home-cooked and home-prepared favourites, as well as blackboard specials.

Once a month there are theme nights where the menu reflects the influences of various cultures and countries - please ring for details. Every second Sunday there's live music between 4 and 7 p.m. Hosts Vanda and Peter and their staff offer all their guests a warm welcome.

THE THREE HORSESHOES

Church Road, Fordham, Colchester,
Essex CO6 3NJ
Tel: 01206 240195

The Three Horseshoes in Fordham is a beautiful whitewashed 16th-century inn with a fine reputation for great food, drink and atmosphere. Owner Danny Murphy has over 19 years experience in the trade, and has owned and personally run this marvellous pub since 1994. He and his friendly, attentive staff make all their guests feel at home.

Formerly separate cottages, there has been an alehouse here since the 1700s. This traditional inn, which has seen its day as a coaching inn and mail stop, is known locally as The Shoes. It is open every session Monday to Thursday and all day Friday to Sunday. There is an excellent range of real ales on tap, together with a choice of domestic and imported lagers, stout, cider, wine and spirits.

The restaurant is open Wednesday to Saturday evenings and Sunday lunch. The chef, Carole, is a marvel at creating and preparing a selection of tempting dishes. The menu offers many home-cooked favourites, using the freshest ingredients. The atmosphere is warm and cosy, with the very comfortable seating, lovely decor and original features adding to the appeal of this welcoming first-class pub.

collection of period railway architecture, engineering and memorabilia in beautifully restored station buildings. For every railway buff, young or old, this is the place to try your hand at being a signalman and admire the handsome restored engines and carriages. There is also a delightful miniature railway. Special steam days and other events are held throughout the year. The dramatic 32-arched Chappel Viaduct standing 75 feet above the Colne Valley and a designated European Monument, was begun in 1846 and opened in 1849.

EARLS COLNE
7 miles W of Colchester off the A604

The de Veres, Earls of Oxford, and the River Colne bestowed this village with its name. Aubery de Vere founded a Benedictine priory here in the 12th century, and both he and his wife, sister of William the Conqueror, were buried there. Today the site is marked by a redbrick Gothic mansion. Though the commuter culture has spread modern housing around the village, the cluster of timbered cottages hearkens back to this village's distinguished past.

LAMARSH
9 miles NW of Colchester off the B1087

Paradise Centre on Twinstead Road in Lamarsh is a fun day out for children and grown-ups alike. There are miniature goats, bantams and a play area, while gardeners will find a wide variety of unusual plants, particularly woodland ones, beautifully laid out and for sale. As with other River Stour communities, there is some superb walking here.

DEDHAM
6 miles NE of Colchester off the A14

This is true Constable country, along the border with Suffolk, the county's prettiest area. The village has several fine old buildings, especially the 15th century flint church, its pinnacled tower familiar from so many Constable paintings. There's also the school Constable went to, and good walks through the protected riverside meadows of Dedham Vale to **Flatford**, where **Bridge Cottage** is a restored thatched 16th century building housing a display about Constable, who featured this cottage in several of his

THE LAMARSH LION

Lamarsh, Bures, Suffolk CO8 5EP
Tel: 01787 227918

The Lamarsh Lion is a picturesque and friendly Free House and restaurant situated in the Stour Valley made famous by Constable, not far from the Stour Valley long-distance pathway. Views from the front of this fine inn (and from one of the three charming guest bedrooms) overlooks the beautiful rolling panorama as the valley slopes gently away into the distance. Built sometime during the 14th century, it has been voted one of the Britain's top 100 country pubs. The walls in the bar and restaurant area are covered with unusual and delightful scenes. The open plan area has an inglenook fireplace complete with original baking ovens. The unique Charles II fire screen was discovered in a previously walled-up section of the wall. Many of the ancient beams retain their original carved angels.

The bar itself is made of wood from a north Finchley church, and contains all the original carved prayers and imprecations in old-fashioned script. Three cottage style rooms (two doubles, one twin) have been created in former wooden bar, and still contain original open beams. Traditional touches such as old lamps and Shaker-style quilts add to the cosy, homely atmosphere. Raised terraced gardens to the side and rear lead to woodland for acres all around. These peaceful surroundings create a perfectly unspoilt rural atmosphere. The daily menu includes fish specialities, grills, snacks, sandwiches (like the superb avocado and bacon on granary bread) and main courses. Food is served at lunchtime every day, and Tuesday to Saturday evenings 7-9.30. Open: 11-3 and 6-11 Monday to Saturday, midday-3.30 and 7-10.30 Sundays.

THE FOUNTAIN HOUSE AND DEDHAM HALL

Brook Street, Dedham, Essex CO7 6AD
Tel: 01206 323027 Fax: 01206 323293
e-mail: sarton@dedhamhall.demon.co.uk
website: www.dedhamhall.demon.co.uk
The Fountain House and Dedham Hall can offer
guests a peaceful holiday in tranquil surroundings.
Dedham Hall is a spectacular manor dating back
in its oldest parts to 1450. All bedrooms have
ensuite bath or shower room. The residents' lounge,
dining room and bar are in the 15th-century cottage
and overlook a secluded walled garden.

Set in six acres of beautiful gardens which
include a large pond, guests are welcome to enjoy the changing series of painting courses held
throughout the year. The painting holidays offered take advantage of the lovely setting as inspiration.

The Fountain House Restaurant is airy and
attractive, overlooking the pond and gardens of the
Hall. The restaurant is open to residents and non-
residents alike, Tuesday to Saturday nights. Booking
is advised at all times, but is essential at weekends.
All meals are freshly prepared, with eight starters
and eight main courses to choose from, all expertly
presented and memorably delicious. The restaurant,
formerly at East Bergholt, is renowned for
imaginative cooking at very reasonable prices. The
fine menu is complemented by a modern and
adventurous wine list.

paintings (his father's mill is across the river
lock).

Dedham Vale Family Farm on Mill Street
is a nicely undeveloped 16-acre farm boasting
a comprehensive collection of British farm
animals, including many different breeds of
livestock such as pigs, sheep, cattle, Suffolk
horses, goats and poultry. Children may enter
certain of the paddocks to stroke and feed the
animals (bags of feed provided).

The **Art and Craft Centre** on Dedham's
High Street is well worth a visit.
Marlborough Head, a wool merchant's
house dating back to 1475, is now a pub. The
Toy Museum, also on the High Street, has a
fascinating collection of dolls, teddies, toys,
games, doll houses and other artefacts of
childhoods past.

At **Castle House**, approximately ¾ of a
mile from the village centre on the corner of
East Lane and Castle Hill, The **Sir Alfred
Munnings Art Museum** is housed in the
former home, studios and grounds of the
famous painter, who lived here between 1898
and 1920. The museum prides itself on the
diversity of paintings and sculptures on view.
The house itself is a mixture of Turdor and

Georgian periods, carefully restored.
Munnings' original furniture is still in place.
The spacious grounds boast well mainted
gardens.

WIVENHOE
4 miles SE of Colchester off the A133

This riverside town on the banks of the River
Colne was once renowned as a smugglers'
haunt, and there is a very pretty quayside
that is steeped in maritime history. There are
still strong connections with the sea, with
boat-building having replaced fishing as the
main industry. The pretty church, with its
distinctive cupola atop a sturdy tower, stands
on the site of the former Saxon church and
retains some impressive 16th century brasses.

The small streets lead into each other and
end at the picturesque waterfront, where
fishing boats and small sailing craft bob at
their moorings. On the Quay visitors will find
the **Nottage Institute**, the River Colne's
nautical academy; classes here teach students
about knots, skippering and even how to
build a boat! It is open to visitors on Sundays
in summer. The Wivenhoe Trail, by the river,
is an interesting walk starting at the railway

station and continuing along the river to Colchester Hythe. Wivenhoe Woods is dotted with grassy glades set with tables, the perfect place for a picnic.

East of the Quay the public footpath takes visitors to the new Tidal Surge Barrier, one of only two in the country. Volunteers run a ferry service operating across the River Colne between the Quay at Wivenhoe, Fingringhoe and Rowhedge. Nearby Wivenhoe Park has been the site of the campus for the University of Essex since 1962. Visitors are welcome to stroll around the grounds.

BRAINTREE

This town, along with its close neighbour Bocking, are sited at the crossing of two Roman roads and were brought together by the cloth industry in the 16th century. Flemish weavers settled here, followed by many Huguenots. One, Samuel Courtauld, set up a silk mill in 1816 and, by 1866, employed over 3,000 Essex inhabitants. The **Working Silk Museum** on South Street features demonstrations of silk production - from start to finish - in a former mill building that has been faithfully restored. The original hand looms, some over 150 years old, are still used to weave silk fabrics for many of the royal houses throughout the world.

The magnificent former Town Hall is another of the many Courtauld legacies. It was built in 1928 with oak-panelled walls, murals by Grieffenhagen showing stirring scenes of local history, and a grand central tower with a five-belled striking clock. A smaller but no less fascinating reminder of Courtauld's generosity is the 1930s bronze fountain, with bay, shell and fish, at the centre of Braintree.

Huguenot names such as Courtauld are connected with international enterprises to this day. Their reason for coming to Britain is a fascinating and poignant tale. Formed in France in 1559 as an organised Protestant group taking direction from Calvin and the Calvinistic Reformation in Geneva, the Huguenots were at first allowed to live and worship freely. However, as political and religious rivalries grew in France, the Catholic majority started to persecute them; a century of war, massacre and bloodshed followed.

Finally in 1685 all their rights were stripped. In the chaos that ensued, many died and thousands fled. It was to turn out to be France's loss, for the Huguenots were among the most industrious and economically advanced elements in French society. Others gained at France's expense; Huguenots poured into England, and especially East Anglia, where their skills soon made them welcome and valued members of the community.

The **Braintree District Museum** on Manor Street tells the story of Braintree's diverse industrial heritage and traditions. The **Town Hall Centre** is a Grade II listed building housing the Tourist Information Centre and the Art Gallery, which boasts a continuous changing programme of exhibitions and works.

AROUND BRAINTREE

COGGESHALL
5 miles E of Braintree on the A120

This medieval hamlet, a pleasant old cloth and lace town, has some very fine timbered buildings. **Paycocke's House** on West Street, a delightful timber-framed medieval merchant's home dating from about 1500 with unusually rich panelling and wood carvings, is owned by the National Trust. Inside there's a superb carved ceiling and a display of Coggeshall lace. Outdoors there's a lovely garden. The village also has some good antique shops and a working pottery.

The National Trust also own the restored **Coggeshall Grange Barn**, which dates from around 1140 and is the oldest surviving timber-framed barn in Europe. Built for the monks of the nearby Cistercian Abbey, it is a magnificent example of this type of architecture.

Marks Hall Estate began life in Saxon times, and is mentioned in the Domesday Book. In the 15th century, then-owner Sir Thomas Honywood was a leading Parliamentarian who commanded the Essex Regiment during the Civil War. Local legend has it that the two artificial lakes on the grounds were dug by Parliamentary troops during the siege of Colchester in 1648. One of his successors, General Philip Honywood, in 1758 forbade (under the terms of his will) any of his successors to fell timber - thus his lasting legacy of avenues of mature oaks, limes and horse chestnuts, surrounded by one of the largest continuous areas of ancient woodland in the county.

The estate fell on hard times in the 19th and early 20th century, but owner Thomas Phillips Price began an association with Kew Gardens and left the Estate to be held and used for 'advancement in the National interest of Agriculture, Aboriculture and Forestry'. The Thomas Phillips Price Trust was formed and registered as a charity in 1971, and a major programme of revitalisation and restoration began. The Estate now flourishes with native plants and wildlife, ornamental lakes, a 17th century walled garden, cascades,

TIMBERS TEA ROOM AND CRAFT SHOP

Blake House Craft Centre, Blake End,
Braintree, Essex CM7 8SH
Tel/Fax: 01376 552553

The excellent **Blake House Craft Centre** in Blake End is a handsome complex of 22 shops in restored 17th, 18th and 19th-century Grade II listed buildings set around a delightful courtyard. Each self-contained unit specialises in different crafts, workshops and products, such as the art gallery, aromatherapy centre, medieval costumery, pottery shop, florist, fabric emporium, dancewear, equestrian equipment, cycle shop and more. Open all year round, it is a wonderful place to find that special gift or memento. Visitors are encouraged to browse, and indeed this wonderful little complex could easily occupy and reward many hours of exploration. One treat is watching craftsmen and -women at

work, painting canvas, throwing pots and engaging in all manner of fascinating creative pursuits. From bird tables to baby and children's wear, dried, fresh and silk flowers and shrubs, musical instruments, hand-painted ceramics, jewellery, toys, collectibles and more, there's a vast range of individually crafts products to choose from. At Timbers Tea Room and Craft Shop, set in an exquisite renovated barn dating back to the 17th century, guests can enjoy morning coffee, tasty lunches and afternoon tea, from a menu featuring a wide selection of tempting home-made dishes, cakes and snacks. Tea room open Tuesday to Sunday 10 a.m. to 5 p.m.

THE GREEN DRAGON

Upper London Road, Young's End, Braintree,
Essex CM7 8QN
Tel: 01245 361030 Fax: 01245 362575
e-mail: green.dragon@virgin.net

Bob and Mandy Greybrook offer a warm welcome to all their guests at **The Green Dragon** in Young's End. They bring a wealth of experience in inns and catering to running this fine public house, which has an air of real warmth and hospitality. Built in the mid-17th century, it has always been an ale house and inn at the centre of village life. The decor and furnishings are attractive and very comfortable, with open fires, exposed beamwork and other original features. Known as a 'destination eatery' for discerning diners, there are two dining areas, upper and lower, occupying the former stables and hayloft respectively. The excellent menu is varied and imaginative, with dishes such as 'beef and bitter', code in beer batter, Scottish beef steaks, grilled supreme of salmon, fresh seafood (lobster, oysters, dressed crab, mussels and more) and cashew nut paella, together with a tempting range of desserts, soups and salads.

Coach House and Information centre. This last is housed in a painstakingly refurbished 15th century barn, and features informative displays as well as a gift shop and tea room.

Plans for the on-site Arboretum were first drawn up in the late 1980s, to cover 120 acres. Still being established, it will contain a collection of trees from all over the world, laid out in geographical themes - Europe, Asia, America, and the southern hemisphere.

CRESSING
4 miles E of Braintree off the B1018

Cressing Temple Barns, set in the centre of an ancient farmstead, are two splendid medieval timber barns commissioned in the 12th century by the Knights Templar. They contain the timber of over 1,000 oak trees; an interpretive exhibition explains to visitors how the barns were made, as a special viewing platform brings visitors up into the roof of the magnificent Wheat Barn for a closer look. There's also a beautiful walled garden re-creating the Tudor style, with an arbour, fount and physic garden. Special events are held throughout the year.

FEERING
6 miles E of Braintree off the A12

Feeringbury Manor near Feering has a fine, extensive riverside garden with ponds, streams, a little waterwheel, old-fashioned plants and bog gardens.

KELVEDON
6 miles SE of Braintree off the A12

This village alongside the River Blackwater houses the **Feering and Kelvedon Museum**, which is dedicated to manorial history and houses artefacts from the Roman settlement of Canonium, agricultural tools through the ages and other interesting exhibits.

FAIRSTEAD
4 miles S of Braintree off the A131

Fairstead (or Fairsted) is an undulating parish about three miles east of the A131, some four miles northwest of Witham. The **Church of St Mary and St Peter** is an ancient building of flint, in the Norman style, consisting of chancel, nave, north porch and a western tower with a lofty shingled spire with four bells, one of which dates back to before the Reformation. During restoration in the late 1800s various handsome mural paintings were discovered, including, over the chancel arch, those entitled, *Our Lord's Triumphal Entry into Jerusalem, The Last Supper, The Betrayal, Our Lord being crowned with thorns, and Incidents on the way to Calvary*. The hamlet of Fuller Street lies 1 mile west of the church.

BOCKING CHURCH STREET
1½ miles N of Braintree off the A1017

This handsome village, a beauty spot not far from Braintree, boasts an impressive parish church, and a walk down Church Street

THE ROSE AND CROWN

94 Church Street, Bocking Church Street,
Braintree, Essex CN7 5JY
Tel: 01376 324661

Dating back to the early 1700s, when it was known as The Crown and Anchor, **The Rose and Crown** in Bocking is an attractive and cosy pub. Handsomely decorated and furnished, it has a welcoming ambience that makes guests feel right at home. The walls are lined with photographs, prints and memorabilia of bygone days, and the pub has won many awards for the lovely blooms adorning the exterior. Margaret and Keith Stevens have lived in Bocking since 1978 and have been tenants of the pub since 1990. Open all day, every day, there are always three real ales on tap, together with a good range of lagers, stout, cider, wines and spirits. Margaret is an excellent chef, as reflected in the superb range of dishes at lunchtime and evening which feature home-made dishes such as beef and ale with dumplings, steak and kidney pudding and other traditional favourites. The Sunday lunch is justly popular.

THE SQUARE AND COMPASSES

Fuller Street, Fairstead, Chelmsford, Essex CM3 2BB
Tel: 01245 361477

Here in Fuller Street can be found **The Square and Compasses** pub. It is large and impressive, with a handsome whitewashed exterior. Dating back at least 200 years and possibly much further, this hidden gem is set along the Essex Way long-distance footpath. There's also a mystery associated with the pub. It lies on a straight line, 10 miles long, of three pubs called The (Square and) Compasses. A fourth pub, also called The Compasses, creates a circle pinpointing an ancient centre of Knights Templar activity, on the site of a church indicated in the record books but lost for these 650 years.

Links with geomancy, the Masons, the Knights Templar (for which there is evidence going back 800 years) and the Peasants Revolt of 1381 have all been put forward as possible explanations for this mysterious "coincidence".

Long known to those who seek out the best in traditional ales, food and ambience, the 1990s saw this fine pub meet with mixed fortunes. Happily, it has now been extensively and carefully renovated and modernised, to offer guests the highest standard of comfort and quality while retaining the pub's many interesting original features. A huge amount of effort has been put into the decor and furnishings, with excellent results. The pub is divided so as to create a series of cosy and comfortable areas where guests can enjoy a quiet drink, snack or meal. The wealth of artefacts on display are worth the trip

alone, as many are of museum-standard quality. Nor do these artefacts make the pub feel "fake" or as if it is trying too hard - they just add to the authenticity of the historic surroundings. Little touches like fresh flowers on the bar enhance the homely feel, and show that a great deal of care and conscientiousness go into making every guest feel welcome. Landlord Howard Potts and his staff are friendly, competent and helpful. In these welcoming surroundings, the food and drink on offer are of the highest quality. The menu offers a range of home-cooked and freshly prepared dishes - nothing too experimental or over the top, just hearty, delicious traditional cooking at its best. Fine beers on offer include Ridleys IPA fresh from the barrel, along with a changing guest ale. There is also, of course, a good range of lagers, stouts, wines, spirits and non-alcoholic beverages. In fine weather, guests can also enjoy the spacious beer garden, looking out over the lovely surrounding countryside.

repays the curious with a sight of the fine postmill.

GREAT SALING
4 miles NW of Braintree off the A120

Saling Hall Garden is a 12 acre garden including walled garden and dating from 1698. The small park boasts a collection of fine trees, and there are water gardens and an extensive collection of unusual plants with an emphasis on trees.

WETHERSFIELD
5 miles NW of Braintree on the B1053

Boydells Dairy Farm is a working farm where visitors are welcome to join in with tasks

THE WHITE HART
The Street, Great Saling, Braintree, Essex CM7 5DT
Tel: 01371 850341

Here in the picturesque village of Great Saling, **The White Hart** is a wonderful, welcoming public house and separate restaurant dating back to the 16th century. This comfortable coaching inn is run by Corinne and Simon Webber and family. Real fires, original stone floors and age-old memorabilia add to the traditional feel of the place. The cosy and intimate (no smoking) restaurant, located in the original bakehouse to the rear, epitomises olde worlde style. Features here include exposed beams, bleached pine table and chairs to seat 40 comfortably. Roomy and light, this leads out to the large lawned enclosed garden with barbecue area and safe children's play facilities.

The menu has gained a well-earned reputation for excellence, offering a range of international dishes. Popular choices include pan-roasted duck, red Thai chicken curry and Mexican fajitas. There's also a specials board, changed daily. All food is freshly prepared, home cooked and expertly presented. Open for lunch and evenings, booking is advised. The restaurant's baby grand piano means that music occasionally accompanies the dining experiences. The restaurant plays host to occasional gourmet themed evenings - please ring for details. Meals are also available at the main bar, which features The Minstrels Gallery - this bar featured in the Lovejoy television series. Among the light meals on offer are The White Hart's special spin on traditional 'Huffers', which started life as a large triangular bread roll for hungry farmworkers - they are served here full to overflowing with a range of delicious fillings. There is a good wine list and a wide selection of ales, lagers and bitters.

BROOK FARM
Wethersfield, Braintree, Essex CM7 4BX
Tel/Fax: 01371 850284

Brook Farm is a charming and beautiful listed farmhouse dating back in parts to the 13th century, with 16th- and 17th-century additions. This working farm is set in undulating countryside, a quarter of a mile south of the lovely village of Wethersfield. Hidden away from the hustle and bustle, it is still within easy reach of many Essex and Suffolk sights and attractions. Owner Anne Butler is a friendly, hospitable host and an ardent horsewomen. The three spacious guest bedrooms (one double, one twin, one family room) are warm, airy, comfortable and quiet. The rooms are tastefully furnished with period furnishings and very comfortable beds. There's also a handsome and welcoming guests' lounge. The full English breakfast is hearty and delicious - Anne is famous for her excellent porridge! For evening meals there are several good pubs and restaurants nearby.

such as milking, feeding and more. A guided tour mixes fun with education, and all questions are most welcome. From bees to llamas, just about every kind of farm animal can be found here. Goat rides and donkey cart rides, a lovely picnic area and refreshments such as "Yoggipops" (sheep's milk yogurt ice lollies made on-site) make for a perfect family day out. Open to the public April to September.

GREAT BARDFIELD
6 miles NW of Braintree off the B1053

This old market town on a hill above the River Pant is a pleasant mixture of cottages and shops, nicely complemented by the 14th century church of **St Mary the Virgin**. Perhaps Great Bardfield's most notable feature is, however, a restored windmill that goes by the strange name of 'Gibraltar'.

Here in one of the prettiest villages in all of Essex, Great Bardfield's **Cottage Museum** occupies a 16th century cottage and features exhibits of mainly 19th and 20th century domestic and farm implements and some rural crafts.

FINCHINGFIELD
6 miles NW of Braintree off the B1053

This charming village is graced with thatched cottages spread generously around a sloping village green that dips to a stream and duck pond at the centre of the village. Nearby stands an attractive small windmill. Just up the hill visitors will find the Norman church

Finchingfield

of **St John the Baptist**, the **Guildhall** (mentioned in the Domesday book), which has a small museum open Sundays, and, opposite these, the Red Lion Inn.

Finchingfield is easily one of the most picturesque and most photographed villages in Essex, featured in many television programmes and the home of the series Lovejoy. Here visitors will also find the privately owned Tudor stately home, **Spains Hall**, has a lovely flower garden containing a huge Cedar of Lebanon planted in 1670 and an Adams sundial. Many good roses surround the kitchen garden, which contains an ancient Paulonia tree and a bougainvillea in the greenhouse. The garden is generally open on summer Sunday afternoons.

Finchingfield also has an easily followed

THE BELL INN

Great Dunmow Road, Great Bardfield,
Essex CM7 4SA
Tel: 01371 811097

Here in one of the prettiest villages in all of Essex, **The Bell Inn** is a charming traditional coaching inn, the oldest part of which (the lounge area) dates back to the 16th century. Always an inn, this excellent pub is at the centre of village life, with a loyal and friendly band of regulars and frequently host to visitors to this part of the county. There's a fine range of real ales on tap at this Free House to be enjoyed amid the comfortable surroundings. The lounge bar has exposed beams and a handsome inglenook fireplace, complete with 16th-century priest's hole behind the chimney. The menu offers a variety of classic English dishes making use of the freshest local ingredients. For those wishing to extend their visit to the region there's accommodation available here, in two ensuite doubles and two singles. Each room is cosy and welcoming.

THE RED LION INN

6 Church Hill, Finchingfield, Essex CM7 4NN
Tel/Fax: 01371 810400 e-mail: franktyler@excite.co.uk

Frank and Zara Tyler have brought their extensive hotel and catering experience to this quiet and picturesque corner of Essex and to the impressive **Red Lion Inn**. Here they have created a comfortable, cosy and convivial inn, as their enthusiasm for good food, good wine and good company is truly infectious. A hub of local community activity for the surrounding villages, as well as attracting a number of foreign visitors (Stanstead Airport is not far away), this quintessentially English inn -

located in what has been called the country's prettiest village, boasting a number of craft shops, antiques shops and tea rooms, and located near some excellent walking country - dates back to circa 1520 (though it was extensively 'modernised' in 1820). The interior of the bar is a splendid mix of oak beams, brick and brass. The restaurant boast Georgian elegance. The three guest bedrooms are comfortably furnished with locally-produced and hand-painted pine furnishings. The pub has featured several times in *The Good Beer Guide* (1997-2001). The wide-ranging menu features generously filled 'Huffers' and full a la carte selections, all making the most of locally-supplied produce wherever possible. ETC 3 Diamonds.

Another family enterprise is Tylers @ Home (Tel: 01799 542252), a distinguished interiors shop run by Zara in Newport, Essex. Occupying newly refurbished premises at the Saffron Walden end of Newport High Street, next to

the White Horse pub, visitors will find an appealing and reasonably priced range of handmade cushions, vases, prints and frames, glassware, candles, handmade china, cards, toys, bedding, soft furnishings and babywear are on sale here, for anyone looking for the perfect gift - for themselves or anyone else! The shop is also proud to be authorised stockists of L'OCCITANE en Provence, an exciting range of gorgeous-smelling soups, toiletries and scented candles and incense. All products in this range are made using

only natural plants products, no animal fats - an example being the Shea butter range of beauty products, made from the African Shea tree and said to prevent the signs of ageing. The Fete de la Lavande collection of bath and beauty products are made from the finest Provence lavender. An interior design service is another distinctive service offered by this delightful shop. Closed Mondays and Wednesdays.

THE FOX INN

The Green, Finchingfield, Braintree, Essex CM7 4JX
Tel: 01371 810151
website: www.foxinnfinchingfield.co.uk

The Fox Inn in Finchingfield is a superb Free House dating back to the 15th century. Overlooking the picturesque village green, with its pond frequented by ducks, geese and other natural wildlife, this fine inn offers an excellent selection of food and drink, with a varied and imaginative menu. Dishes such as pan-fried tuna steak, breast of duck, steak and kidney pie and the very popular slow roasted shoulder of lamb make up the evening menu, while lunches include a wide range of tempting snacks, sandwiches, salads and hot meals. All food is freshly prepared to order. Diners can enjoy their meal either in the restaurant, the bar or, on fine days, outside with a view of the green and village life.

Hearty and delicious breakfasts are served weekends from 8.30-10.30 a.m. There's a wide selection of draught and bottled beers, including changing guest ales and regular favourites such as Greene King IPA and Triumph. The wine list is extensive and impressive. Dave and Chris Mutch took over at this friendly pub in May of 2000. The clientele includes a good local following and many tourists, including walkers and other visitors attracted to this fair village and the lovely surroundings.

THE GREEN MAN

Gosfield, Halstead, Essex CO9 1TP
Tel: 01787 472746

Built at the same time as the local church - the 1600s - **The Green Man** is a striking pink-washed public house with attractive later additions. This spacious pub and restaurant has always been an inn, and retains many original features such as the fine inglenook fireplace near the bar.

With a warm and cosy interior, this pub is popular with those who enjoy a good glass of real ale and traditional English cooking. Greene King IPA and Abbot ale are among the excellent ales on tap. Landlady Janet Harrington has been working here since 1971, and has been leaseholder since 1998. Affable and attentive, she has won numerous awards for her cooking, and looks after the restaurant with care and a keen instinct for what her clients will like.

Her expertise has earned the pub a reputation far and wide for its excellent cuisine. The menu changes daily, using locally supplied produce freshly prepared on the premises. The beer garden is particularly lovely; just the place to enjoy a quiet drink or fine meal on warm days. Booking is advised at all times for this very popular establishment, which features in all good guides and has won awards as Essex (dining) Pub of the Year.

path along the Finchingfield Brook leading from the village to Great Bardfield, a short distance away.

GOSFIELD
4 miles N of Braintree off the A1017

Gosfield Lake Leisure Resort, the county's largest freshwater lake, lies in the grounds of Gosfield Hall. This Tudor mansion was remodelled in the 19th century by its owner Samuel Courtauld. He also built the attractive mock-Tudor houses in the village.

HALSTEAD

The name 'Halstead' comes from the Anglo-Saxon for Healthy Place. Like Braintree and Coggeshall, Halstead was an important weaving centre. **Townsford Mill** is certainly the most picturesque reminder of Halstead's industrial heritage. Built in the 1700s, it remains one of the most handsome buildings in town. This white, weatherboarded three-storey mill across the River Colne at the Causeway was once a landmark site for the Courtauld empire, producing both the famous funerary crepe and rayon. Today the Mill is an antiques centre.

Though it may now seem somewhat improbable, Halstead's most famous product was once mechanical elephants. Life-sized and weighing half a ton, they were built by one W Hunwicks. Each one consisted of 9,000 parts and could carry a load of eight adults and four children at speeds of up to 12 miles per hour. Rather less unusual but certainly better remembered is the Tortoise Foundry Company for its warm 'tortoise stoves'.

AROUND HALSTEAD

CASTLE HEDINGHAM
3 miles NW of Halstead off the B1058

This town is named for its Norman **Castle**, which dominates the town. One of England's strongest fortresses in the 11th century, even now it is impossible not to sense its power and strength. The impressive stone keep is one of the tallest in Europe, with four floors and rising over 100 feet, with 12-ft thick walls. The banqueting hall and minstrels' gallery can still be seen. It was owned by the Earls of Oxford, the powerful de Veres family, one of whom was among the barons who forced King John to accept the Magna Carta. Amongst those entertained at the castle were Henry VII and Elizabeth I.

The village itself is a maze of narrow streets radiating from Falcon Square, named after the half-timbered Falcon Inn. Attractive buildings include many the Georgian and 15th century houses comfortably vying for space, and the **Church of St Nicholas**, built by the de Veres, which avoided Victorian 'restoration' and is virtually completely Norman, with grand masonry and

THE THREE PIGEONS

6 Mount Hill, Halstead, Essex CO9 1AA
Tel: 01787 472336

The Three Pigeons on Mount Hill in Halsted is a lovely and classically English public house offering traditional ales, bar meals and a warm and cosy ambience. Recently repainted and refurbished, it boasts a spacious open-plan design and very comfortable seating. Dating back to the 1700s, the building has been used as a licensed premises since 1851. Tenant Debbie Webb has been here since 1998, and has brought real flair and verve to running this popular and welcoming pub. There is a good range of tempting hot and cold bar snacks on offer, together with a selection of real ales including Greene King IPA and Old Speckled Hen. Popular with locals and visitors alike, the pub plays a big part in the local community, hosting one of the best ladies' darts team in the area. The patio area and beer garden are spacious and attractive. Open for lunch and evening sessions Monday to Thursday and all day Friday to Sunday.

Castle Hedingham

interestingly carved choir seats. There is a working pottery in St James' Street.

At the **Colne Valley Railway and Museum**, a mile of the Colne Valley and Halstead line between Castle Hedingham and Great Yeldham has been restored and now runs steam trains operated by enthusiasts. These lovingly restored Victorian railway buildings feature a collection of vintage engines and carriages; short steam train trips are available. **Colne Valley Farm Park**, set in

30 acres of traditional river meadows, is open from April to September.

The B1058 towards Sudbury, then left through Gestingthorpe and the Belchamps, makes for a pleasant excursion.

SIBLE HEDINGHAM
3 miles NW of Halstead off the A1017

Mentioned in the Domesday Book as the largest parish in England, Sible Hedingham was the birthplace of Sir John Hawkwood, one of the 14th century's most famous soldiers of fortune. He led a band of mercenaries to Italy, where he was paid to defend Florence and where he also died. There is a monument to him in the village church, decorated with hawks and various other beasts.

Swan Street is the main artery of this charming village, boasting several delightful establishments devoted to providing visitors and natives of the town with places to shop, dine, enjoy a quiet drink and even stay for the night.

The White Horse Inn

Mill Road, Ridgewell, Essex CO9 4SG
Tel: 01440 785532

The White Horse Inn in Ridgewell dates back as an inn to 1790, though the building is believed to be a good deal older even than this. The interior is comfortable and cosy, with real fires adding to the homely ambience. The top of the bar has a display of over 4,000 old pennies - a talking point for locals and visitors alike.

Closed Monday (except for Bank Holidays) and Tuesday lunchtime, this fine pub is open for both sessions Monday to Saturday and all day Sunday. There are always between two and three changing well-kept real ales, along with Websters Yorkshire bitter, Guinness, Scrumpy Jack cider, lagers, wines and spirits. Delicious food is available Monday to Sunday midday to 2 p.m., and Monday to Saturday 7 to 10 p.m. Booking is advised for Saturday evenings. The extensive menu offers a superb range of traditional English dishes, including fresh fish dishes and huge steaks; there are also tempting home-made curries.

Owner Robin Briggs and his friendly, hospitable staff make all their guests feel most welcome at this charming inn.

GESTINGTHORP
5 miles N of Halstead off the A131

The Church of **St Mary the Virgin** in Gestingthorp is distinctive in many respects. Witness to centuries of Christian worship, the Domesday Book of 1086 tells that 'Ghestingetorp' was held by Ledmer the priest before 1066. The oldest part extant of the existing building is the blocked-up lancet window in the north wall of the chancel, which dates back to the 1200s. Apart from this, most of the chancel, nave and south aisle dates from the 14th century. The tower, constructed in about 1500, is 66 feet high. Of the six bells hung in the tower, four were cast in 1658-9 by Miles Gray, a Colchester bellfounder. The 16th century fifth and sixth bells were cast in Bury St Edmunds, and recast in 1901. The west door, set in a stepped brick arch, is the original. The unusual tracery in the East window consists of arches placed atop the apexes of the arches beneath them. The late 15th century/early 16th century nave roof is of the double hammer-beam type, and one of the finest in Essex. The font is late 14th century. One of the church's handsome memorials commemorates Captain L E G Oates, who died in an attempt to save the lives of his companions on an ill-fated expedition to the Antarctic in 1912.

LITTLE MAPLESTEAD
3 miles NE of Halstead off the A131

Little Maplestead has an unusual round church, dedicated to **St John the Baptist**, modelled on the Holy Sepulchre in Jerusalem, and used as a stopping-point for pilgrims on their way there. Built more than 600 years ago by the military order of the Knights Hospitallers, their 'Perceptory' at Little Maplestead was suppressed more than 400 years ago by Henry VIII.

THE NORTH ESSEX COAST

This region is redolent with distinguished history and a stong maritime heritage, as exemplified in towns like Harwich, Manningtree and Mistley. Further examples are the fine Martello Towers - circular brick edifices built to provide a coastal defence against Napoleon's armies - along the Tendring coast at Walton, Clacton, Jaywick and Point Clear. Dating from 1808 to 1812, each is mounted with a gun on the roof. Examples of Martello Towers can be found along the Tendring coast from Walton through Clacton to Point Clear

The Tendring Peninsula, which takes its name from the old Tendring Hundred (a name coming from the county divisions of Saxon times, of which Tendring was a centre), has a rich and varied heritage ranging from prehistoric remains to medieval churches and elegant Victorian villas. It was settled by successive waves of invading Romans, Angles, Saxons and Vikings. Place names include the Danish ending 'by', meaning a settlement, and the Old English 'ea' and 'ey' for an island. Among the many attractive villages in the district are Thorpe-le-Soken, Kirby-le-Soken and Great Bentley - the last reputed to have the largest village green in England. The Tendring Coast contains an interesting mix of extensive tidal inlets, sandy beaches and low cliffs, and the Tendring District Council publishes a series of ``Tendring Trails'' beginning at Mistley, Manningtree, Dedham, Ardleigh and other points around the North Essex Coast.

The **Stour Estuary**, **Hamford Water** and **Colne Estuary** are all renowned for seabirds and other wildlife. Many areas are protected nature reserves. The Manningtree-to-Ramsey road passes through some of the best coastal scenery in Essex, with some outstanding views of the Suffolk shore.

This is of course also the part of the county known as 'the sunshine holiday coast'. Resorts, both boisterous and more placid, dot the coastline here: Clacton-on-Sea, Frinton-on-Sea and Walton-on-the-Naze to name but three - and offer many opportunities for relaxation and recreation.

CLACTON-ON-SEA
16 miles SE of Colchester on the A133

Clacton is a traditional sun-and-sand family resort with a south-facing, long sandy beach, lovely gardens on the seafront and a wide variety of shops and places to explore. It also boasts a wide variety of special events and entertainments taking place throughout the year.

Settled by hunters during the Stone Age - which is borne witness to by the wealth of flint implements and the fossilised bones of the cave lion, straight-tusked elephant and wild ox unearthed on the Clacton foreshore and at Lion Point - the town grew over the centuries from a small village into a prosperous seaside resort in the 1800s, when the craze for the health benefits of coastal air and bathing was at its peak. The Pier was constructed in 1871; at first paddle steamers provided the only mode of transport to the resort, the railway arriving in 1882. **The Pier** was widened from 30 to over 300 foot in the 1930s. On the pier, apart from the marvellous traditional sideshows, big wheel, restaurants and fairground rides, there is the fascinating **Seaquarium and Reptile Safari**.

Amusement centres include the arcades and **Clacton Pavilion**. The two theatres, Princes Theatre and West Cliff, are open all year. Clacton Pavilion boasts a range of attractions, including crazy golf, dodgems and a rock & roll Fun House. The **Clifftop Public Gardens** also repay a visit.

Great Clacton is the oldest part of town, comprising an attractive grouping of shops, pubs and restaurants within the shadow of the 12th century parish church.

A walk round the town repays the visitor with some very handsome sights. There are three Martello Towers along this bit of the Essex coast. Just south of the town, **Jaywick Sands** is the ideal spot for a picnic by the sea, boasting one of the finest natural sandy beaches in the county.

HOLLAND-ON-SEA
1½ miles NE of Clacton off the B1032

This attractive community is home to **Holland Haven Country Park**, 100 acres of open space near the seashore, ideal for watching the marine birds and other wildlife of the region. Throughout the area there are a number of attractive walks which take full advantage of hte varied coastal scenery

FRINTON-ON-SEA
3 miles NE of Clacton off the B1032

Once a quiet fishing village, this town was developed as a select resort by Sir Richard Cooper, and expanded in the 1880s to the genteel family restort it is today. Situated on a long stretch of sandy beach, Frinton remains peaceful and unspoilt. The tree-lined residential avenues sweep elegantly down to the Esplanade and extensive clifftop greensward. Along its main shopping street in Connaught Avenue, the 'Bond Street' of the East Coast, shopkeepers maintain a tradition of friendly and courteous service. Summer theatre and other open-air events take place throughout the season, and there are also some excellent tennis and golf clubs in the town. The grace and elegance of this sophisticated resort is evidenced all round, as are hints of its distinguished past: Victorian beach huts still dot the extensive beach.

The area south of **Frinton Gates** has a unique local character, being laid out with detached houses set along broad tree-lined avenues.

Gardens, Clacton-on-Sea

The Church of Old St Mary in the town contains some panels of stained glass in the East window designed by the Pre-Raphaelite artist Burne Jones.

A good example of 20th century English vernacular architecture is The Homestead at the corner of Second Avenue and Holland Road, built in 1905 by C F Voysey.

WEELEY
5 miles NW of Clacton off the A133

St Andrew's is the handsome parish church just south of the centre of this picturesque village. There is a lovely tree-lined path that passes Weeleyhall Wood and Weeley Lodge, with its beautifully kept gardens. Here visitors will also pass a navigational beacon that forms part of Aircraft Flight Operations for both civil and military flights.

A mile south, off the B1411, Weeley Heath is a small and attractive community boasting a lovely village green and stunning surrounding countryside.

LITTLE CLACTON
3 miles NW of Clacton off the A133

Though it shares its name with its near neighbour, this is a town apart. Quiet and secluded, multiple-winner of the Best Kept Village award, Little Clacton features a lovely Jubilee Oak, planted to celebrate Victoria's 50th year on the throne.

The fine church of **St James** has been described as one of the most beautiful medieval churches in Essex, and sits at the heart of the village

Oakwood Crafts Resource Centre in Little Clacton provides an environment for people with learning disabilities to learn and develop work skills, motivation, responsibility, team spirit, self-esteem and confidence through horticulture, woodwork, ceramics, crafts and catering.

Set in three acres of land, it opened in 1975 and, as a horticultural centre, sells a wide range of bedding plants, shrubs and hanging baskets seasonally, along with a selection of wooden garden implements, furnishings and other items, and ceramics. Teas and coffees are available.

TENDRING
7 miles NW of Clacton off the A133

This village that gives its name to both the peninsula and the district council, contains the handsome church of **St Edmund** with its elegant spire which can be seen for miles around. The church is dedicated to the last King of independent East Anglia, martyred by the Danes in the 9th century.

WALTON-ON-THE-NAZE
8 miles NE of Clacton on the B1034

Walton is all the fun of the fair. It is a traditional, singular and cheerful resort which focuses on the pier and all its attractions, including a ten-pin bowling alley. The gardens at the seafront are colourful and the beach has good sand. The Backwaters to the rear of Walton are made up of a series of small harbours and saltings, which lead into Harwich harbour.

Walton has an outstanding sandy beach. The town's seafront was developed in the 1825 and provides a fine insight into the character of an early Victorian seaside resort. The charming narrow streets of the town

Marina, Walton-on-the-Naze

contain numerous shops, restaurants and pubs overlooking the second longest pier in the country. **Marine Parade**, originally called The Crescent, was built in 1832. **The Pier**, first built in 1830, was originally constructed of wood and measured 330 feet long. It was extended to its present lenght of 2,610 feet in 1898, at the same time as the electric train service began.

The wind-blown expanse of **The Naze** just north of Walton is an extensive coastal recreation and picnic area, pleasant for walking, especially out of season when the visitor is likely to have all 150 acres virtually to him- or herself, with great views out over the water. The shape of the Naze is constantly changing, eroded by wind, water and tide.

The year 1796 saw the demise of the medieval church, and somewhere beyond the 800-foot pier lies medieval Walton. The sandstone cliffs are internationally important for their shell fossil deposits. Inhabitants have been enjoying the bracing sea air at Walton since before Neolithic times: flint-shaping instruments have been found here, and the fossil teeth and the ears of sharks and whales have been discovered in the the Naze's red crag cliffs. The **Naze Tower** is brickbuilt and octagonal in shape, originally built as a beacon in 1720 to warn seamen of the West Rocks off shore. A nature trail has been created nearby and the Essex Skipper butterfly and Emperor moth can be seen here.

The **Old Lifeboat House Museum** at East Terrace, in a building over 100 years old, houses an interpretive museum of local history and development, rural and maritime, covering Walton, Frinton and the Sokens.

KIRBY-LE-SOKEN
2 miles W of Walton on the Naze off the B1034

There is a footpath in this attractive village which begins to the west of the 14th century Ship Inn and affords views of the backwaters of Hamford Water, with views of Horsey and Hedge End Islands in the middle distance.

THORPE-LE-SOKEN
3 miles W of Walton on the Naze off the B1034

This crossroads village has shops and some good-quality pubs and restaurants set amid a mix of historic buildings, including a fine parish church.

BEAUMONT-CUM-MOZE
4 miles NW of Walton on the Naze off the B114

This small village once had a quay originally constructed for loading and unloading vessels plying the Walton backwaters. The disused **Trading Quay** was rebuilt in 1832 using stone from the old London Bridge. The 11th century parish church of **St Leonard** contains the grave of Viscount Byng of Vimy, Governor General of Canada.

BRIGHTLINGSEA
7 miles W of Clacton on the B1029

Brightlingsea enjoys a long tradition of shipbuilding and seafaring. In 1347, 51 men and five ships were sent to the siege of Calais. Among the crew members of Sir Francis Drake's fleet which vanquished the Spanish Armada was one 'William of Brightlingsea'. Brightlingsea has the distinction of being the only limb of the Cinque Ports outside Kent and Sussex.

MILL HOUSE
High Street, Thorpe-le-Soken, Clacton-on-Sea, Essex CO16 0DY
Tel: 01255 861334

Mill House in Thorpe-le-Soken is a gracious and impressive family home offering superior bed and breakfast accommodation. This Tudor building with a later (Georgian) frontage is handsome inside and out, providing a real home from home in its spacious and well-appointed family room. The decor and furnishings are first class, presenting a high standard of comfort and quality. Hosts Sharon and Keith Diplock love to pamper their guests. No smoking.

The 13th century **Jacobes Hall** in the town centre is one of the oldest occupied buildings in Essex. It is timber-framed with an undulating tile roof and an external staircase. Used as a meeting hall during the reign of Henry III, its name originates from its first owner, Edmund Vicar of Brightlingsea, who was known locally as Jacob le Clerk.

All Saints Church, which occupies the highest point of the town on a hill about a mile from the centre, is mainly 13th century. Here are to be found some Roman brickwork and a frieze of ceramic tiles commemorating local residents whose lives were lost at sea. Its 97 foot tower can be seen from 17 miles out to sea. A light was once placed in the tower to guide the town's fishermen home

The **Town Hard** is where you can see all the waterfront comings and goings, including the activities of the Colne Smack Preservation Society, which maintains a seagoing link with the past.

Brightlingsea Museum in Duke Street offers an insight into the lives, customs and traditions of the area, housing a collection of exhibits relating to the town's maritime connections and the oyster industry.

There are plenty of superb walks along Brightlingsea Creek and the River Colne, which offer a chance to watch the birdlife on the saltings and the plethora of boats on the water. Today the town is a haven for the

yachting fraternity and is the home of national and international sailing championships, with one of the best stretches of sailing on the East Coast.

Day and half-day sailing and canoeing sessions are held at the **Brightlingsea Outdoor Education Centre**.

ELMSTEAD MARKET
6 miles N of Brightlingsea off the A120

The Church of **St Anne and St Lawrence** to the north of this village has a rare carved oak recumbent effigy of a knight in armour.

Elmstead Market is perhaps best known as the location of **Beth Chatto Gardens**, at White Barn House, designed and still presided over by the famous gardener herself. Here visitors will find five acres of landscaped gardens including extensive water gardens, shady walks and a Mediterranean-style garden where aromatic drought-loving plants thrive. The adjoining nursery contains a wide variety of plants for sale. Close by is the **Rolts Nursery Butterfly Farm**.

GREAT BENTLEY
4 miles N of Brightlingsea off the A133

Reputed to have the largest village green in England, this lovely village has a number of shops, a pub with a restaurant, a beautiful church and a chapel.

THORRINGTON
3 miles NW of Brightlingsea off the AB1027

Thorrington Tide Mill, built in the early 19th century, is the only remaining Tide Mill in Essex, and one of very few left in East Anglia. It has been fully restored, and although no longer in use the Wheel can be run for guided groups. There is a public footpath, which runs along the creek here.

China Maroc Bonsai is a specialist nursery, part of which is devoted to a peaceful Japanese garden with a waterfall and pool, where one can enjoy the tranquil atmosphere and the many fascinating outdoor bonsai. Crossing the bridge over the pool, one enters a tropical tunnel containing hundreds of indoor bonsai, many of which are imported from the hotter regions of the world, as well as bonsai and seedlings grown and cultivated on the premises.

POINT CLEAR
2 miles SE of Brightlingsea off the B1027

The **East Essex Aviation Museum**, located in the Martello Tower at Point Clear, not only retains its original flooring and roof, but today contains interesting displays of wartime aviation, military and naval photographs, uniforms and other memorabilia with local and US Air Force connections. There are artefacts on show from the crash sites of wartime aircraft in the Tendring area, including the engine and fuselage section of a Mustang fighter. The museum also explores civil and military history from both World Wars. There are very good views from the tower over the Colne Estuary and Brightlingsea.

ST OSYTH
3 miles SE of Brightlingsea off the B1027

This pretty little village has a fascinating history and centres around its Norman church and the ancient ruins of **St Osyth Priory**. The town and Priory were named by Augustinian Canons after St Osytha, martyred daughter of Frithenwald, first Christian King of the East Angles, who was himself beheaded by the Danes in AD 653.

The Priory was founded in the 12th century and built on the site of a nunnery founded by the Princess. Little of the original Priory remains, except for the magnificent late 15th century flint gatehouse, complete with battlements. Heralded as one of the finest monastic buildings in the country, the Priory buildings extant include a 16th century tithe barn and bishops' lodgings, all set in a landscaped park where deer roam free in the deer park and peacocks patrol the shady lawns. The grounds are open to the public during the summer months. Within the gatehouse building there is an interesting collection of ceramics and jade. Other attractions include the Fitzwilliam art collection in the Georgian wing, with paintings by Reynolds, Stubbs and Van Dyck.

The village is centred on a crossroads and contains an attractive group of shops and restaurants. The Church of **St Peter and St**

PRIORY RESTAURANT

4 Clacton Road, St Osyth, Essex
Tel: 01255 820259

The accent is distinctly on the delights of Mediterranean cookery at **Priory Restaurant** in St Osyth, run with flair by Maria and Manuel Carvalho. This restaurant, tearooms and delicatessen makes its home in a magnificent building dating back to the 14th century which was once a public house. The decor is colourful and warm; the comfortable furnishings add to one's relaxation and enjoyment of one's meal or snack. The restaurant menu and daily specials offer a range of delicious fish, meat, poultry and pasta dishes such as breaded scampi, duck in orange sauce, grilled lamb and tagliatelle with smoked

salmon. The wine list is very good. Every dish - from the main courses to the cakes for the cream teas - is lovingly prepared and expertly presented. Maria and Manuel and their staff are friendly, attentive and welcoming.

The deli is open seven days a week from 7.00 am to 5.00 pm. The characterful and stylish restaurant is open Monday to Thursday 9.00 am to 5.00 pm, Friday 9.00 am to 9.00 pm, Saturday 9.00 am to 5.00 pm and 6.00 pm to 9.00 pm, and Sunday midday – 4.00 pm. Booking is advised at weekends. This marvellous establishment is well worth seeking out.

THE BLACKWATER HOTEL AND RESTAURANT

20-22 Church Road, West Mersea, Colchester, Essex CO5 8QH
Tel: 01206 383338 Fax: 01206 384288

Matt and Denise Wareing are the convivial and welcoming hosts at **The Blackwater Hotel and Restaurant**. This fine hotel boasts eight charming guest bedrooms, furnished and decorated to a high standard of taste and comfort. The elegant and intimate restaurant enjoys a fine reputation for its

superb food. The extensive menu offers something for all tastes. Locally caught seafood and Dutch mussels are just two of the delicious specialities. Lobster and the world-renowned Mersea oysters are available with 24 hours' notice. The wine list is particularly good. Dinner is served Monday to Thursday 7 - 9 p.m.; Fridays and Saturdays 7 - 10 p.m. On Sundays there's informal dining, with a choice from the specials board. Residents and non-residents alike are welcome to enjoy the lounge, bar or - weather permitting - lovely secluded courtyard. For hotel guests, the hearty breakfast is served from 7 - 10 a.m.

Paul in the village centre has unusual internal red brick piers and arches. The nearby creek has a small boatyard.

MERSEA ISLAND
2 miles SW of Brightlingsea off the B1025

Much of this island is a National Nature Reserve, home to its teeming shorelife. The island is linked to the mainland by a narrow causeway which is covered over at high tide. The towns of both **East** and **West Mersea** have excellent facilities for sailing enthusiasts. East Mersea is also a haven for birdwatchers.

HARWICH

Harwich's name probably originates from the time of King Alfred, when 'here' meant army, and 'wic' a camp. This attractive old town was built in the 13th century by the Earls of Norfolk to exploit its strategic position on the Stour and Orwell estuary; the town has an important and fascinating maritime history , the legacy of which continues into the present.

During the 14th and 15th century French campaigns it was an important naval base. The famous Elizabethen seafarers Hawkins, Frobisher and Drake sailed from Harwich on various expeditions; in 1561 Queen Elizabeth I visited the town, describing it 'a pretty place and want[ing] for nothing'. Christopher Newport, leader of the Goodspeed expedition

which founded Jamestown, Virginia, in 1607, and Christopher Jones, master of the Pilgrim ship The Mayflower, lived in Harwich (the latter just off the quay in Kings Head Street), as did Jones' kinsman John Alden, who sailed to America in 1620. The famous diarist Samuel Pepys was MP for the town in the 1660s, thus it also was during this time headquarters for the Kings Navy. Charles II took the first pleasure cruise from Harwich's shores. Other notable visitors included Lord Nelson and Lady Hamilton, who stayed at The Three Cups in Church Street.

Harwich remains popular as a vantage point for watching incoming and outgoing shipping in the harbour and across the waters to Felixstowe. Nowadays, lightships, buoys and miles of strong chain are stored along the front, and passengers arriving on North Sea ferries at Parkeston Quay see the 90 foot high, nine-sided **High Lighthouse** as the first landmark. Now housing the **National Vintage Wireless and Television Museum**, it was built in 1818 along with the **Low Lighthouse**. When the two lighthouses were in line they could indicate a safe shipping channel into the harbour. Each had replaced earlier wooden structures, and were themselves replaced by cast iron structures (one of which still stands on the front in nearby Dovercourt) in 1863 when the shifting sandbanks altered the channel. Shipping now relies on light buoys to find its way. The Low lighthouse is now the town's **Maritime Museum**, with specialist displays on the Royal Navy and commercial shipping.

Harwich Lighthouse

Two other worthwhile museums in the town are the Lighthouse Museum off Wellington Road, which contains the last Clacton offshore 34 foot lifeboat and a history of the lifeboat service in Harwich, and the **Ha'penny Pier Visitor Centre** on the Quay, with information on everything in Harwich and a small heritage exhibition.

The **Treadwell Crane** now stands on Harwich Green, but for over 250 years it was sited in the Naval Shipyard. It is worked by two people walking in two 16 foot diameter wheels, and is the only known example of its kind. Amazingly it was operational up until the 1920s. Another fascinating piece of the town's history is the **Electric Palace Cinema**, built in 1911 and now the oldest unaltered purpose-built cinema in Britain. It was restored by a trust and re-opened in 1981.

The importance of Harwich's port during the 19th century is confirmed by **The Redoubt**, a huge grey fort built between 1808 and 1810. Its design is an enlarged version of the Martello towers which dotted the English

coast awaiting a Napoleonic invasion which never came (some of these towers of course still exist). Today the Harwich Society has largely restored it and opened it as a museum.

The old town also contains many ancient buildings, including the **Guildhall**, which was rebuilt in 1769 and is located in Church Street. The Council chamber, Mayor's Parlour and other rooms may be viewed. The former gaol contains unique graffiti of ships, probably carved by prisoners, and is well worth putting aside an afternoon to explore. Interesting documents on show include those detailing the connection of Harwich with Pepys, the Pilgrim Fathers, and the Virginia settlement.

AROUND HARWICH

PARKESTON
1 mile W of Harwich off the A120

Not far from Harwich Harbour and embracing the River Stour coastline, Parkeston is a quiet suburb of its bustling neighbour.

DOVERCOURT
1 mile S of Harwich off the A120

This residential and holiday suburb of Harwich has Market Day on Fridays. With its attractive cliffs and beach, it also boasts the **Iron Lighthouse** or 'Leading Lights' located just off lower Marine Parade. The town has been settled from prehistoric times, as attested to by the late Bronze Age axe-heads found here (now in Colchester Museum). The Romans found the town a useful source of the stone `Septaria', taken from the cliffs and used in building. The town that visitors see today developed primarily in Victorian times as a fashionable resort.

MISTLEY
7 miles W of Harwich off the B1352

Here at the gateway to Constable Country, local 18th century landowner and MP Richard Rigby had grand designs to develop Mistley into a fashionable spa to rival Harrogate and Bath, adopting the swan as its symbol. Sadly, all that remains of Rigby's ambitious scheme is the Swan Fountain, a small number of attractive Georgian houses and **Mistley Towers**, the remains of a church (otherwise demolished in 1870) designed by the flamboyant architect Robert Adams. From the waterfront, noted for its colony of swans, there are very pleasant views across the estuary to Suffolk.

Mistley Quay Workshops in the High Street feature a pottery workshop, lute/cello maker, harpsichord maker, wood worker, bookbinder, and stained-glass window maker and restorer. There is also a tea-shop on the premises (the key to Mistley Towers can be obtained from the Workshops).

Mistley Place Park Animal Rescue Centre is 25 acres of parkland affording country walks, wildlife habitats, lake, farm animals and great views across the Stour Estuary.

The **Essex Secret Bunker** in Mistley, former county nuclear war headquarters, is now a public museum offering a fascinating insight into the postwar world of top-secret preparations against nuclear attack. Operational from 1951, it was 'declassified' in 1993 and opened to the public in 1996. Interesting things to see and do, include the giant underground operations room, office and dormitories, telephone exchange communications centre and radio room, powerhouse and filtration plant.

MANNINGTREE
9 miles W of Harwich off the B1352

The Walls, on the approach to Manningtree along the B1352, offer unrivalled views of the Stour estuary and the Suffolk coast, and the swans for which the area is famous. Lying on the River Stour amid beautiful rolling countryside, it has often been depicted by artists over the centuries.

Back in Tudor times, Manningtree was the centre of the cloth trade, and later a port filled with barges carrying their various cargoes along the coast to London. Water still dominates today and the town is a centre of leisure sailing.

Manningtree has been a market town since 1238, and is still a busy shopping centre. It is the smallest town in Britain, and a stroll through the streets reveals the variety of its past. There are still traditional (and mainly Georgian) restaurants, pubs and shops, as well as handcraft and specialist outlets. The views over the river are well known to birdspotters, sailors and ramblers. The town has an intriguing past - as a river crossing, market, smugglers' haven and home of Matthew Hopkins, the reviled and self-styled Witchfinder General who struck terror into the local community during the 17th century. Some of his victims were hanged on Manningtree's small village green.

It is believed that the reference in Shakespeare's *Henry IV* to Falstaff as 'that roasted Manningtree ox' relates to the

THE CAPTAIN FRYATT

Garland Road, Parkeston, Harwich,
Essex CO12 4PA
Tel: 01255 503535

The Captain Fryatt in Parkeston takes its name from Charles Algernon Fryatt, master of the Great Eastern Railway Company's steamship, Brussels. A bona fide hero, Captain Fryatt survived many skirmishes with German subs during the First World War, but was captured off the Hook of Holland on the way back to Tilbury and taken to Germany, where he was tried and executed. Tenant Susanne had worked here since 1992 before she and her partner Billy became landlords in April of 2000. Open all day every day, this fine pub serves Tetleys real ale along with a good range of lagers, cider, stout, wines and spirits. Food is available all day up until 9 p.m. Guests choose from a varied list of traditional favourites. This excellent inn also has 12 superior guest bedrooms (doubles, twins, family rooms and singles).

practice of roasting an entire ox at the town's
medieval annual fair.

ARDLEIGH
10 miles W of Harwich off the A137

Tendring's most western village comprises an
attractive group of 16th and 17th century
cottages grouped around the fine 15th
century **Butterfield Church**. **Spring Valley
Mill**, a now privately owned 18th century
timber-framed and weatherboarded edifice,
was once a working watermill, later adapted
to steam. Day and half-day canoeing and
sailing lessons can be taken at the **Ardleigh
Outdoor Education Centre**.

Nearby is **Ardleigh Reservoir** with its
opportunities for water sports and trout
fishing.

3 South and West Suffolk

John Constable, England's greatest landscape painter, was born at East Bergholt in 1776 and remained at heart a Suffolk man throughout his life. He was later to declare *"I associate my careless boyhood with all that lies on the banks of the Stour. Those scenes made me a painter and I am grateful."* He painted the occasional portrait and even attempted a couple of religious works, but he concentrated almost entirely on the scenes that he

Willy Lotts Cottage, Flatford Mill

knew and loved as a boy. The Suffolk tradition of painting continues to this day, with many artists drawn particularly to Walberswick and the beautiful Constable country. That beauty is not always easy to appreciate when crowds throng through the Stour valley at summer weekends, but at other times the peace and beauty are much as they were in Constable's day.

Much of Suffolk's character comes from its rivers, and in the part of the county surrounding Ipswich, the Orwell and the Stour mark the boundaries of the Shotley Peninsula. The countryside here is largely unspoilt, with wide-open spaces between scattered villages. The relative flatness of Suffolk gives every encouragement for motorists to leave their machines, and the peninsula, still relatively peaceful, is ideal for a spot of walking or cycling or boating. Southeast of Ipswich, the peninsula created by the River Deben and the River Orwell is one of the prettiest areas in Suffolk, its winding lanes leading through a delightful series of quiet rural villages and colourful riverside communities.

Cambridgeshire, Norfolk, the A134 and the A14 frame the northern part of West Suffolk, which includes Bury St Edmunds, a pivotal player in the country's religious history, and Newmarket, one of the major centres of the horseracing world. Between and above them are picturesque villages, bustling market towns, rich farming countryside, the fens, and the expanse of sandy heath and pine forest that is Breckland. Many of the remains of the Anglo-Saxon period are on display, notably at West Stow and in Bury St Edmunds (Abbey ruins and Moyses Hall) and elsewhere in

Gainsborough's House, Sudbury

Blythburgh, Sutton Hoo and Snape, and in museums in Ipswich and Woodbridge.

The area south and west of Bury towards the Essex border contains some of Suffolk's most attractive and peaceful countryside. The beauty is largely unspoilt and the motorist will come upon a succession of picturesque villages, historic churches, stately homes, heritage centres and nature reserves. In the south, along the River Stour, stand the historic wool towns of Long Melford, Cavendish and Clare.

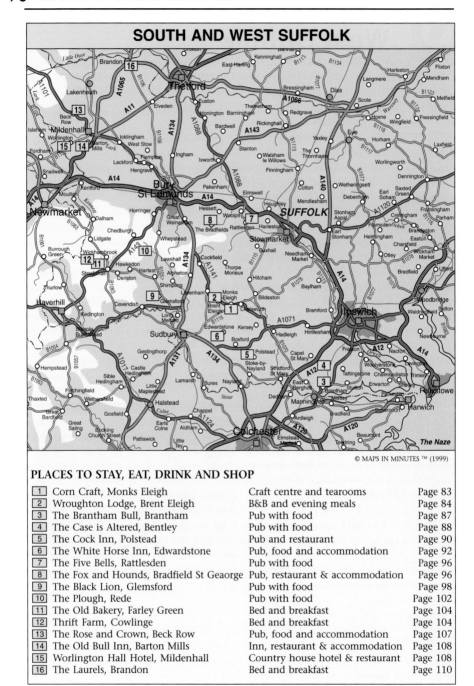

SOUTH AND WEST SUFFOLK

© MAPS IN MINUTES ™ (1999)

PLACES TO STAY, EAT, DRINK AND SHOP

1	Corn Craft, Monks Eleigh	Craft centre and tearooms	Page 83
2	Wroughton Lodge, Brent Eleigh	B&B and evening meals	Page 84
3	The Brantham Bull, Brantham	Pub with food	Page 87
4	The Case is Altered, Bentley	Pub with food	Page 88
5	The Cock Inn, Polstead	Pub and restaurant	Page 90
6	The White Horse Inn, Edwardstone	Pub, food and accommodation	Page 92
7	The Five Bells, Rattlesden	Pub with food	Page 96
8	The Fox and Hounds, Bradfield St Geaorge	Pub, restaurant & accommodation	Page 96
9	The Black Lion, Glemsford	Pub with food	Page 98
10	The Plough, Rede	Pub with food	Page 102
11	The Old Bakery, Farley Green	Bed and breakfast	Page 104
12	Thrift Farm, Cowlinge	Bed and breakfast	Page 104
13	The Rose and Crown, Beck Row	Pub, food and accommodation	Page 107
14	The Old Bull Inn, Barton Mills	Inn, restaurant & accommodation	Page 108
15	Worlington Hall Hotel, Mildenhall	Country house hotel & restaurant	Page 108
16	The Laurels, Brandon	Bed and breakfast	Page 110

IPSWICH

History highlights Ipswich as the birthplace of Cardinal Wolsey, but the story of Suffolk's county town starts very much earlier. It has been a port since the time of the Roman occupation and by the 7th century the Anglo-Saxons had expanded it into the largest port in the country. King John granted a civic charter in 1200, confirming the townspeople's right to their own laws and administration, and for several centuries the town prospered as a port exporting wool, textiles and agricultural products.

Thomas Wolsey arrived on the scene in 1475, the son of a wealthy butcher and grazier. Educated at Magdalen College, Oxford, he was ordained a priest in 1498 and rose quickly in influence, becoming chaplain to Henry VII and then Archbishop of York, a cardinal and Lord Chancellor under Henry VIII. He was quite indispensable to the king and had charge of foreign policy as well as powerful sway over judicial institutions. He also managed to amass enormous wealth, enabling him to found a grammar school in

Ipswich and Cardinal's College (later Christ Church) in Oxford. Wolsey had long been hated by certain nobles for his low birth and arrogance, and they were easily able to turn Henry against him when his attempts to secure an annulment from the Pope of the king's marriage to Catherine of Aragon met with failure. Stripped of most of his offices following a charge of overstepping his authority as a legate, he was later charged with treason but died while travelling from York to London to face the king. His death put an end to his plans for the grammar school, and all that remains now is a red-brick gateway.

When the cloth market fell into decline in the 17th century a respite followed in the following century, when the town was a food distribution port during the Napoleonic Wars. At the beginning of the 19th century the risk from silting was becoming acute at a time when trade was improving and industries were springing up. The Wet Dock, constructed in 1842, solved the silting problem and, with the railway arriving shortly after, Ipswich could once more look forward to a safe future. The Victorians were responsible for considerable development and symbols of their civic pride include the handsome **Old Custom House** by the Wet Dock, the Town Hall and the splendid **Tolly Cobbold brewery**, rebuilt at the end of the 19th century, 150 years after brewing started on the site. Guided tours take visitors through the whole brewing process. In Grimwade Street stands **Peter's Ice Cream Factory**, built 100 years ago. Guided tours take place several times a day, and there's a museum, restaurant and shop. Victorian enterprise depleted the older buildings, but a number survive, notably the Tudor houses where Wolsey was born, the Ancient House with its wonderful pargeting, and a dozen

St Peter's Dock, Ipswich

The Ancient House, Ipswich

On the outskirts of town, signposted from Nacton Road, is **Orwell Country Park**, a 150-acre site of wood, heath and reedbeds by the Orwell estuary. At this point the river is crossed by the imposing Orwell Bridge, a graceful construction in pre-stressed concrete that was completed in 1982 and is not far short of a mile in length.

Notables from the world of the arts with Ipswich connections include Thomas Gainsborough, who got his first major commissions here to paint portraits of local people; David Garrick, the renowned actor-manager, who made his debut here in 1741 as Aboan in Thomas Southerne's *Oroonoko*; and the peripatetic Charles Dickens, who stayed at the Great White Horse while still a young reporter with the Morning Chronicle. Soon afterwards, he featured the tavern in The Pickwick Papers as the place where Mr Pickwick wanders inadvertently into a lady's bedroom. Sir V S Pritchett was born in Ipswich, while Enid Blyton trained as a kindergarten teacher at Ipswich High School.

AROUND IPSWICH

medieval churches. St Margaret's is the finest of these, boasting some very splendid flintwork and a double hammerbeam roof.

Christchurch Mansion is a beautiful Tudor home standing in a 65-acre park. Furnished as an English country house, it contains a major collection of works by Constable and Gainsborough and many other paintings, prints and sculptures by Suffolk artists from the 17th century onwards.

The town's main **museum** is in a Victorian building in the High Street. Displays include a natural history gallery, a wildlife gallery complete with a model of a mammoth, a reconstruction of a Roman villa and replicas of Sutton Hoo treasures. A recent addition is a display of elaborately carved timbers from the homes of wealthy 17th century merchants.

In a former trolleybus depot on Cobham Road is the **Ipswich Transport Museum**, a fascinating collection of vehicles, from prams to fire engines, all made or used around Ipswich.

NACTON
4 miles SE of Ipswich off the A14

South of Nacton's medieval church lies **Orwell Park House**, which was built in the 18th century by Admiral Edward Vernon, sometime Member of Parliament for Ipswich. The admiral, who had won an important victory over the Spanish in the War of Jenkins Ear, was known to his men as Old Grog, because of his habit of wearing a cloak of coarse grogram cloth. His nickname passed into the language when he ordered that the rum ration dished out daily to sailors should be diluted with water to combat the drunkenness that was rife in the service. That was in 1740, and a ration of 'grog' was officially issued to sailors until 1970.

George Tomline bought the splendid house in 1857 and made it even more splendid, adding a conservatory, a ballroom and towers. He also changed the facade to handsome Georgian. The house became the setting for some of the grandest shooting parties ever seen in this part of the world, and such was the power of the Tomlines that they were able to move the village away from the house to its present site.

Nacton picnic site in Shore Lane (signposted from the village) commands wonderful views of the Orwell and is a prime spot in winter for birdwatchers. The birds feed very well off the mud flats.

LEVINGTON
5 miles SE of Ipswich off the A14

A pretty village on the banks of the Orwell. Fisons established a factory here in 1956, and developed the now famous Levington Compost. On the foreshore below the village is an extensive marina which has brought an extra bustle to the area. The coastal footpath along the bank of the Orwell leads across the nature reserve of **Trimley Marshes** and on to Felixstowe.

TRIMLEY ST MARY & TRIMLEY ST MARTIN
6 miles SE of Ipswich off the A14

Twin villages with two churches in the same churchyard. The Cavendish family were famous Trimley residents, their best known member being the adventurer Thomas Cavendish. In 1590 he became the second man to sail round the world and two years later he died on another voyage. He is depicted on the village sign.

Trimley Marshes were created from farmland and comprise grazing marsh, reed beds and wetland that's home to an abundance of interesting plant life and many species of wildfowl, waders and migrant birds. Access is on foot from Trimley St Mary.

NEWBOURNE
7 miles E of Ipswich off the A12

A small miracle occurred here on the night of the hurricane of October 1987. One wall of the ancient St Mary's Church was blown out and with it the stained glass, which shattered into fragments. One piece, showing the face of Christ, was found undamaged and was later incorporated into the rebuilt wall. Two remarkable inhabitants of Newbourne were the Page brothers, who both stood over 7 feet tall; they enjoyed a career touring the fairs and are buried in Newbourne churchyard.

WALDRINGFIELD
7 miles E of Ipswich off the A12

Waldringfield lies on a particularly beautiful stretch of the Deben estuary, and the waterfront is largely given over to leisure boating and cruising. The quay was once busy with barges, many of them laden with coprolite. This fossilised dung, the forerunner of fertilizer, was found in great abundance in and around Waldringfield, and a number of exhausted pits can still be seen.

FELIXSTOWE
12 miles SE of Ipswich off the A14

Until the early 17th century Felixstowe was a little known village of no great importance, but it was the good Colonel Tomline of Orwell Park who put it on the map by creating a port to rival its near neighbour Harwich. He also started work on the Ipswich-Felixstowe railway (with a stop at Nacton for the grand parties), and 1887 saw the completion of both projects. Tomline also

Sailing at Felixstowe

developed the resort aspects of Felixstowe, rivalling the amenities of Dovercourt, and when he died in 1887 most of his dreams had become reality. (He was, incidentally, cremated, one of the first in the county to be so disposed of in the modern era.) What he didn't live to see was the pier, opened in 1904 and still in use.

The town has suffered a number of ups and downs this century, but on the run-up to the Millennium thrives as one of England's busiest ports, having been much extended in the 1960s. The resort is strung out round a wide, gently curving bay, where the long seafront road is prettified by trim lawns and gardens.

The Martello tower is a noted landmark, as is the **pier**, which was once long enough to merit an electric tramway. It was shortened as a security measure during the Second World War. All the usual attractions are provided for the holidaymaker, and a very unusual one. This is the **Felixstowe Water Clock**, a curious piece assembled from dozens of industrial bits and pieces.

The original fishing hamlet from which the Victorian resort was developed lies beyond a golf course north of the town. This is **Felixstowe Ferry**, a cluster of holiday homes, an inn, a boatyard, fishing sheds and a Martello tower. The sailing club is involved mainly with dinghy racing and the whole place becomes a hive of activity during the class meetings. A ferry takes foot passengers (plus bicycles) across to Bawdsey.

At the southernmost tip of the peninsula is **Landguard Point**, where a nature reserve supports rare plants and migrating birds.

Just north on this shingle bank is **Landguard Fort**, built in 1718 (replacing an earlier construction) to protect Harwich harbour and now home to **Felixstowe Museum**. The museum is actually housed in the Ravelin Block (1878), which was used as a mine storage depot by the army when a mine barrier was laid across the Orwell in World War I. A fascinating variety of exhibits includes local history, model aircraft and model paddle steamers, Roman coins and the history of the fort itself, which was the scene of the last invasion of English soil, by the Dutch in 1667. Beyond the fort is an excellent viewing point for watching the comings and goings of the ships.

FRESTON
3 miles S of Ipswich off the B1080

An ancient village on the south bank of the Orwell, worth visiting for some fine old buildings and some curiosities. The most curious and best known of these buildings is the six-storey Tudor tower by the river in **Freston Park** (it's actually best viewed from across the river). The red-brick house, built around 1570, has just six rooms, one per storey. It might be a folly, but it was probably put up as a lookout tower to warn of enemies sailing up the river. The nicest theory is that it was built for Ellen, daughter of Lord Freston, to study a different subject each day, progressing floor by floor up the tower (and with Sundays off, presumably). A 4,000-year-old archaeological site at Freston was revealed by aerial photography.

WOOLVERSTONE
4 miles S of Ipswich on the B1456

Dating back to the Bronze Age, Woolverstone has a large marina along the banks of the Orwell. One of the buildings in the complex is **Cat House**, where it is said that a stuffed white cat placed in the window would be an all-clear sign for smugglers. Woolverstone House was originally St Peter's Home for 'Fallen Women', run by nuns. It was designed by Sir Edwin Lutyens and has its own chapel and bell tower.

TATTINGSTONE
4 miles S of Ipswich off the A137

Tattingstone Wonder, on the road between Tattingstone and Stutton, looks like a church from the front, but it isn't! It was built by a local landowner to provide accommodation for estate workers. He presumably preferred to look at a church from his mansion than some plain little cottages. Tattingstone lies at the western edge of Alton Water, a vast man-made lake created as a reservoir in the late 1970s. A footpath runs round the perimeter, and there's a wildlife sanctuary. On the water itself all sorts of leisure activities are on offer, including angling, sailing and windsurfing.

STUTTON
6 miles S of Ipswich on the B1080

The elongated village of Stutton lies on the southern edge of the reservoir. The Domesday

Book records six manor houses standing here, and there are still some grand properties down by the Stour. St Peter's Church stands isolated overlooking Holbrook Bay, and a footpath from the church leads all the way along the river to Shotley Gate. A little way north, on the B1080, Holbrook is a large village with a brook at the bottom of the hill. Water from the brook powered Alton Mill, a weather-boarded edifice on a site occupied by watermills for more than 900 years. The mill is now a restaurant.

CHELMONDISTON
5 miles S of Ipswich on the B1456

The church here is modern, but incorporates some parts of the original, which was destroyed by a flying bomb in 1944. In the

House by the Waterside, Pin Mill

same parish is the tiny riverside community of **Pin Mill**, a well-known beauty spot and sailing centre. The river views are particularly lovely at this point, and it's also a favourite place for woodland and heathland walks. Pin Mill was once a major manufacturer of barges, and those imposing craft can still be seen, sharing the river with sailing boats and pleasure craft. Each year veteran barges gather for a race that starts here at Buttermans Bay and ends at Harwich. Arthur Ransome, author of *Swallows and Amazons*, stayed here and had boats built. His *We Didn't Mean to Go to Sea* starts aboard a yacht mooring here.

The local hostelry is the 17th century Butt & Oyster, much visited, much painted and one of the best known pubs in the county. To the east of the Quay is Cliff Plantation, an ancient coppice wood of alder and oak.

ERWARTON
6 miles S of Ipswich off the B1456

An impressive red-brick Jacobean gatehouse with a rounded arch, buttresses and pinnacles is part of **Erwarton Hall**, the family home of the Calthorpes. Anne Boleyn was the niece of Philip Calthorpe and visited as a child and as queen. Just before her execution Anne apparently requested that her heart be buried in the family vault at St Mary's Church. A casket in the shape of a heart was found there in 1836 and when opened contained dust. It was resealed and laid in the Lady Chapel.

SHOTLEY
8 miles S of Ipswich on the B1456

Right at the end of the peninsula, with the Orwell on one side and the Stour on the other, Shotley is best known as the home of *HMS Ganges*, where generations of sailors received their training. The main feature is the 142' mast up which trainees would shin at the passing-out ceremony. A small museum records the history of the establishment from 1905 to 1976, when it became a policy academy. At the very tip is a large marina where a classic boat festival is an annual occasion.

HINTLESHAM
7 miles W of Ipswich on the A1071

Hintlesham's glory is a magnificent hall dating from the 1570s, when it was the home of the Timperley family. It was considerably altered during the 18th century, when it acquired its splendid Georgian facade. For some years the hall was owned by the celebrated chef Robert Carrier, who developed it into the county's leading restaurant. It still functions as a high-class hotel and restaurant.

Hadleigh Guild Hall

HADLEIGH
10 miles W of Ipswich on the A1071

Old and not-so-old blend harmoniously in a variety of architectural styles. Timber-framed buildings, often with elaborate plasterwork, stand in the long main street as a reminder of the prosperity generated by the wool trade in the 14th to 16th centuries, and there are also some fine houses from the Regency and Victorian periods. The 15th century **Guildhall** with two overhanging storeys, the Deanery Tower and the church are a magnificent trio of huge appeal and contrasting construction – timber for the Guildhall, brick for the tower and flint for the church.

Guthrun, the Danish leader who was captured by Alfred and pardoned on condition that he became a Christian, made Hadleigh his HQ and lived here for 12 years. He was buried in the church, then a wooden construction but later twice rebuilt. In the south chapel of the present church is a 14th century bench-end carving depicting the scene of the wolf guarding the head of St Edmund. The wolf is wearing a monk's habit, indicating a satirical sense of humour in the carpenter. Also of interest

is the **clock bell**, which stands outside the tower. A famous resident of Hadleigh was the rector Dr Rowland Taylor, who was burnt at the stake on Aldham Common for refusing to hold a mass. A large stone, inscribed and dated 1555, marks the spot.

There are two good walks from Hadleigh, the first being along the Brett with access over medieval **Toppesfield Bridge**. The other is a walk along the disused railway line between Hadleigh and Raydon through peaceful, picturesque countryside. At Raydon a few buildings survive from the wartime base of the 353rd, 357th and 358th Fighter Groups of the USAAF.

Two miles east of Hadleigh is **Wolves Wood**, an RSPB reserve with woodland nature trails and no wolves.

KERSEY
12 miles W of Ipswich off the A1141

The ultimate Suffolk picture-postcard village, a wonderful collection of timbered merchants' houses and weavers' cottages with paint and thatch. The main street has a **water**

Kersey Ford

splash, which, along with the 700-year-old Bell Inn, has featured in many films and travelogues. The Church of St Mary, which overlooks the village from its hilltop position, is of massive proportions, testimony to the wealth that came with the wool and cloth industry. Kersey's speciality was a coarse twill broadcloth much favoured for greatcoats and army uniforms. Headless angels and mutilated carvings are reminders of the Puritans' visit to the church, though some treasures survive, including the ornate flintwork of the 15th century south porch. Traditional craftsmanship can still be seen in practice at the Kersey Pottery, which sells many items of stoneware plus paintings by Suffolk artists.

Chelsworth Village Street

CHELSWORTH
14 miles W of Ipswich off the A1141

An unspoilt delight in the lovely valley of the River Brett, which is crossed by a little double hump-backed bridge. The timbered houses and thatched cottages look much the same as when they were built, and every year the village opens its gardens to the public.

MONKS ELEIGH
16 miles W of Ipswich on the A1141

The setting of thatched cottages, a 14th century church and a pump on the village green is so traditional that Monks Eleigh was regularly used on railway posters as a lure to a wonderful part of the country.

CORN CRAFT

Monks Eleigh, Ipswich, Suffolk IP7 7AY
Tel: 01449 740456

Corn Craft is a unique centre bringing together some of East Anglia's most creative artists and craftspeople. Surrounded by acres of corn, some of which is grown specially to make traditional corn dollies, this fascinating craft centre was founded over 20 years ago by Royston and Win Gage in converted farm buildings on the family farm. Here visitors can discover for themselves traditional Suffolk crafts. In the restored mill visitors

will find beautiful and unusual crafts, ideal as gifts or keepsakes. The pottery and ceramics include model houses, wall plates and distinctive tea pots and lamps. There are also soft toys, jewellery, clocks, toiletries and a tempting array of homemade preserves. The centre's showroom is dedicated to dried and silk flowers and corn and maize dollies. Flowers come in basket arrangements and in loose bunches, so that people can make their own decorations and unique creations for their home or as gifts. In the charming tea room, guests can enjoy a range of delicious cakes, biscuits and lights snacks all day, along with a variety of refreshing hot and cold drinks. On fine days guests can enjoy their tea outdoors in the fresh air and surrounded by the lovely countryside. All the staff at this fine craft centre are friendly and helpful.

Timbered House, Bildeston

BILDESTON
14 miles W of Ipswich on the B1115

More fine old buildings here, including timber-framed cottages with overhanging upper floors. The Church of St Mary has a superb carved door and a splendid hammerbeam roof. A tablet inside the church commemorates Captain Edward Rotherham, Commander of the *Royal Sovereign* at the

Battle of Trafalgar. He died in Bildeston while staying with a friend and is buried in the churchyard.

BRENT ELEIGH
17 miles W of Ipswich off the A1141

The church at Brent Eleigh, on a side road off the A1141, is remarkable for a number of quite beautiful ancient wall paintings, discovered during maintenance work as recently as 1960. The most striking and moving of the paintings is one of the Crucifixion.

LAVENHAM
18 miles W of Ipswich on the A1141

An absolute gem of a town, the most complete and original of the medieval 'wool towns', with crooked timbered and whitewashed buildings lining the narrow streets. From the 14th to the 16th centuries, Lavenham flourished as one of the leading wool and cloth-making centres in the land, but with the decline of that industry the prosperous times soon came to an end. It is

WROUGHTON LODGE

Brent Eleigh, nr Lavenham, Sudbury, Suffolk CO10 9PB
Tel: 01787 247495 Fax: 01787 248462
email: elizabethknight@wroughtonlodge.fsnet.co.uk

Wroughton Lodge offers a taste of gracious living in a truly welcoming and relaxed atmosphere. Luxury doesn't come in a nicer package: this attractive and characterful house is set in a quiet village location just two miles from the historic village of Lavenham, making it an ideal base for exploring Constable Country and the many sights and attractions of this part of East Anglia.

The accommodation is spacious; all rooms are ensuite and equipped with every facility guests have come to expect. The extensive one-and-a-half acres of cultivated gardens boast a hard tennis court and a heated outdoor swimming pool, both available for guests' enjoyment. The guests' sitting room is graciously appointed and supremely comfortable; it leads to an attractive library room, open to guests. The dining room leads to the large family sunroom and patio which overlook the gardens. Guests can come and go as they please - internal telephones connect to owners Mr and Mrs Knight, should they be needed. Evening meals by prior arrangement if required. No smoking. English Tourist Council 4 Diamonds and Silver Award (January 2000).

Restored Medieval Houses, Lavenham

largely due to the fact that Lavenham found no replacement industry that so much of the medieval character remains: there was simply not enough money for the rebuilding and development programmes that changed many towns, often for the worse. The medieval street pattern still exists, complete with market place and market cross.

More than 300 buildings are officially listed as being of architectural and historical interest, and none of them is finer than the **Guildhall**. This superb 16th century timbered building was originally the meeting place of the Guild of Corpus Christi, an organisation that regulated the production of wool. It now houses exhibitions of local history and the wool trade, and its walled garden has a special area devoted to dye plants. **Little Hall** is hardly less remarkable, a 15th century hall house with a superb crown post roof. It was restored by the Gayer Anderson brothers, and has a fine collection of their furniture. The Church of St Peter and St Paul dominates the town from its elevated position. It's a building of great distinction, perhaps the greatest of all the 'wool churches' and declared by the 19th century architect August Pugin to be the finest example of Late Perpendicular style in the world. It was built, with generous help from wealthy local families (notably the Spryngs and the de Veres) in the late 15th and early 16th centuries to celebrate the end of the Wars of the Roses. Its flint tower is a mighty 140 feet in height and it's possible to climb to the top to take in the glorious views over Lavenham and the surrounding countryside. Richly carved screens and fine (Victorian) stained glass are eye-catching features within.

The Priory originated in the 13th century as a home for Benedictine monks and the beautiful timber-framed house on the site dates from about 1600. In the original hall, at the centre of the building, is an important collection of paintings and stained glass. The extensive grounds include a kitchen garden, a herb garden and a pond.

John Constable went to school in Lavenham, where one of his friends was Jane Taylor, who wrote the words to "Twinkle Twinkle Little Star".

SUDBURY
21 miles W of Ipswich on the A131

Another wonderful town, the largest of the 'wool towns' and still home to a number of weaving concerns. Unlike Lavenham, it kept its industry because it was a port, and the result is a much more varied architectural picture. The surrounding countryside is some of the loveliest in Suffolk, and the River Stour is a further plus, with launch trips, rowing boats and fishing all available. Sudbury boasts three medieval churches, but what most visitors make a beeline for is **Gainsborough's House** on Market Hill. The painter Thomas Gainsborough was born here in 1727 in the house built by his father John. More of the artist's work is displayed in this Georgian-fronted house than in any other gallery, and there are also assorted 18th century memorabilia and furnishings. A

Gainsborough's House, Sudbury

changing programme of contemporary art exhibitions includes fine art, photography and sculpture and highlighting East Anglian artists in particular. A bronze statue of Gainsborough stands in the square.

About those churches: All Saints dates from the 15th century and has a glorious carved tracery pulpit and screens; 14th century St Gregory's is notable for a wonderful medieval font; and St Peter's has some marvellous painted screen panels and a piece of 15th century embroidered velvet.

Other buildings of interest are the **Victorian Corn Exchange**, now a library; **Salter's Hall**, a 15th century timbered house; and the **Quay Theatre**, a thriving centre for the arts.

CONSTABLE COUNTRY

England's greatest landscape painter was born at East Bergholt in 1776 and remained at heart a Suffolk man throughout his life. His father, Golding Constable, was a wealthy man who owned both Flatford Mill and Dedham Mill, the latter on the Essex side of the Stour. The river was a major source of inspiration to the young John Constable, and his constant involvement in country matters gave him an expert knowledge of the elements and a keen eye for the details of nature. He was later to declare "I associate my careless boyhood with all that lies on the banks of the Stour. Those scenes made me a painter and I am grateful." That interest in painting developed early and was fostered by his friendship with John Dunthorne, a local plumber and amateur artist. He became a probationer at the Royal Academy Schools in 1799 and over the following years developed the technical skills to match his powers of observation. He painted the occasional portrait and even attempted a couple of religious works, but he concentrated almost entirely on the scenes that he knew and loved as a boy.

The most significant works of the earlier years were the numerous sketches in oil which were forerunners of the major paintings of Constable's mature years. He had exhibited at the Royal Academy every year since 1802, but it was not until 1817 that the first of his important canvases, *Flatford Mill*

on the River Stour, was hung. This was succeeded by the six large paintings which became his best known works. These were all set on a short stretch of the Stour, and all except The Hay Wain show barges at work. These broad, flat-bottomed craft were displayed in scenes remarkable for the realism of the colours, the effects of light and water and, above all, the beautiful depiction of clouds. His fellow-artist Fuseli declared that whenever he saw a Constable painting he felt the need to reach for his coat and umbrella. Though more realistic than anything that preceded them, Constable's paintings were never lacking soul, and his work was much admired by the painters of the French Romantic School. Two quotations from the man himself reveal much about his aims and philosophy:

"In a landscape I want to give one brief moment caught from fleeting time a lasting and sober existence."

And

"I never saw any ugly thing in my life; in fact, whatever may be the shape of an object, light, shade or perspective can always make it beautiful."

At the time of his death in 1837, Constable's reputation at home was relatively modest, though he had many followers and admirers in France. Awareness and understanding of his unique talent grew in the ensuing years, and his place as England's foremost landscape painter is rarely disputed.

Suffolk has produced many other painters of distinction. Thomas Gainsborough, born in Sudbury in 1727, was an artist of great versatility, innovative and instinctive, and equally at home with portraits and landscapes. He earned his living for a while from portrait painting in Ipswich before making a real name for himself in Bath. His relations with the Royal Academy were often stormy, and in 1784 he had a major dispute over the height at which a painting should be hung. He withdrew his intended hangings from the exhibition and never again showed at the Royal Academy.

A man of equally indomitable spirit was Sir Alfred Munnings, born at Mendham in the north of Suffolk in 1878. The last of the great sporting painters, in the tradition of Stubbs and Marshall, Munnings was outspoken in his opinions of modern art. In 1949, as outgoing President of the Royal Academy, he launched an animated attack on modern art as 'silly daubs' and 'violent blows at nothing'. The occasion was broadcast on the radio and many listeners complained about the strong language used by Munnings. In 1956 he jolted the art world again by describing that year's Summer Exhibition as 'bits of nonsense' hung on the wall.

Mary Beale, born at Barrow in 1633, was a noted portrait painter and copyist; some of her work has been attributed to Lely and Kneller, and it was rumoured that Lely was in love with her.

Philip Wilson Steer (1860-1942) was among the most distinguished of the many painters who were attracted to Walberswick. He studied in Paris and acquired the reputation of being the best of the English impressionist painters.

The Suffolk tradition of painting continues to this day, with many artists drawn particularly to Walberswick and the beautiful Constable country. That beauty is not always easy to appreciate when crowds throng through the Stour valley at summer weekends, but at other times the peace and beauty are much as they were in Constable's day.

BRANTHAM
8 miles SW of Ipswich on the A137

Also known as 'Burnt Village' – possibly because it was sacked during a Danish invasion 1,000 years ago. The Church of St Michael owns one of the only two known religious paintings by Constable, *Christ Blessing the Children*, which he executed in the style of the American painter Benjamin West. It is kept in safety in Ipswich Museum. Just off the junction of the A137 and the B1070 is **Cattawade picnic site**, a small area on the edge of the Stour estuary. It's a good spot for birdwatching, and redshanks, lapwings and oystercatchers all breed on the well-known Cattawade Marshes. Fishing and canoeing are available, and there are public footpaths to Flatford Mill.

EAST BERGHOLT
8 miles SW of Ipswich on the B1070

Narrow lanes lead to this picturesque and much visited little village. The **Constable County Trail** starts here, where the painter was born, and passes through Flatford Mill and on to Dedham in Essex. The actual house where he was born no longer stands, but the site is marked by a plaque on the fence of its successor, a private house called Constables. A little further along Church Street is Moss Cottage, which Constable once used as his studio. **St Mary's** Church is one of the many grand churches built with the wealth brought by the wool trade. This one should have been even grander, with a tower to rival that of Dedham across the river. The story goes that Cardinal Wolsey pledged the money to build the tower but fell from grace before the funds were forthcoming. The tower got no further

THE BRANTHAM BULL

The Street, Brantham, Manningtree,
Essex CO11 1PN
Tel: 01473 328494

Situated alongside the A137 - despite its postal address, a mile into Suffolk - **The Brantham Bull** is a lively and welcoming public house dating back to the 18th century. Personally run by Ben and Karl, who are friendly and hospitable hosts, this fine pub is open every session weekdays and all day at weekends. The warm ambience, great food and selection of real

ales and lagers, stout, cider, wines and spirits make this a justly popular place. There's always a relaxed atmosphere at this traditional coaching inn. Meals are served in both the handsome and characterful restaurant and in the bar. All dishes are freshly prepared and make use of the best local ingredients. On the second and last Tuesday of the month there is live jazz from 8.30 onwards. On Wednesday nights in winter there is live music and free hot food.

Georgian House, East Bergholt

century. One of the grandest is **Stour House**, once the home of Randolph Churchill. Its gardens are open to the public, as is **East Bergholt Place Garden** on the B1070.

A leafy lane leads south from the village to the Stour, where two of Constable's favourite subjects, **Flatford Mill** and **Willy Lott's cottage**, both looking much as they did when

than did his college in Ipswich, but a bellcage constructed in the churchyard as a temporary house for the bells became their permanent home, which it remains to this day. In this unique timber-framed structure the massive bells hang upside down and are rung by hand by pulling on the wooden shoulder stocks; an arduous task, as the five bells are among the heaviest in England.

The church is naturally something of a shrine to Constable, his family and his friends. There are memorial windows to the artist and to his beloved wife Maria Bicknell, who bore him seven children and whose early death was an enormous blow to him. His parents, to whom he was clearly devoted, and his old friend Willy Lott, whose cottage is featured famously in *The Hay Wain*, are buried in the churchyard.

East Bergholt has an interesting mix of houses, some dating back as far as the 14th

Artist, Flatford Mill

THE CASE IS ALTERED

Capel Road, Bentley, Ipswich, Suffolk IP9 2DW
Tel: 01473 310282

Several theories exist as to how **The Case Is Altered** public house in Bentley got its most unusual name. Local legend has it that the pub was once owned by a genial landlady who was not too fussy about payment for beer - until she married, when the case was altered. Another possibility is that the pub was christened by Spanish soldiers billeted in England referred to it as 'Casa Altera' (High House). Whatever the origin of the name, a pub is thought to have existed in this area since 1777. Today, as then, good food and excellent drink are on offer.

The menu, which changes every 2-3 months, features a good range of snacks, sandwiches, jackets and other light meals served between midday and 2 p.m., and a more expensive full menu of starters and main courses such as prime chicken fillet wrapped in wild smoked salmon, lamb, Chinese-style duck, and The Case steak - 10 ounces of tender Aberdeen Angus. The ambience of this popular pub is friendly and welcoming; owners Fergus and Amanda Little and all their staff offer their guests warm hospitality.

he painted them, are to be found. Neither is open to the public, and the brick watermill is run as a residential field study centre. Nearby Bridge Cottage at Flatford is a restored 16th century building housing a Constable display, a tea room and a shop. There's also a restored dry dock, and the whole area is a delight for walkers; it is easy to see how Constable drew

Willy Lott's Cottage

constant inspiration from the wonderful riverside setting.

CAPEL ST MARY
6 miles SW of Ipswich on the A12

Constable sketched here, but modern building has more or less overrun the old. A feature of the Church of St Mary is the weeping chancel, a slight kink between the nave and the chancel that apparently signifies Christ's head leaning to the right on the cross.

STRATFORD ST MARY
10 miles SW of Ipswich off the A12

Another of Constable's favourite locations, the most southerly village in Suffolk on the Essex border. *The Young Waltonians* and *A House in Water Lane* (the house still stands today) are the best known of his works set in this picturesque spot. The village church is typically large and imposing, with parts dating back to 1200. At the top of the village

are two splendid half-timbered cottages called the **Ancient House** and the **Priest's House**. Stratford was once on the main coaching route to London, and the largest of the four pubs had stabling for 200 horses. It is claimed that Henry Williamson, author of *Tarka the Otter*, saw his first otter here.

NAYLAND
14 miles SW of Ipswich on the B1087

On a particularly beautiful stretch of the Stour in Dedham Vale, Nayland has charming colour-washed cottages in narrow, winding streets, as well as two very fine 15th century buildings in Alston Court and the Guildhall. Abels Bridge, originally built of wood in the 15th century by wealthy merchant John Abel, divides Suffolk from Essex. In the 16th century a hump bridge replaced it, allowing barges to pass beneath, and the current bridge carries the original keystone bearing the initial A. In the Church of St James stands an

Medieval House, Nayland

altarpiece by Constable entitled *Christ Blessing the Bread and Wine*.

One mile west of Nayland, at the end of a track off the Bures road, stands the Norman Church of St Mary at Wissington. The church has a number of remarkable features, including several 13th century wall paintings, a finely carved 12th century doorway and a tiebeam and crown post roof.

STOKE BY NAYLAND
12 miles SW of Ipswich on the B1087

The drive from Nayland reveals quite stunning views, and the village itself has a large number of listed buildings. The magnificent **Church of St Mary**, with its 120

THE COCK INN

The Green, Polstead, Suffolk CO6 5AL
Tel/Fax: 01206 263150

The Cock Inn in Polstead is a gracious and stylish public house set facing the pretty village green. The main part of this attractive inn dates back to the 17th century; the Victorian-era extension houses the restaurant. Visitors are transported to a gentler age in this gracious and welcoming pub. This handsome inn is a labour of love for hosts Mark and Jo, who have been leaseholders here since

1999. Jo has been the chef here since 1997, putting together a superb daily chioce of delicious hot and cold dishes. There are always three real ales. Greene King IPA is a permanent feature, together with two changing guest ales. John Smiths Extra Smooth can also be found here, along with a full range of draught lagers, cider, stout, and very good wines and spirits. Food is available from midday to 2 p.m. and 6.30 to 9 p.m. weekdays, midday to 2.30 and 6.30 to 9.30 weekends. Guests come from far and wide to sample the delights of Jo's menu, which features such specialities as home-made steak and kidney pudding and salmon fishcakes. All dishes are freshly prepared and expertly presented.

The menu changes monthly to take advantage of the best and freshest seasonal meats and produce. The decor and furnishings enhance the very pleasant dining experience, with a wealth of original features such as the exposed brickwork, beamed ceiling and open fires. The spacious and comfortable restaurant area seats 48; there is also more seating in the bar. The atmosphere is always relaxed and welcoming, and the service attentive and friendly. Open every session Tuesday to Sunday. Closed Mondays except Bank Holidays. Booking is advised at weekends.

foot tower, dominates the scene from its hilltop position; it dominated more than one Constable painting, the most famous showing the church lit up by a rainbow. William Dowsing destroyed 100 'superstitious pictures' here in his Puritan purges, but plenty of fine work is still to be seen, including several monumental brasses.

The Guildhall is another very fine building, now private residences but in the 16th century a busy centre of trade and commerce. When the wool trade declined, so did the importance of the Guildhall, and for a time the noble building saw service as a workhouse.

The decline of the cloth trade in East Anglia had several causes. Fierce competition came from the northern and western weaving industries, which generally had easier access to water supplies for fulling; the wars on the continent of Europe led to the closure of some trading routes and markets; and East Anglia had no supplies of the coal that was used to drive the new steam-powered machinery. In some cases, as at Sudbury, weaving or silk took over as smaller industries.

POLSTEAD
11 miles SW of Ipswich off the B1068

A very pretty village in wooded, hilly countryside, with thatched, colour-washed cottages around the green and a wide duck pond at the bottom of the hill. Standing on a rise above the pond are Polstead Hall, a handsome Georgian mansion, and the 12th century Church of St Mary. The church has two features not found elsewhere in Suffolk – a stone spire and the very early bricks used in its construction. The builders used not only these bricks, but also tiles and tufa, a soft, porous stone much used in Italy. In the grounds of the hall stand the remains of a 'Gospel Oak' said to have been 1,300 years old when it collapsed in 1953. Legend has it that Saxon missionaries preached beneath it in the 7th century; an open-air service is still held here annually.

Polstead has two other claims to fame. One is for Polstead Blacks, a particularly tasty variety of cherry which was cultivated in orchards around the village and which used to be honoured with an annual fair. The other

is much less agreeable, for it was here that the notorious Red Barn murder hit the headlines in 1827. A young girl called Maria Marten, daughter of the local molecatcher, disappeared with William Corder, a farmer's son who was the girl's lover and father of her child. It was at first thought that they had eloped, but Maria's stepmother dreamt three times that she had been murdered and buried in a red barn. A search of the barn soon revealed this to be true. Corder was tracked down to Middlesex, tried and found guilty of Maria's murder and hanged. His skin was used to bind a copy of the trial proceedings and this, together with his scalp, is on display at Moyses Hall in Bury St Edmunds. The incident aroused a great deal of interest and today's visitors to the village will still find reminders of the ghastly deed: the thatched cottage where Maria lived stands, in what is now called Marten's Lane, and the farm where the murderer lived is now called Corder's Farm.

BOXFORD
12 miles W of Ipswich on the A1071

A gloriously unspoilt weaving village, downhill from anywhere, surrounded by the peaceful water meadows of the River Box. St Mary's Church dates back to the 14th century and its wooden north porch is one of the oldest of its kind in the country. In the church is a touching brass in memory of David Byrde, son of the rector, who died a baby in 1606. At the other end of the scale is Elizabeth Hyam, four times a widow, who died in her 113th year.

BURES
17 miles W of Ipswich on the B1508

At this point the River Stour turns sharply to the east, creating a natural boundary between Suffolk and Essex. The little village of Bures straddles the river, lying partly in each county. Bures St Mary in Suffolk is where the church is, overlooked by brick and half-timbered houses. Bures wrote itself very early into the history books when on Christmas Day 855 it is thought that our old friend Edmund the Martyr, the Saxon king, was crowned at the age of 15 in the Chapel of St Stephen. For some time after that momentous occasion Bures was the capital seat of the East

Anglian kings. Bures has a long connection with the Waldegrave family, possibly from as far back as Chaucer's day. One of the Waldegrave memorials shows graphically the results of a visitation by Dowsing and the Puritan iconoclasts: all the figures of the kneeling children have had their hands cut off.

EDWARDSTONE
14 miles W of Ipswich off the A1071

Just to the north of Boxford and close to Edwardstone Hall and the Temple Bar Gate House, Edwardstone is now a 700-acre estate originally home to the Winthrop family. Winthrop was born in Edwardstone and emigrated to the New World, eventually becoming Governor of Massachusetts.

BURY ST EDMUNDS

A gem among Suffolk towns, rich in archaeological treasures and places of religious and historical interest. The town takes its name from St Edmund, who was

born in Nuremberg in 841 and came here as a teenager to become the last king of East Anglia. He was a staunch Christian, and his refusal to deny his faith caused him to be tortured and killed by the Danes in 870. Legend has it that although his body was recovered, his head (cut off by the Danes) could not be found. His men searched for it for 40 days, then heard his voice directing them to it from the depths of a wood, where they discovered it lying protected between the paws of a wolf. The head and the body were seamlessly united and, to commemorate the wolf's deed, the crest of the town's armorial bearings depicts a wolf with a man's head.

Edmund was possibly buried first at Hoxne, the site of his murder, but when he was canonised in about 910 his remains were moved to the monastery at Beodricsworth, which changed its name to St Edmundsbury. A shrine was built in his honour, later incorporated into the Norman Abbey Church after the monastery was granted abbey status by King Canute in 1032. The town soon became a place of pilgrimage and for many years St Edmund was the patron saint of

THE WHITE HORSE INN

Edwardstone, Sudbury,
Suffolk CO10 5PX
Tel: 01787 211211

The White Horse Inn in Edwardstone is a distinctive and easy-going place to enjoy great ales, superb food and genuine hospitality. Originally a farmhouse built in the 16th century, timber and thatch were added in the late 1700s. There were then three storeys - the top was the maltings. Now only two exist. Fabulous rolling pastures surround this quiet and welcoming spot. The interior boasts a collection of old and rare metal advertising signs from the 1920's - 1950's.

There's a warm and friendly atmosphere, and the inn is a mecca for real ale enthusiasts, hosting a beer festival over the May Bank Holiday weekend with a wide range of real ales - especially, and uniquely, dark ales and mild. Set in two acres of land, the inn can offer accommodation for tents and caravans, and there are also two wooden lodges which sleep up to six people, available all year round. Other events held at the inn include a vintage and veteran sports car club which hosts special events throughout the year. Bar snacks and a full menu of steaks, fish and other traditional favourites, cooked to perfection, are served Tuesday to Sunday. Reservations are advised for Saturday evenings and Sunday lunch.

Abbey, Bury St Edmunds

England, until replaced by St George. Growing rapidly around the great abbey, which became one of the largest and most influential in the land, Bury prospered as a centre of trade and commerce, thanks notably to the cloth industry.

The next historical landmark was reached in 1214, when on St Edmund's Feast Day the Archbishop of Canterbury, Simon Langton, met with the Barons of England at the high altar of the Abbey and swore that they would force King John to honour the proposals of the Magna Carta. The twin elements of Edmund's canonisation and the resolution of the Barons explain the motto on the town's crest: "sacrarium regis, cunabula legis" - "shrine of a king, cradle of the law".

Rebuilt in the 15th century, the Abbey was largely dismantled after its dissolution by Henry VIII, but imposing ruins remain in the colourful Abbey Gardens beyond the splendid Abbey Gate and Norman Tower. **St Edmundsbury Cathedral** was originally the Church of St James, built in the 15th/16th century and accorded cathedral status (alone in Suffolk) in 1914. The original building has been much extended down the years (notably

when being adapted for its role as a cathedral) and outstanding features include a magnificent hammerbeam roof, whose 38 beams are decorated with angels bearing the emblems of St James, St Edmund and St George. The monumental Bishop's throne depicts wolves guarding the crowned head of St Edmund, and there's a fascinating collection of 1,000 embroidered kneelers. Millennium funds granted in 1997 should guarantee that the tower which the cathedral lacks is finally built.

St Mary's Church, in the same complex, is also well worth a visit: an equally impressive hammerbeam roof, the detached tower standing much as Abbot Anselm built it in the 12th century, and several interesting monuments, the most important commemorating Mary Tudor, sister of Henry VIII, Queen of France and Duchess of Suffolk. Her remains were moved here when the Abbey was suppressed; a window in the Lady Chapel which records this fact was the gift of Queen Victoria.

The **Abbey Visitor Centre**, open daily from Easter to the end of October, is situated in Samson's Tower, part of the west front of the Abbey. The centre has displays and hands-on activities concerning the Abbey's history. The **Abbey Gardens**, which were laid out in 1831, have as their central feature a great circle of flower beds following the pattern of the Royal Botanical Gardens in Brussels. Some of the original ornamental trees can still be seen, and other - later - features include an Old English rose garden, a water garden and a garden for the blind where fragrance counts for all. Ducks and geese live by the little River Lark, and there are tennis courts, putting and bowls greens and children's play equipment.

Bury is full of fine non-ecclesiastical buildings, many with Georgian frontages concealing medieval interiors. Among the most interesting are the handsome **Manor House Museum** with its collection of clocks, paintings, furniture, costumes and objets d'art; the **Victorian Corn Exchange** with its imposing colonnade; the Athenaeum, hub of social life since Regency times and scene of Charles Dickens's public readings; **Cupola House**, where Daniel Defoe once stayed; the **Angel Hotel**, where Dickens and his marvellous creation Mr Pickwick stayed; and the **Nutshell**, owned by Greene King Brewery and probably the smallest pub in the country. The **Theatre Royal**, now in the care of the National Trust, was built in 1819 by William Wilkins, who was also responsible for the National Gallery. It once staged the premiere of *Charley's Aunt* and still operates as a working theatre.

The **Bury St Edmunds Art Gallery** is housed in one of Bury's noblest buildings, built to a Robert Adam design in 1774. It filled many roles down the years, and was rescued from decline in the 1960s to be restored to Adam's original plans. It is now one of the county's premier art galleries, with eight exhibitions each year and a thriving craft shop.

Perhaps the most fascinating building of all is **Moyses Hall** at one end of the Buttermarket. Built of flint and limestone about 1180, it has claims to being the oldest stone domestic building in England. Originally a rich man's residence, it later saw service as a prison, a workhouse, a police station and a railway office, and for the past 100 years it has been a museum. It houses some 10,000 items, from a Bronze Age hoard, Roman pottery and Anglo-Saxon jewellery to a 19th century doll's house and some grisly relics of the notorious Red Barn murder.

Outside the Spread Eagle pub on the western edge of town is a horse trough erected to the memory of the Victorian romantic novelist Ouida (Maria Louisa Ramee, 1839-1908).

Steeped though it is in history, Bury also moves with the times, and its sporting and leisure facilities are impressive. A mile and a half outside town on the A14 (just off the East Exit) is **Nowton Park**, 172 acres of countryside landscaped in Victorian style and supporting a wealth of flora and fauna; the avenue of limes, carpeted with daffodils in

the spring, is a particular delight. There's also a play area and a ranger centre.

Bury is a wonderful place to visit, with almost 1,000 preserved buildings and a disciplined network of streets (the layout was devised in the 11th century) that provide long, alluring views. Locals protesting against the poll tax of their day did sporadic damage, but a great fire destroyed much of Bury in 1608; it was rebuilt using traditional timber-framing techniques. Arriving here in 1698 Celia Fiennes, the inveterate traveller and critic of architecture, remarked that "there are no good houses but only what are old and rambling" but she made an exception of Cupola House, which was just about completed at the time of her visit. William Cobbett (1763-1835), a visitor when chronicling his Rural Rides, did not disagree with the view that Bury St Edmunds was "the nicest town in the world" - a view which would be endorsed by many of its inhabitants and by many of the millions of visitors who have been charmed by this jewel in Suffolk's crown.

AROUND BURY ST EDMUNDS

HENGRAVE
3 miles NW of Bury St Edmunds on the A1101

A captivating old-world village of flint and thatch. Excavations and aerial photography indicate that a settlement has been here since Neolithic times, and the parts of the village of archaeological interest are now protected. The chief attraction is **Hengrave Hall**, a rambling Tudor mansion built partly of Northamptonshire limestone and partly of yellow brick between 1525 and 1538 by Sir Thomas Kytson, a wool merchant. A notable visitor in the early days was Elizabeth I, who brought her court here in 1578. Several generations of the Gage family were later the owners and one of them, with a particular interest in horticulture, imported various kinds of plum tree from France. Most of the bundles were properly labelled with their names but one had lost its label. When it produced its first crop of luscious green fruit someone had the bright idea of calling it the green Gage. The name stuck, and the descendants of the trees, planted in 1724, are still at the Hall, which may be visited by appointment. In the grounds stands a lovely little church with a round Saxon tower and a wealth of interesting monuments. The church was for some time a family mausoleum; restored by Sir John Wood, it became a private chapel and it now hosts services of various denominations.

FLEMPTON
4 miles NW of Bury St Edmunds on the A1101

An interesting walk from this village just north of the A1101 follows the **Lark Valley Park** through Culford Park, providing a good view of Culford Hall, which has been a school since 1935. A handsome cast-iron bridge dated from the early 19th century and recently brought to light from among the reeds crosses a lake in the park.

WEST STOW
4 miles NW of Bury St Edmunds off the A1101

The villages of West Stow, Culford, Ingham, Timworth and Wordwell were for several centuries part of a single estate covering almost 10,000 acres. Half the estate was sold to the Forestry Commission in 1935 and was renamed the King's Forest in honour of King George V's Jubilee in that year.

An Anglo-Saxon cemetery was discovered in the village in 1849 and the years since have revealed traces of Roman settlements and the actual layout of the original Anglo-Saxon village. A trust was established to investigate further the Anglo-Saxon way of life and their building and farming techniques. Several buildings were constructed using, as accurately as could be achieved, the tools and methods of the 5th century. The undertaking has become a major tourist attraction, with assistance from both human (in Anglo-Saxon costume) and cassette guides. There are pigs and hens and growing crops, craft courses, a Saxon market at Easter, a festival in August and special events all year round. This fascinating village, which is entered through the Visitor Centre, is part of **West Stow Country Park**, a large part of which is designated a Site of Special Scientific Interest (SSSI). Over 120 species of bird and 25 species of animal have been

sighted in this Breckland setting, and a well-marked 5-mile nature trail links this nature reserve with the woods, a large lake and the River Lark. Very near the park and village is Cow Wise, a working dairy farm with lots of animals for young visitors to feed.

LACKFORD
6 miles NW of Bury St Edmunds on the A1101

More interest here for the wildlife enthusiast. Restored gravel pits have been turned into a reserve for wildfowl and waders. Two hides are available.

ICKLINGHAM
8 miles NW of Bury St Edmunds on the A1101

Two churches in this village - the parish church of St James (mentioned in the Domesday Book) and the redundant thatched-roofed All Saints, with medieval tiles on the chancels and beautiful east windows in the south aisle. At the point where the Icknield Way crosses the River Lark, Icklingham has a long history, brought to light in frequent archaeological finds, from pagan bronzes to Roman coins. The place abounds in tales of the supernatural, notably of the white rabbit who is seen at dusk in the company of a witch, causing horses to bolt and men to die!

Just south of Icklingham, at the A1101, is **Rampart Field** picnic site, where pleasant walks through gorse-filled gravel workings reveal the varied plant life of a typical Breckland heath.

GREAT WELNETHAM
2 miles S of Bury St Edmunds off the A134

One of the many surviving Suffolk windmills is to be found here, just south of the village. The sails were lost in a gale 80 years ago but the tower and a neighbouring old barn make an attractive sight.

THE BRADFIELDS
7 miles SE of Bury St Edmunds off the A134

The Bradfields - St George, St Clare and Combust - and Cockfield thread their way through a delightful part of the countryside and are well worth a little exploration, not only to see the picturesque villages themselves but for a stroll in the historic

Bradfield Woods. These woods stand on the eastern edge of the parish of Bradfield St George and have been turned into an outstanding nature reserve, tended and coppiced in the same way for more than 700 years and home to a wide variety of flora and fauna. They once belonged to the Abbey of St Edmundsbury and part of them is still today called Monk's Park Wood.

Coppicing involves cutting a tree back down to the ground every ten years or so. Woodlands were managed in this way to provide an annual crop of timber for local use, and the regrowth after coppicing is very fast as the root is already strongly established. Willow and hazel are the trees most commonly coppiced. Willow is often pollarded, a less drastic form of coppicing where the trees are cut far enough from the ground to stop grazing animals having a free lunch.

Bradfield St Clare, the central of the three Bradfields, has a rival claim to that of Hoxne as the site of the martyrdom of St Edmund. The St Clare family arrived with the Normans and added their name to the village, and the

THE FIVE BELLS

Rattlesden, Suffolk IP30 0RA Tel: 01449 737373

Built in the 1700s, **The Five Bells** in Rattlesden is a place away from it all for those seeking refreshment and a welcoming ambience. Located close to the village church, this small pub is popular and busy, a free house with a good variety of beers - the choice changes regularly. The interior boasts black-beamed ceilings in the main bar, and an attractive wooden ceiling in the extended games area, which overlooks the terraced and grassed garden with its barbecue and petanque pitch. In winter the open fire is the ideal place to enjoy a quiet drink. One unusual feature of this superior pub is the aviary in the garden, home to a pair of barn owls and a Turkermanian eagle who answers to the name 'Maud'. Proprietor Debbie Caley is a gregarious and warm host to all her guests.

THE FOX & HOUNDS FREE HOUSE AND COUNTRY RESTAURANT

Felsham Road, Bradfield St George, Bury St Edmunds, Suffolk IP30 0AB
Tel: 01284 386379

The Fox & Hounds Free House and Country Restaurant is a beautifully restored Victorian Inn which has recently been refurbished to offer a unique combination of a real ale pub with an á la carte restaurant. Here, owners John and Jackie Mansfield and their young, classically trained chef Elliot Barrs offer a high standard of service and excellence. The interior is comfortable and attractive,

comprising two wood-fronted bar areas - one of which has a wood burning stove, wood block flooring and pine seating. There is also a dining room, separated by stylish Victorian glass panelling, which has a traditional period open fireplace. One fun addition is the Pye Black Box, over 50 years old and still in working order, together with a great collection of 78rpm records.

The superb meals feature home-grown and local ingredients wherever possible. Three menus are offered - a lunch menu, an evening á la carte menu and the mid-week specials. All are changed every six weeks approximately to match the changing seasons. Once a month a special evening of foreign foods is featured and proves extremely popular. To accompany the meal there are real cask ales and a good selection of wines and spirits. In the converted barn to the rear there are two charming and comfortable en suite apartments, with views of virtually untouched fields and ancient woodland. Each contains a double bedroom, hall and shower room.

church, originally All Saints, was rededicated to St Clare; it is the only church in England dedicated to her. Bradfield Combust, where the pretty River Lark rises, probably takes it curious name from the fact that the local hall was burnt to the ground during the 14th century riots against the Abbot of St Edmundsbury's crippling tax demands. Arthur Young (1741-1820), noted writer on social, economic and agricultural subjects, is buried in the village churchyard.

RATTLESDEN
9 miles SE of Bury St Edmunds off the A14/B1115

Rattlesden is a small and pretty village - population approximately 700 - with a handsome village church, the Church of St Nicholas.

COCKFIELD
8 miles SE of Bury St Edmunds off the A1141

Cockfield is perhaps the most widely spread village in all Suffolk, its little thatched cottages scattered around and between no fewer than nine greens. Great Green is the largest, with two football pitches and other recreation areas, and Parsonage Green has a literary connection: the **Old Rectory** was once home to a Dr Babbington, whose nephew Robert Louis Stephenson was a frequent visitor and who is said to have written Treasure Island while staying there. Cockfield also shelters one of the last windmills to have been built in Suffolk (1891). Its working life was very short but the tower still stands, now in use as a private residence.

THORPE MORIEUX
9 miles SE of Bury St Edmunds off the B1071

St Mary's Church in Thorpe Morieux is situated in as pleasant a setting as anyone could wish to find. With water meadows, ponds, a stream and a fine Tudor farmhouse to set it off, this 14th century church presents a memorable picture of old England. Look at the church, then take the time to wander around the peaceful churchyard with its profusion of springtime aconites, followed by the colourful flowering of limes and chestnuts in the summer.

LAWSHALL
8 miles S of Bury St Edmunds off the A134

A spread-out village first documented in 972 but regularly giving up evidence of earlier occupation. A Bronze Age sword dated at around 600BC was found here and is now in Bury Museum. The Church of All Saints, Perpendicular with some Early English bits, stands on one of the highest points in Suffolk, and next to it is Lawshall Hall whose owners once entertained Queen Elizabeth I. Another interesting site in Lawshall is the **Wishing Well**, a well-cover on the green put up in memory of Charles Tyrwhitt Drake, who worked for the Royal Geographic Society and was killed in Jerusalem.

ALPHETON
10 miles S of Bury St Edmunds on the A134

Several points of interest at this little village straddling the main road. It was first settled in 991 and its name means the farm of Aefflaed. That lady was the wife of Ealdorman Beorhtnoth of Essex, who was killed resisting the Danes at the Battle of Maldon and is buried in Ely Minster.

The hall, the farm and the church stand in a quiet location away from the main road and about a mile from the village. This remoteness is not unusual: some attribute it to the villagers moving during times of plague but the more likely explanation is simply that the scattered cottages, originally in several tiny hamlets, centred, for whatever reason, in a more convenient site than that of the church. Equally possible is that it was built to suit the local landed family (that is to say, next door). The main features at the Church of **St Peter and St Paul** are the flintwork around the parapet (the exterior is otherwise fairly undistinguished), the carefully restored 15th century porch and some traces of an ancient wall painting of St Christopher with the Christ Child. All in all, a typical country church of unpretentious dignity and well worth a short detour from the busy main roads.

Back in the village, two oak trees were planted and a pump installed in 1887, to commemorate Queen Victoria's 50 years on the throne. Another of the village's claims to fame is that its American airfield was used as the setting for the classic film *Twelve o'Clock*

High, in which Gregory Peck memorably plays a Second World War flight commander cracking up under the strain of countless missions. Incidentally, one of the reasons for constructing the A134 was to help in the development of the airfield. The A134 continues south to Long Melford. An alternative road from Bury to Long Melford is the B1066, quieter and equally scenic, with a number of pleasant places to visit en route.

WHEPSTEAD
6 miles S of Bury St Edmunds on the B1066

Whepstead is a charming little village with three manor houses and a church dedicated to St Petronilla. Brockley Green, a village of some 300 souls, has a church that was built in the 13th and 14th centuries on a Saxon site. The tower dates from the 16th century and in the churchyard the base of a Tudor cross is to be seen.

HARTEST
9 miles S of Bury St Edmunds on the B1066

Hartest, which has a history as long as Alpheton's, celebrated its millennium in 1990 with the erection of a village sign (the hart,

or stag). It's an agreeable spot in a valley, with colour-washed houses and chestnut trees on the green. Also on the green are All Saints Church (mentioned in the Domesday Book) and a large glacial stone, the **Hartest stone**, which was dragged by a team of 45 horses from where it was found in a field in neighbouring Somerton. From 1789 until the 1930s Hartest staged a St George's Day Fair, an annual jolly celebrating King George III's recovery from one of his spells of madness. Just outside the village is **Gifford's Hall**, a smallholding which includes 12 acres of vines and a winery producing white and rosé wines and fruit liqueurs. There are also organic vegetable gardens, wild flower meadows, black St Kilda sheep, black Berkshire pigs, goats and free-range fowl. The Hall is particularly famous for its sweet peas and roses, and an annual festival is held on the last weekend in June. Open from Easter to the end of October.

SHIMPLING
9 miles S of Bury St Edmunds off the B1066

Shimpling is a peaceful farming community whose church, St George's, is approached by a

THE BLACK LION

Lion Road, Glemsford,
Sudbury, Suffolk CO10 7RF
Tel: 01787 280684

Just opposite Glemsford Primary School, **The Black Lion** is a traditional English pub in the best sense of the phrase. Ian Ward and his sister have combined their experience and talents to make a success of this delightful village pub. The large manicured garden is the perfect place to relax over a good meal or drink, and includes a safe children's play area. The

interior is restful and cosy. The wood used on the ceiling was originally in nearby Clare Priory. Some of this same wood was used in Monks Hall close by (unfortunately not open to the public). The large open-plan bar is adorned with sepia photographs of old Glemsford, circa 1890. Real ales on tap include Greene King IPA, Abbot and weekly changing guest ales. There's also lager, wines, spirits and soft drinks to quench the thirst. The excellent menu comprises everything from snacks and starters to sweets, including filled baguettes, fish specials and an exceptionally good vegetarian range. All dishes are expertly prepared and presented. Open every day, meals are served Monday to Thursday 12.00-14.30 and 18.00-21.00, Friday 12.00-15.00 and 17.30-21.30, Saturday 12.00-21.30, Sunday 12.00-21.00 (Sunday lunch 12.00-17.00).

lime avenue. It is notable for Victorian stained glass and a Norman font, and in the churchyard is the **Faint House**, a small stone building where ladies overcome by the tightness of their stays could decently retreat from the service. The banker Thomas Hallifax built many of Shimpling's cottages and also the village school and Chadacre Hall, which Lord Iveagh later turned into an agricultural college (that role ceased in 1989 and the Hall is again in private hands).

GLEMSFORD
12 miles S of Bury St Edmunds off the B1066

Driving in from the north on the B1066, the old Church of St Mary makes an impressive sight on what, for Suffolk, is a quite considerable hill. Textiles and weaving have long played a prominent part in Glemsford's history, and thread from the silk factory, which opened in 1824 and is still growing strongly, has been woven into dresses and robes for various members of the present royal family, including the late Princess Diana's wedding dress. During the last century several factories produced matting from coconut fibres and in 1906 Glemsford was responsible for the largest carpet in the world to cover the floor at London's Olympia. To this day one factory processes horse hair for use in judges' wigs, sporrans and busbies.

LONG MELFORD
13 miles S of Bury St Edmunds off the A134

The heart of this atmospheric wool town is a very long and, in stretches, fairly broad main street, set on an ancient Roman site in a particularly beautiful part of south Suffolk. In Roman times the Stour was a navigable river and trade flourished. Various Roman finds have been unearthed, notably a blue glass vase which is now on display in the British Museum. The street is filled with antique shops, book shops and art galleries and is a favourite place for collectors and browsers. Some of the houses are washed in the characteristic Suffolk pink, which might originally have been achieved by mixing ox blood or sloe juice into the plaster.

Holy Trinity Church, on a 14-acre green at the north end of Hall Street, is a typical exuberant manifestation of the wealth of the wool and textile trade. It's big enough to be a cathedral, but served (and still serves) comparatively few parishioners. John Clopton, grown rich in the woollen business, was largely responsible for this magnificent Perpendicular-style edifice, which has a 180-foot nave and chancel and half timbers, flint flashwork of the highest quality and 100 large windows to give a marvellous sense of light and space. Medieval glass in the north aisle depicts religious scenes and the womenfolk of the Clopton family. There are many interesting monuments and brasses, and in the chantry entrance is a bas relief of the Three Wise Men, the Virgin and Child, and St Joseph. In the Lady Chapel, reached by way of the churchyard, a children's multiplication table written on a wall is a reminder that the chapel served as the village school for a long period after the Reformation.

John Clopton's largesse is recorded rather modestly in inscriptions on the roof parapets. His tower was struck by lightning in the early 18th century and the present brick construction dates from around 1900. The

Long Melford

detail of this great church is of endless fascination, but it's the overall impression that stays in the memory, and the sight of the building floodlit at night is truly spectacular. The distinguished 20th century poet Edmund Blunden spent his last years in Long Melford and is buried in the churchyard. The inscription on his gravestone reads "I live still to love still things quiet and unconcerned".

Melford Hall, east of town beyond an imposing 16th gateway, was built around 1570 by Sir William Cordell on the site of an earlier hall that served as a country retreat, before the Dissolution of the Monasteries, for the monks of St Edmundsbury Abbey. There exists an account of Cordell entertaining Queen Elizabeth I at the Hall in 1578, when she was welcomed by "200 young gentlemen in white velvet, 300 in black and 1,500 serving men". Much of the fine work of Sir William (whose body lies in Holy Trinity Church) has been altered in restoration, but the pepperpot chimneys are original, as is the panelled banqueting hall. The rooms are in various styles, some with ornate walnut furniture, and there's a notable collection of Chinese porcelain on show. Most delightful of all is the Beatrix Potter room, with some of her water colours, first editions of books and, among the toys, the original of Jemima Puddleduck. She was a frequent visitor here (her cousins the Hyde Parkers were the owners), bringing small animals to draw. The Jeremy Fisher illustrations were mostly drawn at Melford Hall's fishponds, and the book is dedicated to Stephanie Hyde Parker. The Hall, which is a National Trust property, stands in a lovely garden with some distinguished clipped box hedges. William Cordell was also responsible for the red-brick almshouses, built in 1593 for '12 poor men', which stand near Holy Trinity.

Kentwell Hall is a red-brick Tudor moated mansion approached by a long avenue of limes. Its grounds include a unique Tudor rose maze. It sets out to illustrate and recreate Tudor times, with a walled garden, a bakery, a dairy and several varieties of rare-breed farm animals. The buildings include a handsome 14th century aisle barn. The Hall was the setting for the film version of *Toad of Toad Hall*.

Long Melford is a great place for leisurely strolls, and for the slightly more energetic there's a scenic 3-mile walk along a disused

The Moat, Kentwell Hall

railway track and farm tracks that lead straight into Lavenham - see earlier in this chapter.

CAVENDISH
3 miles W of Long Melford on the A1092

A most attractive village, where the Romans stayed awhile - the odd remains have been unearthed - and the Saxons settled. The look is splendidly traditional, with the church, thatched cottages, almshouses, Nether Hall and the **Sue Ryder Foundation Museum** spread around the green. The last, in a 16th

Village Green, Cavendish

century rectory by the pond, illustrates the work of the Sue Ryder Foundation, and was formally opened by Queen Elizabeth in 1979. Once a refuge for concentration camp victims, it houses abundant war photographs and memorabilia. Nether Hall is a well-restored 16th century building and the headquarters of **Cavendish Vineyards.**

In the Church of **St Mary**, whose tower has a pointed bellcote and a room inside complete with fireplace and shuttered windows, look for the two handsome lecterns, one with a brass eagle (15th century), the other with two chained books; and for the Flemish and Italian statues. In 1381 Wat Tyler, leader of the Peasants revolt, was killed at Smithfield, in London, by John Cavendish, son of Sir John Cavendish, lord of the manor and Chief Justice of England. Sir John was hounded by the peasants, who caught him and killed him near Bury St Edmunds. He managed en route to hide some valuables in the belfry of St Mary's, Cavendish, and bequeathed to the church £40, sufficient to restore the chancel. A later Cavendish – Thomas – sailed round the world in the 1580s and perished on a second voyage. In the shadow of the church, on the edge of the village green, is a cluster of immaculate thatched cottages at a spot known as Hyde Park Corner. Pink-washed and pretty as a picture, they look almost too good to be true – and they almost are, having been rebuilt twice since the Second World War due to a combination of fire and dilapidation.

CLARE
6 miles W of Long Melford on the A1092

A medieval wool town of great importance, Clare repays a visit today with its fine old buildings and some old ruins. Perhaps the most renowned tourist attraction is **Ancient House**, a timber-framed building dated 1473 and remarkable for its pargeting. This is the decorative treatment of external plasterwork, usually by dividing the surface into rectangles and decorating each panel. It was very much a Suffolk speciality, particularly in the 16th and 17th centuries, with some examples also being found in Cambridgeshire and Essex. The decoration could be simple brushes of a comb, scrolls or squiggles, or more elaborate, with religious motifs, guild signs or family

crests. Some pargeting is incised, but the best is in relief – pressing moulds into wet plaster or shaping by hand. Ancient House sports some splendid twining flowers and branches, and a representation of two figures holding a shield. The best-known workers in this unique skill had their own distinctive styles, and the expert eye could spot the particular 'trademarks' of each man (the same is the case with the master thatchers). Ancient House is now a museum, open during the summer months with an exhibition of local history.

Another place of historical significance is **Nethergate House**, once the work place of dyers, weavers and spinners. The Swan Inn, in the High Street, has a sign which lays claim to being the oldest in the land. Ten feet in length and carved from a solid piece of wood, it portrays the arms of England and France. **Clare Castle** was a motte and bailey fortress that sheltered a household of 250. **Clare Castle Country Park**, with a visitor centre in the goods shed of a disused railway line, contains the remains of the castle and the moat, the latter now a series of ponds and home to varied wild life. At the Prior's House, the original cellar and infirmary are still in use. Established in 1248 by Augustine friars and used by them until the Dissolution of 1538, the priory was handed back to that order in 1953 and remains their property.

A mile or so west of Clare on the A1092 lies **Stoke-by-Clare**, a pretty village on one of the region's most picturesque routes. It once housed a Benedictine priory, whose remains are now in the grounds of a school. There's a fine 15th century church and a vineyard: **Boyton Vineyards** at Hill Farm, Boyton End, is open early April-end October for a tour, a talk and a taste.

CHEDBURGH
6 miles SW of Bury St Edmunds on the A1430

Farm parks are an excellent way of discovering the county's rural and agricultural legacy and **Rede Hall Farm Park**, near Chedburgh, is modelled on a working farm of the 1930-1950 period. The Suffolk Punch can be seen at work here, and there are rare breeds of farm animals, a nature trail, cart rides and working displays. Also picnic and play areas, a tea room and a gift shop. Open April-September.

Approach to Ickworth House

HORRINGER

3 miles SW of Bury St Edmunds on the A143

Rejoining the A143 by Chedburgh, the motorist will soon arrive at Horringer, whose village green is dominated by the flintstone Church of St Leonard. Beside the church are the gates of one of the country's most extraordinary and fascinating houses, now run by the National Trust. **Ickworth House** was the brainchild of the eccentric 4th Earl of Bristol and Bishop of Derry, a collector of art treasures and an inveterate traveller (witness the Bristol Hotels scattered around Europe). His inspiration was Belle Isle, a house built on an island in Lake Windermere, and the massive structure is a central rotunda linking two semi-circular wings. It was designed as a treasure house for the arts and work started in 1795; the first

THE PLOUGH

Rede, Bury St Edmunds,
Suffolk IP29 4BE
Tel: 01284 789208

The Plough in Rede is a 16th-century half-thatched tiled inn, renowned far and wide for its excellent beers, wines and menu. Set on the highest point in Suffolk, near the charming Rede Hall Farm Park, modelled on a working farm of the 1930s-1950s, this fine pub offers a range of fresh dishes using local produce. Owners Brian and Joyce Desborough have been here since 1982. Ably assisted by their daughter Amy, they take pride in offering wonderful service and genuine hospitality to all their guests.

The setting is unspoilt rural splendour, as the pub shares space with the village green. No paving stones or other modernisations intrude upon the sense of a more gracious past. Outside the pub there's an ancient hand plough on display. The graceful overhanging willow outside all but hides the pub beneath its enormous branches. Outdoors there are wooden benches and giant 'African' umbrellas - the perfect place to enjoy a relaxing drink or delicious meal on fine days. The gardens to the rear include a well-stocked aviary and dovecote. Inside, red velvet and the casement windows enhance the cosy and charming atmosphere. A range of ales, including changing guest ales, together with fine wines, spirits and soft drinks, are on hand to accompany the delicious food. Joyce, who does the cooking, is reluctant to send anyone home hungry - portions are hearty. This truly hidden place is well worth seeking out: please ring for full directions.

collection of the Earl's treasures was seized by Napoleon in 1798 so never reached England.

Derry died in 1803 and his son, after some hesitation, saw the work through to completion in 1829. Its chief glories are some marvellous paintings by Titian, Gainsborough, Velasquez, Reynolds and Kauffman, but there's a great deal more to enthral the visitor: late Regency and 18th century French furniture, a notable collection of Georgian silver, friezes and sculptures by John Flaxman, frescoes copied from wall paintings discovered at the Villa Negroni in Rome in 1777. The Italian garden, where Mediterranean species have been bred to withstand a distinctly non-Mediterranean climate, should not be missed, with its hidden glades, orangery and temple rose garden, and in the Capability Brown park are designated walks and cycle routes, bird hides, a deer enclosure and play areas. The latest attractions are a vineyard and plant centre. The House is open Easter-end October, the park and gardens throughout the year.

Arable land surrounds Horringer, with a large annual crop of sugar beet grown for processing at the factory in Bury, the largest of its kind in Europe.

HAVERHILL
18 miles SW of Bury St Edmunds on the A604

Notable for its fine Victorian architecture. Fire destroyed many of the town's buildings in 1665, but **Anne of Cleves House** was restored and is well worth a visit. Anne was the fourth wife of Henry VIII and after a brief political marriage she was given an allowance and spent the remainder of her days at Haverhill and Richmond. **East Town Park** is a new country park on the east side of Haverhill.

KEDINGTON
2 miles N of Haverhill on the B1061

Haverhill intrudes somewhat, but the heart of the old village gains in appeal from the presence of the River Stour. Known to many as the 'Cathedral of West Suffolk', the Church of **St Peter and St Paul** is the chief attraction of Kedington. Almost 150' in length, it stands on a ridge overlooking the Stour Valley. It has several interesting features, including a 15th century font, a Saxon cross in the chancel

window, a three-decker pulpit (with a clerk's desk and a reading desk) and a sermon-timer, looking rather like a grand egg-timer. The foundations of a Roman building have been found beneath the floorboards.

The Bardiston family, one of the oldest in Suffolk, has strong links with the village and many of the family tombs are in the church. In the church grounds is a row of ten elm trees, each, the legend says, with a knight buried beneath its roots.

Following the Stour along the B1061, the visitor will find a number of interesting little villages. In Little Wratting, Holy Trinity Church has a shingled oak-framed steeple (a feature more usually associated with Essex churches). John Sainsbury was a local resident, while in Great Wratting another magnate, W H Smith, financed the restoration of St Mary's Church in 1887. This church boasts some diverting topiary in the shape of a church, a cross and an armchair.

GREAT AND LITTLE THURLOW
3 miles N of Haverhill on the B1061

Great and Little Thurlow form a continuous village on the west bank of the Stour four miles north of Haverhill. Largely undamaged thanks to being in a conservation area, they have many 17th century cottages and a Georgian manor house. In the main street is a schoolhouse built in 1614 by Sir Stephen Soame, sometime Lord Mayor of London, whose family are commemorated in the village church.

A short distance further up the B1061 stands the village of **Great Bradley**, divided in two by the River Stour, which rises just outside the village boundary. Chief points of note in the tranquil parish church are a fine Norman doorway sheltering a Tudor brick porch and some beautiful stained glass poignantly depicting a soldier in the trenches during the First World War. The three bells in the tower include one cast in the 14th century, one of the oldest in Suffolk.

DENSTON
6 miles NE of Haverhill just off the A143

Denston lies just east of the A143 on the River Glem and is notable chiefly for its magnificent Perpendicular church, one of 18 dedicated to St Nicholas, patron saint of

The Old Bakery

Off Mill Lane, Farley Green, nr Wickhambrook, Suffolk CB8 8PX
Tel/Fax: 01440 820852 Mobile: 07759 618709

The Old Bakery in Farley Green is a 17th century country home offering superb bed and breakfast accommodation. As its name tells us it was once a bakery although previously an ale house and even earlier a blacksmiths. This fine B&B retains a traditional rustic atmosphere while offering every modern convenience. The two large ground floor en suite bedrooms were originally the bakehouse. Peaceful and secluded, it offers the perfect opportunity to truly get away from it all. The large garden, with views over the extensive and very beautiful countryside, is the perfect place to relax after a day's

sightseeing or shopping in Newmarket, Cavendish, Bury St Edmunds or the many other attractive areas of East Anglia.

Owners Linda and Brian Lambert are caring and conscientious hosts making their own jams, marmalades and freshly squeezed orange juice to complement the delicious breakfast dishes. Reference books on native birds and wildflowers as well as local interest are available for guest's use. There are also bicycles for hire. Both rooms have their own private entrances. There is excellent access to one of the rooms for people with mobility problems. ETB 4 Diamonds. Exclusively for non-smokers.

Thrift Farm

Cowlinge, nr Newmarket,
Suffolk CB8 9JA
Tel/Fax: 01440 783274

Set in five acres of meadow and garden, **Thrift Farmhouse** is the perfect place to relax amid friendly, homely surroundings. This family home offers superior bed and breakfast accommodation with three lovely guest bedrooms (two doubles, one twin). Owner Jan Oddy has lived here for 42 years; she is a welcoming and hospitable host, with a conscientious attention to service and quality.

The farmhouse is a listed building, believed to be constructed in the 16th century, which has been sensitively converted and refurbished to offer the highest standards of comfort. Truly hidden away down a quiet country lane, visitors are advised to ask directions in the village or to ring for further information. One double and one twin room are in the farmhouse; the third double is ensuite and occupies the former piggery. Tasteful decor and charming furnishings are the hallmark of this B&B. The rooms are enhanced by the addition of artefacts from around the world, brought home by Jan's son Stuart from his many travels. There's a luxurious sunken bath, and guests will also enjoy the truly home-from-home feel of breakfast by the Aga in the handsome country kitchen. There are several excellent country pubs, great walking and good bird-watching in the local area, and of course this makes a handy base from which to explore this part of Suffolk and further afield.

sailors. Stop and admire the fan vaulting in the roof (a comparative rarity in Suffolk), the outstanding brasses and the wide variety of carved animals.

Also on the Glem is the neighbouring village of Stansfield, where stand the ruins of another mill, this one a tower mill but without its cap and in a sorry state.

HAWKEDON
7 miles NE of Haverhill off the A143

On to Hawkedon, designated a place of outstanding beauty, where the Church of St Mary is located untypically in the middle of the village green. The pews and intricately carved bench-ends take the eye here, along with a canopied stoup (a recess for holding holy water) and a Norman font. There is a wide variety of carved animals, many on the bench-ends but some on the roof cornice. One of the stalls is decorated with the carving of a crane holding a stone in its claw; legend says that if it was on watch and fell asleep, the stone would drop and the noise would wake it.

WICKHAMBROOK
8 miles NE of Haverhill on the B1063

Wickhambrook is a series of tiny hamlets with no fewer than 11 greens and three manor houses. The greens have unusual names - Genesis, Nunnery, Meeting, Coltsfoot - whose origins keep local historians busy. One of the two pubs has a split personality, being officially half in Wickhambrook and half in Denston.

Blythburgh Parish Church, Newmarket

NEWMARKET

On the western edge of Suffolk, Newmarket is home to some 16,000 human and 3,000 equine inhabitants. The historic centre of British racing lives and breathes horses, with 60 training establishments, 50 stud farms, the top annual thoroughbred sales and two racecourses (the only two in Suffolk). Thousands of the population are involved in the trade, and racing art and artefacts fill the shops, galleries and museums; one of the oldest established saddlers even has a preserved horse on display - 'Robert the Devil', runner-up in the 1880 Derby.

History records that Queen Boadicea of the Iceni, to whom the six-mile Devil's Dyke stands as a memorial, thundered around these parts in her lethal chariot behind her shaggy-haired horses and she is said to have established the first stud here. In medieval times the chalk heathland was a popular arena for riders to display their skills and in 1605 James I paused on a journey north to enjoy a spot of hare coursing. He enjoyed the place and said he would be back; in moving the royal court to his Newmarket headquarters he began the royal patronage which has remained strong down the years. Charles I maintained the royal connection but it was Charles II who really put the place on the map when he, too, moved the Royal court in the spring and autumn of each year. He initiated the Town Plate, a race which he himself won twice as a rider and which, in a modified form, still exists.

One of the racecourses, the **Rowley Mile**, takes its name from Old Rowley, a favourite horse of the Merry Monarch. Here the first two classics of the season, the 1,000 and 2,000 Guineas, are run, together with important autumn events including the Cambridgeshire and the Cesarewich. There are some 16 race days at this track, while on the leafy July course, with its delightful garden-party atmosphere, a similar number of race days takes in all the important summer fixtures.

The visitor to Newmarket can learn almost all there is to know about flat racing and racehorses by making the grand tour of the several establishments which are open to the public (sometimes by appointment only). **The Jockey Club**, which was the first governing body of the sport and until recently the ultimate authority, was formed in the middle of the 18th century and occupies an imposing building which was restored and rebuilt in Georgian style in the 1930s. Originally a social club for rich gentlemen with an interest in the turf, it soon became the all-powerful regulator of British racing, owning all the racing and training land. When holding an enquiry the stewards sit round a horseshoe table and the jockey or trainer under scrutiny faces them on a strip of carpet by the door - hence the expression 'on the mat'.

Next to the Jockey Club in the High Street is the **National Horseracing Museum**. Opened by the Queen in 1983, its five galleries chronicle the history of the Sport of Kings from its royal beginnings through to the top trainers and jockeys of today. Visitors can ride a mechanical horse, try on racing silks, record a race commentary, ask awkward questions and enjoy a snack in the café, whose walls are hung with murals of racing personalities. The chief treasures among the art collection are equine paintings by Alfred Munnings, while the most famous item is probably the skeleton of the mighty Eclipse, whose superiority over his contemporaries gave rise to the saying 'Eclipse first, the rest nowhere'.

A few steps away is **Palace House**, which contains the remains of Charles II's palace and which, as funds allow, is being restored for use as a visitor centre and museum. In the same street, and still standing, is **Nell Gwynn's house**, which some say was connected beneath the street to the palace. The diarist John Evelyn spent a night in (or on?) the town during a royal visit and declared the occasion to be "more resembling a luxurious and abandoned rout than a Christian court". The palace is the new location for the Newmarket Tourist Information Centre. Other must-sees on the racing enthusiast's tour are **Tattersalls**, where leading thoroughbred sales take place from April to December; the **British Racing School**, where top jockeys are taught the ropes; the **National Stud**, open from March till August plus race days in September and October (booking essential); and the **Animal Health Trust** based at Lanwades Hall, where a Visitor Centre has recently opened. The National Stud at one time housed no fewer than three Derby winners - Blakeney, Mill Reef and Grundy.

Horses aren't all about racing, however. One type of horse you won't see in Newmarket is the wonderful Suffolk Punch, a massive yet elegant working horse which can still be seen at work at Rede Hall Park Farm near Bury St Edmunds and at Kentwell Hall in Long Melford (see under those locations). All Punches descend from Crisp's horse, foaled in 1768. The Punch is part of the Hallowed Trinity of animals at the very centre of Suffolk's agricultural history; the others are the Suffolk Sheep and the Red Poll Cow. And it is entirely appropriate that the last railway station to employ a horse for shunting wagons should have been at Newmarket. That hardworking one-horse-power shunter retired in 1967.

Newmarket has things to offer the tourist outside the equine world, including the churches of **St Mary and All Saints**, and **St Agnes**, and a landmark at each end of the High Street - a Memorial Fountain in honour of Sir Daniel Cooper and the Jubilee Clock Tower commemorating Queen Victoria's Golden Jubilee.

AROUND NEWMARKET

EXNING
2 miles NW of Newmarket on the A14

A pause is certainly in order at this ancient village, whether on a trip out of Newmarket or arriving from Cambridgeshire on the A14. Anglo-Saxons, Romans, the Iceni and the Normans were all here, and the Domesday Book records the village under the name of Esselinga. The village was stricken by a plague during the Iceni occupation, so its market was moved to the next village. Thus Newmarket acquired its name. Exning's written history begins when Henry II granted the manor to the Count of Boulogne, who divided it between four of his knights. References to them and to subsequent Lords of the Manor are to be found in the little Church of **St Martin**, which might well have been founded by the Burgundian Christian missionary monk St Felix in the 7th century. Water from the well used by that saint to baptise members of the Saxon royal family is still used for similar ceremonies by the current vicar. The A14 is a busy main road, but pulling away from the traffic and spending time around this village will be rewarded by some quiet, pleasant walks.

KENTFORD
5 miles E of Newmarket by the A14

At the old junction of the Newmarket-Bury road stands the grave of a young boy who hanged himself after being accused of sheep-stealing. It was a well-established superstition that suicides should be buried at a crossroads to prevent their spirits from wandering. Flowers are still sometimes laid at the **Boys Grave**, sometimes by punters hoping for good luck at Newmarket races.

MOULTON
4 miles E of Newmarket on the B1085

This most delightful village lies in wonderful countryside on chalky downland in farming land and its proximity to Newmarket is

apparent from the racehorses which are often to be seen on the large green. The River Kennett flows through the green, before running north to the Lark, a tributary of the Ouse. Flint walls are a feature of many of the buildings, but the main point of interest is the 15th century 4-arch packhorse bridge on the way to the church.

DALHAM
5 miles E of Newmarket on the B1063

Eighty per cent of the buildings are thatched (the highest proportion in Suffolk) and there are many other attractions in this pretty village. Above the village on one of the county's highest spots stands **St Mary's** Church, which dates from the 14th century. Its spire toppled over during the gales which swept the land on the night that Cromwell died, and was replaced by a tower in 1627. Sir Martin Stutteville was the leading light behind this reconstruction and an inscription at the back of the church notes that the cost was £400. That worthy's grandfather was Thomas Stutteville, whose memorial near the altar declares that "he saw the New World with Francis Drake". (Drake did not survive

THE ROSE AND CROWN

82 Holmsey Green, Beck Row, Suffolk IP28 8AP
Tel: 01638 713407 email: theflinns@btinternet.com

The Rose and Crown is a true local community public house which sponsors the village football team and is also host to a fair few Americans from the nearby base - reputedly the largest airfield in the UK, and subsequently the only diversion, if one were needed, to accommodate a US space shuttle landing. The interior of this very comfortable pub has two large separate bars; the lounge bar also serves as a dining area. Children are not permitted in the Public bar. The spacious lounge bar leads off via French windows to the expansive and very attractive gardens and covered barbecue area. Here there's a safe children's play area. The decor and furnishings are handsome and tasteful. As befitting

the largely American clientele, steaks play a major role on the menu, together with other hearty traditional favourites and a good selection of vegetarian dishes. real ales include Greene King IPA, along with lagers, stout, wines, spirits, tea, coffee and other soft drinks. Proprietors Bev and Alison, assisted by Bev's husband Robbie and son Dylan, offer a warm welcome to all their guests. This friendly pub also boasts three attractive guest bedrooms, for those wishing to stay awhile in this welcoming part of the county.

THE OLD BULL INN AT BARTON MILLS

Barton Mills, Suffolk IP28 6AF
Tel: 01638 713230

The Old Bull at Barton Mills began life as a coaching inn on the road from London to Norwich. It has recently been extensively renovated and modernised, offering excellent food and drink and warm hospitality. The modernisation has been carefully done, so that original features like the old arches for coaches and horses remain. This arch now serves as the entryway to a lovely glassed reception area; the courtyard beyond is a delightful haven in which to sit on warm evenings. The interior is also distinguished and supremely relaxing. Here guests can enjoy real cask ales or a choice of lagers, wines and spirits.

The restaurant boasts a welcoming atmosphere. The all-day menu varies with the seasons, but always offers excellent steaks, grills and other traditional favourites. The restaurant bar has a very good wine list. There is also a separate "Ladies" bar for cosy chats. This fine inn is also in the process of creating 20

comfortable and tasteful guest bedrooms (to be completed by early 2001), to provide exceptional and affordable accommod-ation. The surrounding area is rich in history and attractions, including Thetford Forest, Newmarket and Bury St Edmunds.

WORLINGTON HALL COUNTRY HOUSE HOTEL

Worlington, Mildenhall, Suffolk IP28 8RX
Tel: 01638 712237 Fax: 01638 712631

Worlington Hall is an elegant 16th-century former manor house which epitomizes old country grace and charm. Set in five acres of beautiful grounds and gardens, impressive features include the imposing archway and cobbled and stone entranceway. Inside, the comfortable lounge bar has red leather chairs, grandfather clocks and other elegant touches, so that it is almost as it was when this was the residence of a rich country gentleman. There are three handsome dining rooms - The Alcove is the intimate a la carte restaurant,

The Bistro and The Garden Room, the hotel function room which leads to the extensive grounds and down to the River Lark. This superb hotel also offers guests a beauty salon, 9-hole pitch and putt course, meditation centre and children's amenities. There are eight individually designed guest bedrooms plus the unique Coachhouse Suite with four-poster bed. Guests are greeted with complimentary sherry, fresh flowers and fruit in their rooms. The excellent, attentive staff are friendly and efficient. For a real taste of luxury, look no further.

that journey - his third to South America.) Thomas's grandson died in the fullness of his years (62 wasn't bad for those times!) while hosting a jolly at The Angel Hotel, Bury St Edmunds.

Dalham Hall was constructed in the first years of the 18th century at the order of the Bishop of Ely, who decreed that it should be built up until Ely Cathedral could be seen across the fens on a clear day. That view was sadly cut off in 1957 when a fire shortened the hall to two storeys. Wellington lived here for some years, and much later it was bought by Cecil Rhodes, who unfortunately died before taking up residence. His brother Francis erected the village hall in the adventurer's memory, and he himself is buried in the churchyard.

All in all, Dalham is a place of charm and interest, clearly unlike the one described in *The Times* in the 1880s as full of ruffians and drunks, where the vicar felt obliged to give all the village children boxing lessons to increase their chances of survival.

MILDENHALL
8 miles NE of Newmarket off the A11

On the edge of the Fens and Breckland, Mildenhall is a town which has many links with the past. It was once a port for the hinterland of West Suffolk, though the River Lark has long ceased to be a trade route. Most of the town's heritage is recorded in the excellent **Mildenhall & District Museum** in King Street. Here will be found exhibits of local history (including the distinguished RAF and USAAF base), crafts and domestic skills, the natural history of the Fens and Breckland and, perhaps most famously, the 'Mildenhall Treasure'. This was a cache of 34 pieces of 4th century Roman silverware - dishes, goblets and spoons - found by a ploughman in 1946 at Thistley Green and now on display in the British Museum. There is evidence of much earlier occupation than the Roman era, with flint tools and other artefacts being unearthed in 1988 on the site of an ancient lake.

The parish of Mildenhall is the largest in Suffolk so it is perhaps fitting that it should boast so magnificent a parish church as **St Mary's**, built of Barnack stone; it dominates the heart of the town and indeed its west tower commands the flat surrounding countryside. Above the splendid north porch (the largest in Suffolk) are the arms of Edward the Confessor and of St Edmund. The chancel, dating back to the 13th century, is a marvellous work of architecture, but pride of place goes to the east window, divided into seven vertical lights. Off the south aisle is the Chapel of St Margaret, whose altar, itself modern, contains a medieval altar stone. At the west end, the font, dating from the 15th century, bears the arms of Sir Henry Barton, who was twice Lord Mayor of London and whose tomb is located on the south side of the tower. Above the nave and aisles is a particularly fine hammerbeam roof whose outstanding feature is the carved angels. Efforts of the Puritans to destroy the angels failed, but traces of buckshot and arrowheads have been found embedded in the woodwork.

Sir Henry North built a manor house on the north side of the church in the 17th century and his successors included a dynasty of the Bunbury family who were Lords of the Manor from 1747 to 1933. Sir Henry Edward Bunbury was the man chosen to let Napoleon Bonaparte know of his exile to St Helena, but the best known member of the family is Sir Thomas, who in 1780 tossed a coin with Lord Derby to see whose name should be borne by a race to be inaugurated at Epsom. Lord Derby won, but Sir Thomas had the satisfaction of winning the first running of the race with his colt Diomed.

The other focal point in Mildenhall is the Market Place, with its 16th century timbered cross.

BARTON MILLS
1 mile S of Mildenhall off the A11

Known as Barton Parva (Little Barton) in Saxon times, the village changed its name during the 18th century. St Mary's Church can trace its origins back to at least 1150, and one of its early rectors had the Pope as his patron. Sir Alexander Fleming had a country house in the village and it is possible that he worked on the invention of penicillin in a shed in the garden.

WORLINGTON
2 miles W of Mildenhall on the B1102

A small village near the River Lark, known chiefly as the location of **Wamil Hall**, an Elizabethan mansion which stands on the riverbank. Popular lore has it that a person called Lady Rainbow haunts the place, though the spot she favoured for appearances, a flight of stairs, was destroyed in one of the many fires the mansion has suffered. Cricket is very much part of the village scene (there's a splendid village green) and has been since the early days of the last century.

BRANDON
9 miles NE of Mildenhall on the A1065

On the edge of **Thetford Forest** by the Little Ouse, Brandon was long ago a thriving port, but flint is what really put it on the map. The town itself is built mainly of flint, and flint was mined from early Neolithic times to make arrowheads and other implements and weapons of war. The gun flint industry brought substantial wealth, and a good flint-knapper could produce up to 300 gun flints in an hour. The invention of the percussion cap killed off much of their work so they turned to shaping flints for church building and ornamental purposes. **The Heritage Centre**, in a former fire station in George Street, provides visitors with a splendid insight into this industry, while for an even more tangible feel a visit to **Grimes Graves**, just over the Norfolk border, reveals an amazing site covering 35 acres and 300 pits (one of the shafts is open for visits). With the close proximity of numerous warrens and their rabbit population, the fur trade also flourished here, and that, too, along with forestry, is brought to life in the Heritage Centre.

The whole of this north west corner of Suffolk, know as **Breckland**, offers almost unlimited opportunities for touring by car, cycling or walking. A mile south of town on the B1106 is **Brandon Country Park**, a 30-acre landscaped site with a tree trail, forest walks, a walled garden and a visitor centre. There's also an orienteering route leading on into Thetford Forest, Britain's largest lowland pine forest. The **High Lodge Forest Centre**, by Santon Downham (off the B1107), also attracts with walks, cycle trails and adventure facilities.

ELVEDEN
5 miles S of Brandon on the A11

The road from Brandon leads south through the forest to a historic estate village with some unusual architectural features. Where the three parishes of Elveden, Eriswell and Icklingham meet a tall war memorial in the form of a Corinthian column is a landmark.

Elveden Hall became more remarkable than its builders intended when Prince Duleep Singh, heir to the throne of the Punjab, a noted sportsman and shot, and the man who handed over the Koh-I-Noor diamond to Queen Victoria, arrived on the scene. Exiled to England with a handsome pension, he bought the Georgian house in 1863 and commissioned John Norton to transform it into a palace modelled on those in Lahore and Delhi. Although it is stated that in private Duleep Singh referred to Queen Victoria as "Mrs Fagin......receiver of stolen goods" (the diamond), he kept close contact with the royal household and the Queen became his son's godmother. The Guinness family (Lord Iveagh) later took it over and joined in the fun, adding even more exotic adornments including a replica Taj Mahal, while at the same time creating the largest arable farm in the whole of the country.

THE LAURELS

162 London Road, Brandon, Suffolk IP27 0LP
Tel: 01842 812005

The Laurels in Brandon offers superior bed and breakfast accommodation. This family-run business is cosy, quiet and friendly. The clean, comfortable and welcoming accommodation comprises three guest bedrooms (one double, one twin, one single - ETC 2 Diamonds). There are several excellent eateries nearby, as well as excellent walking in nearby Thetford Forest, Peddars Way and the Norfolk Coastal Path. Central for many amenities and attractions in this part of the county, this superb hostelry is well worth seeking out.

4 Central and Eastern Suffolk

The heart of Suffolk is *the* place in the county to get away from it all, lying between the heathland and the coast. Many of the villages are little changed from olden days, and the Rivers Deben and Gipping run through much of the region, which naturally has its fair share of churches, museums, fayres and festivals. The little market towns of Stowmarket and Needham Market are full of interest and in this part of Suffolk some of the best-preserved windmills and watermills are to be found. Several examples of both windmills and watermills survive in Suffolk, and Pakenham is lucky in having a splendid example of each.

St Mary the Virgin Flint Tower, Wortham

The sea brings its own dangers and also brings them in human form, and it was against the threat of a Napoleonic invasion that Martello Towers were built in southeastern Suffolk, in the tradition of Saxon and Tudor forts and precursors of concrete pillboxes. Starting just before the end of the 18th century, over 100 of these sturdy circular fortified towers were built along the coast from Suffolk to Sussex. Aldeburgh's at Slaughden is the most northerly (and the largest), the tower at Shoreham in Sussex the southernmost.

The marshes by the coast have traditionally been a source of reeds, the raw material for the thatch that is such a pretty sight on so many Suffolk buildings. Reed cutting happens between December and February, the beds being drained in preparation and

Somerleyton Hall and Maze

reflooded after the crop has been gathered. Thatching itself is a highly skilled craft, but 10 weeks of work can give a thatched roof 50 years of life. Organised walks of the reed beds take place from time to time – wellies essential.

While inland Suffolk has few peers in terms of picturesque countryside and villages, Suffolk is also very much a maritime county, with over 50 miles of coastline. The whole coast is a conservation area, which the 50-mile Suffolk Coastal Path makes walkable throughout. With all the miles of meandering rivers and superb stretches of coastline, it is only natural that watery pursuits are a popular pastime, and everything from sailing to scuba diving, from angling to powerboat racing, is available. Many of the local museums have a nautical theme, and the Suffolk coast has been a source of inspiration for many of our most distinguished writers and composers.

CENTRAL AND EASTERN SUFFOLK

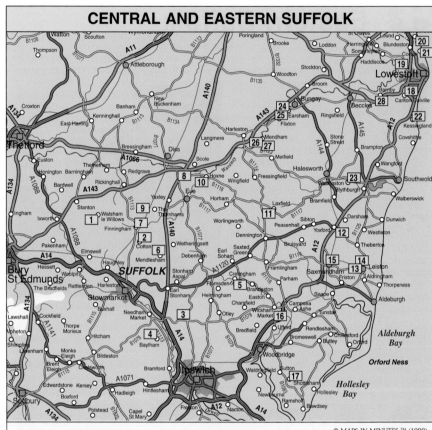

© MAPS IN MINUTES ™ (1999)

PLACES TO STAY, EAT, DRINK AND SHOP

NORTH AND EAST OF BURY ST EDMUNDS

PAKENHAM
4 mile NE of Bury St Edmunds off the A143

On a side road just off the A143 (turn right just north of Great Barton), lies the village of Pakenham, whose long history has been unearthed in the shape of a Bronze Age barrow and kiln, and another kiln from Roman times.

Elsewhere in Pakenham are the 17th century **Nether Hall**, from whose lake in the park the village stream flows through the fen into the millpond, and from the same period **Newe House**, a handsome Jacobean building with Dutch gables and a two-storey porch. The Church of St Mary has an impressive carved Perpendicular font and in its adjacent vicarage is the famous Whistler Window - a painting by Rex Whistler of an 18th century parish priest. The fens were an important source of reeds, and many of Pakenham's buildings show off the thatcher's art.

Pakenham's current unique claim to fame is in being the only parish in England with a windmill *and* a watermill, both in working order. The **watermill** was built around 1814 on a site mentioned in the Domesday Book (the Roman excavations suggest that there could have been a mill here as far back as the 1st century AD). The mill, which is fed from Pakenham fen, has many interesting features, including the Blackstone oil engine, dating from around 1900, and the Tattersall Midget rollermill from 1913, a brave but not successful attempt to compete with the larger roller mills in the production of flour. The mill and the neighbouring recreation park are well worth a visit.

No less remarkable is the **windmill**, one of the most famous in Suffolk. The black-tarred tower was built in 1831 and was in regular use until the 1950s. One of the best preserved mills in the county, it survived a lightning strike in 1971.

IXWORTH
5 miles NE of Bury St Edmunds on the A143

One of the Iceni tribe's major settlements, with important Roman connections and, in the 12th century, the site of an Augustinian priory. The remains of the priory were incorporated into a Georgian house known as Ixworth Abbey, which stands among trees by the River Blackbourne. The village has many 14th century timber-framed dwellings, and the Church of St Mary dates from the same period, though with many later additions.

A little way north of the village, on the A1088, are a nature trail and bird reserve at Ixworth Thorpe Farm. At this point a brief diversion northwards up the A1088 is very worth while.

BARDWELL
7 miles NE of Bury St Edmunds just off the A1088

Here's another tower windmill. This one dates from the 1820s and was worked by wind for 100 years, then by an oil engine until 1941. It was restored in the 1980s, only to suffer severe damage in the great storm of October 1987, when its sails were torn off. Stoneground flour is still produced by an auxiliary engine, and there's an on-site bakery. Also in this delightful village are a 16th century inn and the Church of St Peter and St Paul, known particularly for its medieval stained glass.

HONINGTON
7 miles NE of Bury St Edmunds on the A1088

Back on the A1088, the little village of Honington is the birthplace of the pastoral poet Robert Bloomfield (1766-1823), whose best known work is *The Farmer's Boy*. The house where he was born is now divided, one part called Bloomfield Cottage, the other Bloomfield Farmhouse. A brass plaque to his memory can be seen in All Saints Church, in whose graveyard his parents are buried.

EUSTON
9 miles N of Bury St Edmunds on the A1088

Euston Hall, on the A1088, has been the seat of the Dukes of Grafton for 300 years. It's open to the public on Thursday afternoons and is well worth a visit, not least for its portraits of Charles II and its paintings by Van Dyck, Lely and Stubbs. In the colourful landscaped grounds is an ice house disguised as an Italianate temple, the distinguished work of John Evelyn and William Kent.

Euston's church, in the grounds of the Hall, is the only one in the county dedicated to St

Genevieve. It's also one of only two Classical designs in the county, being rebuilt in 1676 on part of the original structure. The interior is richly decorated, with beautiful carving on the hexagonal pulpit, panelling around the walls and a carved panel of the Last Supper. Parts of this lovely wood carving are attributed by some to Grinling Gibbons. Behind the family pew is a marble memorial to Lord Arlington, who built the church.

STANTON
7 miles NE of Bury St Edmunds on the A143

Stanton was mentioned in the Domesday Book and the Romans were here before that. A double ration of medieval churches - All Saints and St John the Baptist - will satisfy the ecclesiastical scholar, while for more worldly indulgences **Wyken Vineyards** will have a strong appeal. Four acres of gardens - herb, knot, rose, kitchen and woodland - are on the same site, and the complex also includes an Elizabethan manor house, a 16th century barn, a country shop and a café. There's also a splendid woodland walk.

SIX BELLS INN

Summer Road, Walsham le Willows, Suffolk IP31 3AH
Tel: 01359 259726

The Six Bells Inn is a 16th-century part-thatched and timber-framed house offering drink and accommodation here in picturesque Walsham-le-Willows. Occupying a corner location opposite the large village Church of St Mary, this pub takes its name from the six bells of the church. The large and

attractive curved oak bar is adjacent to a brick fireplace. Other original features include the exposed beamed ceilings.

Peaceful and welcoming, this charming pub offers Greene King real ales as well as seasonal guest beers. The guest bedrooms (one twin, two double and one family room) are cosy and comfortable - and no one leaves hungry after the full and hearty English breakfast!

BARNINGHAM
8 miles NE of Bury St Edmunds on the B1111

Near the Norfolk border, Barningham was the first home of the firm of Fisons, which started in the late 18th century. Starting with a couple of windmills, they later installed one of the earliest steam mills in existence. The engine saw service for nearly 100 years and is now in an American museum; the mill building exists to this day, supplying animal feed.

This is marvellous walking country, and **Knettishall Heath Country Park**, on 400 acres of prime Breckland terrain, is the official starting place of the Peddars Way National Trail and of a path that stretches 77 miles to Great Yarmouth by way of the Little Ouse and Waveney valleys.

WALSHAM-LE-WILLOWS
9 miles NE of Bury St Edmunds off the A143

A pretty name for a pretty village, with weatherboarded and timber-framed cottages along the willow-banked river which flows throughout its length. **St Mary's** Church is no less pleasing to the eye, with its sturdy western tower and handsome windows in the Perpendicular style. Of particular interest inside is the superb tie and hammerbeam roof of the nave, and (unique in Suffolk and very rare elsewhere) a tiny circular medallion which hangs suspended from the nave wall, known as a 'Maiden's Garland' or 'Virgin's Crant'. These marked the pew seats of unmarried girls who had passed away, and the old custom was for the young men of the village to hang garlands of flowers from them on the anniversary of the girl's death. This particular example celebrates the virginity of one Mary Boyce, who died (so the inscription says) of a broken heart in 1685, just 20 years old. There is also a carving on the rood screen which looks rather like the face of a wolf: this may well be a reference to the benevolent creature that plays such an important role in the legend of St Edmund. A museum by the church has changing exhibitions of local history.

RICKINGHALL
12 miles NE of BurySt Edmunds on the A143

More timber-framed buildings, some thatched, along the streets of the two villages,

Superior and Inferior, which follow an underground stream running right through them. Each has a church dedicated to St Mary and featuring fine flintwork and tracery. The upper church, now closed, was used as a school for London evacuees during the Second World War.

REDGRAVE
13 miles NE of Bury St Edmunds on the B1113

Arachnophobes beware! Redgrave and Lopham Fens form a 360-acre reserve of reed and sedge beds where one of the most interesting inhabitants is the Great Raft Spider. The village is the source of the Little Ouse and Waveney rivers, which rise on either side of the B1113 and set off on their seaward journeys in opposite directions.

Half Moon Street, Redgrave

THELNETHAM
12 miles NE of Bury St Edmunds off the B111

West of Redgrave, between the B1113 and the B1111, lies Thelnetham – another village, another windmill. This one, a tower mill, was built in 1819 to replace a post mill on the same site, and worked for 100 years. It has been lovingly restored. Stoneground flour is produced and sold at the mill. If you wish to visit you should set sail on a summer Sunday.

COTTON
16 miles E of Bury St Edmunds off the B1113

South of Finningham, where Yew Tree House displays some fine pargeting, and just by

The Mechanical Music Museum and Bygones,
Blacksmith Road, Cotton, Stowmarket,
Suffolk IP14 4QN Tel: 01449 613876

The Mechanical Music Museum & Bygones is a treasure trove of fairground organs, reed organs, barrel organs, player organs, street pianos, pianolas, music boxes and a mighty Wurlitzer theatre organ. This wonderful place will delight anyone with an ear for music or an eye for the unusual. Open: Sundays 2.30 to 5.30 p.m. June to September inclusive.

Bacton, a lovely village originally built round seven greens, lies the village of Cotton, which should be visited for several reasons, one of which is to see the splendid 14th century flint Church of St Andrew, impressive in its dimensions and notable for its double hammerbeam roof with carved angels.

HESSETT
4 miles E of Bury St Edmunds off the A14

Dedicated to St Ethelbert, King of East Anglia, Hessett's church has many remarkable features, particularly some beautiful 16th century glass and wall paintings, both of which somehow escaped the Puritan wave of destruction. Ethelbert was unlucky enough to get on the wrong side of the mighty Offa, King of the Mercians, and was killed by him at Hereford, in 794.

WOOLPIT
6 miles E of Bury St Edmunds on the A14

The Church of St Mary the Virgin is Woolpit's crowning glory, with a marvellous porch and one of the most magnificent double hammerbeam roofs. The village was long famous for its brick industry, and the majority of the old buildings are faced with 'Woolpit Whites'. The yellowish-white brick looked very much like more expensive stone and for several centuries was widely exported. Some was used in the building of the Senate wing of the Capitol in Washington DC. Red bricks were also produced, and the **Bygones Museum** has a brick-making display and also tells the story of the evolution of the village.

Nearby is a moated site known as **Lady's Well**, a place of pilgrimage in the Middle Ages. The water from the spring was reputed to have healing properties, most efficacious in curing eye troubles.

A favourite Woolpit legend concerns the *Green Children*, a brother and sister with green complexions who appeared one day in a field, apparently attracted by church bells. Though hungry, they would eat nothing until some green beans were produced. Given shelter by the lord of the manor, they learned to speak English and said that they came from a place called St Martin. The boy survived for only a short time, but the girl thrived, lost her green colour, was baptised and married a man from King's Lynn – no doubt leaving many a Suffolk man green with envy!

ELMSWELL
7 miles E of Bury St Edmunds off the A14

Clearly visible from the A14, the impressive Church of St John the Baptist with its massive flint tower stands at the entrance to the village facing Woolpit across the valley. A short drive north of Elmswell lies **Great Ashfield**, an unspoilt village whose now disused airfield played key roles in both World Wars. In the churchyard of the 13th century All Saints is a memorial to the Americans who died during the Second World War and inside is a commemorative altar. Some accounts say that Edmund was buried here in 903 after dying at the hands of the Danes; a cross was put up in his memory. The cross was replaced in the 19th century and now stands in the garden of Ashfield House.

HAUGHLEY
12 miles E of Bury St Edmunds off the A14

On the run into Stowmarket, Haughley once had the largest motte and bailey castle in Suffolk. All that now remains is a mound behind the church. **Haughley Park** is a handsome redbrick mansion set in eight acres of gardens and surrounding woodland featuring ancient oaks and splendid magnolias. Woodland paths take you past a half-mile stretch of rhododendrons, and in springtime the bluebells and lilies of the valley are a magical sight. The gardens are open on Tuesdays between May and September, the house by appointment only.

HARLESTON
9 miles E of Bury St Edmunds off the A14

The churches of Shelland and Harleston lie in close proximity on a minor road between Woolpit and Haughley picnic site. At Shelland, the tiny Church of King Charles the Martyr is one of only four in England to be dedicated to King Charles I. The brick floor is laid in a herringbone pattern, there are high box pews and a three-decker pulpit, but the most unusual accessory is a working barrel organ dating from the early 19th century.

The Church of St Augustine at Harleston stands all alone among pine trees and is reached by a track across a field. It has a thatched roof, Early English windows and a tower with a single bell.

STOWMARKET

The largest town in the heart of Suffolk, Stowmarket enjoyed a period of rapid growth when the River Gipping was still navigable to Ipswich and when the railway arrived.

Much of the town's history and legacy are brought vividly to life in the splendid **Museum of East Anglian Life**, which is situated in the centre of town to the west of the market place, in a 70-acre meadowland site on the old Abbot's Hall Estate (the aisled original barn dates from the 13th century). Part of the open-air section features several historic buildings which have been moved

from elsewhere in the region and carefully re-erected on site. These include an engineering workshop from the 1870s, part of a 14th century farmhouse, a watermill from Alton and a wind pump which was rescued in a collapsed state at Minsmere in 1977.

There's also a collection of working steam engines, farm animals and year-round demonstrations of all manner of local arts and crafts, from coopering to candle-making, from sheep shearing to saddlery.

Stowmarket's Church of St Peter and St Mary acquired a new spire in 1994, replacing the 1715 version (itself a replacement) which was dismantled on safety grounds in 1975.

The town certainly merits a major stroll, while for a peaceful picnic the riverbank beckons. Serious scenic walkers should make for the **Gipping Valley River Park** walk, which runs all the way to Ipswich.

AROUND STOWMARKET

BUXHALL
3 miles W of Stowmarket just off the B1115

The village church is notable for its six heavy bells, but the best-known landmark in this quiet village is undoubtedly the majestic tower mill, without sails since a gale removed them in 1929 but still standing as a silent, sturdy reminder of its working days. This is good walking country, with an ancient wood and many signposted footpaths.

NEEDHAM MARKET
4 miles SE of Stowmarket off the A14

A thriving village whose greatest glory is the wonderful carvings on the ceiling of the Church of **St John the Baptist**. The church, both outside and within, is otherwise not remarkable, so the ornate double hammerbeam roof seems all the more magnificent, especially when bathed in light from the strategically placed skylight. The roof is massive, as high as the walls of the church itself; the renowned authority on Suffolk churches, H Munro Cautley, described the work at Needham as "the culminating achievement of the English carpenter".

The River Gipping flows to the east of the High Street and its banks provide miles of

Floral Delight Country Tea Room

Hemingstone, Ipswich,
Suffolk IP6 9RT (on B1078)
Tel: 01449 761800

The charming **Floral Delight Tea Room** lives up to its name, occupying a beautifully converted 200-year-old stable/haybarn festooned with flowers and set amid tranquil Suffolk countryside. Owned and personally run by Barbara Lucey, who bakes most of the tempting cakes, scones and other delicacies. The menu includes freshly-prepared soups, savoury pies such as duck and sage, country pork, and chicken and ham, quiches and more. This is the perfect place to enjoy hot or cold light lunches and teas and coffees from around the world. In addition there are own-label preserves and local apple juices to buy as well as a take-away menu available.

The gift area of the tea room displays some superb Italian glassware, exclusive ceramics, bone china, porcelain miniatures, photo frames, pot pourri, candles, cards and other unique collectibles. The decor and furnishings are tasteful and comfortable, the atmosphere is very welcoming, Barbara and her staff offer attentive and friendly service. Open daily 10.30 a.m. - 17.30. 1st March - October; 10.30 a.m. - 16.00. November - mid-December.

Baylham House Rare Breeds Farm

Mill Lane, Baylham, Ipswich, Suffolk IP6 8LG
Tel/Fax: 01473 830264
e-mail: hplaces@baylham-house-farm.co.uk
website: www.baylham-house-farm.co.uk

Baylham House Farm is open to the public and breeds endangered farm animals including pigs, cattle, sheep, pygmy goats and poultry. The farm includes a pleasant riverside walk and a picnic area and the majority of the farm is wheelchair and pushchair friendly. A disabled toilet is available in the Visitor's Centre which also sells gifts, souvenirs and refreshments.

In addition, Baylham House Farm offers self-catering accommodation in either the Annexe - which sleeps four plus a cot - or the Flat, which sleeps two plus a cot. Inspected by the Tourist Board, these charming units are cosy and comfortable. Guests have access to the whole of the farm and can get involved in looking after the animals if they want to. The Gipping Valley public footpath network runs by the farm and Baylham is centrally placed to provide an excellent base from which to explore the rest of Suffolk's wonderful countryside and attractions.

walks: the towpath is a public right of way walkable all the way from Stowmarket to Ipswich and the on riverbank at Needham is a 25-acre picnic site and a nature reserve.

Nearby **Barking**, on the B1018 south of Needham, was once more important than its neighbour, being described in 1874 as "a pleasant village ... including the hamlet of Needham Market". This explains the fact that Barking's church is exceptionally large for a village church: it was the mother church to Needham Market and was used for Needham's burials when that place had no ground of its own.

BAYLHAM
7 miles SE of Stowmarket off the B11130

The Roman site of Combretrovium is home to **Baylham House Rare Breeds Farm**, and visitors (April-early October) will find displays and information relating to both Rome and rare animals. The farm's chief concern is the survival of rare breeds and there are breeding groups of cattle, sheep, pigs, goats and poultry (see panel opposite)

BRAMFORD
11 miles SE of Stowmarket off the A14

Bramford has a pretty little church, St Mary's, with a 13th century stone screen. It was once an important spot on the river route, when barges from Ipswich stopped to unload corn; the walls of the old lock are still visible. In the vicinity is **Suffolk Water Park**, where the lake welcomes canoeists and windsurfers.

EARL STONHAM
6 miles E of Stowmarket on the A1120

A scattered village set around three greens in farming land. The Church of St Mary the Virgin boasts one of Suffolk's finest single hammerbeam roofs, and is also notable for its Bible scene murals, the doom (Last Judgement scene) over the chancel arch and a triple hour-glass, presumably to record just how protracted were some of the sermons.

STONHAM ASPAL
7 miles E of Stowmarket on the A1120

On the other side of the A140 lies Stonham Aspal, where in 1962 the remains of a Roman bath house were unearthed. The parish church has an unusual wooden top to its tower, a necessary addition to house the ten bells that a keen campanologist insisted on installing. At Stonham Barns, the **British Birds of Prey and Nature Centre** is home to every British owl and raptors from Britain and around the world. These wonderful birds flap their wings in regular flying displays, and in the Pets Paradise the kiddies can say hello to the hamsters and horses, the mice and the meerkats, the parrots and the piglets.

EARL SOHAM
12 miles E of Stowmarket on the A1120

Earl Soham comprises a long, winding street that was once part of a Roman road. It lies in a valley, and on the largest of its three greens the village sign is a carved wooden statue of a falconer given as a gift by the Womens Institute in 1953. The 13th century Church of St Mary is well worth a visit.

SAXTEAD GREEN
14 miles E of Stowmarket off the A1120

One of the prettiest sights in Suffolk is the white **18th century mill** that stands on the marshy green. This is a wonderful example of a post mill, perhaps the best in the world, dating back to 1796 and renovated first in the 19th century. It worked until 1947 and has since been kept in working order, with the sails turning though the mill no longer grinds. You can climb into the buck (body) of the elegant weatherboarded construction and explore the machinery. It's open for visits in the summer.

FRAMLINGHAM
18 miles NE of Stowmarket on the B1119

The marvellous **castle**, brooding on a hilltop, dominates this agreeable market town, as it has since Roger Bigod, 2nd Earl of Norfolk, built it in the 12th century (his grandfather built the first a century earlier but this wooden construction was soon demolished). The Earls and Dukes of Norfolk, the Howards, were here for many generations before moving to Arundel in 1635. The castle is in remarkably good condition, partly because it was rarely attacked – though King John put it under siege in 1215. Its most famous occupant was Mary Tudor, who was in residence when proclaimed Queen in 1553.

Framlingham Castle

In the reign of Elizabeth I it was used as a prison for defiant priests and in the 17th century, after being bequeathed to Pembroke College, Cambridge, it saw service as a home and school for local paupers. Nine of the castle's 13 towers are accessible and the climb up the spiral staircase and walk round the battlements are well worth the effort. On one side the view is of the Meres, which is a bird sanctuary. In the north wing is the Lanman Museum, devoted to farm and craft tools and domestic bygones.

The castle brought considerable prestige and prosperity to Framlingham, evidence of which can be found in the splendid Church of **St Michael**, which has two wonderful works of art. One is the tomb of Henry Fitzroy, bastard son of Henry VIII, beautifully adorned with scenes from Genesis and Exodus and in a superb state of repair. The other is the tomb of the 3rd Duke with carvings of the apostles in shell niches. Also of note is the Carolean organ of 1674, a gift of Sir Robert Hitcham, to whom the Howards sold the estate. Cromwell and the Puritans were anti-organ so this instrument was lucky to escape the mass destruction of organs at the time of the Commonwealth. Sir Robert is also buried in the church. On a humbler level, the people of Framlingham are very proud of their two Victorian post boxes, which were installed in 1856.

DENNINGTON
2 miles N of Framlingham on the B1116

The pretty little village of Dennington boasts one of the oldest post offices in the country,

this one having occupied the same site since 1830. The village church has some very unusual features, none more so than the hanging pyx canopy above the altar. A pyx served as a receptacle for the Reserved Sacrament which would be kept under a canopy attached to weights and pulleys so that the whole thing could be lowered when the sacrament was required for the sick and the dying.

The church also has many interesting carvings, the most remarkable being that of a skiapod, the only known representation in this county of a mythical creature of the African desert, humanoid but with a huge boat-shaped foot with which he could cover himself against the sun. This curious beast was 'known' to Herodotus and to Pliny, who remarked that it had 'great pertinacity in leaping'. In the chapel at the top of the south aisle stands the tomb of Lord Bardolph, who fought at Agincourt, and his wife, their effigies carved in alabaster.

CHARSFIELD
5 miles S of Framlington off the B1078

A minor road runs from Framlingham through picturesque Kettleburgh and Hoo to Charsfield, best known as the inspiration for Ronald Blyth's book *Akenfield*, later memorably filmed by Sir Peter Hall. A cottage garden in the village displays the Akenfield village sign and is open to visitors in the summer.

OTLEY
7 miles SW of Framlingham on the B1079

The 15th century **moated hall** is open to the public at certain times. Standing in ten acres of gardens that include a canal, a nuttery and a knot garden, the hall was long associated with the Gosnold family, whose coat of arms is also that of the village. The best-known member of that family is Bartholomew Gosnold, who sailed to the New World, named Martha's Vineyard, discovered Cape Cod and founded the settlement of

Otley Hall

Jamestown, Virginia. The 13th century Church of St Mary has a remarkable baptistry font measuring 6 feet in length and 2 feet 8 inches in depth. Though filled with water, the font is not used and was only discovered in 1950 when the vestry floor was raised. Perhaps it was used for adult baptisms.

HELMINGHAM
7 miles SW of Framlingham on the B1077

Another moated hall, this one a Tudor construction. The house is not open to the public but on summer Sundays the gardens can be visited; attractions include herbaceous and spring borders, many varieties of rose, safari rides and deer, Highland cattle and Soay sheep. The Tollemache family were here for many years, and one of their number founded a brewery, which, after a merger, became the Tolly Cobbold brewery based in Ipswich.

FRAMSDEN
7 miles SW of Framlingham on the B1077

The scenery in these parts is real picture postcard stuff, and in the village of Framsden the picture is completed by a fine **post mill**, this one built high on a hill in 1760, refitted and raised in 1836 and in commercial use until 1934. The milling machinery is still in place and the mill is open for visits at weekends by appointment only.

CRETINGHAM
4 miles SW of Framlingham off the A1120

The village sign is the unusual item here, in that it has two different panels: one shows an everyday Anglo-Saxon farming scene, the other a group (of Danes?) sailing up the River

THE CRETINGHAM BELL

Cretingham, Woodbridge, Suffolk IP13 7BJ
Tel/Fax: 01728 685419

The Cretingham Bell is a delightful traditional country Free House with accommodation. Originally four cottages dating back to 1545, the pub was established in 1968. Hidden away off the main road in a relaxing and quiet spot, it is well worth making the effort to seek out. The interior is exceptionally attractive, with a bare polished wooden floor and large brick open fireplace in the main bar, and tile flooring, open fire and wooden bench seating in the second bar. The restaurant area completes

the rustic ambience, with exposed beams, low lighting and carved furniture.

All the beers served are local East Anglian ones such as Adnams, Woodfords Wherry, Victoria and Buffy's Hopleaf. Malt whiskies, and extensive wine list, spirits, lagers and non-alcoholic drinks complete the list of liquid refreshment on offer. Delicious home-cooked food is available between 12.00-14.00 each day and from 19.00-21.00 Sun-Thu evenings or 19.00-21.30 Fri and Sat evenings. Opening times: 11.00-14.30 and 18.00-23.00 Monday to Saturday; 12.00-15.00 and 19.00-22.30 Sundays. The comfortable and welcoming accommodation comprises two ensuite guest bedrooms (a double and a twin). No smoking in the rooms. No children under 14.

Just off the A1120, the pub is close to Framlingham Castle and Saxted Mill, other local attractions include the tea pot factory at Debenham, birds of prey centre at Stonham Aspel, Helmingham Hall and Easton Farm Park.

THE FLEECE INN

Front Street, Mendlesham, Suffolk IP14 5RX
Tel/Fax: 01449 766511

Set at the end of Front Street in Mendlesham, in an area known as Fleece Corner close to Mendlesham Field, the delightful **Fleece Inn** is a cheerful pink 16th-century building. Extended from a small house to include a dairy, buttery and "new" hall in 1550, it retains many original features and is just one of several Tudor buildings in this charming village. The decor inside and out has a distinctly Art Deco

feel. Countryside implements and photographs adorn the walls, including dozens of pictures tracing the history of village life over the years.

Hosts Gordon and Gemma Cox offer a warm welcome to all their guests. Gordon, a Cordon Bleu-trained chef, has created a wonderful menu of freshly cooked and prepared roasts, steaks, Mediterranean and Singapore dishes, including locally caught fish and a good range of changing daily specials. The range of beers and lagers includes Greene King IPA and guest ales like Hobgoblin and Bombardier, together with a variety of wines, spirits and soft drinks. This excellent rural pub is well worth seeking out.

THE WHITE HORSE INN

Station Road, Finningham,
Suffolk IP14 4TL
Tel: 01449 781250

The **White Horse Inn** in Finningham is a Grade II listed building dating back some 500 years, the second oldest building in the village after the church. The exterior is particularly attractive, set in several acres of gardens. The interior boasts low beams and a cosy atmosphere.

Sepia photos of the village in days gone by and a photographic history of local football teams adorn the walls. The profusion of fresh flowers and the collection of bric a brac add to the homely traditional ambience. Hosts Don and Pat Lamb and their friendly staff make all their guests feel very welcome. Pat also does all the cooking, creating a menu of tempting favourites such as beef and ale pie, steaks and chops, fish and chicken. There are also good vegetarian options and a delicious range of puddings. Real ales include Flowers IPA and Speckled Hen. There's also a good range of lagers, wines, spirits and non-alcoholic drinks.

The pub is the hub of the local community, hosting the village's unusual events such as the bubble car rally and pony and trap rally.

Deben, with the locals fleeing. The signs are made from mosaic tiles.

BRANDESTON
3 miles SW of Framlingham off the A1120

A further mile to the east, through more pretty countryside, Brandeston is another delightful spot, with a row of beautiful thatched cottages and the parish Church of All Saints with a 13th century font. The best-known vicar of Brandeston was John Lowes (1572-1646) who was accused of witchcraft by the villagers, interrogated by Witchfinder General Matthew Hopkins and hanged at Bury St Edmunds. His sad end was made even sadder by the fact that before being strung up he had himself to read out the burial service of a condemned witch, as no priest was allowed to conduct the service. Hopkins made a handsome living out of this bizarre business, preying on the superstitions of the times and using the foulest means to obtain confessions. One account of his end is that he himself was accused of being a witch and hanged. The less satisfactory alternative is that he died of tuberculosis. "Witch" do you prefer?

DEBENHAM
10 miles E of Stowmarket on the B1077

A sizeable village of architectural distinction, with a profusion of attractive timber-framed buildings dating from the 14th to the 17th century. The River Deben flows beside and beneath the main street and, by one of the little bridges, weavers still practise their craft. There is also a pottery centre. St Mary's Church is unusual in having an original Saxon tower, and the roof alternates hammerbeams and crested tie beams.

MENDLESHAM
6 miles NE of Stowmarket off the A140

On the green in Old Market Street lies an enormous stone which is said to have been used as a preaching stone, mounted by itinerant Wesleyan preachers. In the Church of St Mary there is a collection of parish armour assembled 400 years ago, and also some fine carvings. The least hidden local landmark is a 1,000ft TV mast put up by the IBA in 1959.

WETHERINGSETT
7 miles NE of Stowmarket off the A140

On the other side of the A140, Wetheringsett is where you'll find **Mid-Suffolk Light Railway Museum**, open on summer Sundays and during summer school holidays.

Wetheringsett has had two well-known rectors, famous for very different reasons. Richard Hakluyt, incumbent from 1590 to 1616, is remembered for his major work *Voyages* (full title *Principal Navigation, Voiages, Traffiques and Discoveries of the English Nation*). The rector between 1858 and 1883 was a certain George Wilfrid Ellis, sometime tailor and butler, and finally a bogus clergyman. After he was unmasked as a sham it needed a special Act of Parliament to validate the marriage ceremonies he had illegally conducted and to legitimise the issue of those marriages.

THORNHAM MAGNA & PARVA
10 miles N of Stowmarket off the A140

The **Thornham Walks and Field Centre**, with 12 miles of walks and a herb garden and nursery, cater admirably for hikers, horticulturists and students of the countryside. The tiny thatched Church of St Mary at Thornham Parva houses a considerable treasure in the shape of an exquisite medieval altar painting, known as a retable, with a central panel depicting the Crucifixion and four saints on each side panel. Its origins are uncertain but it was possibly the work of the Royal Workshops at Westminster Abbey, and made for Thetford Priory, or a nearby Dominican monastery. Also to be admired is the 14th century octagonal font and a series of fascinating wall paintings. In the churchyard is a monument to Sir Basil Spence (1907-76), architect of Coventry Cathedral.

YAXLEY
12 miles N of Stowmarket on the A140

Another Church of **St Mary** and more treasures. One is an extremely rare sexton's wheel, which hangs above the south door and was used in medieval times to select fast days in honour of the Virgin. When a pair of iron wheels were spun on their axle, strings attached to the outer wheel would catch on the inner, stopping both and indicating the chosen day. The 17th century pulpit is one of the finest in the country, with the most glorious, sumptuous carvings.

Yaxley's most famous son is Sir Frederick Ashton, who is buried in the churchyard.

EYE
13 miles NE of Stowmarket on the B1117

The name is derived from the Saxon for an island, as this super little town was once surrounded by water and marshes. The Church of **St Peter and St Paul** stands in the shadow of a mound on which a castle once stood (the remains are worth a look and the mound offers a panoramic view of the town – almost a bird's eye view, in fact). The church's 100 foot tower is described by Pevsner as "one of the wonders of Suffolk" and the interior is a masterpiece of restoration, with all the essential medieval features in place. The rood screen, with painted panels depicting St Edmund, St Ursula, Edward the Confessor and Henry VI, is particularly fine.

DAWNRO COTTAGE

Eye Road, Brome, Eye, Suffolk IP23 8AL
Tel: 01379 870727
email: dawnrodogs@aol.com

Dawnro Cottage is a welcoming and very attractive thatched country cottage offering superior bed and breakfast, or self catering accommodation. Next door to the home of a Dalmatian kennel which has been running for 25 years, this beamed Suffolk pink family cottage boasts a strong Dalmatian theme. The cottage is self-contained and features all modern facilities. The rooms are warm in winter and cool in summer. The accommodation comprises a large family bedroom that sleeps four (plus a cot at no extra charge), bathroom, fully equipped kitchen and sitting/dining room. There are two lovely gardens. Dogs welcome!

SIX BELLS

High Street, Gislingham, Suffolk IP23 8JD
Tel: 01379 783349

Owners Roy and Margaret offer all guests to the **Six Bells** public house a warm welcome. Roy is a devotee of real ales and a CAMRA member. In the 13 years he has run this fine pub he has showcased over 100 different real ales - these are all on display around the walls. The pub has featured beers from micro breweries all over the country; the selection changes monthly. The interior of this welcoming pub is Margaret's drawing room, cosy and decorated in chintz and with tasteful decorations and comfortable furnishings.

Cosy and friendly, the pub dates back to the mid-1850s and takes its name from the six bells hanging in the church tower which were cast between 1553 and 1814. The restaurant area is called The Columbine Room and was constructed in 1991 by a local builder. During the construction a 32-foot well was uncovered; covered by glass and lit from below, it is an unusual and attractive feature. The restaurant is Victorian in style and furnishings, decorated in deep greens and wrought ironwork. All dishes served use only the best and freshest ingredients.

The Columbine also takes its name from the village church, were a stained window dating from the 15th century is believed to contain one of the earliest known pictorial records of flowers in the country.

Other interesting Eye sights are the ornate redbrick town hall; the timbered Guildhall, with the archangel Gabriel carved on a corner post; a crinkle-crankle (serpentine) wall fronting Chandos Lodge, where Sir Frederick Ashton once lived; and a thriving theatre, one of the smallest professional theatres in the country.

HOXNE
4 miles NE of Eye on the B1118

Palaeolithic remains indicate the exceptionally long history of Hoxne (call it Hoxon), which stands along the banks of the River Waveney near the Norfolk border. It is best known for its links with King Edmund, who was reputedly killed here, though Bradfield St Clare and Shottisham have rival claims. The Hoxne legend is that Edmund was betrayed to the Danes by a newlywed couple who were crossing the Goldbrook bridge and spotted his golden spurs reflected from his hiding place below the bridge. Edmund put a curse on all newlyweds crossing the bridge, and to this day some brides take care to avoid it.

The story continues that Edmund was tied to an oak tree and killed with arrows. That same oak mysteriously fell down in 1848 while apparently in good health, and a monument at the site is a popular tourist attraction. In the Church of St Peter and St Paul an oak screen (perhaps that very same oak?) depicts scenes from the martyr's life. A more cheerful event is the Harvest Breakfast on the village green that follows the annual service.

HORHAM
6 miles E of Eye on the B1117

Three distinct musical connections in this dapper little village. The Norman church has had its tower strengthened for the rehanging of the peal of eight bells, which is believed to be the oldest in the world. Benjamin Britten, later associated with the Aldeburgh Festival, lived and composed in Horham for a time, and on a famous day during World War II, Glenn Miller brought his band here to celebrate the 200th flying mission from the American aerodrome.

THE SWAN INN

Low Street, Hoxne, Suffolk IP21 5AS
Tel: 01379 668275
email: hoxneswan@supernet.com

The Swan in Hoxne occupies a 15th Century Grade II listed lodge, formerly known as Bishops Lodge. Huge gardens run down to the river Dove. A vast willow tree dominates the lawns, and throughout there's an air of peace and rural seclusion. Unique local brickwork surrounds the side garden. The 17th- and 18th-century outbuildings add to the idyllic rural atmosphere of the place. This fine pub is set at the bottom end of the village green, opposite the village Post Office and Grocery Store.

The restaurant and front bar aptly reflect Hoxne's ecclesiastical history with its ornate ceiling beams and ancient wide-planked floors. The 10-foot inglenook fireplace is another impressive feature of this elegant establishment. Here amid these charming surroundings guests can enjoy a menu which offers a wide choice of expertly prepared home cooked dishes. The very good wine list includes no fewer than seven reds and nine whites, all excellent vintages. There's also an impressive range of ever changing cask ales from all areas of the country. Food is available every day, however visitors should note that the pub is closed between 3 and 6 p.m. weekdays.

WORLINGWORTH
8 miles SE of Eye off the B1118

It's well worth taking the country road to Worlingworth, a long, straggling village whose Church of St Mary has a remarkable font cover reaching up about 30 feet. It is brilliantly coloured and intricately carved, and near the top is an inscription in Greek which translates as 'wash my sin and not my body only'. Note, too, the Carolean box pews, the carved pulpit and an oil painting of Worlingworth's Great Feast of 1810 to celebrate George III's jubilee.

WINGFIELD
6 miles E of Eye off the B1118

Wingfield College is one of the country's most historic seats of learning, founded in 1362 as a college for priests with a bequest from Sir John de Wingfield, Chief Staff Officer to the Black Prince. Sir John's wealth came from ransoming a French nobleman at the Battle of Poitiers in 1356. Surrendered to Henry VIII at the time of the Dissolution, the college became a farmhouse and is now in private hands. The facade is now Georgian, but the original medieval Great Hall still stands, and the college and its three acres of gardens are open to the public at weekends during the summer. Attractions include regular artistic events and printing demonstrations.

The Church of St Andrew was built as the collegiate church and has an extra-large chancel to accommodate the college choir. The church contains three really fine monuments: to Sir John (in stone); to Michael de la Pole, 2nd Earl of Suffolk (in wood); and to John de la Pole, Duke of Suffolk (in alabaster). In the churchyard is a hudd – a shelter for the priest for use at the graveside in bad weather.

On a hill outside the village are the imposing remains of a castle built by the 1st Earl.

FRESSINGFIELD
10 miles E of Eye on the B1116

The Fox and Goose restaurant is one of the best in Suffolk, but the spiritual centre is the Church of St Peter and St Paul. It has a superb

THE VILLA STABLES

The Villa, High Street, Laxfield, Suffolk IP13 8DU
Tel: 01986 798019 email: laxfieldleisure@talk21.com

The Villa Stables in Laxfield offers charming and impressive accommodation in one of two excellently refurbished traditional dwellings. Here in the heart of Suffolk, owners John Reeve and his wife escaped from Islington in London to this fabulous former doctor's residence. John is chair of the Heart of Suffolk Tourism Association and is committed to high standards of excellence for the two cottages available. The house itself was refurbished in 1828, and remains a mix of the modern and traditional. Former residents include one Mr Gillingwater, superintendent of the (now sadly defunct) Mid-Suffolk Light Railway.

The guests' accommodation is located in the former stables. There are two separate residences. The first, called The Old Stables, comprises kitchen and dining area separated by the original horse enclosures. Stone floors add to the traditional ambience; the tasteful redecoration was undertaken by local craftsmen to create a light, airy and warm atmosphere. The lounge area's French windows lead to a paved patio/terrace. The second accommodation is called The Loose Box. It was once the food/grain store; today it is a stylish and handsome studio apartment with private garden area. Furnished in cottage style, both retain a traditional feel while offering every modern facility. Characterful and quiet, these cottages offer a truly relaxing and supremely comfortable home from home - just the place to unwind, and perfect as a base from which to explore the many sights and attractions of this part of Suffolk.

hammerbeam roof and a lovely stone bell tower that was built in the 14th century. On one of the pews the initials AP are carved. These are believed to be the work of Alice de la Pole, Duchess of Norfolk and granddaughter of Geoffrey Chaucer. Was this a work of art or a bout of vandalism brought on by a dull sermon?

At nearby **Ufford Hall** lived the Sancroft family, one of whom became Archbishop of Canterbury. He led the revolt of the bishops against James II and was imprisoned in the Tower of London. Released by William IV and sacked for refusing to swear the oath of allegiance, he returned home and is entombed by the south porch of the church.

The village sign is a pilgrim and a donkey, recording that Fressingfield was a stopping place on the pilgrim route from Dunwich to Bury St Edmunds.

LAXFIELD
12 miles E of Eye on the B1117

Laxfield & District Museum, in the 16th century Guildhall, gives a fine insight into bygone ages with geology and natural history exhibits, farm and domestic tools, a Victorian kitchen, a village shop and a costume room. The museum is open Saturday and Sunday afternoons in summer.

All Saints Church is distinguished by some wonderful flint flashwork on its tower, roof and nave. In the 1808 Baptist church is a plaque remembering John Noyes, burnt at the stake in 1557 for refusing to take Catholic vows. History relates that the villagers, with a

Drawing Room, Heveningham Hall

single exception, dowsed their fires in protest, and the one remaining fire was used to light the stake.

A couple of miles east of Laxfield, **Heveningham Hall** is a fine Georgian mansion, a model of classical elegance designed by James Wyatt with lovely grounds by Capability Brown. As it runs through the grounds, the River Blyth widens into a lake.

ALONG THE COAST

DUNWICH
4 miles SW of Southwold off the B1105

Surely the Hidden Place of all Hidden Places! Dunwich was once the capital of East Anglia, founded by the Burgundian Christian missionary St Felix and for several centuries a major trading port (wool and grain out; wine, timber and cloth in) and a centre of fishing and shipbuilding. The records show that in 1241 no fewer than 80 ships were built for the king. By the middle of the next century the best days were over as the sea attacked from the east and a vast bank of sand and shingle silted up the harbour. The course

Heveningham Hall

of the river was diverted, the town was cut off from the sea and the town's trade was effectively dead. For the next 700 years, the relentless forces of nature continued to take their toll, and all that remains now of ancient Dunwich are the ruins of a Norman leper hospital, the archways of a medieval friary and a buttress of one of the nine churches which once served the community.

Today's village comprises a 19th century church and a row of Victorian cottages, one of which houses the **Dunwich museum**. Local residents set up the museum in 1972 to tell the Dunwich story; the historical section has displays and exhibits from Roman, Saxon and medieval times, the centrepiece being a large model of the town at its 12th century peak. There are also sections for natural history, social history and the arts. Experts have calculated that the main part of old Dunwich extended up to seven miles beyond its present boundaries, and the vengeance of the sea has thrown up inevitable stories of drama and mystery. The locals say that when a storm is threatening, the sound of submerged church bells can still be heard tolling under the waves as they shift in the current. Other tales tell of strange lights in

the ruined priory and the eerie chanting of long-gone monks.

Dunwich Forest, immediately inland from the village, is one of three – the others are further south at Tunstall and Rendlesham – named by the Forestry Commission as Aldewood Forest. Work started on these in 1920 with the planting of Scots pine, Corsican pine and some Douglas fir; oak and poplar were tried but did not thrive in the sandy soil. The three forests, which between them cover nearly 9,000 acres, were almost completely devastated in the hurricane of October 1987, Rendlesham alone losing more than a million trees, and the replanting will take many years to restore them.

South of the village lies **Dunwich Heath**, one of Suffolk's most important conservation areas, comprising the beach, splendid heather, a field study centre, a public hide, and an information centre and restaurant in converted coastguard cottages. 1998 marks the 30th anniversary of the heath being in the care of the National Trust.

Around Dunwich Heath are the attractive villages of Westleton, Middleton, Theberton and Eastbridge.

THE KINGS HEAD

Brook Street, Yoxford,
Suffolk IP17 3EX
Tel/Fax: 01728 668008

The Kings Head, situated on the A12 in Yoxford, dates back hundreds of years and now has the distinction of being Suffolk's first completely "Smoke Free Eating & Drinking Freehouse".

Set in this area of outstanding natural beauty, known as the Garden of Suffolk, this welcoming pub's interior is pristine and airy and boasts of a log

burning stove, pews, settles, oak bar counter, and interior feature stained glass, with polished bare wooden floors and tasteful, comfortable furnishings and decor. This true Freehouse offers a range of food and drink of an unusually high standard for a village pub, incorporating innovative touches which include a comprehensive fine wines list, a range of hand pulled cask beers which change on a weekly basis, draft Erdinger wheat beer from Germany, a wide selection of continental bottled beers and bean to cup espresso and coffee.

The menu's emphasis centres on fresh local produce (no meal over £10) all backed up with a great level of service for its fast growing customer base.

In **Westleton**, the 14th century thatched Church of St Peter, built by the monks of Sibton Abbey, has twice seen the collapse of its tower. The first fell down in a hurricane in 1776 and its smaller wooden replacement collapsed when a bomb fell in World War II. The village is the main route of access to the RSPB-managed **Minsmere Bird Sanctuary**, the most important sanctuary for wading birds in eastern England. The marshland was flooded during World War II, and nature and this wartime emergency measure created the perfect habitat for innumerable birds. More than 100 species nest here, and a similar number visit. It's a birdwatcher's paradise, with many hides, and the **Suffolk Coastal Path** runs along the foreshore.

A little way inland from Westleton lies **Darsham**, where another nature reserve is home to many varieties of birds and flowers.

YOXFORD
10 miles SW of Southwold on the A12

Once an important stop on the London-Yarmouth coaching route, Yoxford now attracts visitors with its pink-washed cottages and its arts and crafts, antique and food shops. Look for the cast-iron signpost outside the church, with hands pointing to London, Yarmouth and Framlingham set high enough to be seen by the driver of a stagecoach.

SIBTON
12 miles SW of Southwold on the A1120

Two miles west of Yoxford, on the A1120, Sibton is known chiefly for its abbey (only the ruins remain), the only Cistercian house in Suffolk. The Church of St Peter is certainly not a ruin and should be seen for its fine hammerbeam and collar roof.

SAXMUNDHAM
12 miles SW of Southwold off the A12

A pretty name for a little town that was granted its market charter in 1272. On the font of the church is the carving of a woodwose, a tree spirit or green man – he, and others like him, have given their name to a large number of pubs, in Suffolk and elsewhere. The only thing in ruins in Sax is the bus garage!

BRUISYARD
4 miles NW of Saxmundham off the B1119

Just west of the village is the **Bruisyard Vineyard, Winery and Herb Centre**, a complex of a 10-acre vineyard with 13,000 Müller Thurgau grape vines, a wine-production centre, herb and water gardens, a tea shop and a picnic site.

PEASENHALL
6 miles NW of Saxmundham on the A1120

A little stream runs along the side of the main street, whose buildings present several styles and ages. Most distinguished is the old timbered **Woolhall**, splendidly restored to its 15th century grandeur. The oddest is certainly a hall in the style of a Swiss chalet, built for his workers by James Josiah Smyth, grandson of the founder of James Smyth & Sons. This company, renowned for its agricultural drills, was for more than two centuries the dominant industrial presence in Peasenhall. On the south side of St Michael's churchyard stands the 1805 drill mill where James Smyth manufactured his Nonpareil seed drills, one of which is on display in Stowmarket's museum.

LEISTON
4 miles E of Saxmundham off the B1119

The first **Leiston Abbey** was built on Nunsmere marshes in 1182 but in 1363 the Earl of Suffolk rebuilt it on its present site. It became one of the largest and most prestigious monasteries in the country, and its wealth probably spelt its ruin, as it fell within Henry VIII's plan for the dissolution of the monasteries. A new abbey was built by the ruins of the old, and the restored old hall is used as a base for PROCORDA, a group promoting musical excellence.

For 200 years the biggest name in Leiston was that of Richard Garrett, who founded an engineering works here in 1778 after starting business in Woodbridge. In the early years ploughs, threshers, seed drills and other agricultural machinery were the main products, but the company later started one of the country's first production lines for steam machines. The Garrett works are now the **Long Shop Museum**, the factory buildings having been lovingly restored, and

Field End Guest House

(ETC and AA 4 Diamonds - Silver Award)

1 Kings Road, Leiston, Suffolk IP16 4DA
Tel/Fax: 01728 833527
website: www.field-end.freeserve.co.uk email: pwright@field-end.freeserve.co.uk

Field End Guest House in Leiston offers excellent bed and breakfast accommodation. Open since February 1999 and run with care and consideration by Mrs Pat Wright, it is a comfortable, newly refurbished Edwardian home. There are five attractive and welcoming guest bedrooms (one twin, one double, one family room and two singles). All rooms have every amenity guests have come to expect. The family room is en suite; there are two further bathrooms which can be booked for private use.

Extra touches like books and magazines, flowers and a folder of sample menus from local restaurants and pubs provided in the rooms make this a home from home.

The receipt of a Silver Award by the ETC reflects the high standard of awareness of guests needs and comfort. The guests' private dining room is available throughout the day as a cosy sitting room. It is equipped with games, puzzles, books and a radio. Breakfast is hearty and delicious - differing dietary needs are happily catered for. Central for the many sights and attractions of this part of Suffolk, it makes a perfect base. Open all year. No smoking or pets. Off street parking.

The White Horse Hotel

Station Road, Leiston,
Suffolk IP16 4HD
Tel: 01728 830694 Fax: 01728 833105
e-mail: whihorse@globalnet.co.uk
website: www.whitehorsehotel.co.uk
The White Horse Hotel has been a thriving hub of village life since the 18th century.

This impressive Georgian inn is warm and welcoming. Its name tells guests of its origins, as many hostelries of this era demonstrated their loyalty to the new Hanoverian kings by incorporating the white horse - the family insignia - into their names and signs.

Handsome inside and out, just inside the entrance hall there's a list of the inn's landlords, beginning with a Mr Gildersleeves in 1772. The present proprietor John Doyle, who arrived here in 1984, upholds the inn's longstanding reputation for great ales, food and atmosphere. The attractive and extensive menu features traditional dishes like grills, pies and steaks, and inventive options such as gingered swordfish and turkey balsamico. Meals can be enjoyed in either the bars or the attractive and comfortable dining room - or, when the weather is fine, in the very pleasant garden which includes a spacious safe children's play area. This well-appointed hotel also boasts tastefully decorated and furnished ensuite guest bedrooms, as this village makes a perfect base from which to explore the many delights of the region.

many of the Garrett machines are now on display, including traction engines, a steam-driven tractor and a road roller. There's also a section where the history and workings of steam engines are explained. A small area of the museum recalls the USAAF's 357th fighter group, who flew from an airfield outside Leiston during World War II. One of their number, a Captain Chuck Yeager, was the first man to fly at more than the speed of sound

The Garrett works closed in 1980 and what could have been a disastrous unemployment situation was to some extent alleviated by the nuclear power station at **Sizewell**.

House in the Clouds, Thorpeness

The coast road in the centre of Leiston leads to this establishment, where visitors can take tours, on foot with access to buildings at Sizewell A or by minibus, with guide and videos, round the newer PWR Sizewell B.

ALDRINGHAM
4 miles E of Saxmundham on the B1122

The village church is notable for its superb 15th century font, and the village inn was once a haunt of smugglers. It now helps to refresh the visitors who flock to the **Aldringham Craft Market**, founded in 1958 and extending over three galleries, with a serious selection of arts and crafts, clothes and gifts, pottery, basketry, books and cards.

THORPENESS
6 miles E of Saxmundham on the B1353

Thorpeness is a unique holiday village with mock-Tudor houses and the general look of a series of eccentric film sets. Buying a considerable pocket of land called the Sizewell estate in 1910, the architect, barrister and playwright Glencairn Stuart Ogilvie created what he hoped would be a fashionable resort with cottages, some larger houses and a shallow boating and pleasure lake called the Meare. The 85' water tower,

built to aid in the lake's construction, looked out of place, so Ogilvie disguised it as a house, known ever since as the House in the Clouds, and now available for rent as a holiday home. The neighbouring mill, moved lock, stock and millstones from Aldringham, stopped pumping in 1940 but has been restored and now houses a visitor centre. Every August, in the week following the Aldeburgh Carnival, a regatta is held on the Meare, culminating in a splendid fireworks show. Thorpeness is very much a one-off, not at all typical Suffolk, but with a droll charm that is all its own.

ALDEBURGH
6 miles SE of Saxmundham on the A1094

And so down the coast road to Aldeburgh, another of those coastal towns that once prospered as a port with major fishing and shipbuilding industries. Drake's *Greyhound* and *Pelican* were built at Slaughden, now taken by the sea, and during the 16th century some 1,500 people were engaged in fishing. Both industries declined as shipbuilding moved elsewhere and the fishing boats became too large to be hauled up the shingle. Suffolk's best-known poet, George Crabbe, was born at Slaughden in 1754 and lived in the poor times. He clearly reflected the melancholy of those days when he wrote of his fellow townsmen:

"Here joyless roam a wild amphibious race,
With sullen woe displayed in every face;
Who far from civil arts and social fly,
And scowl at strangers with suspicious eye."

He was equally evocative concerning the sea and the river, and the following lines written about the River Alde could apply to several others in the county:

"With ceaseless motion comes and goes the tide
Flowing, it fills the channel vast and wide;
Then back to sea, with strong majestic sweep
It rolls, in ebb yet terrible and deep;
Here samphire-banks and salt-wort bound the flood
There stakes and seaweed withering on the mud;
And higher up, a ridge of all things base,
Which some strong tide has rolled upon the place."

Crabbe it was who created the character of the solitary fisherman Peter Grimes, later the subject of an opera composed by another Aldeburgh resident, Benjamin Britten.

Aldeburgh's role gradually changed into that of a holiday resort, and the Marquess of Salisbury, visiting early in the 19th century, was one of the first to be attracted by the idea of sea-bathing without the crowds. By the middle of the century the grand houses that had sprung up were joined by smaller residences, the railway arrived, a handsome water tower was put up (1860) and Aldeburgh prospered once more. There were even plans for a pier, and construction started in 1878, but the project proved too difficult or too expensive and was halted, the rusting girders being removed some time later.

One of the town's major benefactors was Newson Garrett, a wealthy businessman who was the first mayor under the charter of the Local Government Act of 1875. This colourful character also developed the **Maltings at Snape**, but is perhaps best remembered through his remarkable daughter Elizabeth, who was the first woman doctor in England (having qualified in Paris at a time when women could not qualify here) and the first woman mayor (of Aldeburgh, in 1908). This lady married the shipowner James Skelton Anderson, who established the golf club in 1884.

If the poet were alive today he would have a rather less crabbed opinion of his fellows, especially at carnival time on a Monday in August, when the town celebrates with a colourful procession of floats and pedestrians, a fireworks display and numerous other social events.

As for the arts, there is, of course, the **Aldeburgh Festival**, started in 1948 by Britten and others; the festival's main venue is Snape Maltings, but many performances take place in Aldeburgh itself.

The maritime connection remains very strong. There has been a lifeboat here since 1851 and down the years many acts of great heroism are recorded. The very modern lifeboat station is one of the town's chief attractions for visitors, and there are regular practice launches from the shingle beach. A handful of fishermen still put out to sea from the beach, selling their catch from their little wooden huts, while down at Slaughden a thriving yacht club is the base for sailing on the Orde and sometimes on the sea. At the very southern tip of the town the Martello tower serves as a reminder of the power of the

Beach, Aldeburgh

Aldeburgh

sea: old pictures show it standing well back from the waves, but now the seaward side of the moat has disappeared and the shingle is constantly being shored up to protect it. Beyond it a long strip of marsh and shingle stretches right down to the mouth of the river at Shingle Street.

Back in town, there are several interesting buildings, notably the **Moot Hall** and the parish Church of **St Peter and St Paul**. Moot Hall is a 16th century timber-framed building that once apparently stood in the centre of town. It hasn't moved, but the sea long ago

took away several houses and streets. Inside the hall is a museum of town history and finds from the nearby Snape burial ship. Britten set the first scene of Peter Grimes in the Moot Hall. A sundial on the south face of the hall proclaims, in Latin, that it only tells the time when the sun shines.

The church, which stands above the town as a very visible landmark for mariners, contains a memorial to George Crabbe and a beautiful stained-glass window, the work of John Piper, depicting three Britten parables for church performance, *Curlew River*, *The Burning Fiery Furnace* and *The Prodigal Son*. Britten is buried in the churchyard, part of which is set aside for the benefit of wildlife.

Aldeburgh has a number of good hotels and fine restaurants specialising in locally-caught fish and shellfish.

FRISTON
3 miles SE of Saxmundham off the A1094

The tallest post mill in England is a prominent sight on the Aldeburgh-Snape road, moved from Woodbridge in 1812, just after its construction. It worked by wind until

THE SCHOOL HOUSE

Friston, Saxmundham, Suffolk IP17 1NP
Tel: 01728 688173
email: oldschool@fristonoldschool.freeserve.co.uk

As its name tells us, **The School House** began life (in the early 1900s) as the village school, and now offers superior bed and breakfast accommodation. When Derek and Nina bought the place it was almost derelict; they spent the next three years refurbishing and renovating this delightful building. Here on

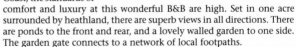

Suffolk's Heritage Coast, the standards of comfort and luxury at this wonderful B&B are high. Set in one acre surrounded by heathland, there are superb views in all directions. There are ponds to the front and rear, and a lovely walled garden to one side. The garden gate connects to a network of local footpaths.

There are three ensuite guest bedrooms (two doubles, one twin). All rooms are comfortably furnished and attractively decorated. The main double has a huge window overlooking the heath and common land. The guests' sitting room is light, airy and welcoming. The breakfast room downstairs occupies a former classroom. Evening meals by arrangement; there are also some fine pubs nearby.

With Aldeburgh (3 miles away), sailing on the River Alde, and excellent 18-hole golf course, tennis courts and fishing from the beach, this charming establishment provides an ideal base for enjoying the many attractions of the area.

1956, then by engine until 1972. St Mary's Church dates from the 11th century.

SNAPE
3 miles S of Saxmundham on the A1094

The "boggy place" has a long and interesting history, and in 1862 an Anglo-Saxon ship was discovered. Since that time regular finds have been made, with some remarkable cases of almost perfect preservation. Snape, like Aldeburgh, benefited from the philanthropy

The Maltings, Snape

of the Garrett family, one of whose members built the primary school and set up the Maltings, centre of the Aldeburgh Music Festival.

The last 30-odd years have seen the development of the **Snape Maltings Riverside Centre**, a group of shops and galleries that offers a unique shopping experience. The site is a complex of restored Victorian granaries and malthouses that is also the setting for the renowned Aldeburgh festival.

The Maltings began their designated task in the 1840s and continued thus until 1965, when the pressure of modern techniques brought them to a halt. There was a real risk of the buildings being demolished but George Gooderham, a local farmer, bought the site to expand his animal feeds business and soon saw the potential of the redundant buildings (his son Jonathan is the current owner of the site, Julia Pipe the Director of Retailing).

The concert hall came first, in 1967, and in 1971 the Craft Shop was established as the first conversion of the old buildings for retailing. Conversion and expansion continue to this day, and in the numerous stylish outlets visitors can buy anything from fudge to country-style clothing, from herbs to household furniture, from silver buttons to top hats. Plants and garden accessories are also sold, and art galleries feature the work of local painters, potters and sculptors. The centre hosts regular painting, craft and decorative art courses, and the latest expansion saw the creation of an impressive country-style department store.

A short distance west of Snape, off the B1069, lies Blaxhall, slightly famous for its growing stone. The **Blaxhall Stone**, which lies in the yard of Stone Farm, is reputed to have grown to its present size (5 tons) from a comparative pebble, the size of a football, when it first came to local attention 100 years ago. Blaxhall getting mixed up with 'Blarney'?

CAMPSEA ASHE
6 miles NE of Woodbridge on the B1078

On towards Wickham Market, the road passes through Campsea Ashe in the parish of Campsey Ashe. The 14th century Church of St John the Baptist has an interesting brass showing a 14th century rector in full priestly garb.

WICKHAM MARKET
5 miles N of Woodbridge off the A12

Places to see in this straggling village are a picturesque watermill by the River Deben and All Saints Church, whose 137' octagonal tower has a little roof to shelter the bell. At Boulge, a couple of miles southwest of Wickham Market, is the grave of Edward Fitzgerald, whose free translation of *The Rubaiyat of Omar Khayyam* is an English masterpiece. Tradition has it that on his grave is a rose bush grown from one on Omar

Khayyam's grave in Iran. More of 'Old Fitz' in Woodbridge.

EASTON
5 miles N of Woodbridge off the B1078

A scenic drive leads to the lovely village of Easton, one of the most colourful, flower-bedecked places in the county. A remarkable sight to the west of the village is the 2-mile-long **crinkle-crankle wall** that surrounds Easton Park. This extraordinary type of wall, also known as a ribbon wall, wavers snake-like in and out and is much stronger than if it were straight. This particular wall, said to be the world's longest, was built by lord of the manor the Earl of Rochford in the 1820s.

Tucked away three miles off the A12 in the beautiful Deben valley, **Easton Park Farm** is one of Suffolk's greatest attractions. 2001 sees its 28th year, and in that time more than a million visitors have passed through the gates to have a great day out and to leave knowing a lot more about the ways of the countryside than when they arrived. It's a marvellous place to bring the family, as the children can have endless fun feeding and making friends with the little animals in Pets Paddock, riding ponies or simply running around in the adventure playground. The showpiece of the park is the Victorian dairy, an ornate octagonal building, while the Dairy Centre is contrastingly modern, with walkways over the top of the stalls and a viewing gallery over the milking parlour.

PARHAM
8 miles N of Woodbridge on the B1116

Parham airfield is now agricultural land, but in the control tower and a hut are memorabilia of the 390th Bomb Group of the USAAF.

UFFORD
4 miles N of Woodbridge off the A12

Pride of place in a village that takes its name from Uffa (or Wuffa), the founder of the leading Anglo-Saxon dynasty, goes to the 13th century **Church of the Assumption**. The font cover, which telescopes from 5 feet to 18 feet in height, is a masterpiece of craftsmanship, its elaborate carving crowned by a pelican. Many 15th century benches have survived but Dowsing smashed the

THE THREE TUNS COACHING INN

Main Road, Pettistree, Woodbridge, Suffolk IP13 0HW
Tel: 01728 747979 Fax: 01728 746244
email: jon@threetuns-coachinginn.co.uk website: www.threetuns-coachinginn.co.uk

John and Brenda Pallett offer all guests an invitation to experience the find food, wines and local ales at **The Three Tuns Coaching Inn**. Whether to enjoy a drink at the bar, a meal in the restaurant or just to relax in the warm and friendly atmosphere of the exceptionally well-appointed lounge with its comfy sofas and, on cooler evenings, welcoming open log fires, all visitors will find something special here. Those wishing to stay for longer can spoil themselves in one of the 11 delightful ensuite guest bedrooms equipped to the highest standards of comfort and quality. The distinctive 3 Tuns sign

topped by an eagle is a relic from the former Lacon Breweries, long since disappeared. Originally along the main road route from Ipswich to Great Yarmouth, this inn was one of several significant stopping-off places enroute. The inn boasts photos of the coaches and charabancs of the 1920s and 1930s which would stop here, and of the drivers and passengers enjoying the inn's hospitality. This tradition of hospitality continues today. Close to the Heritage coast and many of the region's sights and attractions, it makes an ideal place to take a break from shopping or sightseeing, or to use as a base for exploring the area. Disabled facilities.

organ and most of the stained glass – what's there now is mainly Victorian, some of it a copy of 15th century work at All Souls College, Oxford. Ufford is where the Suffolk Punch originated, Crisp's 404 being, in 1768, the progenitor of the breed.

BREDFIELD
3 miles N of Woodbridge off the A12

The funny thing about Bredfield is that sometimes nothing happens, and a plaque on the wall of the village pub actually records nothing at all happening on a day in 1742. On a day in 1809, however, something *did* happen: Edward Fitzgerald was born. Something else happened in 1953: a wrought-iron canopy with a golden crown, made at the village forge, was put on the crossroads pump to celebrate Queen Elizabeth II's coronation.

WOODBRIDGE

Udebyge, Wiebryge, Wodebryge, Wudebrige ... just some of the ways of spelling this splendid old market town since first recorded in 970. As to what it means, it could simply be 'wooden bridge' or 'bridge by the wood', but the most likely and most interesting explanation is that it is derived from Anglo-Saxon words meaning 'Woden's (or Odin's) town'.

Standing at the head of the Deben estuary, it is a place of considerable charm, with a wealth of handsome, often historic buildings and a considerable sense of history, as both a market town and a port.

The shipbuilding and allied industries flourished here as at most towns on the Suffolk coast, and it is recorded that both Edward III, in the 14th century, and Drake in the 16th sailed in Woodbridge ships. There's still plenty of activity on and by the river, though nowadays it is all leisure-

oriented. The town's greatest benefactor was Thomas Seckford, who rebuilt the abbey, paid for the chapel in the north aisle of St Mary's Church and founded the original almshouses in Seckford Street. In 1575 he gave the town the splendid Shire Hall on Market Hill. Originally used as a corn exchange, it now houses the **Suffolk Horse Museum**, which is an exhibition devoted to the Suffolk Punch breed of heavy working horse, the oldest such breed in the world. The history of the breed and its rescue from near-extinction in the 1960s is covered in fascinating detail, and there's a section dealing with the other famous Suffolk breeds – the Red Poll cattle, the Suffolk sheep and the Large Black pigs. Opposite the Shire Hall is **Woodbridge Museum**, a treasure trove of information on the history of the town and its more notable residents, and from here it is a short stroll down the cobbled alleyway to the magnificent parish Church of St Mary, where Seckford was buried in 1587.

Seckford naturally features prominently in the museum, along with the painter Thomas Churchyard, the map-maker Isaac Johnson and the poet Edward Fitzgerald. 'Old Fitz' was something of an eccentric and, for the most part, fairly reclusive. He loved Woodbridge

River Deben, Woodbridge

and particularly the River Deben, where he often sailed in his little boat Scandal.

Woodbridge is lucky enough to have two marvellous mills, both in working order, and both great attractions for the visitor. The **Tide Mill**, on the quayside close to the town centre, dates from the late 18th century (though the site was mentioned 600 years previously) and worked by the power of the tide until 1957. It has been meticulously restored and the waterwheel still turns, fed by a recently created pond which replaced the original huge mill pond when it was turned into a marina. **Buttrum's Mill**, named after the last miller, is a tower mill standing just off the A12 by-pass a mile west of the town centre. She is a marvellous sight, and her six storeys make her the tallest surviving tower mill in Suffolk. There is a ground-floor display of the history and workings of the mill.

Many of the town's streets are traffic-free, so shopping is a real pleasure. If you should catch the Fitzgerald mood and feel like 'a jug of wine and a loaf of bread', Woodbridge can oblige with a good variety of pubs and restaurants.

AROUND WOODBRIDGE

SUTTON HOO
1 mile E of Woodbridge off the B1083

A mile or so east of Woodbridge on the opposite bank of the Deben is the **Sutton Hoo burial site**, a group of a dozen grassy barrows which hit the headlines in 1939. Excavations brought to light the outline of an 80' long Anglo-Saxon ship, filled with one of the greatest hoards of treasure ever discovered in Britain. The priceless find includes gold coins and ornaments, silverware, weapons and armoury, drinking horns and leather cups; it is housed in the British Museum, but there are exhibitions, replicas and plenty of other interest at the site. Research continues, and it is now believed that the ship was the burial place of Raedwald, of the Wuffinga dynasty, who was King of East Anglia from about 610 to 625. Access to the site is on foot from the B1083.

BROMESWELL
3 miles NE of Woodbridge off the B1084

This quiet village occupies a scenic setting. Bromeswell's church has a 12th century archway at its entrance, a 15th century font and an unusual Flemish well. The angels in the hammerbeam roof are plastic replicas of the originals, whose wings were clipped by Cromwell's men.

RENDLESHAM
5 miles NE of Woodbridge on the A1152

The Church of **St Gregory the Great** dates from the 14th century, but there is evidence (not physical, unfortunately) of an earlier Christian presence in the shape of Raedwald's palace.

Rendlesham Forest, part of the Forest of Aldewood, was ravaged by the great hurricane of October 1987 but seven years before that, on Christmas night 1980, another visitation had occurred. Security guards at RAF Woodbridge, at that time a front line NATO base, spotted strange lights in the forest and went to investigate. They came upon a 9 foot high triangular object with a series of lights around it. As they approached, it did what all good UFOs do and flew off before it could be photographed. The next day the guards returned to the spot where it had landed and found three depressions in the ground. The UFO was apparently sighted again two days later and security in the area was tightened. No explanation has ever been forthcoming about the incident, but interest in it continues and from time to time guided walks to the landing site are arranged.

BUTLEY
5 miles NE of Woodbridge on the B1084

At the northern edge of Rendlesham Forest, the village has a splendid 14th century gatehouse, all that remains of **Butley Priory**, an Augustinian priory founded by Ranulf de Glanville in 1171. The gatehouse is, by itself, a fairly imposing building, with some interesting flintwork on the north facade (1320) and baronial carvings. Butley still has a working mill, remarkable for its fine Regency porch, and the parish church is Norman, with a 14th century tower.

There are some splendid country walks here, notably by **Staverton Thicks**, which has a deer park and woods of oak and holly. The oldest trees date back more than 400 years. Butley Clumps is an avenue of beech trees planted in clumps of four, with a pine tree at the centre of each clump – the technical term for such an arrangement is a *quincunx*. Butley was long renowned for its oysters, and the beds have recently been revived.

CHILLESFORD
6 miles E of Woodbridge on the B1084

Brick was once big business here, and while digging for clay the locals made many finds, including hundreds of varieties of mollusc and the skeleton of an enormous whale. Chillesford supplies some of the clay for Aldeburgh brickworks.

ORFORD
12 miles E of Woodbridge at the end of the B1084

Without doubt one of the most charming and interesting of all the places in Suffolk, with something to please everyone. The ruins of one of the most important **castles** in medieval England are a most impressive sight, even though the keep is all that remains of the original building commissioned by Henry II in 1165. The walls of the keep are 10 feet deep, and behind them are many rooms and passages in a remarkable state of preservation. A climb up the spiral staircase to the top provides splendid views.

St Bartholomew's Church was built at the same time, though the present church dates from the 14th century. A wonderful sight at night when floodlit, the church is regularly used for the performance of concerts and recitals, and many of Benjamin Britten's works were first heard here. At the east end lie the still-splendid Norman remains, all that is left of the original chancel.

These two grand buildings indicate that Orford was a very important town at one time. Indeed it was once a thriving port, but the steadily growing shingle bank of Orford Ness gradually cut it off from the sea, and down the years its appeal has changed. The sea may have gone, but the river is still there, and in summer the quayside is alive with yachts and pleasure craft. On the other side of the river is **Orford Ness**, the largest vegetated shingle spit in England which is home to a variety of rare flora and fauna. The lighthouse marks the most easterly point in Britain (jointly with Lowestoft).

Access to the spit, which is in the hands of the National Trust, is by ferry from Orford quay only. For many years the ness was out of bounds to the public, being used for various military purposes, including pre-war radar research under Sir Robert Watson-Watt. Boat trips also leave Orford quay for the RSPB reserve of **Havergate Island**, haunt of avocet and tern (the former returned in 1947 after being long absent).

Back in the market square are a handsome town hall, two pubs with a fair quota of smuggling tales, a well-loved restaurant serving Butley oysters and a smokehouse where kippers, salmon, trout, ham, sausages, chicken and even garlic are smoked over Suffolk oak.

Orford

SHOTTISHAM
2 miles SE of Woodbridge on the B1083

Apart from The Sorrel Horse Inn (see panel below) Shottisham has an alternative claim to Hoxne as the place of Edmund's martydom.

BAWDSEY
7 miles SE of Woodbridge on the B1083

The B1083 runs from Woodbridge through farming country and several villages (Sutton, Shottisham, Alderton) to Bawdsey, beyond which lie the mouth of the River Deben, the end of the Sussex Coastal Path, and the ferry to Felixstowe. The late-Victorian Bawdsey Manor was taken over by the Government and became the centre for radar development when Orford Ness was deemed unsuitable. By the beginning of World War II there were two dozen secret radar stations in Britain and radar HQ moved to Dundee from Bawdsey. The manor is now a leisure centre.

RAMSHOLT
7 miles SE of Woodbridge off the B1083

Ramsholt is a tiny community on the north bank of the Deben a little way up from Bawdsey. The pub is a popular port of call for yachtsmen, and half a mile from the quay, in quiet isolation, stands the Church of All Saints with its round tower. Road access to Ramsholt is from the B1083 just south of Shottisham.

HOLLESLEY
5 miles SE of Woodbridge off the B1083

The Deben and the Ore turn this part of Suffolk almost into a peninsula and on the seaward side lie Hollesley and Shingle Street. The latter stands up on a shingle bank at the entrance to the Ore and comprises a row of little houses, a coastguard cottage and a Martello tower. Its very isolation is an attraction, and the sight of the sea rushing into and out of the river is worth the journey.

Brendan Behan did not enjoy his visit. Brought here on a swimming outing from the Borstal at Hollesley, he declared that the waves had "no limit but the rim of the world". Looking out to the bleak North Sea, it is easy to see what he meant.

THE SORREL HORSE INN

Hollesley Road, Shottisham,
Woodbridge, Suffolk IP12 3HD
Tel: 01394 411617

Next door to Shottisham's very picturesque St Margaret's Church, **The Sorrell Horse Inn** was built in the 14th century, as its fine thatched roof and other original features attest. The low ceilings, wood floors and intimate decor enhance the cosiness of the ambience. This historic building was once a smugglers' inn and is reputed to have been associated with the smuggling fraternity, in particular one Margaret Catchpole, who was the first woman to be transported to Australia - her crime having been the theft of a horse. The bar splits the interior into the 'public' bar and lounge with its wood-burning cast iron stove.

Ken and Janet give all their guests a warm welcome. Janet does all the cooking herself - guests can be assured of excellent food. The inn is particularly renowned for its winter roasts. The emphasis is always on the freshest and tastiest ingredients, used to create an excellent range of traditional and more innovative dishes, freshly and individually prepared. There are always at least three different real ales served direct from the barrel behind the bar. In an area ideal for walking, cycling, or just taking in the superb scenery, this is a relaxing haven in which to enjoy great food, real ales and the welcoming atmosphere. Pub hours: midday - 2.30 and 7-11; all day in summer at weekends. No food Monday or Tuesday evenings. Booking required Friday-Sunday.

LOWESTOFT

The most easterly town in Britain had its heyday as a major fishing port during the late 19th and early 20th centuries, when it was a mighty rival to Great Yarmouth in the herring fishing industry. That industry has been in major decline since World War I but Lowestoft is still a fishing port, and the trawlers still chug into the harbour in the early morning with the catches of the night. Guided tours of the **fish market** and the **harbour** are available.

Fishing Boats, Lowestoft

Lowestoft is also a popular holiday resort, the star attraction being the lovely South Beach with its golden sands, safe swimming, two piers and all the expected seaside amusement and entertainment. **Claremont Pier**, over 600 feet in length, was built in 1902, ready to receive day trippers on the famous Belle steamers. The buildings in this part of town were developed in mid-Victorian times by the company of Sir Samuel Morton Peto, also responsible for Nelson's Column, the statues in the Houses of Parliament, the Reform Club and Somerleyton Hall, about which more anon.

At the heart of the town is the old harbour, home to the **Royal Norfolk & Suffolk Yacht Club** and the **lifeboat station**. Further upriver is the commercial part of the port, used chiefly by ships carrying grain and timber. The history of Lowestoft is naturally tied up with the sea, and much of that history is recorded in fascinating detail in the

Lowestoft & East Suffolk Maritime Museum with model boats, fishing gear, a lifeboat cockpit, paintings and shipwrights' tools. The setting is a flint-built fisherman's cottage in Sparrow's Nest Gardens. The **Royal Naval Patrol Museum** nearby remembers the minesweeping service in models, photographs, documents and uniforms.

Lowestoft had England's first lighthouse, installed in 1609. The present one dates from 1874. Also in Sparrow's Nest Gardens is the **War Memorial Museum**, dedicated to those who served during the Second World War. There's a photographic collection of the bombing of the town, aircraft models and a chapel of remembrance.

St Margaret's Church, notable for its decorated ceiling and copper-covered spire, is a memorial to seafarers, and the north aisle has panels recording the names of fishermen lost at sea from 1865 to 1923.

Lowestoft has some interesting literary and musical connections. The Elizabethan playwright, poet and pamphleteer, Thomas Nash(e), was born here in 1567. His last work, *Lenten Stuffe*, was a eulogy to the herring trade and specifically Great Yarmouth. Joseph Conrad (Jozef Teodor Konrad Korzeniowski), working as a deckhand on a British freighter bound for Constantinople, jumped ship here in 1878, speaking only a few words of the language in which he was to become one of the modern masters. Benjamin Britten, the greatest English composer of the 20th century, is associated with several places in Suffolk, but Lowestoft has the earliest claim, for it is here that he was born in 1913.

Just north of town with access from the B1385, **Pleasurewood Hill** is the largest theme park in East Anglia.

Oulton Broad, on the western edge of Lowestoft, is a major centre of amusement afloat, with boats for hire and cruises on the Waveney. It also attracts visitors to Nicholas Everitt Park to look around **Lowestoft Museum**, housed in historic Broad House. Opened by the Queen and Prince Philip in 1985, the museum displays archaeological finds from local sites, some now lost to the sea, costumes, toys, domestic bygones, and a fine collection of Lowestoft porcelain. (The porcelain industry lasted from about 1760 to 1800, using clay from the nearby Gunton Hall Estate. The soft-paste ware, resembling Bow porcelain, was usually decorated in white and blue.)

Another museum, the **ISCA Maritime Museum**, has a unique collection of ethnic working boats, including coracles, gondolas, junks, dhows, sampans and proas.

AROUND LOWESTOFT

CARLTON COLVILLE
3 miles SW of Lowestoft on the B1384

Many an old bus-spotter has shed a nostalgic tear at the **East Anglia Transport Museum**, where children and ex-children climb aboard to enjoy rides on buses, trams and trolleybuses (one of the resident trolleybuses was built at the Garrett works in Leiston). The East Suffolk narrow-gauge railway winds its

way around the site, and there's a 1930s' street with all the authentic accessories, plus lorries, vans and steamrollers. If you think it's far too long since you saw a tram or trolleybus, this is the place for you.

Also in Carlton Colville is the 15th century Church of St Peter, which incorporated parts of other buildings when restored in the 19th century.

Carlton Marshes is Oulton Broad's nature reserve with grazing marsh and fen, reached by the Waveney Way footpath.

BLUNDESTON
4 miles N of Lowestoft off the A12

Known chiefly as the village used by Charles Dickens as the birthplace of that writer's 'favourite child', David Copperfield. The morning light shining on the sundial of the church – which has the tallest, narrowest Saxon round tower of any in East Anglia – greeted young David as he looked out of his bedroom window in the nearby Rookery. He said of the churchyard: "There is nothing half so green that I know anywhere, as the grass of that churchyard, nothing half so shady as its

EARLY DAWN GARDEN CENTRE

Rushmere Road, Carlton Colville,
Lowestoft, Suffolk NR33 8HA
Tel: 01502 476340 Fax: 01502 476887

The **Early Dawn Garden Centre** is a paradise for gardeners. Just outside the village of Carlton Colville on the road to Mutford, it's run by Dawn Gissing, who put down roots here 18 years ago, together with her business partner Karen Gapper. Visitors are greeted by two grandiose lions adorning the entrance. A leisurely stroll around the centre reveals plenty of interesting and useful items for sale in addition to almost every sort of flower and plant

you can think of, including ornamental fruit trees and dried flowers. There are pumps for rockery pools, garden tools and fencing, Grecian urns and terracotta pots, hanging baskets, gazebos, sundials with brass pedestals, gargoyles, stone pagoda lanterns, bird houses, Malaysian pots, garden furniture and barbecues. There's also a section devoted to wild birds. All the staff are friendly and helpful, able to offer advice and encouragement to any gardener, from the novice to the long-established expert. Open Monday to Saturday 8-5.30; Sundays 10.30-4.30

PARKHILL HOTEL

Park Hill, Oulton, Lowestoft, Suffolk NR32 5DQ
Tel: 01502 730322 Fax: 01502 731695
email: mail@parkhillhotel.co.uk
website: www.parkhillhotel.co.uk

One mile from the village of Corton and just over two miles from Lowestoft, **Parkhill Hotel** is a haven of peace and rural splendour with a well-deserved reputation for quality and service. Set in nine acres of beautiful rolling gardens, which includes a large swimming pool, this elegant hotel dates back in parts to the 18th century. Its great character and warmth have made it popular with both holiday and business visitors to the area. There are 20 ensuite guest

bedrooms in this impressive establishment, some of them dedicated no smoking rooms. A number are elegant suites with a lounge area and writing facilities. The beautifully appointed restaurant serves a good range of delicious starters, main courses and chef's specials, such as Dover soul, English fillet steak and breast of duckling. The tempting desserts are worth saving room for, and include choux buns filled with cream, lemon tart or hot pudding of the day. This family business has been run by Ruth and David Truman for 20 years. Guests are assured a warm welcome and only the highest standard of courtesy and gracious hospitality.

HOLLYBANK

High Street, Hopton, Suffolk IP22 2QX
Tel/Fax: 01953 688147

email: hollybankbandb@talk21.com

Hollybank is a delightful home offering superior bed and breakfast accommodation. A warm welcome awaits all guests at this former public house, first built in the 18th century - the original pub collapsed during renovation and was replaced by the present building in 1960. Each of the three guest bedrooms (two doubles, one twin; the larger double also serves as a family room) is well equipped and very comfortable. The guests' lounge is also handsomely appointed, cosy and welcoming.

The full Suffolk breakfast is delicious and hearty. The former bowling green clubhouse is now an annexe housing a sauna, which guests may use for a small charge. Owners Sue and Tony Tomlinson are happy to pick guests up from the local railway station. Tony was in the RAF, and a strong aviation

theme can be found in the decor and mementos about the house.

This fine B&B straddling the border of Suffolk and Norfolk is ideally placed to serve as a base from which to explore the sights and attractions of both counties. There are also several good pubs and restaurants in the locality.

The village of Hopton itself is mentioned in the Domesday Book and is within a conservation area. The parish church has a unique hammer beam roof with painted figures.

trees; nothing half so quiet as its tombstones."

Blundeston has another notable literary connection: Blundeston Lodge was once the home of Norton Nichols, whose friend the poet Gray is reputed to have taken his inspiration for *An Elegy Written in a Country Church Yard* while staying there.

LOUND
5 miles N of Lowestoft off the A12

Lound's parish Church of **St John the Baptist**, in the very north of the county, is sometimes known as the 'golden church'. This epithet is the result of the handiwork of designer/architect Sir Ninian Comper, seen most memorably in the gilded organ-case with two trumpeting angels, the font cover and the rood screen. The last is a very elaborate affair, with several heraldic arms displayed. The surprise package here is the modern St Christopher mural on the north wall. It includes Sir Ninian at the wheel of his Rolls Royce, and, in 1976, an aeroplane was added!

SOMERLEYTON
5 miles NW of Lowestoft on the B1074

Somerleyton Hall, one of the grandest and most distinctive of stately homes, is a splendid Victorian mansion built in Anglo-Italian style by Samuel Morton Peto. Its lavish architectural features are complemented by fine state rooms, magnificent wood carvings (some by Grinling Gibbons) and notable paintings. The grounds include a renowned yew-hedge maze, where people have been going round in circles since 1846, walled and sunken gardens and a 300-foot pergola. There's also a sweet little miniature railway, and **Fritton Lake Countryworld**, part of the Somerleyton Estate, is a 10-minute drive away. The Hall is open to the public on most days in summer.

Samuel Morton Peto learned his skills as a civil engineer and businessman from his uncle and was still a young man when he put the Reform Club and Nelson's Column into his cv. The Somerleyton Hall he bought in 1843 was a Tudor and Jacobean mansion. He and his architect virtually rebuilt the place, and also built Somerleyton village, a cluster

CHURCH FARM

Corton, Lowestoft, Suffolk NR32 5HX
Tel: 01502 730359 Fax: 01502 733426

Church Farm is an elegant and welcoming 19th-century farmhouse situated on the rural Suffolk coastline and offering superior bed and breakfast accommodation. This working arable farm offers a very high standard of comfort and hospitality. Formerly part of the Colmans Mustard estates, this no-smoking establishment is owned and run by Elisabeth Edwards, who maintains exceptional standards throughout this beautifully appointed home. Handy for beach and cliff walks, exploring the Heritage Coastline, the ancient village church of St Bartholomew's and Lowestoft, here at the most easterly point in the UK guests are still within easy reach of the many sights and attractions of Suffolk, Norfolk and further afield.

There are three comfortable and tastefully furnished ensuite double guest bedrooms. All three are stylishly decorated to fit the period of the house. Guests are welcome to enjoy the extensive and beautifully laid out gardens for afternoon tea and evening relaxation in fine weather. Breakfast is served in the gracious dining room. Church Farm is renowned for its hearty English breakfasts; special dietary requirements are happily catered for. English Tourist Board 5 Diamonds.

Somerleyton Hall and Gardens

pump, whose job was to assist in draining the marshes. This example was built in 1820 and worked regularly until the 1950s. It contains a fireplace and a wooden bench, providing a modicum of comfort for a millman on a cold night shift. To arrange a visit call 01473 583352.

KESSINGLAND
3 miles S of Lowestoft off the A12

A small resort with a big history. Palaeolithic and Neolithic remains have come to light, and traces of an ancient forest have been unearthed on the sea bed. At the time of William the Conqueror, Kessingland prospered with its herring industry and was a major fishing port rivalled only by Dunwich. The estuary gradually silted up, sealing off the river with a shingle bank and cutting off the major source of wealth. The tower of the Church of St Edmund reaches up almost 100 feet – not unusual on the coast, where it provides a conspicuous landmark for sailors and fishermen. Most of the maritime trappings have disappeared: the lighthouse on the cliffs was scrapped 100 years ago, the lifeboat lasted until 1936 (having saved 144 lives), and there were several coastguard stations, one of them bought as a holiday home by the writer Rider Haggard.

The major tourist attraction is the **Suffolk Wildlife Park**, 100 acres of coastal parkland that are home to a wide range of wild animals, from aardvarks to zebras by way of bats, flamingos, giraffes, meerkats and sitatunga. The flamingos have their own enclosure. The park has been home to several film stars, including two chimps who appeared in *Gorillas in the Mist* and Joey, leading player in the PG Tips TV commercials. Burmese pythons are used for snake-handling sessions – an attraction that's definitely not for everyone!

COVEHITHE
7 miles S of Lowestoft off the A12

Leave the A12 at Wrentham and head for the tiny coastal village of Covehithe which is remarkable for its 'church within a church'.

of thatched redbrick cottages. Nor was this the limit of Peto's achievements, for he ran a company which laid railways all over the world and was a Liberal MP, first for Norwich, then for Finsbury and finally for Bristol. His company foundered in 1863 and Somerleyton Hall was sold to Sir Francis Crossley, one of three brothers who made a fortune in mass-producing carpets. Crossley's son became Baron Somerleyton in 1916, and the Baron's grandson is the present Lord Somerleyton.

HERRINGFLEET
5 miles NW of Lowestoft on the B1074

Standing above the River Waveney, the parish Church of St Margaret is a charming sight with its Saxon round tower, thatched roof and lovely glass. **Herringfleet Windmill** is a beautiful black-tarred smock mill in working order, the last survivor of the Broadland wind

LIVINGSTONE'S CARVERY RESTAURANT AND FREE HOUSE

White's Lane, Kessingland, Suffolk NR33 7TF
Tel: 01502 741491

Just south of Lowestoft in the village of Kessingland, **Livingstone's Carvery Restaurant and Free House** is a spacious and modern establishment tastefully converted from an impressive Suffolk farmhouse. The decor and furnishings are "Colonial", hearkening back to gracious Victorian buildings on the African plains - hence the name Livingstone's after the distinguished 19th-century physician. The restaurant walls are adorned with artistry depicting waterfall and a jungle encampment complete with tents, canoes and other artefacts. The bar area is extensive and very attractive. A range of hearty traditional dishes can be accompanied by a good choice of beers, wines, spirits and soft drinks.

The African theme at this superb eatery is extended in the adjacent Suffolk Wildlife Park and The African Adventure. A wonderful place set in 100 acres of stunning parkland where visitors can experience a walking safari, encountering hyaenas, bat-eared and Fennec foxes, giraffes, lions, lemurs, cheetah and pythons along the way. The Safari Roadtrain provides guided tours the length and breadth of this impressive attraction. Visitors should reserve a whole day to explore all the sights and sounds of this African adventure, which includes three explorer trails through woods, lakeland and over grassy plains.

The massive Church of **St Andrew**, partly funded by the Benedictine monks at Cluniac, was left to decline after being laid waste by Dowsing's men. The villagers could not afford a replacement on the same grand scale so in 1672 it was decided to remove the roof and sell off some of the material. From what was left a small new church was built within the old walls. The original tower still stands, spared by Cromwell for use as a landmark for sailors.

SOUTHWOLD
15 miles S of Lowestoft on the A1095

A town full of character, and full of interest for the holidaymaker and for the historian. Though one of the most popular resorts on the east coast, Southwold has very little of the kiss-me-quick commercialism that spoils so many seaside towns. It's practically an island, bounded by creeks and marshes, the River Blyth and the North Sea, and has managed to retain the atmosphere of the last century. There are some attractive buildings, from pink-washed cottages to elegant Georgian town houses, many of them ranged around a series of greens which were left undeveloped to act as firebreaks after much of the town was lost in the great fire of 1659.

In a seaside town whose buildings present a wide variety of styles, shapes and sizes, William Denny's **Buckenham House** is among the most elegant and interesting. On the face of it a classic Georgian town house, it's actually much older, dating probably from the middle of the 16th century. Richard Buckenham, a wealthy Tudor merchant, was the man who had it built and it was truly impressive in size, as can be deduced from the dimensions of the cellar (now the Coffee House). Many fine features survive, including moulded cornices, carefully restored sash windows, Tudor brickwork and heavy timbers in the ceilings.

The town, which was granted its charter by Henry VII in 1489, once prospered, like many of its neighbours, through herring fishing, and the few remaining fishermen share the harbour on the River Blyth with pleasure craft. Also adding to the period atmosphere is the pier, though as a result of storm damage this is much shorter than in the days when steamers from London called in on their way up the east coast.

Sole Bay Inn and Lighthouse, Southwold

There are also bathing huts, and a brilliant white lighthouse that's approaching its 100th birthday. It stands 100 feet tall and its light can be seen 17 miles out to sea. Beneath the lighthouse stands a little Victorian pub, the Sole Bay Inn, whose name recalls a battle fought off Southwold in 1672 between the British and French fleets and the Dutch. This was an episode in the Third Anglo-Dutch War, but why Sole Bay? Because the Duke of York, Lord High Admiral of England and later to be crowned James II, had taken Sutherland House in Southwold as his headquarters and it was from there that his fleet (along with the French) set sail. A distinguished victim of the battle was Edward Montagu, 1st Earl of Sandwich, great-grandfather of the man whose gambling mania did not allow him time for a formal meal. By inserting slices of meat between slices of bread, the 4th Earl ensured that his name would live on.

The Sole Bay Inn is one of several owned by the local brewery Adnams. One of the best known is the Lord Nelson, where traces can be seen of a smugglers' passageway leading to the cliffs. Where there were smugglers there are usually ghosts, and here it's a man in a frock coat who disappears into the cliff face. Adnams still use horse-drawn drays for local beer deliveries.

Southwold's maritime past is recorded in the **museum** set in a Dutch-style cottage in Victoria Street. Open daily in the summer, it records the famous battle and also local archaeology, geology and natural history, and the history of the Southwold railway. The Southwold Sailors' Reading Room contains pictures, ship models and other items, and at Gun Hill the Lifeboat Museum has a small collection of RNLI-related material with particular reference to Southwold. The main attraction at Gun Hill is a set of six 18-pounder guns, captured in 1746 at the Battle of Culloden and presented to the town (hitherto more or less undefended) by the Duke of Cumberland.

No visitor to Southwold should leave without spending some time in the splendid Church of **St Edmund King and Martyr**, which emerged relatively unscathed from the ravages of the Commonwealth. The lovely painted roof and wide screen are the chief glories, but the slim-stemmed 15th century pulpit and the Elizabethan Holy Table must also be seen. Outside the church, a splendid Jack o'the Clock – a little wooden man in War of the Roses armour – strikes his bell on the hour.

WANGFORD
2 miles NW of Southwold off the A12

There's some great walking in the country around Southwold, both along the coast and inland. At Wangford, a mile or so inland, **Henham Walks** are waymarked paths through Repton Park, lake and woods. A splendid place for a ramble or a picnic, or to see the wildlife, rare-breed sheep and Highland cattle. Also at Wangford is the Perpendicular Church of St Peter and St Paul, built on the site of a Benedictine priory. Even closer to Southwold is Reydon Wood Nature Reserve.

BLYTHBURGH
2 miles SW of Southwold, A1095 then A12

Blythburgh's Church of **Holy Trinity** is one of the wonders of Suffolk, a stirring sight as it rises from the reed beds, visible for miles around and floodlit at night to spectacular effect. This 'Cathedral of the Marshes' reflects the days when Blythburgh was a prosperous port with a bustling quayside wool trade. With the silting up of the river trade rapidly fell off and the church fell into decay. In 1577 the steeple of the 14th century tower was struck by lightning in a severe storm; it fell into the nave, shattering the font and taking two lives. The scorch marks visible to this day on the north door are said to be the claw marks of the Devil in the guise of hellhound Black Shuck, left as he sped towards Bungay to terrify the congregation of St Mary's.

Disaster struck again in 1644, when Dowsing and his men smashed windows, ornaments and statues, blasted the wooden angels in the roof with hundreds of bullets and used the nave as a stable, with tethering rings screwed into the pillars of the nave. Luckily, the bench-end carvings escaped the desecration, not being labelled idolatrous. These depict the Labours of the Months, and the Seven Deadly Sins. Blythburgh also has a Jack o'the Clock, a brother of the figure at Southwold, and the priest's chamber over the south porch has been lovingly restored complete with an altar made with wood from *HMS Victory*. The angels may have survived, but the font was defaced to remove the signs of the sacraments.

A mile south, at the junction of the A12 and the Walberswick road, **Toby's Walks** is an ideal place for a picnic and, like so many places in Suffolk, has its own ghost story. This concerns Tobias Gill, a dragoon drummer who murdered a local girl and was hanged here after a trial at Ipswich. His ghost is said to haunt the heath, but this should not deter picnickers.

The Norman Gwatkin Nature Reserve is an area of marsh and fen with two hides, walkways and a willow coppice.

WENHASTON
5 miles W of Southwold off the A12

The Church of **St Peter** cannot compete as a spectacle with Blythburgh's Holy Trinity, but is well worth a detour. Saxon stones are embedded in its walls but the most remarkable feature is the doom (Last Judgement), said to have been painted around 1500 by a monk from Blythburgh.

THE OLD VICARAGE

Wenhaston, Halesworth,
Suffolk IP19 9EG
Tel: 01502 478339
Fax: 01502 478068
e-mail: Theycock@aol.com

Hidden away behind the church in the charming village of Wenhaston, **The Old Vicarage** offers a taste of luxury and very comfortable bed and breakfast accommodation. Built in 1600, the impressive Georgian entrance was added in 1800. Set in five acres of lawns dotted with lovely trees, it is a true haven of rest and relaxation. The peaceful solitude is broken only by the sound of birdsong and the church bells.

The interior boasts chandeliers, heavy drapery and distinguished paintings. Each of the three guest bedrooms is handsomely decorated and furnished; each has a private bath. The Chinese Room is a twin . One double bedroom has a beautiful four-poster bed and elegant furnishings. The other double bedroom has a stylish canopied bed. The histories of the house and the present owner, Mrs Heycock, are interesting ones: the famous painter Arthur Becker (1865-1928), lived here for many years, and one of Mrs Heycock's relations was Betty Kirby-Green, a renowned aviator rivalling Amy Johnston. The sights and attractions of the Heritage Coastline, Southwold, Minsmere, Walberswick and further afield in Suffolk and Norfolk await exploration. Smoking permitted only in the kitchen. No children under 12. No pets.

The River Blithe, Walberswick

WALBERSWICK
1 miles SW of Southwold on the B1387

The story is familiar: flourishing fishing port; grand church; changing of the coastline due to erosion and silting; decline of fishing and trading; no money to maintain the church; church falls into disrepair. Towards the end of the 16th century, a smaller church was built within the original St Andrew's, by then in ruins through neglect. The situation in Walberswick had been exacerbated by the seizing of church lands and revenues by the king, and by a severe fire.

Fishing hardly exists today, and boating in Walberswick is almost entirely a weekend and holiday activity. The tiny 'church within a church' is still in use, its churchyard a nature reserve. South of the village is the bird sanctuary of **Walberswick & Westleton heaths**. Walberswick has, for two centuries, been a magnet for painters, the religious ruins, the beach and the sea being favourite subject for visiting artists. The tradition continues unabated, and many academics have made their homes here.

HALESWORTH
16 miles SW of Lowestoft on the A144

Granted a market in 1222, Halesworth reached the peak of its trading importance when the River Blyth was made navigable as far as the town in 1756. A stroll around the streets reveals several buildings of architectural interest. The Market Place has a handsome Elizabethan timber-framed house, but the chief attraction for the visitor is the **Halesworth and District Museum** at Steeple End, a conversion of a row of 17th century almshouses. Local geology and archaeology are the main interests, with various fossils and flints on display, and there's a fascinating account of the Halesworth witchcraft trials of 1645. An art gallery is in the same building.

BRAMFIELD
3 miles S of Halesworth on the A144

The massive Norman round tower of **St Andrew's** Church is separate from the main building and was built as a defensive structure, with walls over 3 feet thick. Dowsing ran riot here in 1643, destroyed 24 superstitious pictures, one crucifix, a picture of Christ and 12 angels on the roof. The most important monument is one to Sir Arthur Coke, sometime Lord Chief Justice, who died in 1629, and his wife Elizabeth. Arthur is kneeling, resplendent in full armour, while Elizabeth is lying on her bed with a baby in her arms. This monument is the work of Nicholas Stone, the most important English mason and sculptor of his day. The Cokes at one time occupied Bramfield Hall, and another family, in residence for 300 years, were the Rabetts, whose coat of arms in the church punningly depicts rabbits on its shield.

BUNGAY
9 miles N of Halesworth on the A144

An ancient fortress town on the River Waveney. The river played an important part in the town's fortunes until well into the 18th century, with barges laden with coal, corn, malt and timber plying the route to the coast. The river is no longer navigable above Geldeston but is a great attraction for anglers and yachtsmen.

Bungay is best known for its **castle**, built in its original form by Hugh Bigod, 1st Earl of Norfolk, as a rival to Henry II's castle at Orford. In 1173 Hugh took the side of the rebellious sons of Henry, but this insurrection ended with the surrender of the castle to the king. Hugh was killed not long after this episode while on the Third Crusade; his son Roger inherited the title and the castle, but it was another Roger Bigod who came to Bungay in 1294 and built the round tower and mighty outer walls which stand today.

To the north of the castle are Bungay's two surviving churches of note (the Domesday Book recorded five). The Saxon round tower of **Holy Trinity** Church is the oldest complete structure in the town, and a brass plate on the door commemorates the church's narrow escape from the fire of 1688 that destroyed much of the town (similar disasters overtook many other towns with close-set timber-and-thatch buildings). The Church of **St Mary** - now redundant - was not so lucky, being more or less completely gutted. The tower survives to dominate the townscape, and points of interest in the church itself include a woodcarving of the Resurrection presented by Rider Haggard, and a monument to General Robert Kelso, who fought in the American War of Independence.

A century before the fire the church received a visit, during a storm, from the devilish Black Shuck, a retriever-like hound who, hot from causing severe damage at Blythburgh, raced down the nave and killed two worshippers. A weather vane in the market place puts the legend into verse:

"All down the church in midst of fire
The Hellish Monster Flew
And Passing onwards to the Quire
He many people slew."

Nearby is the famous octagonal **Butter Cross**, rebuilt after the Great Fire and topped by Justice with her scales and sword. This building was once used as a prison, with a dungeon below.

EARSHAM
1 mile SW of Bungay off the A143

All Saints Church and Earsham Hall are well worth a visit, but what brings most people here is the **Otter Trust**, on the banks of the Waveney, where the largest collection of otters in natural enclosures are bred for re-introduction into the wild. Waterfowl, herons are deer are also kept here, and there are some lovely walks by the lakes and river.

THE QUEEN'S HEAD

Station Road, Earsham,
Bungay, Suffolk NR35 2TS
Tel: 01986 892623

Very much at the centre of village life, **The Queen's Head** is a traditional Free House boasting real ale and real food. Other pubs in the nearby village of Denton and Arlborough have recently closed, so this fine pub attracts villagers from these areas as well, being noted for its exceptional ales from micro breweries across the nation. The interior has several original features like the low ceilings and open fires. The atmosphere is friendly and cosy.

The separate dining area has high ceilings, a wood-burning stove and old wooden high-backed benches. The piano in the small main bar comes in for regular use to accompany sing-songs. Outside, there's a long fenced garden area to enjoy when the weather is fine, complete with safe playing area for children. This characterful pub is very welcoming, and the service and hospitality are first-rate. In addition to the fine range of ales, there's a good variety of lagers, wines, spirits and soft drinks. The menu offers home-cooked and freshly prepared favourites such as steaks and scampi, together with imaginative dishes such as green Thai chicken curry and lime-crusted haddock. The tempting puddings are well worth saving room for.

EARSHAM PARK FARM

Harleston Road, Earsham, Bungay, Suffolk NR35 2AQ
Tel/Fax: 01986 892180
email: watchorn_s@freenet.co.uk

Earsham Park Farm is a most hospitable and friendly country residence offering bed and breakfast accommodation. Owner Bobbie Watchorn takes an early morning ride and then comes back to prepare a delicious breakfast of home-made sausages and other tempting delicacies for her guests. The atmosphere is relaxed and informal, the setting exquisitely appointed. Each of the three spacious and light ensuite guest bedrooms (two doubles, one twin) has its own name, all are truly lovely and elegant, with superb decor and furnishings. Each has a cast iron fireplace; one boasts a beautiful four-

poster bed. Touches like the stained glass windows and potted palms add to the luxurious feel of this superior establishment. The Earsham Park estate dates back to 1648 and was originally part of the Duke of Norfolk's deer park - Bobbie has an original map showing the layout 1648-1670. It is now a 600-acre working farm with thriving wildlife and lovely walks. Rebuilt after a fire in the 1860s, the bell tower and cellar remain of the original building. The dining room with its polished and stencilled floor overlooks a panorama of country life. Open all year round. No smoking.

SIR ALFRED MUNNINGS

Studio Corner, Mendham, Harleston,Suffolk IP20 0NH
Tel/Fax: 01379 852358

Nestling in the heart of the Waveney Valley on the Norfolk/Suffolk border, **Sir Alfred Munnings** is an excellent public house and restaurant dating back to the 16th century. Outstanding views of the surrounding woodlands and fields are among the many delights of the area, as well as some first-class coarse fishing lakes, superb golf courses and windsurfing and sailing on the nearby Weybread lakes. Ramblers and walkers will also find much to enjoy.

And after all this activity? What better than a relaxing drink or meal amid supremely comfortable surroundings. The pub is named after the famous artist, son of a local miller - his full history is proudly displayed on a wall of the pub. The excellent menu boasts a range of tempting dishes such as

honey and mustard roast rack of lamb, pan-fired gammon steak with fresh pineapple, butterfly chicken breast with lemon and tarragon sauce, fillet of beef stroganoff, "surf and turf" (six ounce rump steak with butterfly king prawns) and creamy mushroom and Stilton pancakes. All food is cooked to order, home prepared and expertly presented. Real ales, a very good wine list and a variety of lagers and spirits complement the fine selection of dishes.

FLIXTON
2 miles SW of Bungay on the B1062

Javelin, Meteor, Sea Vixen, Westland Whirlwind: names that evoke earlier days of flying, and just four of the 20 aircraft on show at The **Norfolk and Suffolk Aviation Museum**, on the site of a USAAF Liberator base during the Second World War. There's a lot of associated material, both civil and military, covering the period from the First World War to the present day. The museum incorporates the Royal Observer Corps Museum, RAF Bomber Command Museum, and the Museum and Memorial of the 446th Bomb Group - the Bungay Buckeroos.

Flixton is named after St Flik, the first Bishop of East Anglia, and he is depicted in the village sign.

MENDHAM
6 miles SW of Bungay off the A143

This pretty little village on the Waveney is the birthplace of Sir Alfred Munnings RA, who was born at Mendham Mill, where his father was the miller. Sir Alfred's Charlotte and her Pony was the inspiration for the

village sign, which was unveiled by his niece Kathleen Hadingham.

BECCLES
9 miles W of Lowestoft on the A146

The largest town in the Waveney district at the southernmost point of the Broads. The Saxons were here, the Vikings were here, and at one time the market was a major supplier of herring (up to 60,000 a year) to the Abbey at Bury St Edmunds. At the height of its trading importance Beccles must have painted a splendidly animated picture, with wherries constantly on the move transporting goods from seaports to inland towns. The same stretch of river is still alive, but now with the yachts and pleasure boats of the holidaymakers and weekenders who fill the town in summer. The regatta in July and August is a particularly busy time.

The fires that are such a sadly common part of small-town history ravaged Beccles at various times in the 16th and 17th centuries, destroying much of the old town. For that reason the dwellings are largely Georgian in origin, with handsome redbrick facades. One that is not is **Roos Hall**, a gabled building

MENDHAM WATERMILL

Mill Lane, Mendham, Harleston,
Suffolk IP20 0NN
Tel: 01379 855410 Fax: 01379 855414
email: publicpersona@dial.pipex.com

Mendham Watermill is the place to enjoy charming and classically rural surroundings. Birthplace of the artist and member of the Royal Society Sir Alfred Munnings, whose father was the local miller, this superb mill offers excellent self-catering accommodation. The Miller's Nest is a ground floor apartment (adjacent to the room housing the mill's ancient waterwheel)

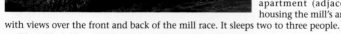

with views over the front and back of the mill race. It sleeps two to three people.

The Miller's House sleeps six to eight people, and comprises three floors - there are bedrooms on the ground and second floors. Both the "Nest" and house are cheerful and comfortable, and feature fully fitted kitchens with automatic washing machines, tumble dryer and all modern amenities, bathroom, and sitting/dining room. There is a small supermarket, a good butcher's, greengrocer's and more in Harleston, two miles away, for all basic needs, and a range of excellent pubs and restaurants in the area. Owners Carol and David Spenser provide their guests with all kinds of nice, homely touches, including CDs and videotapes, deckchairs and loungers, OS maps and local guides - and they are happy to offer any recommendations and do all they can to make any stay here an enjoyable and memorable one. Babysitting services are available, and of course there are a number of leisure pursuits to be enjoyed in the area, including fishing (right here at the mill), swimming, horseriding, clay pigeon shooting, tennis, sailing, birdwatching, golf and lovely walks.

dating from 1583. Just outside the town, far enough away to escape the great fire of 1586, it was built to a Dutch design, underlining the links between East Anglia and the Low Countries forged by the wool and weaving trades. Elizabeth I stayed at the hall just after it was completed, when she visited Beccles to present the town's charter; the occasion is depicted in the town sign. One of the hall's owners was Sir John Suckling (later to become Controller of the Household to James I), one of whose descendants was Lord Nelson. Any old hall worth its salt has a ghost, and the Roos representative is a headless coachman who appears on Christmas Eve.

The parish Church of **St Michael** was built in the second half of the 14th century by the Abbot of Bury. Its tower stands separate, built in the 16th century, rising almost 100 feet and containing a peal of bells. An unusual feature at the north facade is an outside pulpit taking the form of a small balcony. The priest could enter the pulpit from inside the church and preach to lepers, who were not allowed inside. Nelson's parents, the Reverend Edmund Nelson and Catherine

Suckling, were married in St Michael's, so too the Suffolk poet George Crabbe.

Another building with Dutch-style gables houses **Beccles & District Museum**, whose contents include 19th century toys and costume, farm implements, items from the old town jail and memorabilia from the sailing wherries. Beccles, like Bungay, is a printing town, and has its own **printing museum** at the Newgate works of printer William Clowes. Here the visitor will learn about the history of printing since the 1800s, with woodcuts, books and machinery, and it is also possible to tour the factory.

RINGSFIELD
2 miles SW of Beccles off the A146

In a wooded valley away from the main village, the parish Church of All Saints has a dual appeal: the marvellous array of spring flowers in the churchyard and the story of the robins. A pair nested in the lectern 50 years ago and raised a family, an event recalled in carvings on the new lectern and on the porch gates. The original nest, in the old lectern, is still in the church.

The Swan Inn

Swan Lane, Barnby, Beccles, Suffolk NR34 7QE
Tel: 01502 476646 Fax: 01502 711698

Manager Beverley Calver puts out the welcome mat at the popular **Swan Inn**, which is located just off the A146 between Beccles and Lowestoft. It's very much the centre of village life, attracting both locals and tourists for anything from a convivial drink to a slap-up meal. The pub area and the Fisherman's Cove restaurant are filled to the gunwales with nautical articles and artefacts (note the boat in the ceiling!) and the menu majors on fresh fish from local suppliers. The restaurant is very popular - booking is essential at all times, including lunch time.

Voted Best Free House in Britain 1997, this fine pub has recently added a self-contained flat for up to six people, with three bedrooms, kitchen, lounge/dining room and bath. While in Barnby, those new to the village will enjoy a visit to the garden centre and the handsome church of St John; the latter dates from about 1200 and contains some notable wall paintings. What visitors might not see is the ghost of Black Shuck, a retriever who is said to haunt the local roads at night.

5 Norwich and East Norfolk

Breckland, which extends for more than 940 sq. km. in southwest Norfolk and northwest Suffolk, is underlain by chalk with only a light covering of soil. The name "Breckland" comes from the dialect word *breck*, meaning an area of land which was cultivated for a

while, then allowed to revert to heath after the poor soil had become exhausted. This quiet corner of the county is bounded by the Rivers Little Ouse and Waveney which separate Norfolk from Suffolk.

The eastern central part of the county is effectively a plateau, where the gentle contours never rise or fall more than a few metres. It's far from dull, though. The valleys of the Rivers Nar and Wensum display some of the most enchanting scenery in the county, and the area boasts two of the finest Gothic parish churches in England, at Cawston and Salle. In pre-historic times, this was the most wooded part of Norfolk, and a good number of medieval natural woods still remain, a feature which adds another visual attraction to this pastoral area of the country.

Norwich Cathedral

There is a wealth of quiet, unspoilt villages hidden away on minor roads.

The northeast coast makes up the Highlands of Norfolk - the Cromer Ridge which attains the not very dizzying height of 330ft above sea level. Substantial stretches of the coast are, happily, in the care of the National Trust, but anyone in search of a beach holiday will be much more interested in the coastline east of Sheringham. From this decorous resort, a broad strip of excellent sands runs almost uninterruptedly past Cromer and southwards to Great Yarmouth.

Visitors who want to experience a bird's-eye view which encompasses the essence of the Norfolk Broads should climb the tower of the "Cathedral of the Broads", the Church of St Helen's at Ranworth. Spread out beneath you lies

Horning Broad

a vast panorama of glittering waterways, acres of marshland dotted with windmills, reed beds which are still harvested for thatch, grand medieval churches, and farmhouses of warm, red brick.

This is Britain's finest wetland area, a National Park in all but name. Broadland covers some 220 square miles, in a rough oval to the northwest of Great Yarmouth. Three main rivers, the Ant, the Thurne, and the Bure, thread their way through the marshes, providing some 120 miles of navigable waterways. The Broads remain a refuge for many species of endangered birds and plants, and during the spring and autumn they are a favourite stopping-off place for migrating birds.

NORWICH AND EAST NORFOLK

© MAPS IN MINUTES ™ (1999)

PLACES TO STAY, EAT, DRINK AND SHOP

1	The Chequers Inn, Thompson	Pub, food and accommodation	Page 157
2	Willow House Motel & Restaurant, Watton	Hotel and restaurant	Page 158
3	The White Horse Inn, Kenninghall	Pub with food	Page 158
4	The Kings Head, New Buckenham	Pub, food and accommodation	Page 160
5	JD Young Hotel, Harleston	Hotel and restaurant	Page 162
6	The Crown Inn, Pulham Market	Pub and restaurant	Page 162
7	Victoria Inn, Deopham	Pub, restaurant & accommodation	Page 167
8	Scarning Dale, Scarning	Guest house with self catering	Page 168
9	The Mustard Pot, Whinburgh	Pub with food	Page 169
10	Peacock House, Dereham	Bed and breakfast	Page 170
11	Longham White Horse, Longham	Pub, restaurant & accommodation	Page 171
12	The Bluebell, Langham	Pub, food and self catering	Page 175
13	Cottage Holidays Blakeney, Blakeney	Self catering	Page 176
14	Daubeney Hall, Sharrington	Bed and breakfast	Page 177

THETFORD

Some 2,000 years ago, Thetford may well have been the site of **Boadicea's Palace**. In the 1980s excavations for building development at Gallows Hill, north of the town, revealed an Iron Age enclosure. It is so extensive it may well have been the capital of the Iceni tribe which gave the Romans so much trouble. Certainly, the town's strategic location at the meeting of the Rivers Thet and Little Ouse made it an important settlement for centuries. At the time of the Domesday Book, 1086, Thetford was the sixth largest town in the country and the seat of the Bishop of East Anglia, with its own castle, mint and pottery.

Of the **Castle**, only the 80 foot motte remains, but it's worth climbing to the top of this mighty mound for the views across the town. An early Victorian traveller described Thetford as "An ancient and princely little town....one of the most charming country towns in England". Despite major development all around, the heart of the town still fits that description, with a goodly number of medieval and Georgian houses presenting an attractive medley of flint and half-timbered buildings. Perhaps the most striking is the **Ancient House** Museum in White Hart Street, a magnificent 15th century timber-framed house with superb carved oak ceilings. It houses the Tourist Information Centre and a museum where some of the most interesting exhibits are replicas of the Thetford Treasure, a 4th century hoard of gold and silver jewellery discovered as recently as 1979 by an amateur archaeologist with a metal detector. The originals of these sumptuous artefacts are housed in the British Museum.

Even older than the Ancient House is the 12th century **Cluniac Priory** (English Heritage), now mostly in ruins but with an impressive 14th century gatehouse still standing. During the Middle Ages, Thetford could boast 24 churches; today, only three remain.

Statue of Thomas Paine

Thetford's industrial heritage is vividly displayed in the **Burrell Steam Museum**, in Minstergate, which has full-size steam engines regularly "in steam", re-created workshops and many examples of vintage agricultural machinery. The Museum tells the story of the Burrell Steam Company which formed the backbone of the town's industry from the late 18th to the early 20th centuries, their sturdy machines famous around the world.

In King Street, the Thomas Paine Statue commemorates the town's most famous son, born here in 1737. The revolutionary philosopher, and author of *The Rights of Man*, emigrated to America in 1774 where he helped formulate the American Bill of Rights. Paine's democratic views were so detested in England that even ten years after his death in New York State, the authorities refused permission for his admirer, William Cobbett, to have the remains buried in his home country. And it wasn't until the 1950s that Thetford finally got around to erecting a statue in his honour. Ironically for such a robust democrat, his statue stands in King Street and opposite **The King's House**, named after James I who was a frequent visitor here between 1608 and 1618. At the Thomas Paine Hotel in White Hart Street, the room in which it is believed that Paine was born is now the Honeymoon Suite, complete with four-poster bed.

To the west of the town stretch the 90 square miles of **Thetford Forest**, the most extensive lowland forest in Britain. The Forestry Commission began planting in 1922, and although the woodland is largely given over to conifers, with Scots and Corsican Pine and Douglas Fir predominating, oak, sycamore and beech can also be seen throughout. There is a particularly varied trail leading from the Forestry Commission Information Centre which has detailed information about this and other walks through the area.

On the edge of the forest, about two miles west of Thetford, are the ruins of **Thetford**

Euston Hall, Thetford

Warren Lodge, built around 1400. At that time a huge area here was preserved for farming rabbits, a major element of the medieval diet. The vast warren was owned by the Abbot of Thetford Priory and it was he who built the Lodge for his gamekeeper. Still in the forest, reached by a footpath from the village of Santon Downham, are **Grimes Graves** (English Heritage), the earliest major industrial site to be discovered in Europe. At these unique Neolithic flint mines, Stone Age labourers extracted the materials for their sharp-edged axes and knives. It's a strange experience entering these 4,000 year old shafts which descend some 30 feet to an underground chamber. (The experience is even better if you bring your own high-powered torch.)

MUNDFORD
8 miles NW of Thetford on the A1065/A134

Mundford is a large Breckland village of flint built cottages, set on the northern edge of Thetford Forest and with the River Wissey running by. If you ever watch television, you've almost certainly seen Lynford Hall, a mile or so northwest of Mundford. It has provided an impressive location for scenes in

Dad's Army, Allo, Allo, You Rang My Lord? and *Love on a Branch Line*, as well as featuring in numerous television commercials. The Hall is a superb Grade II listed mansion, built for the Lyne-Stevens family in 1885 (as a hunting-lodge, incredibly), and designed in the Jacobean Renaissance style by William Burn.

THOMPSON
10 miles NE of Thetford on minor road off the A1075

This is a quiet village with a marshy man-made lake, **Thompson Water**, and a wild common. **The Peddars Way** long-distance

footpath passes about a mile to the west and, about the same distance to the north-east, the Church is a splendid early 14th century building notable for its fine carved screen and choice 17th century fittings.

WATTON
14 miles NE of Thetford on the A1075

Watton's striking town sign depicts the "Babes in the Wood" of the famous nursery story. The story, which was already current hereabouts in the 1500s, relates that as Arthur Truelove lay dying, he decided that the only hope for his two children was to leave them

THE CHEQUERS INN

Griston Road, Thompson, Thetford, Norfolk IP24 1PX
Tel: 01953 483360 Fax: 01953 488092

The Chequers Inn at Thompson is indescribably pretty. With its thatched roof (one of the longest in Norfolk) swooping almost to the ground, white walls and multitude of colourful hanging baskets, it

presents the kind of charming chocolate-box appearance loved by many. The interior of this 17th century building is equally lovely, with exposed timber beams that are even older than the house (possibly 14th century), low ceilings whose height varies unpredictably from room to room, and an abundance of gleaming brasses and other vintage agricultural bygones.

Heather and Richard McDowall arrived at this idyllic old inn early in 1998 and have added to its many attractions by providing an excellent choice of wholesome, carefully

prepared and presented food. Richard is the chef; his varied menu ranges from freshly baked filled baguettes to hearty 12-ounce steaks; from appetising starters such as chicken liver paté through a vegetarian selection and a children's menu to a wonderfully indulgent choice of desserts. In addition, on the specials board can be found a wide variety of fresh fish dishes to choose from. A choice of four real ales, a beer garden and a safe, secluded children's play area all help to confirm the impression that at The Chequers one has finally found the ideal English pub.

Accommodation here comprises three double ensuite purpose-built rooms, spacious and commanding great views across the rural landscape. Private fishing and shooting on neighbouring farms can be arranged for guests.

WILLOW HOUSE MOTEL AND RESTAURANT

2 The High Street, Watton, Norfolk IP25 6AE
Tel: 01953 881181 Fax: 01953 885885

Willow House Motel and Restaurant is a delightful thatched Free House with a reputation for excellent food amid elegant surroundings. The accommodation comprises five charming and completely modern lodges hidden away to the rear of the main building. These lodges have been tastefully furnished and decorated; each open out onto a small gravel garden and path leading to the main building. Very roomy and welcoming, they make the perfect base from which to explore the region. Watton is a tiny market town set amid rolling Norfolk countryside close to the huge Thetford forest. Just off the eastern end of the village high street, which retains its old gas street lamps and traditional water pump, this fine hotel's restaurant features crisp white linen, beautiful glassware and cutlery, and a huge inglenook fireplace. The style and grace continues with the excellent menu. Diners can enjoy a pre-dinner drink in the secluded 'waiting' bar, which has a lovely fireplace and is adorned with old-fashioned 'butler's bells'; there's also another, larger bar area. Wood beams and other attractive original features add to the warm and welcoming ambience throughout this superb establishment.

THE WHITE HORSE INN

Market Place, Kenninghall, Norfolk Nr16 2AH
Tel: 01953 888857

The White Horse in Kenninghall is over 400 years old, and has seen its fair share of history. Situated in the village square, this attractive and welcoming public house was the scene of the start of the poor law riots in 1836, and was once linked through a series of underground tunnels to Kenninghall Palace, home to the Duke of Norfolk (the palace was dismantled in the 17th century, though the tunnels still exist).

The pub also has a promising future, as it continues to serve excellent food and drink to all visitors. The atmosphere is relaxed and friendly, aided by the tasteful decor and furnishings. Real ales at this Free House include Adnams and guest ales from local breweries such as Fenland and Wolfe Brewery. All food on the fine menu of creative and tempting dishes is home-cooked and freshly prepared. Amiable owners Jane and Clenton Hood offer a warm welcome to all their guests. They and their clientele take their food seriously: the pub even has its own dining club. Dishes such as Italian chicken, steak and ale pie, tuna fillet and a range of daily specials are bound to appeal to every diner.

in the care of their uncle. Unfortunately, the uncle decided to help himself to their inheritance and paid two men to take the children into nearby **Wayland Wood** and kill them. In a moment of unexpected compassion, one of the men decided that he could not commit the dastardly act. He disposed of his accomplice instead and abandoned the children in the wood to suffer whatever fate might befall them. Sadly, unlike the nursery tale in which the children find their way back home and live happily ever after, this unfortunate brother and sister perished. Their ghosts are said to wander hand in hand through the woods to this day.

Wayland Wood is now owned by the Norfolk Naturalist Trust and is believed to be one of the oldest in England; **Griston Hall** (private), half a mile south of the wood, is a Grade II listed building, reputedly the home of the Wicked Uncle in the Babes in the Wood story.

Watton itself boasts an unusual **Clock Tower**, dated 1679, standing at the centre of its long main street.

ATTLEBOROUGH
16 miles NE of Thetford off the A11

The greatest glory of this pleasant market town is to be found in its Church of **St Mary**. Here, a remarkable 15th century chancel screen stretches the width of the church and is beautifully embellished with the arms of the 24 bishoprics into which England was divided at that time. The screen is generally reckoned to be one of the most outstanding in the country, a remarkable survivor of the Reformation purging of such beautiful creations from churches across the land.

Collectors of curiosities will be interested in a strange memorial in the churchyard. It takes the form of a pyramid, about 6ft high, and was erected in 1929 to mark the grave of a local solicitor with the rather splendid name of Melancthon William Henry Brooke, or "Lawyer" Brooke as he was more familiarly known. Melancthon was an amateur Egyptologist who became convinced by his studies of the Pharoahs' tombs that the only way to ensure an agreeable after-life was to be buried beneath a pyramid, precisely placed, and of the correct physical dimensions. Several years before his death, he gave the

most punctilious instructions as to how this assurance of his immortal existence should be constructed and located.

A couple of miles west of Attleborough, the **Tropical Butterfly Gardens and Bird Park** is set in 2,400 square feet of landscaped tropical gardens and provides a congenial home for hundreds of exotic tropical butterflies. There's also a Falconry Centre with flying displays twice daily; one and a half miles of paths and a waterside walk, a two-acre garden centre with more than 2,000 plant varieties on offer, a gift shop, coffee shop and tea gardens.

EAST HARLING
8 miles E of Thetford on the B1111

This attractive little town boasts a beautiful 15th century church in a pastoral location beside the River Thet. Inside, a magnificent hammer-beam roof crowns the lofty nave, there's some outstanding 15th century glass, and in the Harling Chapel, the fine marble **Tomb of Robert Harling**. Harling was one of Henry V's knights who met his death at the siege of Paris in 1435. Since this was long before the days of refrigeration, the knight's body was instead stewed, then stuffed into a barrel, and brought back to East Harling for a ceremonious burial.

The church houses another, equally sumptuous memorial, the **Tomb of Sir Thomas Lovell**. Sculpted in alabaster, Sir Thomas is an imposing figure, clad in armour with a long sword, his head resting on a helmet, his feet on a spray of peacock's feathers. He and his wife lie beneath a wondrously ornamented canopy, decorated with multi-coloured shields and pinnacles.

BANHAM
12 miles E of Thetford on the B1114

Banham Zoo, about five miles to the east of East Harling, provides the opportunity of coming face to face with some of the world's rarest wildlife - many of the animals who find a home here otherwise facing extinction. The Zoo is particularly concerned with monkeys and apes, but in the 25 acres of landscaped gardens, you'll also come across tigers, cheetahs, lemurs, penguins, and many other species. There are educational talks and displays, a children's play area, Shire Horse dray rides, and a restaurant.

New Buckenham

BRESSINGHAM
4 miles NW of Diss off the A1066

The **Bressingham Steam Museum** boasts one of the world's finest collections of British and Continental locomotives, amongst them the famous "Royal Scot". A number of the locomotives on display here are on loan from the National Railway Museum at York. All are housed under cover in the museum's extensive locomotive sheds which also contain many steam-driven industrial engines, traction engines, and **The Fire Museum** whose collection of fire engines and fire-fighting equipment could form a complete museum in its own right. Visitors can view the interior of the Royal Coach and ride along five miles of track through the woods and gardens. The six acres of landscaped grounds are notable in themselves since they are planted with more than 5,000 alpine and other types of plant. A two-acre plant centre adjoins the gardens and here there are thousands of plant specimens, many of them rare, available for purchase. Bressingham is renowned for its special "Steam Days'" when the engines can be seen

in full steam on the three narrow gauge lines, and talks and footplate rides are given on the standard gauge locomotives.

DISS
19 miles E of Thetford on the A1066/A140

The late Poet Laureate, John Betjeman, voted Diss his favourite Norfolk town, and it's easy to understand his enthusiasm. The River Waveney running alongside forms the boundary between Norfolk and Suffolk, but this attractive old market town keeps itself firmly on the northern bank of the river. The town is a pleasing mixture of Tudor, Georgian and Victorian houses grouped around **The Mere** which gives the town its name, derived from the Anglo-Saxon word for "standing water".

The old town grew up on the hill above The Mere perhaps because, as an 18th century

The Mere, Diss

THE KINGS HEAD

Market Place, New Buckenham, Norfolk NR16 2AM
Tel: 01963 860487

The Kings Head is a cosy country pub with a genuinely welcoming and rustic feel. The village's oldest records show that the pub was here as far back as 1645, as a coaching inn on the London-Norwich road. Real ales at this relaxed and friendly Free House include Adnams, Bass and a changing guest ale. Dishes such as steak and kidney pudding, venison pie and other traditional favourites are home-made by owner Jackie Watts, who together with her husband John offers all her guests a warm welcome. The pub will be offering comfortable accommodation in three ensuite bedrooms, tastefully furnished and decorated, from March 2001.

resident observed, "all the filth of the town centering in the Mere, beside the many conveniences that are placed over it, make the water very bad and altogether useless;...it stinks exceedingly, and sometimes the fish rise in great numbers, so thick that they are easily taken; they are chiefly roach and eels". A proper sewerage system was finally installed in 1851.

There's a public park beside the six-acre Mere and from it a narrow street leads to the small **Market Place**. This former poultry market is dominated by the somewhat over-

River Waveney, Scole

restored **St Mary's** Church. The oldest parts date back some 700 years and the St Nicholas Chapel is particularly enjoyable with its wonderful corbels, angels in the roof, and gargoyles. In the early 1500s, the Rector here was John Skelton, Court poet and tutor to Prince Henry, later Henry VIII. A bitter, quarrelsome man, Skelton was appointed Poet Laureate through the patronage of Cardinal Wolsey despite the fact that most of Skelton's output has been described as "breathless doggerel". Appointed Rector of Diss in 1502, he appears to have been

suspended nine years later for having a concubine. Not far from his church is the delightful Victorian Shambles with a cast-iron veranda and a small museum inside.

SCOLE
2 miles E of Diss on the A140

Scole's history goes back to Roman times since it grew up alongside the Imperial highway from Ipswich to Norwich at the point where it bridged the River Waveney. Traffic on this road (the A140) became unbearable in the 1980s, but a bypass has now mercifully restored some peace to the village. There are two hostelries of note: a coaching inn of 1655, built in an extravagant style of Dutch gables, giant pilasters and towering chimney stacks, and the Crossways Inn which must have a good claim to being the prettiest pub in the county.

LANGMERE
6 miles NE of Diss on minor road off the A140 (through Dickleburgh)

Veterans of the Second World War and their families and friends will be interested in the **100th Bomb Group Memorial Museum**, a small museum on the edge of Dickleburgh Airfield (now disused). The Museum is a tribute to the U.S. 8th Air Force which was stationed here during the war, and includes displays of USAAF decorations and uniforms, equipment, combat records and other memorabilia. Facilities include refreshments, a museum shop, visitor centre and a picnic area.

HARLESTON
7 miles NE of Diss off the A143

This pretty market town with some notable half-timbered and Georgian houses, and a splendid 12th century coaching inn, was a favourite of the renowned architectural authority, Nikolaus Pevsner, who particularly admired the early Georgian Candlers House at the northern end of the town. Another

JD YOUNG HOTEL

2-4 Market Place, Harleston, Norfolk IP20 9AD
Tel/Fax: 01379 852822

The **JD Young Hotel** in Harleston is an elegant and welcoming establishment. No expense has been spared in the tasteful renovation and improvement of this lovely hotel, which re-opened in October 2000. The interior is the height of luxury, with polished wood floors, attractive oil paintings adorning the walls, handsome wood panelling, a wealth of fresh flowers and very comfortable seating - all of which speak of a more gracious past while providing every modern comfort.

The menu offers an excellent range of traditional and more innovative dishes, all expertly cooked and prepared. the restaurant offers a full a la carte menu from midday to 3 p.m. and 6 to 10 p.m.

Monday to Saturday; midday to 8 p.m. Sundays. There is an unusual double-sided fireplace with decorative brickwork built into the wall separating the restaurant from the bar area. In such sumptuous surroundings, who couldn't relax and enjoy a quiet drink or superb meal?

There are also six luxurious guest bedrooms, which overlook Harleston's charming market square. Each room is furnished and decorated to a high standard of comfort and quality. The staff are unfailingly pleasant and attentive.

THE CROWN INN

Pulham Market, Norfolk IP21 4TA
Tel: 01379 676652

Set in the centre of this lovely and quiet village, opposite the village green, **The Crown Inn** in Pulham Market is surrounded by small thatched cottages, a setting of complete rural bliss. Built in 1610, it is a typical country pub in the best sense of the words. The comfortable interior is informally divided into four distinct areas. The Sceptre Bar has sumptuous red leather Chesterfield-style sofas and armchairs, set off by the deep red walls, exposed beams and open fire. The main bar area, which also accommodates diners, is filled with memorabilia and interesting bric a brac. In Cricketers Corner,

photos of various distinguished teams cover the walls. This part of the pub also serves as a no smoking area for diners.

Finally there is the restaurant and carvery area, decorated in Victorian style with elegant green walls and plush carpets. Real ales straight from the barrel are a hallmark of this pub. There are changing guest ales. The superb menu features a good range of expertly prepared and presented favourites. Owner Anne Courtenay is hospitality personified; her friendly, helpful staff make all their guests feel most welcome. This excellent pub is very busy at mealtimes, so booking is essential.

writer has described the area around the market place as "the finest street scene in East Anglia". The town lies in the heart of the Waveney Valley, a lovely area which inspired many paintings by the locally-born artist, Sir Alfred Munnings.

NORWICH

"Norwich has the most Dickensian atmosphere of any city I know" declared J.B. Priestley in his *English Journey of 1933*. "What a grand, higgledy-piggledy, sensible old place Norwich is!" More than half-a-century later, in a European Commission study of "most habitable" cities, Norwich topped the list of British contenders, well ahead of more favoured candidates such as Bath and York. The political, social and cultural capital of Norfolk, Norwich has an individual charm which is difficult to define, a beguiling atmosphere created in part by its prodigal wealth of sublime buildings, partly by its intriguing dual personality as both an old-fashioned Cathedral town and a vibrant, modern metropolis.

Back in prehistoric times, there were several settlements around the confluence of the Rivers Wensum and Yare and, by the late fourth century, one of them was important enough to have its own mint. This was *Northwic* and, by the time of the Domesday Book 700 years later, Northwic/Norwich, had become the third most populous city in England, only outnumbered by London and York. To the Norman conquerors such a major centre of population (about 5,500 residents) needed a **Castle** to make sure its Saxon inhabitants were kept in order.

The first structure, in wood, was replaced in the late 1100s by a mighty fortress in stone which, unlike most blank-walled castles of the period, is decorated with a rich facade of blind arcades and ornamental pilasters. The great fort never saw any military action and as early as the 13th century it was being used as the county gaol, a role it continued to fill until 1889. From its walls, in December 1549, the leader of the rebellion against land enclosures, Robert Kett, was hung in chains and left to starve to death. The Castle is now a lively **Museum** where the old dungeons house a forbidding display of instruments of torture, along with the death masks of some of the prisoners who were executed here.

Among the countless other fascinating exhibits are the **Bulwer and Miller** collection of more than 2,600 English china teapots; the Langton collection of around 100 cats, fashioned in porcelain, ivory, bronze, glass, and wood, and originating from anywhere between Derbyshire and China; and Margaret Elizabeth Fountaine's mind-boggling accumulation of 22,000 butterflies which she had personally netted during her travels around the world. Pride of place must go however to the Museum's incomparable collection of paintings by the celebrated Norwich artist, John Sell Cotman (1782-1842), and others in the group known as the Norwich School. Their subjects were mostly landscape scenes, such as John Crome's *The Poringland Oak*, and quite apart from the artistic quality of their works, they have left a fascinating pictorial record of early 19th century Norfolk.

Norwich Cathedral

Norwich Cathedral

The Castle's function has changed over the years, but the **Cathedral** is still the focus of ecclesiastical life in the county. It's even older than the castle, its service of consecration taking place 900 years ago, in 1101. This peerless building, its flint walls clad in creamy-white stone from Caen is, after Durham, the most completely Norman cathedral in England, its appeal enhanced by later Gothic features such as the flying buttresses. The Norman cloisters are the largest in the country and notable for the 400 coloured and gilded bosses depicting scenes from medieval life. Another 1600 of these wondrous carvings decorate the glorious vaulted roof of the nave.

It's impossible to list all the Cathedral's treasures here, but do seek out the **Saxon Bishop's Throne** in the Presbytery; the lovely 14th century altar painting in St Luke's Chapel; and the richly carved canopies in the Choir.

Outside, beneath the slender 315 foot high spire soaring heavenwards, the **Cathedral Close** is timeless in its sense of peace. There are some 80 houses inside the Close, some medieval, many Georgian, their residents enjoying an idyllic refuge free

from cars. At peace here lie the remains of Nurse Edith Cavell. A daughter of the rector of Swardeston, a few miles south of Norwich, Nurse Cavell worked at a Red Cross hospital in occupied Brussels during the First World War. She helped some 200 Allied soldiers to escape to neutral Holland before being detected and court-martialled by the Germans. As she faced execution by firing squad on 12 October 1915, she spoke her own resonant epitaph: "Standing as I do, in the view of God and eternity, I realize that patriotism is not enough. I must have no hatred or bitterness towards anyone."

A stroll around the Close will take you to **Pull's Ferry** with its picturesque flint gateway fronting the River Wensum. In medieval times, a canal ran inland from here so that provisions, goods, and in the earliest days, building materials, could be moved direct to the Cathedral. A short stroll along the riverside walk will bring you to **Cow Tower**, built around 1378, and the most massive of the old city towers. And at the western end of the Cathedral Close is the magnificent **Erpingham Gate**, presented to the city in 1420 by a hero of the Battle of Agincourt, Sir Thomas Erpingham.

Pull's Ferry, Norwich

Beyond this gate, in Tombland (originally Toom- or waste-land), is **Samson and Hercules House**, its entrance flanked by two 1674 carvings of the giants, and, diagonally opposite, the 15th century Maid's Head Hotel.

About 400 yards to the west is the great open space of the Market Square where every weekday a colourful jumble of traders' stalls offer just about every conceivable item for sale. Dominating the western side of the market square is **City Hall**, modelled on Stockholm City Hall and opened by George VI in 1938. Opinions differ about its architectural merits, but there are no such doubts about its predecessor as Civic Centre, the nearby Guildhall, a fine example of 15th century flintwork which now houses the Tourist Information Centre and a small museum.

Around the corner from London Street, in Bridewell Alley, is the **Bridewell Museum**, a late 14th century merchant's house now dedicated to Norfolk's crafts and industries. And right next door another museum/shop celebrates the county's great contribution to world cuisine, mustard. Back in the early 1800s, Jeremiah Colman perfected his blend of mustard flours and spice to produce a condiment that was smooth in texture and tart in flavour. Together with his nephew James he founded J & J Colman in 1823 and, a century and a half later, **The Mustard Shop** was established to commemorate the company's history. It also serves as a showcase for the range of Colman products which nowadays includes a variety of drinks and foods. The shop has an appropriately Victorian atmosphere with lots of mahogany and marble, and a fascinating display of vintage containers and advertisements, amongst them a series of cod detective stories featuring such characters as Lord Bacon of Cookham and Miss Di Gester, written by no less distinguished a

Elm Hill, Norwich

writer than Dorothy L. Sayers. A very appetising exhibition.

There are still 32 churches in Norwich, all worth attention, although many are now used for purposes other than worship. Outstanding amongst them are **St Peter Mancroft**, a masterpiece of Gothic architecture built between 1430-55, and St Peter Hungate, a handsome 15th century church which, since 1933, has been a museum illustrating all aspects of the arts and crafts involved in ecclesiastical decoration and ritual. St Peter Hungate stands at the top of **Elm Hill**, a narrow, unbelievably picturesque lane where in medieval times the city's wool merchants built their homes, close to their warehouses beside the River Wensum.

St Gregory's Church in Pottergate is another Norwich church to have been declared redundant, and its fate might well have been a sad one. Happily, it is now the home of the **Saint Gregory's Trust**, a vibrant centre where local artists, actors, musicians, dancers, and other arts groups stage a variety of performances and exhibitions.

When the basic structure of the present church was built in the late 14th century, the general rule seems to have been that any parish of around 1000 people would have its own place of worship. St Gregory's was founded on the site of a Saxon church in 1210 and rebuilt in its present form in 1394. The church takes it name from Gregory the

Great, the 6th century Pope best known for his campaign to convert the heathen Anglo-Saxons of Angle-land to Christianity. His enthusiasm for this mission, it's said, was fired by the sight of fair-haired youths from that distant country being paraded for sale in the Roman slave market. On being told that the captives were "Angles", he remarked that they were well-named, for they resembled angels. Impressed by their physical beauty, and pitying their ignorance of Christ's redemption, the Pope despatched a party of 40 monks to Angle-land in AD596, led by Augustine whom he consecrated as the first Archbishop of Canterbury.

On the western edge of the city stands the **University of East Anglia**. It's well worth making your way here to visit the **Sainsbury Centre for Visual Arts**. Housed in a huge hall of aluminium and glass designed by Norman Foster, the Centre contains the eclectic collection of a "passionate acquirer" of art, Sir Robert Sainsbury. For more than 50 years, Sir Robert purchased whatever works of art took his fancy, ignoring fashionable trends and "correct" choices. So you'll find sculptures and pictures by Henry Moore, Bacon and Giacometti, along with African and pre-Columbian artefacts; Egyptian, Etruscan and Roman bronzes; works by Indians and by Inuit eskimos; sculptures from the Cyclades, the South Seas, the Orient and medieval Europe. This extraordinary collection was donated to the University by Sir Robert and Lady Lisa Sainsbury in 1973; their son David complemented his parents' generosity by paying for the building in which it is housed.

To the south of Norwich are the remains of **Venta Icenorum**, the Roman town established here after Boadicea's rebellion in AD 61. Unusually, this extensive site has not been disturbed by later developments, so archaeologists have been able to identify the full scale of the original settlement. Sadly, very little remains above ground, although in dry summers the grid pattern of the streets show up as brown lines in the grass. Most of the finds discovered during excavations in 1920s and 1930s are now in **Norwich Castle Museum**, but the riverside site is still worth visiting, especially if you have a vivid imagination.

AROUND NORWICH

PORINGLAND
6 miles SE of Norwich on the B1332

This sizeable village is surrounded by mustard fields, a dazzling sight in June when the custard-coloured blooms create a cloth of gold and, according to old folk lore, their glow shines all the way up to the moon. The name of the village will be familiar to those who love the paintings of the Norwich artist John Crome (1794-1842) whose arcadian painting of *The Poringland Oak* hangs in the Tate Gallery.

To the southwest of Poringland is **The Playbarn**, an indoor and outdoor adventure centre specially designed for the under-sevens. All the play equipment is based on a farmyard theme with a miniature farm, bouncy tractors, soft play sheep pens, and donkey rides among the attractions. Refreshments and light lunches are available, or you can bring along your own picnic.

WYMONDHAM
9 miles SW of Norwich off the A11

The exterior of **Wymondham Abbey** presents one of the oddest ecclesiastical buildings in the county; the interior reveals one of the most glorious. The Abbey was founded in 1107 by the Benedictines, or Black Monks, as they were known from the colour of their habits. The richest and most aristocratic of the monastic orders, the Black Monks apparently experienced some difficulty in respecting their solemn vows of poverty and humility. Especially the latter.

The monks were constantly in conflict with the people of Wymondham. In 1249, the dissension between them was so bitter that Pope Innocent IV himself attempted to reconcile their differences. When his efforts failed, a wall was then built across the interior of the Abbey, dividing it into an area for the monks and another for the parishioners. Even that drastic measure failed to bring peace. Both parties wanted to ring their own bells, so each built a tower. The villagers erected a stately rectangular tower at the west end; the monks an octagonal one over the crossing, thus creating the Abbey's

Wymondham Abbey

walls, William Kett was hung in chains and left to die: his brother, Robert, the leading figure in the uprising, suffered the same fate at Norwich Castle.

Although many of Wymondham's oldest houses were lost in the fire of 1615 when some 300 dwellings were destroyed, there are still some attractive Elizabethan buildings in the heart of the town. The **Market Place** is given dignity by the picturesque octagonal Market Cross, rebuilt two years after the fire. Crowned by a pyramid roof, this appealing timber-framed building is open on all sides on the ground floor, and its upper floor is reached by an outside stairway. Also of interest is **Becket's Chapel**, founded in 1174 and restored in 1559. In its long history it has served as a pilgrim's chapel, grammar school, and coal store. Currently, it houses the town library. **The Bridewell**, or House of Correction, in Bridewell Street, was built as a model prison in 1785 along lines recommended by the prison reformer, John Howard, who had condemned the earlier gaol on the site as "one of the vilest in the country". Wymondham's Bridewell is said to have served as a model for the penitentiaries established in the United States. Now owned by the town's Heritage Society, Bridewell is

curious exterior appearance. Step inside however and you find a magnificent Norman nave, 112 feet long. (It was originally twice as long, but the eastern end, along with most of the Abbey buildings, was demolished after the Dissolution of the Monasteries.)

The superb hammerbeam roof is supported by 76 beautifully carved angels; there's an interesting 16th century tomb, of the last Abbot, in delicate terracotta work; and a striking modern memorial, a gilded and coloured reredos and tester, commemorating the local men who lost their lives in the First World War.

The rectangular western tower of the Abbey was the setting for one of the last acts in the ill-fated Kett's Rebellion of 1549. From its

VICTORIA INN

Church Road, Deopham, Wymondham, Norfolk NR18 9DT
Tel: 01953 850783 Fax: 01953 851733
website: www.the-victoria-inn.co.uk

The **Victoria Inn** was built in 1670 as an ale house. Completely refurbished by John and Jean Heeson-Greene when the took over the inn in December of 1998, it retains traditional features such as the exposed beamwork which complement the tasteful furnishings and decor. John and Jean are welcoming and experienced hosts. Their clientele is a mix of locals, walkers, cyclists, anglers, golfers and other visitors. All guests will enjoy the relaxed atmosphere and pleasant surroundings. Real ales available at this excellent Free House include Adnams, Greene King IPA and changing guest ales. The walls are adorned with photographs of the American Air Force 452nd Bombardment Group, stationed at Deopham during the Second World War. The attractive restaurant is newly built; the menu offers a range of favourites such as steak and kidney pie, liver and bacon hotpot and Sunday roasts, all freshly cooked and prepared by Jean and the pub's talented chef. There are six ensuite guest bedrooms (two twin, two double, one family and one single), each very comfortable and perfect to use as a base while exploring this part of Norfolk. Bicycle hire from the pub.

SCARNING DALE

Dale Road, Scarning, Dereham,
Norfolk NR19 2QN
Tel: 01362 687269 Fax: 01362 687378
e-mail: jean@scarningdale.freeserve.co.uk
website: www.scarningdale.co.uk

For a real taste of luxury amid truly impressive surroundings, **Scarning Dale** is the place to go. This superb country house boasts an impressive range of facilities and amenities. A delightfully different holiday experience, short break or special venue for parties and functions awaits those who come to this wonderful retreat. Quality is the byword here.

A guest house and accompanying self-catering cottages offer excellent accommodation and service. The house itself is a heavily timbered structure dating back to the 16th century. In the 25 acres of grounds are the remains of what is

reputed to be part of the Abbey of Wendling, founded by Sir William de Wendling in 1267. The house accommodates up to six people in a true home-from-home atmosphere. The guest bedrooms comprise one family-sized twin room, two double rooms and a single room. Everywhere in the house, the standard of decor and furnishings is first class. Guests are welcome to relax in the Music Room, enjoy peace and quiet in the Library or engage in a game of snooker or table tennis. Winter evenings can be spent enjoying the blazing log fire in the heavily timbered sitting room with its inglenook fireplace, while the summer brings the delights of the lovely garden. Guests can also enjoy a swim in the heated indoor pool and there is an on-site aromatherapist.

There are also five delightful self-catering cottages (three accommodate two persons, one sleeps four guests, the other six). A stable block and paddocks are available for guest's use. Most Wednesdays from 10 a.m. to midday there's an art class run on site, and the function suite - in the 18th-century converted barn - seats up to 110 people. In the elegant dining room, guests can savour home-cooked and delicious meals. Owner Jean Magrath uses the freshest ingredients, including fresh organic vegetables grown in the kitchen garden. There is also a lovely tea room, open Monday to Saturday 10-5, Sundays 3-5. A truly warm welcome awaits all guests.

All this and central for delightful local walks and sights and attractions such as the Broads, bird watching, Norwich, golf, riding, sailing, trout fishing, Sandringham and a number of historic houses in the surrounding area, Scarning Dale makes for a unique holiday experience.

home to several community projects, including the **Wymondham Heritage Museum**.

Railway buffs will also want to visit the historic **Railway Station**, built in 1845 on the Great Eastern's Norwich-Ely line. At its peak, the station and its section employed over 100 people. Still providing a rail link to Norwich, London and the Midlands, the station has been restored, and its buildings house a railway museum, restaurant and tea room, and a piano showroom.

EAST DEREHAM
16 miles W of Norwich on the A47

One of the most ancient towns in the county, East Dereham has a recorded history stretching back to 654AD when St Withburga founded a Nunnery here. Her name lives on at **St Withburga's Well**, just to the west of the church. This is where she was laid to rest but, some 300 years later, the Abbot and monks of Ely robbed her grave and ensconced the precious, fund-raising relic in their own Cathedral. In the saint's desecrated grave a spring suddenly bubbled forth, its waters possessed of miraculous healing properties, and St Withburga's shrine attracted even more pilgrims than before. Some still come.

In the Church of St Nicholas, the second largest in Norfolk, there are features from every century from the 12th to the 16th: a magnificent lantern tower, a lofty Bell Tower, painted roofs, and a Seven Sacrament Font.

This is the largest of these notable fonts of which only 30 have survived, 28 of them in Norfolk and Suffolk.

In the northeast transept is buried a poet some of whose lines have become embedded in the language:

> *"Variety's the very spice of life, the monarch of all I survey*
> *God made the country and man made the town".*

They all came from the pen of William Cowper who, despite being the author of such cheery poems as "John Gilpin", suffered grievously from depression, a condition not improved by his association with John Newton, a former slave trader who had repented and become "a man of gloomy piety". The two men collaborated on a book of hymns which included such perennial favourites as "Oh! for a closer walk with God", "Hark, my soul, it is the Lord", and "God moves in a mysterious way". Cowper spent the last four years of his life at East Dereham, veering in and out of madness. In a late-flowering romance, he had married the widow Mary Unwin but the strain of caring for the deranged poet drove her in turn to insanity and death. She too is buried in the church.

William died four years after Mary, in 1800. Three years later another celebrated writer was born at the quaintly named hamlet of **Dumpling Green** on the edge of the town. George Borrow was to become one of the great English travel writers, producing

THE MUSTARD POT

Dereham Road, Whinburgh, Dereham, Norfolk NR19 1AA
Tel/Fax: 01362 692179

Tucked away in the quiet village of Winburgh, **The Mustard Pot** is a charming and welcoming pub. Originally three rural cottages, the building once served as the village shop and village post office - the old postbox adorning one wall is still used - before being converted to a pub around 1978. Low ceilings and exposed beams add to the

cosy and traditional ambience. All guests are made to feel very welcome here by owners Judith and Neil Mitchell. Tea and coffee are served all day, and there's a good range of real ales including changing guest ales. The menus boast a tempting selection of hearty meals and snacks, including beef and ale crockpot, steaks, pasta and an excellent range of vegetarian dishes, all home-made by Judith. There are also daily specials. Open all day; meals served Mon-Thu, 12.00-14.00, 17.00-20.00; Fri-Sat, 12.00-14.00, 17.00-21.00; Sun 12.00-14.30. Light snacks are served 2.30-4 p.m.

during the unhappy reign of Mary Tudor. He was rector of the town before being appointed Bishop of London and he lived in the exquisite thatched terrace now called **Bishop Bonner's Cottages**. The exterior is ornamented with delightful pargetting, a frieze of flower and fruit designs below the eaves, a form of decoration which is very unusual in Norfolk. The cottages now house a small Museum.

Dereham Centre

books full of character and colour such as *Wild Wales* and *The Bible in Spain*. In his autobiographical novel Lavengro he begins with a warm recollection of the town where he was born: "I love to think on thee, pretty, quiet D[ereham], thou pattern of an English market town, with thy clean but narrow streets branching out from thy modest market place, with thine old-fashioned houses, with here and there a roof of venerable thatch". The house in which George Borrow was born, Borrow's Hall, still stands in Dumpling Green.

A much less attractive character connected with East Dereham is Bishop Bonner, the enthusiastic arsonist of Protestant "heretics"

GRESSENHALL
3 miles NW of Dereham off the B1146

The **Norfolk Rural Life Museum** is housed in a former workhouse which, like so many of those detested institutions, is an extremely imposing late 18th century building, this one built in rose-red brick. Gressenhall Workhouse was designed to accommodate some 700 unfortunates, so it was built on a very grand scale indeed. There's ample room for the many exhibits illuminating the working and domestic life of Norfolk people over the last 150 years. The surrounding 50 acres of countryside, Union Farm, is run as a typical 1920s farm, with rare breeds of sheep, pigs, cattle and poultry, and demonstrations of the real nature of bygone agricultural

PEACOCK HOUSE

Old Beetley, Dereham, Norfolk NR20 4DG
Tel: 01362 860371 email: PeackH@aol.com

Peacock House is a strikingly handsome timber-framed farmhouse set within 2½ acres of garden, orchard and meadow, and dating back in parts to the early 17th century. Tastefully renovated to provide every comfort while maintaining the building's original character and charm, it offers superior bed and breakfast accommodation in three lovely ensuite guest bedrooms (two doubles, one twin). Discerning guests appreciate the

relaxed atmosphere and peaceful surroundings. Owners Jenny and Peter enjoy spoiling their guests. The guests' lounge is very comfortable, while the dining room boasts exposed beams, a large inglenook fireplace and long refectory table. Fresh local produce is used in the delicious breakfast, which includes home-made preserves, fruit compote and a selection of teas. Special diets are catered for. This charming B&B also makes an excellent base for exploring Sandringham, Blickling, Houghton Hall, Holkham Hall, and the many other sights and attractions in this part of Norfolk. No smoking.

labour. The museum hosts numerous special events during the season, ranging from Steam Days to an international folk dance festival with more than 200 dancers taking part.

A mile or so south of Gressenhall, the tiny community of **Dillington** has great difficulty in getting itself noticed on even the most large-scale of maps. This very Hidden Place is worth seeking out for **Norfolk Herbs at Blackberry Farm**, a specialist herb farm located in a beautiful wooded valley. Visitors are invited to browse through a vast collection of aromatic, culinary and medicinal herb plants, and to learn all about growing and using herbs.

NORTH ELMHAM
6 miles N of Dereham off the B1110

Near the village of North Elmham stand the sparse remains of a Saxon Cathedral. North Elmham was the seat of the Bishops of East Anglia until 1071 when they removed to Thetford, and 20 years later to Norwich. Although there had been a cathedral here since the late 7th century, what has survived is mostly from the 11th century. Despite its

grand title, the T-shaped ground plan reveals that the cathedral was no larger than a small parish church.

BRISLEY
7 miles N of East Dereham on the B1145

Brisley village is well known to local historians and naturalists for its huge expanse of heathland, some 170 acres of it. It's reckoned to be the best example of unspoilt common in Norfolk and at its centre are scores of pits which were dug out in medieval times to provide clay for the wattle and daub houses of the period. Another feature of interest in the village is Gately Manor (private), an Elizabethan manor house standing within the remains of a medieval moat, and yet another moated house at Old Hall Farm in the southwest corner of the green.

GREAT WITCHINGHAM
11 miles NW of Norwich off the A1067

Norfolk Wildlife Centre & Country Park is home to an interesting collection of rare, or ancient, breeds of farm livestock such as

LONGHAM WHITE HORSE

Wendling Road, Longham, Dereham, Norfolk NR19 2RD
Tel/Fax: 01362 687464

The **Longham White Horse** has been serving fine ales and meals to the villagers of Longham and the surrounding area for over 350 years. It has been run by the same family for more than 80 years. This quintessentially English pub has all the features that make for a relaxed and pleasant dining experience: comfortable seating in the spacious lounge bar or beer garden, a handsome wood and brick bar, cheery wood burning stove and tasteful decor.

There are two restaurant areas (both no smoking), including a delightful conservatory area overlooking the lawned garden. There are five comfortable and attractive ensuite guest bedrooms

(one family room, three doubles, and two twin?). All the rooms are welcoming and very comfortable, equipped with every modern facility.

Real ales on tap in this Free House include Woodfords and two changing guest ales. There's also a good range of lagers, wines and spirits, as well as scrumpy cider. The various menus offer an excellent choice of delicious dishes, snacks, sandwiches and more. Partners Barry White and Chrissie Sandford offer all their guests a warm and genuine welcome. Open: Tuesday to Sunday 12-2.30 and 6.30-11; Mondays 6.30-11 p.m.

white-faced woodland and Shetland sheep, pygmy goats and Exmoor ponies. Set in 40 acres of peaceful parkland, the Centre also has reindeer, otters, and badgers, pools teeming with wildfowl and a huge colony of wild herons nesting in the trees. There are also commando and Adventure Play Areas; one of the finest collection of trees and flowering shrubs in the county; a cafe and gift shop.

A little further southeast, the **Dinosaur Adventure Park** near Lenwade doesn't have any living creatures, but as you wander through the woods here you will come across some startlingly convincing life-size models of dinosaurs. One of them, the "Climb-a-Saurus", is a children's activity centre. A woodland maze; a picnic area with gas-fired barbecues; a play area for toddlers; a restaurant, and a Dinostore offering a wide variety of dinosaur models, books and gifts, are amongst the other attractions.

Anyone who has ever read Parson Woodforde's enchanting *Diary of a Country Parson* will want to make a short diversion to the tiny village of **Weston Longville**, a mile or so south of the Dinosaur Park. The Revd James Woodforde was vicar of this remote parish from 1774 until his death in 1803, and throughout that time he conscientiously maintained a daily diary detailing a wonderful mixture of the momentous and the trivial. "Very great Rebellion in France" he notes, when 10 days after the Fall of the Bastille, the dramatic news eventually arrived at Weston Longville. More often he is recording his copious meals ("We had for dinner a Calf's head, boiled Fowl and Tongue, a saddle of Mutton roasted on the side table, and a fine Swan roasted with Currant Jelly Sauce for the first Course. The Second Course a couple of Wild Fowl, Larks, Blamange, Tarts etc. etc."); the weather (during the winter of 1785, for example, the frost was so severe that it froze the chamberpots under the beds); and his frequent dealings with the smuggler Andrews who kept the good parson well-supplied with contraband tea, gin and cognac. Inside the simple village church there's a portrait of Parson Woodforde, painted by his nephew, and across the road the inn has been named after this beguiling character.

CAWSTON
12 miles NW of Norwich on the B1145

"Lovers of the Norfolk churches can never agree which is the best", wrote Sir John Betjeman. "I have heard it said that you are either a Salle man or a Cawston man". In this county so rich in exceptionally beautiful churches, Salle and Cawston are indeed in a class of their own. **St Agnes Church** in Cawston, amongst other many treasures, boasts a magnificent double hammerbeam roof, where angels with protective wings eight feet across float serenely from the roof, and a gorgeous 15th century rood screen embellished with lovely painted panels of saints and Fathers of the Church. The two churches are just a couple of miles apart so you can easily decide for yourself whether you are "a Salle man or a Cawston man". Surprisingly for such a genial character, Sir John seems to have overlooked the possibility that other visitors to these two remarkable churches might define themselves as either "a Salle woman or a Cawston woman".

On the edge of Cawston village is **Broadland Wineries**, a family-owned business which was established in 1965 and moved to its 4.5 acre site here in 1971.

AYLSHAM
14 miles N of Norwich on the A140

From Hevingham, the A140 leads due north to the attractive little town of Aylsham, set beside the River Bure, the northern terminus of the **Bure Valley Railway**. It has an unspoilt **Market Place**, surrounded by late 17th and early-18th century houses, reflecting the prosperity the town enjoyed in those years from the cloth trade, and a 14th/15th century church, St Michael's, said to have been built by John O'Gaunt. In the churchyard is the tomb of one of the greatest of the 18th century landscape gardeners, Humphrey Repton, the creator of some 200 parks and gardens around the country.

One of Repton's many commissions was to landscape the grounds of **Blickling Hall** (National Trust), a "dream of architectural beauty", which stands a mile or so outside Aylsham. Many visitors have marvelled at their first sight of the great Hall built for Sir Henry Hobart in the 1620s. "No-one is prepared on coming downhill past the

Blichling Hall

church into the village, to find the main front of this finest of Jacobean mansions, actually looking upon the road, unobstructedly, from behind its velvet lawns" enthused Charles Harper in 1904. "No theatrical manager cunning in all the artful accessories of the stage could devise anything more dramatic".

From the outside, Sir Henry's house fully satisfied the current architectural vogue for perfect symmetry. Four towers topped with lead-covered turret-caps rise at each corner, there are lines of matching Dutch gables and mullioned windows, and even the chimneys were placed in corresponding groups of twos, threes or fours.

Inside, the most spectacular feature is the Long Gallery which extends for 135 feet and originally provided space for indoor exercise in bad weather. Its glory is the plaster ceiling, an intricately patterned expanse of heraldic panels bearing the Hobart arms, along with others displaying bizarre and inscrutable emblems such as a naked lady riding a two-legged dragon.

Other treasures at Blickling include a dramatic double-flight carved oak staircase, the Chinese Bedroom lined with 18th century hand-painted wallpaper, and the dazzling Peter the Great Room. A descendant of Sir Henry Hobart, the 2nd Earl of Buckinghamshire, was appointed Ambassador to Russia in 1746, and he returned from that posting with a magnificent tapestry, the gift of Empress Catherine the Great. This room

was re-designed so as to display the Earl's sumptuous souvenir to its full effect, and portraits of himself and his Countess by Gainsborough were added later.

The Earl was a martyr to gout and his death in 1793 at the age of 50 occurred when, finding the pain unbearable, he thrust his bloated foot into a bucket of icy water, and suffered a heart attack. He was buried beneath the idiosyncratic Egyptian Pyramid in the grounds, a 45 foot high structure designed by Ignatius Bonomi who combined Egyptian and classical elements to create a mausoleum which, if nothing else, is certainly distinctive.

Blickling also offers its visitors miles of footpaths through lovely grounds, a plant centre, picnic area, restaurant and shop.

Within a few miles of Blickling Hall are two other stately homes, both the properties of Lord and Lady Walpole. Neither of the houses, **Mannington Hall** and **Wolterton Park**, is normally open to the public but their gardens and grounds are. At Mannington there are country walks and trails, a Heritage Rose Garden featuring thousands of roses set in small gardens reflecting their period of origin, a Garden Shop, and tea room. Wolterton Park, the stately 18th century Hall built for Horatio Walpole, brother of Sir Robert, England's first Prime Minister stands in grounds landscaped by Humphrey Repton. Here there are miles of waymarked walks and trails, orienteering, an adventure playground and various special events are held throughout the year.

Just north of Mannington Hall stands the village of **Little Barningham** where St Mary's Church is a magnet for collectors of ecclesiastical curiosities. Inside, perched on the corner of an ancient box pew, stands a remarkable wood-carved skeletal figure of the Grim Reaper. Its fleshless skull stares hollow-eyed at visitors with a defiant, mirthless grin: a scythe gripped in one clutch of bones, and an hour-glass in the other, symbolise the inescapable fate that awaits us all. This gruesomely powerful *memento mori* was donated to the church in 1640 by one Stephen Crosbie who, for good measure, added the inscription: "As you are now, even so was I, Remember death for ye must dye." Those words were a conventional enough adjuration at that time, but what is one supposed to make of Stephen's postscript inscribed on the back of the pew: "For couples joined in wedlock this seat I did intend"?

THE NORTHEAST COAST

STIFFKEY
16 miles W of Cromer on the A149

Regarded as one of the prettiest villages in the county, Stiffkey lies beside the little river of the same name. Pronounced "Stewkey", the name means "island of tree stumps" and is most likely derived from the marshy river valley of reed beds and fallen trees which indeed gives the village the appearance of an island. At the east end of the village is the church of St John the Baptist and from the churchyard there are fine views of the river and of Stiffkey Hall to the south. All that now remains of this once-impressive building, built by the Bacon family in 1578, are the towers, one wing of the house, and the 17th century gatehouse. The stately ruins of the great hall have been transformed into a rose terrace and sunken garden and are open to the public.

The former Rectory is a grand Georgian building, famous as the residence of the Revd Harold Davidson, Rector of Stiffkey during the 1920s and 1930s. Rather like the central character in Michael Palin's film *The Missionary*, Harold launched a personal crusade to save the fallen women of London's West End, and caused much gossip and scandal by doing so. Despite the fact that his notoriety regularly filled the church to capacity, he constantly fell foul of the ecclesiastical authorities and eventually lost his living. There is a rather bizarre ending to his story. After handing over the keys of Stiffkey Rectory, Harold joined a travelling show and was later killed by a lion whose cage he was sharing.

To the north of the village are the **Stiffkey Salt Marshes**, a National Trust nature reserve which turns a delicate shade of purple in July when the sea lavender is in bloom. Here on the sandflats can be found the famous "Stewkey blues" - cockles which are highly regarded as a delicacy by connoisseurs of succulent bivalve molluscs.

A couple of miles south of Stiffkey stand the picturesque ruins of **Binham Priory** (English Heritage), its magnificent nave still serving as the parish church. This represents only about one-sixth of the original Priory, founded in 1091 by a nephew of William the Conqueror. The church is well worth a visit to see its unusually lofty interior with a Monk's Walk at roof level, its Seven Sacraments font, and noble west front.

MORSTON
13 miles W of Cromer on the A149

Great stretches of salt marshes and mud flats lie between this pleasant village and the sea which is reached by way of a tidal creek that almost disappears at low tide. Morston is a particularly pleasing village with quiet lanes and clusters of cottages built from local cobbles. If the church tower looks rather patched-up, that's because it was struck by lightning in 1743. It's said that local people took this as a sign that the Second Coming of Christ was imminent and that repairing their church was therefore pointless. It was many years before restoration work was finally undertaken, by which time the fabric of the tower had deteriorated even further.

LANGHAM
14 miles W of Cromer off the A149/A148

The minor road leading south from Morston will bring you, after a mile or so, to **Langham Fine Norfolk Rural Crafts** where, in a wonderful collection of restored 18th century barn workshops, you watch a variety of craftspeople exercising their traditional skills. In addition to the now famous Longham Glass works where a master glass-maker will give a running commentary, there's a pyrographer, wood-turner, stained glass maker, and glass engraver. The Factory Gift Shop is well stocked with their creations, the Antiques & Collectibles Shop offers a wide variety of items from Victorian china to

THE BLUEBELL

Holt Road, Langham,
Norfolk NR25 7BX
Tel/Fax: 01328 830502
email: newmanp@brconnect.com

Here in north Norfolk, a region classed as an Area of Outstanding Natural Beauty, **The Bluebell** public house makes its home. Set in the centre of the village of Langham, the pub has in its 400-year history been licenced to only three families.

Pat and Bridget Newman carry on the proud tradition of warm hospitality, fine ales and excellent service. Welcoming and comfortable, the interior decor features RAF memorabilia on the walls (as Langham was the site of an RAF base during the Second World War).

This traditional coaching inn offers a menu of freshly prepared food, with dishes such as rump steak, mixed grill, lobster tails, roast duck, Stilton and vegetable crumble, giant Yorkshire pudding and more. Meals are complemented by a wide range of keg, cask and guest ales, including Tetley's cask bitter. The wine list features a variety of old and new world wines. To the rear of the pub there is a welcoming beer garden. The pub also boasts superior facilities for people with disabilities, including full disabled access and a Braille menu. And for those wishing to stay for a while in this lovely part of the county, a nearby house (sleeping seven) is available for self-catering accommodation.

Lalique, and there's also a walled garden, adventure playground and restaurant.

BLAKENEY
14 miles W of Cromer on the A149

One of the most enchanting of the North Norfolk coastal villages, Blakeney was a commercial port until the beginning of the 20th century when silting up of the estuary prevented all but pleasure craft from gaining access. The silting has left a fascinating landscape of serpentine creeks and channels twisting their way through mud banks and sand hills. In a side street off the quay is the 14th century **Guildhall** (English Heritage), which was probably a private house and contains little of interest apart from the undercroft, or cellar, which is notable as an early example of a brick-built vaulted ceiling. The beautifully restored Church of St Nicholas, set on a hill overlooking village and marshland, offers much

more to the visitor. The chancel, built in 1220, is lovely Early English work, and the magnificent west tower, 100 feet high, is a

Blakeney Harbour

COTTAGE HOLIDAYS BLAKENEY

Swafield Rise, North Walsham, Norfolk
Tel: 01692 405188/403369

Cottage Holidays Blakeney can provide delightful accommodation in traditional flint holiday cottages, all of which are owner supervised and most of which are located in Blakeney's winding High Street leading directly to the picturesque quay. There are six lovely cottages in all, with charming names like The Jolly Boat, Jib Cottage and Ship's Wheel. The charm doesn't end there, though: inside and out, these cottages make for a perfect home from home. Tastefully furnished and decorated, with all modern conveniences, these wonderful cottages provide an excellent base from which to explore Blakeney and the surrounding region. Sleeping between two and six people, there's one to suit every pocket and circumstance. Each of these fine self-catering cottages features duvets, electric blankets, TV and radio. Cosy and welcoming, these listed cottages will enhance the pleasure of any holiday in Blakeney. Available all year round.

landmark for miles around. In a small turret on the northeast corner of the chancel a light would once burn as a beacon to guide ships safely into Blakeney Harbour.

CLEY-NEXT-THE-SEA
12 miles W of Cromer on the A149

Cley's name is no longer appropriate. Cley-a-mile-away-from-the-Sea would be more truthful. But in early medieval times, Cley (pronounced Cly, and meaning clay) was a more important port than King's Lynn, with a busy trade exporting wool to the Netherlands. In return, Cley imported a predilection for houses with curved gables, Flemish bricks and pantiles. The windmill overlooking the harbour adds to the sense that a little piece of Holland has strayed across the North Sea. This is the famous **Cley Mill**, the subject of thousands of paintings. Built in 1713 and in use until 1921, the Mill is open to visitors during the season (afternoons only), and also offers bed and breakfast.

The village's prosperity in the past is reflected in the enormous scale of its 14th/15th century parish church, **St Mary's**, whose south porch is particularly notable for its fine stonework and 16 armorial crests. The gorgeous

fan-vaulted roof is decorated with bosses carved with angels, flowers, and a lively scene of an old woman throwing her distaff at a fox running away with her chickens.

From Cley, it's possible to walk along the shoreline to **Blakeney Point**, the most northerly extremity of East Anglia. This spit of land that stretches three miles out into the sea is a twitcher's paradise. Some 256 species of birds have been spotted here, and the

Cley Windmill

Salthouse Church

A couple of miles south of Glandford you'll find a building of 1802 which year after year has been awarded the title of "Top Tourist Attraction in North Norfolk". **Letheringsett Watermill** stands on the site of an earlier mill recorded in the Doomsday Book and was rescued from near-dereliction in the 1980s. This fully functional, water-powered mill produces 100% wholewheat flour from locally grown wheat; there are

variety of flora is scarcely less impressive: almost 200 flowering species have been recorded.

GLANDFORD
12 miles W of Cromer off the B1156

Near this delightful village, the **Natural Surroundings Wild Flower Centre** is dedicated to gardening with a strong ecological emphasis. There are wild flower meadows and gardens, organic vegetable and herb gardens, nurseries, a nature trail alongside the unspoilt River Glaven, and the Centre also organises a wide range of events with a conservation theme. A short walk down the valley from the Centre is the **Glandford Shell Museum**, a lovely Dutch-style building which houses the private collection of Sir Alfred Jodrell, a unique accumulation of sea shells gathered from beaches all around the world, together with a fascinating variety of artefacts made from them.

Letteringsett Mill

regular demonstrations of the milling process, with a running commentary from the miller; and the end product can be purchased in the gift shop.

DAUBENEY HALL

Sharrington, Norfolk
Tel: 01263 861412

Close to Sherringham Park with its lovely gardens, **Daubeney Hall** is an impressive Grade II listed building dating back to the 16th century. The surrounding gardens and woodlands extend to two acres, home to hedgehogs, moorhens and other native wildlife. Very quiet, peaceful and secluded, the accommodation at this rural haven comprises an en suite double or twin room, or the delightful separate cottage in the former stables. All are spotless, tastefully decorated, and furnished to a high standard of comfort. All guests partake of the excellent breakfast complete with hot home-baked breads and rolls, and fresh fruit from the garden and greenhouse.

THE KINGS HEAD

19 High Street, Holt, Norfolk
Tel/Fax: 01263 712543

Enjoying a prime position on Holt's High Street, **The Kings Head** was named in honour of George III. The interior of this historic 18th century building was refurbished by a conservationist designer, utilising period colours and features. The overall effect is truly impressive and welcoming. There are four dining areas: the lounge/restaurant, the Maria Fitzherbert room (non-smoking), the Garden Room Restaurant, and the garden itself. The pub's reputation for excellent food is well deserved - the fare on offer provides a wonderful combination of the traditional and the innovative, including vegetarian dishes.

Owners Kevin and Sandra Brown have been in the trade for 40 years, and have been building on the success of this fine pub and restaurant since 1997. Kevin's kitchen staff are happy to prepare meals for any special dietary requirements. The menus boast a range of delicious meals and snacks, in addition to which there are tempting daily specials and a good children's menu. Fresh seafood is just one highlight of the culinary delights to be sampled. There are always three or four real ales on tap, an exceptional wine list and a fine selection of keg and bottled beers. This family pub is very child-friendly, with a bouncy castle and safe children's play area in the enclosed garden. Open all day seven days a week, this is the perfect place to enjoy morning coffee, lunch, supper, or just a good pint or glass of wine in very pleasant surroundings.

'HUNNYBELL'/THE BLUE BELL INN

The Green, Hunworth, Holt, Norfolk NR24 2AA
Tel: 01263 712300

The **Blue Bell Inn** in Hunworth, known by the affectionate nickname '**Hunnybell**' - from The Hunworth Bell, for the bell outside the village church - is an attractive rustic whitewashed pub with a truly warm and welcoming ambience. Owner Derek Feast and his pleasant, friendly staff ensure that all their guests are made most welcome. Built as an ale house in the 1650s, it occupies a lovely site opposite the tree-lined village green. Gardens to the side and rear include lawns and a picnic table. The rear garden overlooks open fields. The handsome interior boasts traditional features such as the stone floors, low ceilings, church pew benches and wood-burning stove. The excellent menu offers hearty staples such as home-made steak and ale pie, lamb cutlets and giant Yorkshire pudding with a variety of fillings. There are also tempting daily specials. Wednesdays are Steak Night - booking is essential for this culinary feast.

The range of sandwiches include special 'jaw breakers' - generous portions of meats and cheeses on the freshest breads. The wonderful selection of desserts includes delicious imported ice creams. And to drink, there are always five real ales including those from local breweries, as well as a good range of lagers, wines and spirits. The relaxed atmosphere and superb food and drink make this fine pub well worth seeking out.

Mannington House, Saxthorpe

HOLT
10 miles W of Cromer on the A148

A perennial finalist in the Anglia in Bloom competition, Holt's town centre always looks a picture with hanging baskets and flowers everywhere. Back in 1892, a guide-book to the county described Holt as "A clean and very prettily situated market town, being planted in a well undulating and very woody neighbourhood". More than a century later, one can't quarrel with that characterisation.

The worst day in the town's history was May 1st, 1708 when a raging fire consumed most of the town's ancient houses. The consequent rebuilding replaced them with some elegant Georgian houses, gracious buildings which played a large part in earning the town its designation as a Conservation Area.

The town's most famous building, **Gresham's School**, somehow escaped that disastrous conflagration of 1708. Founded in 1555 by Sir John Gresham, the school began as an altruistic educational establishment, its pupils accepted solely on the basis of their academic promise. Since then, the school has abandoned both its town centre location and its founder's commitment to educating, free, those bright children who could not otherwise afford it. Placing your child here, today, will drain more than £13,000 each year from your income. Solace yourself with the thought that amongst the school's many distinguished alumni are the dour creator of the BBC, Lord Reith, the poets W.H. Auden and Stephen Spender, and the composer Benjamin Britten.

Look out for one of Holt's most unusual buildings, **Home Place**. Designed and built in 1903-5 by E.S. Prior, an architect follower of the Arts & Crafts movement, the exterior of the house is completely covered with an ingeniously contrived cladding of local pebbles.

BODHAM
9 miles W of Cromer off the A148

About midway between Bodham and Weybourne, in the grounds of the Kelling Park Hotel, is the **East Anglian Falconry**

RED HART INN

The Street, Bodham, Norfolk NR25 6AP
Tel/Fax: 01263 588270

Just three miles from the coast, the lovely village of Bodham is home to the excellent **Red Hart Inn**. There's been a pub on this site since about 1685, and this former coaching inn retains many traditional features and a homely, cosy atmosphere. Popular with locals and visitors alike, the interior boasts a bar, lounge and restaurant/ function room. The inglenook fire is just the place to enjoy a drink on cold days, while the garden

with patio is perfect for fine evenings. Partners Craig and Sharon are experienced in the licenced trade, and this shows in their warm hospitality and the pub's excellent standard of service. Craig trained as a chef, and the menu offers a good range of tempting home-cooked dishes served at lunch and evenings seven days a week. Real ales (including regularly changing guest ales) are another feature of this superior pub. The caravan site adjacent to the pub can accommodate up to five vans.

Centre which, in addition to having daily flying displays, is also the largest sanctuary in the country for injured owls and birds of prey. The centre keeps and cares for over 200 birds, amongst them kestrels and sparrowhawks, as well as a number of rarer birds such as goshawks, peregrine falcons, harriers and redtail hawks, eagles and snowy owls.

WEYBOURNE
9 miles W of Cromer on the A149

Here, the shingle beach known as **Weybourne Hope** (or Hoop) slopes so steeply that an invading fleet could bring its ships right up to the shore. Which is exactly what the Danes did many times during the 9th and 10th centuries. A local adage states that "He who would Old England win, Must at Weybourne Hoop begin", and over the centuries care has been taken to protect this stretch of the coast. A map dated 1st May 1588 clearly shows "Waborne Fort" and Holt's Parish Register for that year of the Armada notes that "in this yeare was the town of Waborne fortified with a continuall garrison of men bothe of horse and foote with sconces (earthworks) ordinaunce and all manner of appoyntment to defend the Spannyards landing theare".

As it turned out, the "Spannyards" never got close, but during both World Wars the same concern was shown for defending this vulnerable beach. The garrison then became the Anti-Aircraft Permanent Range and Radar Training Wing, providing instruction for National Servicemen until the camp finally closed in 1959. It was reckoned that by then some 1,500,000 shells had been fired out to sea. The site has since been returned to agricultural use, but the original NAAFI building remains and now houses **The Muckleburgh Collection**, a fascinating museum of military vehicles, weapons, and equipment most of which has seen action in battlefields all over the world. All of the tanks,

armoured cars, and amphibious vehicles on display can be inspected at close quarters, and there are regular tank demonstrations. Meals and snacks are available - served in a NAAFI-style canteen.

Incidentally, despite Weybourne's exposed position, it has in fact only been attacked once, by the Luftwaffe on 11th July 1940. A stick of bombs landed in the main street and badly damaged two cottages.

SHERINGHAM
5 miles W of Cromer on the A149

Sheringham has made the transition from fishing village to popular seaside resort with grace and style. There are plenty of activities on offer but Sheringham has managed to avoid the brasher excesses of many English seaside towns. The beach here is among the cleanest in England and markedly different from the shingle beaches elsewhere on this part of the coast. Consisting mainly of gently sloping sand, it is excellent for bathing and the team of lifeguards makes it ideal for families with children. Rainfall at Sheringham is one of the lowest in the county and the bracing air has also recommended the town to sufferers from rheumatism and respiratory problems.

A small fleet of fishing boats still operates from here, mostly concentrating on crabs and lobsters, but also bringing in catches of cod, skate, plaice, mackerel and herring. Several original fishermens' cottages remain, some with lofts where the nets were mended.

Sheringham Beach and Sea Front

Sheringham Hall

Scott travelled to Cromer on the newly-opened Great Eastern Railway's extension from Norwich. Walking out of the town, he was entranced by the tranquillity of the countryside. In his dispatch to the *Daily Telegraph* he wrote: "It is difficult to convey an idea of the silence of the fields through which I passed, or the beauty of the prospect that surrounded me - a blue sky without a cloud across it, a sea sparkling under a haze of heat, wild flowers in profusion around me, poppies predominating everywhere..." Spurred by Scott's enthusiasm, a succession of notable Victorians made their way here - painters, writers, actors, even a youthful Winston Churchill. Later, during the Second World War, Churchill returned to the area, staying at Pear Tree Cottage in Mundesley.

Sheringham has never had a harbour, so boats are launched from the shore where stacks of creels stand as they have for generations. A "golden lobster" in the town's coat of arms celebrates this traditional industry.

Like so many other former fishing villages in England, Sheringham owes its transformation into a resort to the arrival of the railway. During the Edwardian peak years of rail travel, some 64 trains a day steamed into the station but the line became yet another victim of the Beeching closures of the 1960s. Devotees of steam trains joined together and by dint of great effort and enthusiasm managed to re-open the line in 1975 as the **North Norfolk Railway**, better known as **The Poppy Line**.

The name refers to "Poppyland", a term given to the area by the Victorian journalist Clement Scott who visited in pre-herbicide days when the summer fields were ablaze with poppies. In 1883,

Although greatly diminished in number, plenty of brilliant poppies can still be seen as you travel the scenic five-mile journey from Sheringham to Holt. The railway operates up to eight trains daily in each direction during the season, March to October, and there are special Saturday evening and Sunday lunchtime services when you can dine in style in one of the Pullman coaches from the old "Brighton Belle".

Country Lane, West Beckham

Just to the west of the town, at Upper Sheringham, footpaths lead to the lovely grounds of **Sheringham Park** (National Trust). The Park was landscaped by Humphrey Repton who declared it to be his "favourite and darling child in Norfolk". There are grand views along the coast, dense growths of oak, beech and fir trees, and banks of rhododendrons which are at most dazzling in late May and June. There's yet more grand scenery at the aptly-named **Pretty Corner**, just to the east of the A1082 at its junction with the A148. This is a particularly beautiful area of woodland and also offers superb views over the surrounding countryside.

WEST RUNTON
3 miles W of Cromer on the A149

The parish of West Runton can boast that within its boundaries lies the highest point in Norfolk - **Beacon Hill**. This eminence is 330 feet high, so you won't be needing any oxygen equipment to reach the summit, but there are some excellent views and nearby is the Roman Camp (National Trust), a misleading name since there's no evidence

that the Romans ever occupied this 70 acres of heathland. Excavations have shown, however, that in Saxon and medieval times this was an iron-working settlement.

West Runton's major tourist attraction is undoubtedly the **Norfolk Shire Horse Centre** where twice a day, during the season, these noble beasts are harnessed up and give a half-hour demonstration of the important role they played in agricultural life right up until the 1930s. They are the largest (19 hands/6 feet 4 inches high) and heaviest horses in the world, weighing more than a ton, and for generations were highly valued both as war-horses and draught animals. Several other heavy breeds, such as the Suffolk Punch, Clydesdale and Percheron, also have their home here, along with no fewer than nine different breeds of pony. The Centre also has a video room showing a 30-minute film, a small animals' enclosure and an adventure playground for children, a cafe and gift shop. A horse-drawn cart will transport you around the village and at the West Runton Riding School (on site) you can hire riding horses by the hour.

THE MIRABELLE BISTRO AND RESTAURANT

Station Road, West Runton, Cromer, Norfolk NR27 9QD
Tel: 01263 837396

Here in the coastal village of West Runton, the wonderful **Mirabelle Bistro and Restaurant** serves up a delicious range of tempting dishes. Using a cooking style with a strong Austrian influence, the chef produces mouth-watering meals using the freshest and best ingredients available, including locally caught fish, seasonal vegetables and fruits and succulent meats. The bistro has recently been completely refurbished and redecorated, and presents an extremely attractive ambience for diners. The bistro is the place to come for a lighter meal, while in the slightly more formal restaurant diners choose from

a full a la carte menu or restaurant menu. Boasting dishes such as seafood vol au vent, medallions of beef served with a lightly spiced red wine sauce, pan-fried salmon on a bed of Mediterranean char-grilled vegetables with a citrus sauce, and a tempting selection of fabulous desserts, this superb establishment has been delighting customers for over 25 years. In addition to the excellent wine list there is a fine range from the minicellar (one and a half glasses) and half bottles. Open: lunch and evening Tuesday - Saturday; Sunday evenings November to May.

AYLMERTON
3 miles W of Cromer on minor road off the A148

A couple of miles south of West Runton is one of Norfolk's grandest houses, **Felbrigg Hall** (National Trust). Thomas Windham began rebuilding the old manor house at Felbrigg in the 1620s, erecting in its place a grand Jacobean mansion with huge mullioned windows, pillared porch, and at roof-level a dedication in openwork stone: Gloria Deo in Excelsis, "Glory to God in the Highest". Later that century, Thomas' grandson William Windham I married a wealthy heiress and added the beautifully proportioned Carolean West Wing where visitors can see portraits of the happily married couple, painted by Sir Peter Lely. Their son, William Windham II, returning from his four year long Grand Tour, filled the house with treasures he had collected - so many of them that he had to extend the Hall yet again. The Windham family's ownership of Felbrigg Hall came to a tragi-comic end in the 1860s when William Frederick Windham inherited the estate. William was one of the great English eccentrics. He loved uniforms. Accoutred in the Felbrigg blue and red livery he would insist on serving at table; in guard's uniform he caused chaos on the local railway with his arbitrary whistle-blasts; dressed as a policeman, he sternly rounded up the ladies of easy virtue patrolling London's Haymarket. Inevitably, "Mad" Windham fell prey to a pretty fortune-hunter and Felbrigg was only saved from complete bankruptcy by his death at the age of 26.

The Hall was acquired by the National Trust in 1969, complete with its 18th century furnishings, collection of paintings by artists such as Kneller and van der Velde, and a wonderful Gothic library. There are extensive grounds which include a Walled Garden containing an elegant octagonal dove-house, an Orangery of 1707 sheltering an outstanding collection of camellias, many woodland and lakeside walks, a restaurant, tea room and shop.

CROMER
25 miles N of Norwich on the A149

As you enter a seaside town, what more reassuring sight could there be than to see the pier still standing? **Cromer Pier** is the genuine article, complete with Lifeboat Station and the Pavilion Theatre which still stages traditional end-of-the-pier shows. The Pier's survival is all the more impressive since it was badly damaged in 1953 and 1989, and in 1993 sliced in two by a drilling rig which had broken adrift in a storm.

Cromer has been a significant resort since the late 1700s and in its early days even received an unsolicited testimonial from Jane Austen. In her novel *Emma* (1816) a character declares that "Perry was a week at Cromer once, and he holds it to be the best of all the sea-bathing places." A succession of celebrities, ranging from Lord Tennyson and Oscar Wilde to Winston Churchill and the German Kaiser, all came to see for themselves.

The inviting sandy beach remains much as they saw it (horse-drawn bathing machines aside), and so does the Church of **St Peter & St Paul**, which boasts the tallest tower in Norfolk, 160 feet high. And then as now, Cromer Crabs were reckoned to be the most succulent in England. During the season, between April and September, crab-boats are launched from the shore (there's no harbour here), sail out to the crab banks about 3 miles offshore,

Felbrigg Hall

Cromer Beach and Pier

around the southern edge of the town for another three miles before finally entering the sea.

So Yarmouth is now a promontory, its eastern and western sides displaying markedly different characters. The seaward side is a 5-mile stretch of sandy beaches and countless amusements, with a breezy promenade from which one can watch the constant traffic of ships in Yarmouth Roads, and two fine old traditional piers, the Britannia (810 feet long) and the Wellington (600 feet). Of the host of entertainments on offer, three are particularly suitable for families. The **Sea Life Centre** includes displays of the kinds of marine life found on the Norfolk coast and an underwater viewing channel passing through shark-infested "oceans"; **Amazonia**, which is an indoor tropical paradise amongst whose reptilian residents are a 13 foot alligator and a python which if fully uncoiled would extend to some 24 feet; and the **Merrivale Model Village** which offers attractive landscaped gardens, children's rides, and an exceptionally detailed miniature village with more than 200 models.

and there the two-man teams on each boat deal with some 200 pots.

The **Lifeboat Museum**, however, is a fairly recent addition. Housed in the former Lifeboat Station, it tells the dramatic story of the courageous men who manned the town's rescue service. Pre-eminent among them was Harry Blogg who was coxswain of the lifeboat for 37 years, from 1910 to 1947. During those years his boat, the *H F Bailey*, was called out 128 times and saved 518 lives. In 1991, the H F Bailey was purchased by Peter Cadbury of the chocolate manufacturing family and presented to the Museum as its prime exhibit.

Also well worth visiting is the **Cromer Museum**, housed in a row of restored fishermen's cottages near the church, where you can follow the story of Cromer from the days of the dinosaurs, some of whose bones were found nearby, up to the present, and access the computer for thousands of pictures and facts about this attractive town.

Also on the sea front are the **Maritime Museum of East Anglia**, housed in what was formerly the Shipwrecked Sailors' Home; the **Elizabethan House** (National Trust), a merchant's house of 1596, now a museum of domestic life with 16th century panelled rooms and a functional Victorian kitchen; and, behind South Beach, the 144 foot high **Nelson's Monument** crowned by a statue, not of Norfolk's most famous son, but of Britannia. A sinew-stretching climb up the 217 steps to the viewing platform is rewarded by some striking views.

Most of Yarmouth's older buildings are concentrated in the western, or riverside, part of the town. Here you'll find **The Quay**, which Daniel Defoe considered the most beautiful in England, more than a mile long and in places 150 yards wide; a stately Town Hall worth visiting to see its grand staircase, Court Room and Assembly Room; and **The**

GREAT YARMOUTH

The topography of Great Yarmouth is rather curious. Back in Saxon times, it was actually an island, a large sandbank dotted with fishermen's cottages. Later, the narrow estuary of the River Bure at the northern end was blocked off, causing it to flow down the western side of the town. It runs parallel to the sea for two miles before joining the larger River Yare, and then their united waters curve

Rows, a medieval network of tiny courtyards and narrow alleys, a mere two feet wide in places. The Rows were badly damaged during a bombing raid in 1942 but enough remains to show their unique character. There were originally 145 of these rows, about 7 miles in total, all of them built at right angles to the sea and therefore freely ventilated by onshore breezes which, given the urban sanitary conditions of those times, must have been extremely welcome.

The bombing raid of 1942 also completely destroyed the interior of **St Nicholas'** Church, but left its walls standing. Between 1957-60, this huge building - the largest parish church in England, was completely restored and furnished in traditional style largely by using pieces garnered from redundant churches and other sources. The partly Norman font, for example, came from Highway church in Wiltshire: the organ from St Mary-the-Boltons in Kensington.

Just south of the church, off the Market Place, is the half-timbered house, built in 1641, in which Anna Sewell lived. The author of *Black Beauty* was born in the town in 1820 but it was only when she was in her late 50s that she transmuted her concern for the more humane treatment of horses into a classic and seemingly timeless novel. Anna was paid just £20 for the rights to a book which, in the five months that elapsed between its publication and her death in 1878, had already sold an incredible 100,000 copies.

Another famous author associated with the town is Charles Dickens who stayed at the Royal Hotel on Marine Parade in 1847-48 while writing *David Copperfield*. Dickens had visited the town as a child and had actually seen an upturned boat on the beach being used as a dwelling, complete with a chimney emerging from its keel. In his novel, this becomes Peggotty's house to which young Copperfield is brought following the death of his mother. "One thing I particularly noticed in this delightful house", he writes, "was the smell of fish; which was so searching, that when I took out my pocket-handkerchief to wipe my nose, I found it smelt exactly as if it had wrapped up a lobster".

In fact, the whole town at that time was pervaded with the aroma of smoked herrings, the silvery fish which were the basis of Yarmouth's prosperity. Around the time of Dickens' stay here, the author of the town's directory tried to pre-empt any discouraging effect this might have on visitors by claiming that "The wholesome exhalations arising from the fish during the operation of curing are said to have a tendency to dissipate contagious disorders, and to be generally beneficial to the human constitution which is here sometimes preserved to extreme longevity".

Across the town, some 60 curing houses were busy gutting, salting and spicing herrings to produce Yarmouth's great contribution to the English breakfast, the kipper. The process had been invented by a Yarmouth man, John Woodger: a rival of his, a Mr Bishop, developed a different method which left the fish wonderfully moist and flavoursome, and so created the famous Yarmouth bloater.

For centuries, incredible quantities of herring were landed, nearly a billion in 1913 alone. In earlier years, the trade had involved so many fishermen that there were more boats (1,123) registered at Yarmouth than at London. But the scale of the over-fishing produced the inevitable result and suddenly, within the space of two decades, the 1950s

Sands and Pier, Great Yarmouth

and 1960s, Yarmouth's herring industry found itself dead in the water. Luckily, the end of that historic trade co-incided with the beginning of North Sea oil and gas exploitation, a business which has kept the town in reasonably good economic health up to the present day.

IN AND AROUND GREAT YARMOUTH

BURGH CASTLE
4 miles W of Great Yarmouth off the A12 or A143

When the Romans established their fortress of *Garionnonum*, now known as Burgh Castle, the surrounding marshes were still under water. The fort then stood on one bank of a vast estuary, commanding a strategic position at the head of an important waterway running into the heart of East Anglia. The ruins are impressive, with walls of alternating flint and brick layers rising 15 feet high in places, and spreading more than 11 feet wide

at their base. The Romans abandoned Garionnonum around AD 408 and some two centuries later the Irish missionary St Fursey (or Fursa) founded a monastery within its walls. Later generations cannibalised both his building, and much of the crumbling Roman castle, as materials for their own churches and houses.

CAISTER-ON-SEA
4 miles N of Great Yarmouth on the A149

In Boadicea's time, this modern holiday resort with its stretch of fine sands, was an important fishing port for her people, the Iceni. After the Romans had vanquished her unruly tribe, they settled here sometime in the 2nd century and built a "castra", or castle, or Caister, of which only a few foundations and remains have yet been found. **Caister Castle**, which stands in a picturesque setting about a mile to the west of the town, is a much later construction, built in 1432-5 by the legendary Sir John Fastolf with his spoils from the French wars in which he had served, very profitably, as Governor of Normandy and also

WINTERTON VALLEY HOLIDAYS

15 Kingston Avenue, Caister-on-Sea, Norfolk NR30 5ET
Tel: 01493 377175

Advertised as the holiday estate with a difference, **Winterton Valley Holidays** offers some superb properties on th Winterton Valley Estate, between Great Yarmouth and Cromer on the B1159. Being just 8 miles from Great Yarmouth, 25 miles from Norwich,10 minutes drive to the Norfolk Broads and 40 minutes from Pleasurewood Hills family theme park, the site makes the perfect place for exploring these and other local sights and attractions such as the historic homes, museums, gardens, light railways, wildlife parks, horse centre, bird sanctuary, nature reserves, Sandringham House and more, as well, of course, as the north Norfolk coast itself.

Each chalet on this delightfully landscaped estate of holiday homes is individual in style, decoration and furnishings, and is designed to give maximum sun and the best possible view from its comfortably furnished living rooms. There's private access to Winterton's fine sandy beaches. All chalets have open-plan lounge with bed settee and dining area adjoining the fully equipped kitchen. The bathrooms have a full-size bath; some also have a shower. All chalets have two bedrooms (one with double bed, one with twin or bunk beds), sleeping between two and six people. Quiet, peaceful and relaxed, the site is the perfect place to get away from it all. Pets are very welcome.

distinguished himself leading the English bowmen at the Battle of Agincourt. Academics have enjoyed themselves for centuries disputing whether this Sir John was the model for Shakespeare's immortal rogue, Falstaff. Certainly, the historic Sir John was a larger-than-life character, but there's no evidence that he shared Falstaff's other characteristics of cowardliness, boastfulness and general over-indulgence.

Caister Castle was the first in England to be built of brick and is in fact one of the earliest brick buildings in the county. The 90 foot tower remains, together with much of the moated wall and gatehouse, now lapped by still waters and with ivy relentlessly encroaching. The castle is open daily from May to September and, as an additional attraction, there is a Motor Museum in the grounds which houses an impressive collection of veteran, Edwardian, and vintage cars, an antique fire engine, and the original car used in the film of Ian Fleming's *Chitty Chitty Bang Bang*.

About three miles west of Caister Castle, the pleasantly landscaped grounds surrounding an 1876 Victorian mansion have been transformed into the **Thrigby Hall Wildlife Gardens**, home for a renowned collection of Asian mammals, birds and reptiles. There are snow leopards and rare tigers; gibbons and crocodiles; deer and otters; and other attractions include a tropical house, aviaries, waterfowl lake, willow pattern garden, gift shop and cafe. The Gardens are open every day, all year round.

ORMESBY ST MICHAEL
9 miles NW of Great Yarmouth on the A149

Just to the north of this tiny village, at Decoy Farm, is the **Norfolk Rare Breeds Centre**, home to a wide variety of domestic and rare breed farm animals enjoying a tranquil

WINTERTON HALL

Winterton-on-Sea, Great Yarmouth, Norfolk NR29 4AL
Tel: 01493 393530 Fax: 01493 393604

Winterton Hall is a hidden place well worth seeking out. Built around 1850, this elegant manor house calls to mind a more gracious era. Set in its own gardens, it is just a five-minute walk from the beach and sand dunes. The accommodation here comprises one self-contained flat with its own entrance, suitable for two, complete with expansive lounge/dining room, fully fitted modern kitchen with dishwasher, microwave, washing machine and dryer, bedroom and fitted bath, all decorated and furnished to a very high standard of comfort and quality.

SEADELL HOLIDAY CHALETS & SHOPS

Beach Road, Hemsby, Norfolk NR29 4HS
Tel: 01493 730041 Fax: 01493 740674
email: enquiries@seadell.sagehost.co.uk
website: www.seadell.co.uk

Established since 1974, **Seadell Holiday Chalets** is a family-run business directed by Toni and Ann Reeve. This attractive chalet park has large well-kept grassed area. The delightful and charming detached and semi-detached chalets are pleasantly sited about 700 yards from the beach. Each chalet offers every convenience and comfort, and accommodates up to six people. They boast a fully equipped kitchenette, lounge, bathroom and two bedrooms (one with double bed, one with two singles). Pets are welcome at a small extra charge. The delightful coastal village of Hemsby is the centre for all that's best on the Norfolk and north Suffolk coast. Within easy reach are Great Yarmouth, Norwich, the Norfolk Broads National Park, Pleasurewood Hills theme park, Bygone Village and Thrigby Hall Wildlife Park. The onsite Seadell Shops were established in 1984. With a convenience store, newsagents, off-licence, gift shop and beach supplies, they can meet holiday-makers' every need. There are also several restaurants and pubs nearby.

Horsey Windmill

Broadland setting. Visitors can inspect the extensive collection of unusual species, see chicks hatching in the incubation room, wander round the museum which houses an interesting collection of old farm-carts, follow the Nature Trail, enjoy home-made cakes in the tearoom, and perhaps take a memento home from the well-stocked gift shop. Throughout the year, there are special events such as sheep shearing and a Heavy Horse Day.

THE NORFOLK BROADS

ACLE
10 miles W of Great Yarmouth off the A47

A thousand years ago, this small market town, now 10 miles inland, was a small fishing port on the coast. Gradually, land has been reclaimed from the estuaries of the Rivers Bure, Waveney and Yare so that today large expanses of flat land stretch away from Acle towards the sea. The town's importance as a boating centre began in the 19th century with boat-building yards springing up beside the bridge. When Acle's first Regatta was held in 1890, some 150 yachts took part. The town became known as the "Gateway to the Broads" and also as the gateway to "Windmill Land", a picturesque stretch of the River Bure dotted with windmills. The medieval bridge that formerly crossed the Bure at Acle has less agreeable associations since it was used for

numerous executions with the unfortunate victims left to dangle over the river.

Acle was granted permission for a market in 1272 and it's still held every Thursday, attracting visitors from miles around. Others come to see the unusual Church of **St Edmund** with its Saxon round tower, built some time around AD 900, crowned with a 15th century belfry from which eight carved figures look down on the beautifully thatched roof of the nave. The treasures inside include a superbly carved font, 6 feet high, and inscribed with the date 1410, and a fine 15th century screen.

SOUTH WALSHAM
9 miles E of Norwich on the B1140

This small village is notable for having two parish churches built within yards of each other. Just to the north of the village is the **Fairhaven Garden Trust**, an expanse of delightful water gardens lying beside the private **South Walsham Inner Broad**. Its centrepiece is the 900 year old King Oak, lording it over the surrounding displays of rare shrubs and plants, native wildflowers, rhododendrons and giant lilies. There are tree-lined walks, a bird sanctuary, plants for sale, and a restaurant. A vintage style river boat runs trips every half-hour around the Broad.

The best way to see the remains of **St Benet's Abbey** is from a boat along the River Bure (indeed it's quite difficult to reach it any other way). Rebuilt in 1020 by King Canute, after the Vikings had destroyed an earlier Saxon building, St Benet's became one of the richest abbeys in East Anglia. When Henry VIII closed it down in 1536 he made an unusual deal with its last Abbot. In return for creating the Abbot Bishop of Norwich, the Cathedral estates were to be handed over to the King but St Benet's properties could remain in the Abbot/Bishop's possession. Even today, the Bishop of Norwich retains the additional title of Abbot of St Benet's, and on the first Sunday in August each year, travels the last part of the journey by boat to hold an open-air service near the stately ruins of the Abbey gatehouse.

RANWORTH
14 miles NW of Great Yarmouth off the B1140

This beautiful Broadland village is famous for its church and its position on Ranworth Broad. From the tower of **St Helen's** Church it is possible to see 5 Norfolk Broads, Horsey Mill, the sea at Great Yarmouth, and on a clear day, the spire of Norwich Cathedral. Inside, the church houses one of Norfolk's greatest ecclesiastical treasures, a breathtaking early 15th century Gothic choir screen, the most beautiful and the best preserved in the county. In glowing reds, greens and golds, gifted medieval artists painted a gallery of more than thirty saints and martyrs, inserting tiny cameos of such everyday scenes as falcons seizing hares, dogs chasing ducks and, oddly for Norfolk, lions. Cromwell's bigoted vandals, offended by such idolatrous images, smothered them with brown paint - an ideal preservative for these wonderful paintings as became apparent when they were once again revealed during the course of a 19th century restoration of the church.

Just to the north of the village is the **Broadland Conservation Centre** (Norfolk Naturalists Trust), a thatched building floating on pontoons at the edge of Ranworth Broad. It houses an informative exhibition on the history of the Broads, and there's also an interesting Nature Trail which shows how

these wetlands gradually developed over the centuries.

HORNING
12 miles NE of Norwich off the A1062

The travel writer Arthur Mee described Horning as "Venice in Broadland", where "waterways wandering from the river into the gardens are crossed by tiny bridges". With its

Horning Broad

pretty reed-thatched cottages lining the bank of the River Bure and its position in the heart of the Broads, there are few more attractive places from which to explore this magical area.

POTTER HEIGHAM
13 miles NW of Great Yarmouth off the A149

Modern Potter Heigham has sprung up around the medieval bridge over the River Thurne, a low-arched structure with a clearance of only 7 foot at its highest, a notorious test for novice sailors. The Thurne is a major artery through the Broads, linking them in a continuous waterway from Horsey Mere in the east to Wroxham Broad in the west. Generally regarded as one of the liveliest of the Broadland boating centres, Potter Heigham is also home to the **Museum of the Broads**, located in boat sheds in the historic Herbert Woods boat yard. Amongst the museum's many intriguing exhibits are the only

Norfolk Reed for Thatching, Ranworth

Thurne, Norfolk

concrete dinghy ever constructed; an ice yacht; tools from traditional Broads industries such as eel catching; gun punts for duck-shooting, complete with incredibly long guns; and a display featuring one of Broadland's most destructive pests, the coypu.

A pleasant excursion from Potter Heigham is a visit to **Horsey Mere**, about six miles to the east, and **Horsey Windpump** (both National Trust). From this early 20th century drainage mill, now restored and fully working, there are lovely views across the Mere. A circular walk follows the north side of Horsey Mere, passes another windmill, and returns through the village. There's a small shop at the Windpump, and light refreshments are available.

WROXHAM
8 miles NE of Norwich on the A1151

This riverside village, linked to its twin, Hoveton, by a hump-backed bridge over the River Bure, is the self-styled "capital" of the Norfolk Broads and as such, gets extremely busy during the season. The banks of the river are chock-a-block with boatyards full of cruisers of all shapes and sizes, there's a constant traffic of boats making their way to the open spaces of **Wroxham Broad**, and in July the scene becomes even more hectic when the annual Regatta is under way.

Wroxham is also the southern terminus of the **Bure Valley Railway**, a nine-mile long, narrow-gauge (15") steam train service that closely follows the course of the River Bure through lovely countryside to the market town of Aylsham. It runs along the trackbed of the old East Norfolk Railway, has two half-scale locomotives, and specially constructed passenger coaches with large windows to provide the best possible views. In the high season, there are half a dozen trains each day, in both directions, and throughout the year there are special events such as the "Friends of Thomas the Tank Engine" days, and "Santa Specials". And if you still cherish that childhood ambition of becoming a train driver, the BVR also runs one- or two- day steam driving courses, framed to suit anyone from the absolute beginner upwards.

A couple of miles north of Wroxham is **Wroxham Barns**, a delightful collection of beautifully restored 18th century barns, set in 10 acres of countryside, and housing a community of craftspeople. There are thirteen of them, producing between them a wide range of crafts, from stained glass to woodturning, stitchcraft to handmade children's clothes, pottery to floral artistry, and much more. The complex also includes a cider-pressing centre; a junior farm with lots of "hands on" activities; a traditional Family Fair (with individually priced rides); a gift and craft shop, and a tearoom.

A mile or so east of Wroxham Barns, **Hoveton Hall Gardens** offer visitors a splendid combination of plants, shrubs and trees, with rare rhododendrons, azaleas, water plants, and dazzling herbaceous borders within a walled garden. There are woodland and lakeside walks, plant sales, gardening books, and a tea room.

Anyone interested in dried flower arrangements should make their way to the tiny hamlet of **Cangate**, another couple of miles to the east, where **Willow Farm Flowers** provides an opportunity of seeing the whole process, from the flowers in the field to the final colourful displays. The farm shop has an abundance of dried, silk, parchment and wooden flowers, beautifully arranged, and more than 50 varieties of dried flowers are available in bunches or made into arrangements of all shapes and sizes, or to special order. Willow Farm also has a picnic and play area, a guided farm walk, lays on flower arranging demonstrations and also runs one day classes for those interested in learning more about mastering this delicate-fingered skill.

COLTISHALL
8 miles N of Norwich on the B1150/B1354

This charming village beside the River Bure captivates visitors with its riverside setting, leafy lanes, elegant Dutch-gabled houses, village green and thatched church. Coltishall has a good claim to its title of "Gateway to Broadland" since for most cruisers this is the beginning of the navigable portion of the Bure. Anyone interested in Norfolk's industrial heritage will want to seek out the **Ancient Lime Kiln**, next door to the Railway Tavern in Station Road. Lime, formerly an important part of Norfolk's rural economy, is obtained by heating chalk to a very high temperature in a kiln. Most of the county sits on a bed of chalk, but in the area around Coltishall and Horstead it is of a particularly high quality. The kiln at Coltishall, one of the few surviving in the country, is a listed building of finely finished brickwork, built in a style unique to Norfolk.

The top of the tapered kiln pot is level with the ground, and down below a vaulted walkway allowed access to the grills through which the lime was raked out. This was uncomfortable and even dangerous work since fresh lime, when it comes into contact with a moist surface, such as a human body, becomes burning hot. The lime had to be slaked with water before it could be used as a fertiliser, for mortar or as whitewash. Access to the kiln is by way of the Railway Tavern, but during the months from October to March you may find that the building has been taken over by a colony of hibernating bats which, by law, may not be disturbed.

A couple of miles south of Coltishall, on the B1150, is another animal refuge, the **Redwings Horse Sanctuary**, founded in 1984 to provide a caring and permanent home for

THE HORSE AND GROOM

Market Street, Tunstead, nr Wroxham,
Norfolk NR12 8AH
Tel: 01603 738153
email: martins.horseandgroom@virgin.net

The Horse and Groom, a charming listed building with a history going back some 400 years, is the focal-point of the village of Tunstead, near Wroxham and just a mile from Wroxham Barns, a popular craft centre. There is a large car park and patio area to the rear as well as a beer garden and patio area to the front, perfect for enjoying a quiet drink and to watch the world go by, with unobscured views over the surrounding countryside.

The interior has recently been completely refurbished, while still retaining its original fireplaces and oak beams to give a friendly and cosy atmosphere. You can choose to relax in the non-smoking dining-room, lounge bar or games bar, with its pool table, dart board, shove-halfpenny board and other traditional games. There's also a separate function room, The Barn, ideal for private parties and other events. The pub hosts a range of special events throughout the year, as well as regular quiz nights, live music and karaoke evenings.

The Horse and Groom is a family-run pub, with Stewart and Vivienne personally supervising every aspect of the business. The comprehensive menu includes an impressive range of both hot and cold homemade dishes, grills and freshly-baked filled baguettes, with the emphasis on the freshest of ingredients. There are daily specials and tempting homemade desserts, as well as a very popular Sunday lunch. Families are made to feel very welcome, highchairs can be provided and there is a separate children's menu. Stewart has a very well-stocked bar with a wide range of ales, lagers, wines, spirits, soft drinks and fresh coffee.

horses, ponies, donkeys and mules rescued from neglect and slaughter. The Sanctuary cares for more than 1000 animals at any one time, and there are no indications that this number is likely to diminish. Even with the help of many volunteers, the work is expensive. To raise funds, the Sanctuary holds regular Open Days, has a gift shop with many horse-related items on sale, and also runs an Adopt-a-Horse scheme.

WORSTEAD
12 miles NE of Norwich off the A149 or B1150

Hard to imagine now, but Worstead was a busy little industrial centre in the Middle Ages. The village lent its name to the hard-wearing cloth produced in the region, and many of the original weavers' cottages can still be seen in the narrow side-streets. Worsted cloth, woven from tightly-twisted yarn, was introduced by Flemish immigrants and became popular throughout England from the 13th century onwards. The Flemish weavers settled happily into the East Anglian way of life and seem to have influenced its architecture almost as strongly as its weaving industry.

The lovely 14th century Church of **St Mary** provides ample evidence of Worstead's former prosperity. Its many treasures include a fine hammerbeam roof, a chancel screen with a remarkable painted dado, and a magnificent traceried font complete with cover. The village stages an annual weekend of events in July to raise money for the restoration of the church. The festival started

up some 35 years ago, attracting more than 35,000 visitors in 1999. The memory of Worstead's days of glory is kept alive by a still-functioning Guild of Weavers. The Guild has placed looms in the north aisle of St Mary's, and from time to time there are demonstrations of the ancient skill of weaving.

NORTH WALSHAM
9 miles SE of Cromer on the A149

This busy country town with its attractive **Market Cross** of 1600 has some interesting historical associations. Back in 1381, despite its remoteness from London, North Walsham became the focus of an uprising in support of Wat Tyler's Peasants' Rebellion. These North Norfolk rebels were led by John Litester, a local dyer, and their object was the abolition of serfdom. Their actions were mainly symbolic: invading manor houses, monasteries and town halls and burning the documents that recorded their subservient status. In a mass demonstration they gathered on Mousehold Heath outside Norwich, presented a petition to the King, and then retreated to North Walsham to await his answer. It came in the form of the sanguinary Bishop of Norwich, Henry Despenser, who, as his admiring biographer recorded, led an assault on the rebels, "grinding his teeth like a wild boar, and sparing neither himself nor his enemies,...stabbing some, unhorsing others, hacking and hewing". John Litester was captured, summarily executed and, on the

The New Inn

Church Plain, Worstead, Norfolk NR28 9RW
Tel: 01692 536296

Just off the village square near the church, **The New Inn** attracts a variety of thirsty and hungry guests. Popular with locals and visitors alike, including walkers using the 'Weavers' Trail', this friendly and welcoming inn was built in 1825. A typically English traditional inn, there are several real ales on tap including one guest ale from local breweries. The menu offers an excellent range of sandwiches, snacks and main courses such as ribs, mussels, steaks, fish and mushroom stroganoff, as well as changing daily specials, all home cooked using the freshest local produce. Accommodation is also available at this superb inn, in the form of three guest bedrooms (two doubles, one twin) overlooking meadows and the church. Tastefully furnished and decorated, with full facilities, each room is comfortable and attractive. There's also a touring caravan site on the grounds, for up to five vans.

Lord Nelson's School

orders of the Bishop, "divided into four parts, and sent throughout the country to Norwich, Yarmouth, Lynn and to the site of his own house".

A more glorious fate awaited the town's most famous resident, Horatio Nelson, who came to the Paston School here in 1768 as a boy of ten. Horatio was already dreaming of a naval career and three years later, when he read in the county newspaper that his Uncle Maurice had been appointed commander of a warship, he prevailed on his father to let him join the Raisonnable.

The **Paston School** had been founded in 1606 by Sir William Paston. His ancestors were the writers of the extraordinary collection of more than a thousand letters, written between 1422 and 1509, which present an astonishingly vivid picture of East Anglian life at the end of the turbulent Middle Ages. Sir William himself is buried in the parish church where he personally supervised (and paid for) the construction of the impressive marble and alabaster monument he desired to be erected in his memory.

About four miles east of North Walsham, near the village of Erpingham on the A140, **Alby Crafts & Gardens** has a Crafts Gallery promoting the excellence of mainly East Anglian and British craftsmanship - lacework, woodturning, jewellery, canework, and much more. The "Plantsman's Garden" displays a fine collection of unusual shrubs, plants and bulbs in a 4 acre site, there are workshops where you can watch craftsmen at work, a Bottle Museum (small charge for admission) and a tea-room.

THE DUTCH OVEN

4 Church Street, North Walsham, Norfolk NR28 9DA
Tel: 01692 405955

Just a short walk from North Walsham's splendid church, **The Dutch Oven** is well known locally as an excellent bakery, confectionery and for its fresh wholesome food. It's long been a family business, now run by Chris Williams who took over from this parents in 1992. Over the years the family have built up an impressive reputation for service and quality.

This lively, friendly restaurant has become a regular meeting place for local residents; visitors are also made most welcome. The menu offers a good choice of hot and cold light meals and snacks from a hearty breakfast through mouth-watering pastries and fresh crusty breads made on the premises. Sandwiches, filled rolls or jacket potatoes, ploughmans and salads all feature on the extensive menu. The large, modern and comfortable interior is cheerful and airy, with facilities for people with disabilities. To one side is 'The Mad Fryer', serving traditional fish and chips to eat in or take away. Its convenient town centre location makes it ideal for a relaxing and pleasant break from shopping or sight-seeing. Open: Monday to Saturday 8.30 to 4.30.

MUNDESLEY
7 miles SE of Cromer on the B1159

"The finest air in the kingdom has been wasted for centuries" said a speaker celebrating the arrival of the railway at Mundesley in 1898, "because nobody had the courage to bring the people to the district". The railway has been and gone, but the fresh breezes off the North Sea remain as invigorating as ever.

After the hazards of the coastline immediately to the north where cliffs, fields and houses have all been eroded by the relentless sea, it's a pleasure to arrive at this unassuming holiday resort with its superb sandy beach, considered by many the very best in Norfolk. Mundesley village is quite small (appropriately, its Maritime Museum is believed to be the smallest museum in the country) but it provides all the facilities conducive to a relaxing family holiday. Best of all, there is safe swimming in the sea and when the tide is out children can spend many a happy hour exploring the many "lowes", or shallow lagoons, left behind.

PASTON
9 miles SE of Cromer on the B1159

It was in this small village that the Paston family entered the historical record. The vivid collection of letters they wrote to each other during the years that England was being wracked by the Wars of the Roses has already been mentioned, and the village boasts another magnificent legacy from this remarkable family. In 1581, Sir William Paston built a cavernous tithe-barn here with flint walls and a thatched roof. It still stands, it's roof still thatched: 160 feet long, almost 60 feet high - the longest, most imposing barn in Norfolk. In the nearby church, the most striking of the family memorials is the one dedicated to Katherine Paston. Sculpted in alabaster by Nicholas Stone in 1628, Katherine lies dressed to kill in her Jacobean finery of starched ruff, embroidered bodice, puffed sleeves and pearl necklaces. The monument cost £340, a staggering sum of money at that time.

HAPPISBURGH
14 miles SE of Cromer on the B1159

The coastal waters off Happisburgh (or "Hazeborough" to give the village its unlikely but correct pronunciation), have seen many a shipwreck over the centuries, and the victims lie buried in the graveyard of **St Mary's** Church. The large grassy mound on the north side of the church contains the bodies of the ill-fated crew of HMS Invincible, wrecked on the treacherous sandbanks here in 1801. The ship was on its way to join up with Nelson's fleet at Copenhagen when the tragedy occurred, resulting in the deaths of 119 sailors. Happisburgh's distinctive Lighthouse, built in 1791 and striped like a barber's pole, certainly proved ineffectual on that occasion; as did the soaring 110 foot tower of the church itself which could normally be relied on as a "back-up" warning to mariners.

Inside the Church is a splendid 15th century octagonal font carved with the figures of lions, satyrs, and "wild men"; and embedded in the pillars along the aisle are the marks left by shrapnel from German bombs dropped on the village in 1940.

LESSINGHAM
17 miles SE of Cromer off the B1159

From this small village a lane winds down through spectacular dunes to the sands at Eccles Beach and, a little further north, to Cart Gap with its gently sloping beach and colourful lines of beach huts.

About four miles south of Lessingham stands a windmill that is not just the tallest in Norfolk, but in the whole of England. Eighty feet high, **Sutton Windmill** was built in the year of the French Revolution, 1789, and its millstones only finally ground to a halt in 1940. Chris Nunn bought the mill in 1976 and since then he has devoted himself to renovating this glorious nine-storey building with the ultimate aim of restoring it to working order. During those years, Chris and his family have also built up a fascinating private collection of artefacts which reflect the social history of Norfolk over the past 150 years or so. These are on display in the family's privately-owned **Broadlands Museum**, a magpie's nest in which you'll find anything from vintage kitchen and veterinary tools to a reconstructed Pharmacy Shop of the 1880s, complete with a fine collection of patent medicines, ointments and pills.

6 King's Lynn and West Norfolk

Along most of The Wash's 50-mile shoreline there is no human habitation: good news for the more than 160,000 wading birds and 51,000 wild ducks who have claimed the coast for themselves. It's surprising to find that one of England's most important ports in medieval times, King's Lynn, sat at the southern end of the underwater maze of sandbanks in The Wash. Keels were shallower then, of course, but without such modern aids as echo-sounders it must still have taken sailing skills of a high order to navigate one's way into the safety of King's Lynn harbour.

Holkham Hall

South of King's Lynn the countryside never quite decides whether it belongs to the Cambridgeshire fenland, with its bread-board level contours and over-arching skyscapes, or to the subtly-rounded undulations of central Norfolk where each twist of the road reveals yet another unblemished rural scene.

Within a radius of a few miles from the small town of Fakenham can be found a remarkable variety of places of interest. To the north, in the valley of the River Stiffkey, the Shrine of Our Lady of Walsingham was in medieval times second only to that of Thomas à Becket at Canterbury as a pilgrim destination. To the northeast, the Thursford Collection is home to an astonishing gathering of steam-powered engines of every description, including a monumental Wurlitzer organ. On the eastern outskirts of the town you can visit the premier collection of endangered and exotic waterbirds to be found in Europe, and over to the west stands the Marquess of Cholmondely's majestic home, Houghton Hall.

The shoreline along Norfolk's northwest coast changes from the perfect sands at Hunstanton to salt marshes threaded by winding creeks, and windswept dunes barely held in place by marram grass. It's an exhilarating coast, with huge skies, ozone-tangy breezes sweeping in from the North Sea, and an abundance of wildlife. There are three separate Nature Reserves within an eight-mile stretch, including the huge National Trust-owned bird sanctuary of Scolt Head Island. An admirable

Oxburgh Hall

way to experience the area to the full is to walk all or part of the Coastal Footpath which begins at Holme next the Sea and follows the coastline for some 36 miles eastwards to Cromer, for most of its route well away from any roads.

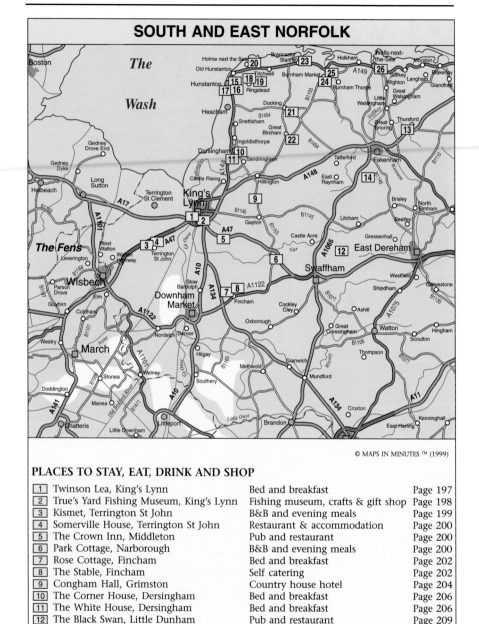

SOUTH AND EAST NORFOLK

© MAPS IN MINUTES ™ (1999)

PLACES TO STAY, EAT, DRINK AND SHOP

KING'S LYNN

In the opinion of James Lee-Milne, the National Trust's architectural authority, "The finest old streets anywhere in England" are to be found at King's Lynn. Tudor, Jacobean and Flemish houses mingle harmoniously with grand medieval churches and stately civic buildings. It's not surprising that BBC Television chose the town to represent early 19th century London in their production of *Martin Chuzzlewit*. It seems, though, that word of this ancient sea-port's many treasures has not yet been widely broadcast, so most visitors to the area tend to stay on the King's Lynn by-pass, making their way to the better-known attractions of the north Norfolk coast. They are missing a lot.

The best place to start an exploration of the town is at the beautiful Church of St Margaret, founded in 1101 and with a remarkable leaning arch of that original building still intact. The architecture is impressive but the church is especially famous for its two outstanding 14th century brasses, generally reckoned to be the two largest and most monumental in the kingdom. Richly engraved, one shows workers in a vineyard, the other, commemorating Robert Braunche, represents the great feast which Robert hosted at King's Lynn for Edward III in 1364.

Marks on the tower doorway indicate the church's, and the town's, vulnerability to the waters of the Wash and the River Great Ouse. They show the high-water levels reached during the great floods of 11 March 1883 (the lowest), 31 January 1953 and 11 January, 1978.

The organist at St Margaret's in the mid 18th century was the celebrated writer on music, Dr Charles Burney, but his daughter

Twinson Lea

109 Tennyson Road, King's Lynn, Norfolk PE30 5PA
Tel: 01553 762900 Fax: 01553 769944

Twinson Lea in Tennyson Road, King's Lynn, is a charming Victorian home offering bed and breakfast accommodation. There are three handsome and very comfortable guest bedrooms (one family room, one double, one single). Owners Susan and David Thomas offer all their guests a very warm welcome. Just 10 minutes from the centre of town, opposite 'The Walks', King's Lynn's delightful parkland area, this makes a perfect base for exploring this part of the county and further afield. All rooms offer full facilities and are furnished and decorated to a high standard of comfort and quality. The dining room is furnished in pine; it is here that the delicious breakfast is served. Vegetarian or other dietary requirements are happily catered for. For a truly relaxing home from home, look no further.

Customs House, King's Lynn

Fanny was perhaps even more interesting. She wrote a best-selling novel, *Evelina*, at the age of 25, became a leading light of London society, a close friend of Dr Johnson and Sir Joshua Reynolds, and at the age of 59 underwent an operation for breast cancer without anaesthetic. She only fainted once during the 20 minute operation, and went on to continue her active social life until her death at the ripe old age of 87.

Alongside the north wall of St Margaret's is the **Saturday Market Place**, one of the town's two market places, and a few steps further is one of the most striking sights in the town, the **Guildhall of the Holy Trinity** with a distinctive chequerboard design of black flint and white stone. The Guildhall was built in 1421, extended in Elizabethan times, and its Great Hall is still used today for wedding ceremonies and various civic events.

Next door to the Guildhall is the Town Hall of 1895, which in a good-neighbourly way is constructed in the same flint and stone pattern. The Town Hall also houses the **Museum of Lynn Life** where, along with displays telling the story of the town's 900 years, you can also admire the municipal

TRUE'S YARD FISHING MUSEUM

North Street, King's Lynn, Norfolk PE30 1QW
Tel: 01553 770479 Fax: 01553 765100 email: trues.yard@virgin.net

For an insight into the life of King's Lynn's old fishing community, a visit to **True's Yard Fishing Museum** is highly recommended. Located on North Street, it is King's Lynn's last remaining fisherman's yard. Two tiny cottages are all that is left of the North End which was once King's Lynn's busy fishing community, with its own boatbuilders, chandlers, sailmakers, pubs, bakehouses and school. Everything else was swept away during the slum clearances of the 1930s. At one time, hundreds of families lived within a stone's throw of their chapel of St Nicholas, which still dominates the area. Now, although the fishing fleet still sails regularly from King's Lynn, the old way of life has gone. One of the cottages is furnished in the style of the 1850s, the other in that of the 1920s.

Beautifully and faithfully restored, these cottages tell the fascinating story of how life was lived in days gone by - with families of up to 11 sharing the tiny two-room cottages (sometimes nine children to a bed!), no bathrooms or sewage systems, no cooking facilities, primitive healthcare and precious few of the comforts people nowadays take for granted. Both cottages are stocked with a wealth of memorabilia from the days of fishing under sail - the tools of the trade, knotwork ornaments, models of the old fishing smacks, vintage photographs and hand-knitted 'ganseys'. Other features of the site

include a marvellous gift shop selling unusual and attractive items on the seafaring theme, including jewellery and ornaments, local crafts and books, and the tea room, open all day and serving a wide variety of homemade cakes and snacks, teas and fresh coffee. True's Yard also offers research facilities for those wishing to trace their ancestry or for students researching the area. Open: daily 9.30; last admissions 3.45. Guided tours available. Group visits welcome. True's Yard is accessible by wheelchair everywhere except the upstairs rooms at the cottages.

regalia. The greatest treasure in this collection is King John's Cup, a dazzling piece of medieval workmanship with coloured enamel scenes set in gold. The Cup was supposed to be part of King John's treasure which had been lost in 1215 when his overburdened baggage train was crossing the Nene Estuary and sank into the treacherous quicksands. This venerable legend is sadly undermined by the fact that the Cup was not made until 1340, more than a century after John was dead.

A short distance from the Town Hall, standing proudly by itself on the banks of the River Purfleet, is the handsome **Custom House** of 1683, designed by the celebrated local architect Henry Bell.

There's not enough space here to list all of the town's many other important buildings, but mention must be made of the **Hanseatic Warehouse** (1428), the **South Gate** (1440), the **Greenland Fishery Building** (1605), and the **Guildhall of St George**, built around 1406 and reputedly the oldest civic hall in England. The Hall was from time to time also used a theatre and it's known that Shakespeare's travelling company played here. It's considered highly likely that the Bard himself trod the boards. If true, his appearance would be very appropriate since the Guildhall is now home to the **King's Lynn Arts Centre**, which is active all year round with events and exhibitions, and since 1951 has arranged an annual Arts Festival in July with concerts, theatre and a composer in

residence. Some of the concerts are held in St Nicholas' Chapel, a medieval building whose acoustics outmatch those of many a modern concert hall.

At **Caithness Crystal** Visitor Centre, visitors can watch craftsmen at close quarters as they shape and manipulate the glass into beautiful objets d'art.

AROUND KING'S LYNN

TERRINGTON ST CLEMENT
6 miles W of Kings Lynn off the A17

Terrington St Clement is a sizeable village notable for the "**Cathedral of the Marshland**", a 14th century Gothic masterwork more properly known as St Clement's Church, and for the **African Violet Centre** where some quarter of a million violets are grown each year, in a wide range of colour and species.

STOW BARDOLPH
8 miles S of King's Lynn off the A10

Holy Trinity Church at Stow Bardolph houses one of the oddest memorials in the country. Before her death in 1744, Sarah Hare, youngest daughter of the Lord of the Manor, Sir Thomas Hare, arranged for a life-sized effigy of herself to be made in wax. It was said to be an exceptionally good likeness:

'KISMET'

Main Road, Terrington St John, Kings Lynn, Norfolk PE14 7RR
Tel/Fax: 01945 881364

'Kismet' Bed & Breakfast is a welcoming RAC 4 diamond accommodation offering a comfortable place to stay while in this part of the world. In addition it has received the RAC Warm Welcome and RAC Sparkling Diamond accolades.

The property was built as a farm manor house around 1850, changed to a village store from 1900 and reverted to a family home in 1986. Characterful and cosy, it is a non-smoking house offering one twin and two double bedrooms (all fully ensuite). There is a guest lounge/dining room. The rooms are very comfortable as well as tastefully decorated and furnished. Owners Frances and Ken Goodwin are friendly and welcoming hosts. Evening meals by prior arrangement. There is a public phone box opposite the house and the village bakery, garage and store are all within 200 yds. There are three pubs serving food and one restaurant all nearby. It is handy for Peckover House, Wisbech, historic Kings Lynn, Sandringham House and many other local sites and attractions making this an ideal base.

SOMERVILLE HOUSE

Church Road, Terrington St John, Wisbech,
Cambridgeshire PE14 7RY Tel/Fax: 01945 880952
e-mail: somervillemc@hotmail.com

Somerville House, lying off the A47 between Kings Lynn
and Wisbech/Peterborough, is an excellent fully licensed
restaurant with accommodation. Hosts Colin and Mibette
are welcoming and conscientious. Colin is a trained chef who
has worked at several fine hotels including London's Mayfair,
Hilton and Claridges. Discerning diners come from far and wide to sample the fine food on offer. The
menus provide a selection of carefully chosen starters, main courses, desserts and cheeses, and are
changed fortnightly to take advantage of the freshest local produce and seasonal foods. All dishes are
home-cooked and home-prepared. This attractive restaurant overlooks the handsome gardens. The
accommodation comprises three en suite guest bedrooms (one double, one twin and a single). All
bedrooms are furnished and decorated to a high standard of comfort and taste. The charming and very
comfortable lounge has a cosy wood-burning stove and is open to guests and visitors alike. Set in
spacious mature gardens of approximately two acres on the edge of the Fens, this excellent establishment
makes a wonderful spot for a relaxed and enjoyable midweek or weekend break.

THE CROWN INN

Lynn Road, Middleton, King's Lynn,
Norfolk PE32 1RH
Tel: 01553 841925 Fax: 01553 840385

Martin and Pauline Robinson offer a warm welcome to all
their guests at the excellent **Crown Inn** in Middleton. Both
Martin and Pauline are experienced in the catering and
licenced trade, and took over at this friendly inn in July
2000. Martin is a trained chef who is in charge of the
interesting and varied menu, made up of traditional home-
cooked English and French dishes ranging from Liver and Bacon to Filet Mignon. His "Famous
Ploughmans" is deservedly popular, consisting of a full salad with pickles, fruit, three crusty rolls and a
choice of Cheddar, English ham or prawns. This venerable coaching inn dates back to at least the
1700s, and occupies a central position in this charming village, just opposite of St Mary's Church.
There are two bars and a restaurant. The Snug has an open brick fire and very comfortable and attractive
furnishings and decor. The public bar has pew bench seating and a lively atmosphere. Real ales on tap
include Adnams and the very popular Batemans Dark Mild, as well as a changing guest ale.

PARK COTTAGE

Narford Road, Narborough, King's Lynn,
Norfolk PE32 1HZ
Tel: 01760 337220

Originally two cottages tastefully refurbished and
redecorated to a high standard of comfort and
quality, **Park Cottage** offers excellent bed and
breakfast accommodation. There are three charming
and comfortable guest bedrooms, a large family
room, small double (also let as a single) and an
ensuite double. All boast full facilities in a warm
and welcoming ambience. The guests' lounge is
beautiful, with plush furnishings and a log-burning stove for those wintry evenings. The marvellous
three-acre garden is a secluded haven for visitors to explore and savour, and leads to peaceful woodland
beyond. There's also a large games room complete with full-size snooker table and exercise machine for
guests to enjoy. The full English breakfast comprises the freshest ingredients; special dietary requirements
are happily catered for. Evening meals are also available on request.

if so, Sarah appears to have been a rather uncomely maiden, and afflicted with boils to boot. Her death was attributed to blood poisoning after she had pricked her finger with a needle, an act of Divine retribution, apparently, for her sin of sewing on a Sunday. Sarah was attired in a dress she had chosen herself, placed in a windowed mahogany cabinet, and the monument set up in the Hare family's chapel, a grandiose structure which is larger than the chancel of the church itself.

DOWNHAM MARKET
10 miles S of King's Lynn off the A10/A1122

Once the site for a major horse fair, this compact little market town stands at the very edge of the Fens, with the River Great Ouse and the New Bedford Drain running side by side at its western edge. Many of its houses are built in the distinctive brick and carrstone style of the area. One of the finest examples of this traditional use of local materials can be seen at Dial House in Railway Road (now a guest house), which was built in the late 1600s.

The parish church has managed to find a small hill on which to perch. It's an unassuming building with a rather incongruously splendid glass chandelier from the 1730s. Another feature of the town, much loved by postcard manufacturers, is the elegant, riotously decorated cast-iron **Clock Tower** in the market place. This was erected in 1878 at a cost of £450 and "was worth every penny of it!" The tower's backdrop of attractive cottages provides a charming setting for a holiday snap.

Two great names are associated with this small town: Charles I, disguised as a clergyman, stayed at Downham Market for a night during his flight after the Battle of Naseby, and Horatio (later Lord) Nelson, son of the parson of Burnham Thorpe, was sent to the little school here.

DENVER
2 miles S of Downham Market off the A10/A1122

Denver Sluice was originally built in 1651 by the Dutch engineer, Cornelius Vermuyden, as part of a scheme to drain 20,000 acres of land owned by the Duke of Bedford. Various modifications were made to the system over the years, but the principle remains the same, and the oldest surviving sluice, built in 1834, is still in use today. Running parallel with it is the modern **Great Denver Sluice**, opened in 1964: together these two sluices control the flow of a large complex of rivers and drainage channels, and are able to divert floodwaters into the Flood Relief Channel that runs alongside the Great Ouse. The two great drainage cuts constructed by Vermuyden are known as the Old and New Bedford rivers, and the strip of land between them, never more than 1,000 yards wide, is called the Ouse Washes. This is deliberately allowed to flood during the winter months so that the fields on either side remain dry. The drains run side by side for more than 13 miles, to Earith in Cambridgeshire, and this has become a favourite route for walkers, with a rich variety of bird, animal and insect life to be seen along the way.

Denver Windmill, built in 1835 but put out of commission in 1941, when the sails were struck by lightning, re-opened in 2000. This wonderful working mill set on the edge of the Fens has been carefully restored. On-site attractions include a visitor centre, craft workshops, bakery and tea shop. Holiday accommodation is also available.

HILGAY
3 miles S of Downham Market off the A10

When the Domesday Book was written, Hilgay was recorded as one of only two settlements in the Norfolk fens. It was then an island, its few houses planted on a low hill rising from the surrounding marshland. The village is scarcely any larger today, there's not a lot to see, but collectors of unusual gravestones make their way to its churchyard seeking the last resting-place of George William Manby who, during the Napoleonic wars, invented the rocket-powered life line fired to ships in distress. His gravestone is carved with a ship, an anchor, a depiction of his rocket device, and an inscription that ends with the reproachful words, "The public should have paid this tribute".

OXBOROUGH
10 miles SE of Downham Market off the A134

How many hamlets in the country, one

ROSE COTTAGE

Fincham, Norfolk PE33 9HF
Tel/Fax: 01366 347426

Rose Cottage is a stately brickbuilt home offering excellent bed and breakfast accommodation. Featured in the *Which? Good Bed & Breakfast Guide*, this charming home from home is tucked away off the A1122 between Fincham and Downham Market, making it the perfect base for exploring Ely, King's Lynn, Swaffham and the many other sights and attractions of the region. This supremely attractive Georgian house is set in its own grounds, with a large well-tended garden, croquet lawn and an atmosphere of peace and rural tranquillity. Comfortable, spotless and warm, it offers two comfortable and handsome guest bedrooms (both twins, one ensuite, one with shared bathroom with Victorian bath), furnished and decorated to a high standard of comfort and luxury. The excellent English breakfast is hearty and delicious, setting guests up for a day's sightseeing, shopping or the wonderful walks which Fincham is famous for. Special dietary requirements are happily catered for. Owner Angela Vaughan-Arbuckle is a conscientious and friendly host, offering all her guests a warm and hospitable welcome. Born in Hannover, she has lived in England with her husband Ian for over 35 years, though naturally she speaks fluent German. Children and small dogs welcome. No smoking. 3 diamonds.

THE STABLE

Rose Cottage, Fincham, Norfolk PE33 9HF
Tel/Fax: 01366 347426

Within the grounds of Rose Cottage, **The Stable** is a carefully and sensitively converted building first constructed in 1826. It retains its original traditional character while being tastefully redesigned to offer every modern facility. Standing in a corner of its own two-acre grounds included a pond, it is equipped and furnished to a good standard of quality and comfort. Affording unrestricted views over open countryside, it is the perfect rural hideaway. This self-catering accommodation is just a mile from the nearest shop and pub. Comprising a lounge with dining area, kitchen, bathroom/toilet and two bedrooms (one double, one twin), it is cosy and welcoming. There's a lovely open fire in the

lounge. All logs, fuel, power, bed linen and towels are included. Other amenities include a washing machine, incoming telephone, TV, radio/stereo music centre, microwave, high chair and cot. Outdoors there's a lovely courtyard with garden chairs and a croquet set. Owner Angela Vaughan-Arbuckle extends the same courtesy and consideration to guests here as to those at her B&B in Rose Cottage nearby. Handy for Ely, the North Norfolk coast, Norwich, Cambridge and Peterborough, this charming self-catering establishment makes a good base for exploring the area. ETC 3 stars Commended.

Oxburgh Hall

to draw the short straw when the Tudors needed someone to discharge an unpleasant or difficult task. It was an earlier Sir Edmund who was charged with the care of Henry VIII's discarded wife, Catherine of Aragon, and his son, Sir Henry, was given the even more onerous task of looking after the King's official bastard, the Princess Elizabeth. After Elizabeth's accession as Queen, Sir Henry presented himself at Court, no doubt with some misgivings. Elizabeth received him civilly but, as he was leaving, tartly observed that "if we have any prisoner whom we would have hardlie and strictly kept, we will send him to you."

As staunch Catholics, the Bedingfelds were, for the next two and a half centuries, consigned to the margins of English political life. Their estates dwindled as portions were sold to meet the punitive taxes imposed on adherents of the Old Faith. By the middle of the 20th century, the Bedingfelds long tenure of Oxburgh was drawing to a close. In 1951, the 9th Baronet, another Sir Edmund, sold Oxburgh to a builder who promptly announced his intention of demolishing the house. Sir Edmund's mother, the Dowager Lady Sybil, was shocked by such vandalism and used her considerable powers of persuasion to raise sufficient funds to buy back the house. She then conveyed it into the safe keeping of the National Trust.

The grounds at Oxburgh provide the perfect foil for the mellow old building, reflected in its broad moat. There's a wonderfully formal, and colourful, French Garden; a walled Kitchen Garden; and woodland walks.

wonders, can boast two such different buildings of note as those to be seen at Oxborough. First there's the Church of **St John the Evangelist**, remarkable for its rare brass eagle lectern of 1498, and its glorious Bedingfeld Chapel of 1525, sheltering twin monuments to Sir Edmund Bedingfeld and his wife fashioned in the then newly popular material of terracotta.

It was Sir Edmund who built **Oxburgh Hall** (National Trust), a breathtakingly lovely moated house built of pale-rose brick and white stone. Sir Edmund's descendants still live in what a later architect, Pugin, described as "one of the noblest specimens of domestic architecture of the 15th century". Henry VII and his Queen, Elizabeth of York, visited in 1497 and lodged in the splendid State Apartments which form a bridge between the lofty gatehouse towers, and which ever since have been known as the King's Room and the Queen's Room. On display here is the original Charter of 1482, affixed with Edward IV's Great Seal of England, granting Sir Edmund permission to build with "stone, lime and sand", and to fortify the building with battlements. These rooms also house some magnificent period furniture, a collection of royal letters to the Bedingfelds, and the huge Sheldon Tapestry Map of 1647 showing Oxfordshire and Berkshire. Another, more poignant, tapestry, known as the Marian Needlework, was the joint handiwork of Elizabeth, Countess of Shrewsbury, and Mary, Queen of Scots, during the latter's captivity here in 1570. The Bedingfelds seemed always

CASTLE RISING
5 miles NE of King's Lynn off the A148/A149

As the bells ring for Sunday morning service at Castle Rising, a group of elderly ladies leave the mellow red brick Bede House and walk in procession to the church. They are all dressed in long scarlet cloaks, emblazoned on

Castle Rising

tableau vivant of the procession of these blameless virgins to the church seems completely in keeping with this picturesque village which rates high on any "must-not-miss" list of places to visit in Norfolk. The church to which the ladies are making their way, St Lawrence's, although much of it has been reconstructed, is an outstanding example of Norman and Early English work. But overshadowing everything else in this pretty village is the massive **Castle Keep** (English Heritage), its well-preserved walls rising 50 feet high, and pierced by a single entrance. The Keep's towering presence is made even more formidable by the huge earthworks on which it stands. The Castle was built in 1150, guarding what was then the sea approach to the River Ouse. (The marshy shore is now some three miles distant and still retreating.)

the left breast with a badge of the Howard family arms. Once a year, on Founder's Day, they add to their regular Sunday costume a tall-crowned hat typical of the Jacobean period, just like those worn in stereotypical pictures of broomstick-flying witches.

These ladies are the residents of the almshouses founded by Henry Howard, Earl of Northampton, in 1614, and their regular Sunday attendance at church was one of the conditions he imposed on the 11 needy spinsters who were to enjoy his beneficence. Howard also required that each inmate of his "Hospital of the Holy and Undivided Trinity" must also "be able to read, if such a one may be had, single, 56 at least, no common beggar, harlot, scold, drunkard, haunter of taverns, inns or alehouses". The weekly

Despite its fortress-like appearance, Castle Rising was much more of a residential building than a defensive one. In 1331, when Edward III found it necessary to banish his ferocious French-born mother, Isabella, to some reasonably comfortable place of safety, he chose this far-from-London castle. She was to spend some 27 years here before her death in 1358, never seeing her son again during that time. How could Edward treat his own

Congham Hall

Grimston, King's Lynn, Norfolk PE32 1AH
Tel: 01485 600250 Fax: 01485 601191
e-mail: reception@conghamhallhotel.co.uk

A fine Georgian manor has been transformed into one of the finest country house hotels in the land. The setting, in 30 acres of parkland, lawns and gardens, is both beautiful and serene, and guests enjoy the highest standards of comfort and service.

Fine antiques are enhanced by exquisite soft furnishings in the day rooms and the 17 non-smoking bedrooms, all with private bathroom, tv, radio and lovely fresh flowers. Smart dress is requested for dinner in the superb Orangery Restaurant. Guests have free use of the tennis courts and outdoor swimming pool.

mother in such a way? Her crime, in his view, was that the '"She-Wolf of France", as all her enemies and many of her friends called Isabella, had joined forces with her lover Mortimer against her homosexual husband Edward II (young Edward's father), and later colluded in the king's grisly murder at Berkeley Castle. A red-hot poker, inserted anally, was the instrument of his death. For three years after that loathsome assassination, Isabella and Mortimer ruled England as Regents. The moment Edward III achieved his majority, he had Mortimer hung, drawn and quartered. His mother he despatched to a lonely retirement at Castle Rising.

Sandringham House

Six and a half centuries later, the spacious grounds around the castle provide an appropriate backdrop for an annual display by members of the White Society. Caparisoned in colourful medieval garments and armed with more-or-less authentic replicas of swords and halberds, these modern White Knights stage a battle for control of the castle.

SANDRINGHAM
8 miles NE of King's Lynn off the A149/B1140

A couple of miles north of Castle Rising is the entrance to **Sandringham Country Park** and **Sandringham House**, the royal family's country retreat. Unlike the State Rooms at Windsor Castle and Buckingham Palace, where visitors marvel at the awesome trappings of majesty, at Sandringham they can savour the atmosphere of a family home. The rooms the visitor sees at Sandringham are those used by the royal family when in residence, complete with family portraits and photographs, and comfy armchairs. Successive royal owners have furnished the house with an intriguing medley of the grand, the domestic and the unusual. Entering the principal reception room, The Saloon, for example, you pass a weighing-machine with a leather-covered seat, a common amenity apparently in great houses of the 19th century. In the same room, with

its attractively carved Minstrels' Gallery, hangs a fine family portrait by one of Queen Victoria's favourite artists, Heinrich von Angeli. It shows the Prince of Wales (later Edward VII), his wife Alexandra and two of their children, with Sandringham in the background.

The Prince first saw Sandringham on 4th February 1862. At Victoria's instigation, the 20-year-old heir to the throne had been searching for some time for a country property, a refuge of the kind his parents already enjoyed at Balmoral and Osborne. A courtier accompanying the Prince reported back that although the outside of house was ugly, it was pleasant and convenient within, and set in pretty grounds. The surrounding countryside was plain, he went on, but the property was in excellent order and the opportunity of securing it should not be missed. Within days, the purchase was completed.

Most of the "ugly" house disappeared a few years later when the Prince rebuilt the main residence; the "pretty grounds" have matured into one of the most beautiful landscaped areas in the country. And the "plain" countryside around - open heath and grassland overrun by rabbits, has been transformed into a wooded country park, part of the coastal Area of Outstanding Natural Beauty.

One of the additions the Prince made to the house in 1883 was a Ballroom, much to the relief of Princess Alexandra. "It is beautiful I think & a great success", she wrote, "& avoids pulling the hall to pieces each time there is a ball or anything". This attractive room is now used for cinema shows and the estate workers Christmas party. Displayed on the walls is a remarkable collection of Indian weapons, presented to the Prince during his state visit in 1875-6,

and hidden away in a recess, are the two flags planted at the South Pole by the Shackleton expedition.

Just across from the house, the old coach-houses and stables have been converted into a fascinating museum. There are some truly splendid royal vehicles here, including the first car bought by a member of the royal

THE CORNER HOUSE

2 Sandringham Road, Dersingham,
King's Lynn, Norfolk PE31 6LL
Tel: 01485 543532

The Corner House in Dersingham is a delightful mid-Victorian home offering bed and breakfast accommodation. Owner Brenda Smith offers a warm and friendly welcome to all her guests. Popular with holidaymakers and those attracted to the excellent walking, cycling, birdwatching and other sights and attractions of the area - particularly Sandringham - this fine establishment features three comfortable and attractive guest bedrooms. Guests are also welcome to enjoy the lovely garden and lounge/dining room, overlooking the garden. Recently refurbished and redecorated to a high standard, the decor is bright, cheerful and welcoming. Featuring every amenity, guests are certain to enjoy their stay here. The full English breakfast makes use of the freshest ingredients, and includes fresh and dried fruits, yogurts, and other extras that make for a hearty start to a day's sightseeing.

THE WHITE HOUSE

44 Hunstanton Road, Dersingham, Norfolk PE31 6HQ
Tel: 01485 541895 Fax: 01485 544880

An excellent place for bed and breakfast in Dersingham is **The White House** on Hunstanton Road. This substantial Victorian detached house is owned by Valerie Brundle, step-mother of the well-known motor racing driver, Martin. Valerie herself is an active rally driver - scattered around the house are some interesting motor racing memorabilia, including Martin's racing helmet and trophies.

Birds are another of Valerie's interests. She is a member of the Royal Society for the Protection of Birds and a keen supporter of the RSPB sanctuary at Snettisham Scalp, just a couple of miles away. The White House has six spacious and well-appointed letting rooms, all ensuite, and all furnished and equipped to a high standard well above their 3

Diamonds Commended rating from the ETB. Two of the bedrooms occupy the ground floor. The hearty traditional breakfast, included in the tariff, will certainly set guests up for a day of exploring this appealing corner of the county, whether your preference is for sandy beaches, prime bird-watching areas or stately homes such as Sandringham House, Holkham Hall and Houghton Hall. This fine establishment is also just 10 minutes from King's Lynn, and within easy reach of natural beauties such as lavender fields and a butterfly park. Please note there is no smoking anywhere in the house.

family - a 1900 Daimler - and an evocative series of old photographs depicting the life of the royal family at Sandringham from 1862 until Christmas 1951. Other attractions at Sandringham include a visitors centre, adventure playground, nature walks, souvenir shop, restaurant and tearoom.

DERSINGHAM
9 miles NE of King's Lynn off the A149

This large village just north of Sandringham was actually the source of the latter's name: in the Domesday Book, the manor was inscribed as "Sant-Dersingham": Norfolk tongues found "Sandringham" much easier to get around. Dersingham village has expanded greatly in recent years and modern housing has claimed much of Dersingham Common, although there are still many pleasant walks here through **Dersingham Wood** and the adjoining Sandringham Country Park.

SNETTISHAM
11 miles N of King's Lynn off the A149

Snettisham is best known nowadays for its spacious, sandy beaches and the **RSPB Bird Sanctuary**, both about two miles west of the village itself. But for centuries Snettisham was much more famous as a prime quarry for carrstone, an attractive soft-white building-block that provided the "light relief" for the walls of thousands of Georgian houses around the country, and for nearby Sandringham House. The carrstone quarry is still working, its product now destined mainly for "goldfish ponds and the entrance-banks of the more pretentious types of bungalow". Unfortunately, one has to go the British Museum in London to see Snettisham's greatest gift to the national heritage: an opulent collection of gold and silver ornaments from the 1st century AD, the largest hoard of treasure trove ever found in Britain, discovered here in 1991.

HEACHAM
13 miles N of King's Lynn off the A149

Heacham Park Fishery on Pocahontas Lake is set within the original boudnary of Heacham Hall. This three and a half acre freshwater late was re-established in 1996. Spring 1997 saw the introduction to the lake

of specimen carp, to be followed in 1998 by rudd, bream, perch and roach. The lake takes its name from the renowned Native American princess, who is said to have stayed at Heacham Hall in the 1600s, as a guest of the Rolfe family.

Just outside this charming village is the famous **Norfolk Lavender**, the largest lavender-growing and distilling operation in the country. Established in 1932, it is also the oldest. The information point at the western entrance is sited in an attractive listed building which has become something of a Norfolk landmark. On entering the site, visitors instinctively breathe in, savouring the unmistakeable aroma that fills the air. Guided tours of the grounds run throughout the day from the Spring Bank Holiday until the end of September, and during the lavender harvest, visitors can tour the distillery and see how the wonderful fragrance is made.

As well as being a working farm, this is also the home of the National Collection of Lavenders, a living botanical dictionary which displays the many different colours, sizes and smells of this lovely plant. Amongst other attractions at Norfolk Lavender are a Fragrant Meadow Garden, Fragrant Plant Centre, Herb Garden, a gift shop selling a wide variety of products, and a tea room serving cream teas and even lavender and lemon scones!

SWAFFHAM

Swaffham's one-time claim to be the "Montpellier of England" was justified by the abundance of handsome Georgian houses that used to surround the large, wedge-shaped market place. A good number still survive, along with the **Assembly Room** of 1817 where the quality would foregather for concerts, balls and soirees. The central focus of the market square is the elegant **Butter Cross** presented to the town by the Earl of Orford in 1783. It's not a cross at all but a classical lead-covered dome standing on eight columns and surmounted by a life-size statue of Ceres, the Roman goddess of agriculture, an appropriate symbol for this busy market town from which ten roads radiate out across the county. From the market place an avenue of limes leads to the quite outstanding

Church of **St Peter & St Paul**, a 15th century masterpiece with one of the very best double hammerbeam roofs in the county, strikingly embellished with a host of angels, their wings widespread. The unknown mason who devised the church's harmonious proportions made it 51 feet wide, 51 feet high and 102 feet long. Carved on a bench-end here is a man in medieval dress accompanied by a dog on a chain. The same two figures are incorporated in the town's coat of arms, and also appear in the elegantly designed town sign just beyond the market place. The man is the "Pedlar of Swaffham", a certain John Chapman who, according to legend, dreamed that if he made his way to London Bridge he would meet a stranger who would make him rich. The pedlar and his dog set off for London, and on the bridge he was eventually accosted by a stranger who asked him what he was doing there. John recounted his dream. Scoffingly, the stranger said "If I were a dreamer, I should go to Swaffham. Recently I dreamt that in Swaffham lived a man named Chapman, and in his garden, buried under a tree, lay a treasure." John hastily returned home, uprooted the only tree in his garden, and unearthed two jugs full of gold coins.

There was indeed a John Chapman who contributed generously to the building of the parish church in the late 1400s. Cynics claim that he was a wealthy merchant, and that similar tales occur in the folklore of most European countries. Whatever the truth, there's no doubt that the people of Swaffham took the story to their hearts.

John Chapman may be Swaffham's best known character locally, but internationally the name of Howard Carter, the discoverer of Tutankhamen's tomb, is much better known. Carter was born at Swaffham in 1874; his death in 1939 was attributed by the popular press to the "Curse of Tutankhamen". If so, it must have been an extremely sluggish curse. Some 17 years had elapsed since Carter had knelt by a dark, underground opening, swivelled his torch and found himself the first human being in centuries to gaze on the astonishing treasures buried in the tomb of the teenage Pharaoh.

Swaffham Museum in the Town Hall is the setting for the story of the town's past. Visitors can follow Howard Carter's road to the Valley of the Kings, see the Symonds Colelction of handmade figurines, and admire the Sporle collection of locally-found artefacts.

Move on some 1,400 years from the death of Tutankhamen to Norfolk in the 1st century AD. Before a battle, members of the Iceni tribe, led by Boadicea, would squeeze the blue sap of the woad plant onto their faces in the hope of frightening the Roman invaders (or any other of their many enemies). At **Cockley Cley Iceni Village and Museums**, three miles southwest of Swaffham, archaeologists have reconstructed a village of Boadicea's time, complete with wooden huts, moat, drawbridge and palisades. Reconstruction though it is, the village is remarkably effective in evoking a sense of what daily life for our ancestors entailed more than 1,900 years ago.

A more recent addition to Swaffham's attractions is the **EcoTech Discovery Centre**, opened in 1998. Through intriguing interactive displays and hands-on demonstrations, visitors can discover what startling innovations current, and possible, technology may have in store for us during the next millennium.

AROUND SWAFFHAM

CASTLE ACRE
4 miles N of Swaffham off the A1065

Set on a hill surrounded by water meadows, Castle Acre seems still to linger in the Middle Ages. William de Warenne, William the Conqueror's son-in-law, came here very soon after the Conquest and built a Castle that was one of the first, and largest, in the country to be built by the Normans. Of that vast fortress, little remains apart from the gargantuan earthworks and a squat 13th century, gateway.

Much more has survived of **Castle Acre Priory**, founded in 1090 and set in fields beside the River Nar. Its glorious West Front gives a powerful indication of how majestic a triumph of late Norman architecture the complete Priory must have been. With five apses and twin towers, the ground plan was modelled on the Cluniac mother church in Burgundy where William de Warenne had stayed while making a pilgrimage to Rome.

Castle Acre

Today the noble ruins of the Priory are powerfully atmospheric, a brooding scene skillfully exploited by Roger Corman when he filmed here for his screen version of Edgar Allan Poe's ghostly story, *The Tomb of Ligeia*.

Castle Acre village is extremely picturesque, the first place in Norfolk to be designated a Conservation Area, in 1971. Most of the village, including the 15th century parish church, is built in traditional flint with a few later houses of brick blending in remarkably happily.

Despite the Priory's great size, it appears that perhaps as few as 25 monks lived here during the Middle Ages. And in some comfort, to judge from the well-preserved Prior's House which has its own bath and built-in wash-basin. The Priory lay on the main route to the famous Shrine at Walsingham with which it tried to compete by offering pilgrims a rival attraction in the form of an arm of St Philip.

LITCHAM
11 miles NE of Swaffham on the B1145

Small though it is, this village strung alongside the infant River Nar can boast an intriguing **Village Museum**, with displays of local artefacts from Roman times to the

THE BLACK SWAN

The Street, Little Dunham, nr Swaffham, Norfolk PE32 2DG
Tel/Fax: 01760 722200

The Black Swan public house and restaurant in Little Dunham is a friendly and welcoming place with an enviable reputation for great food and drink and warm hospitality. Owners Paula and Alan Budd took over at this fine pub in March of 1999; they and their friendly, helpful staff offer all their guests a hearty welcome. Built in the mid-1600s, this traditional coaching house serves several fine real ales including Green King IPA, Speckled Hen, Shepherd Neame and changing guest ales, together with a good range of lagers, bottled beers, wines and spirits.

The original barns and stables have been sensitively converted into the comfortable restaurant, where the menu offers a variety of home-cooked, freshly prepared and delicious dishes such as giant filled Yorkshire puddings, chicken and mushroom pie, vegetable curry, trout, fish specials and the popular sizzling platters. The tempting desserts are also well worth leaving room for. Meals are served at lunch and evening Tuesday to Sunday. In the centre of this delightful small village, there's a nine-hole golf course and Dunham fishing lakes with some excellent trout fishing nearby, making this a relaxing base from which to explore the surrounding area and further afield.

present, an extensive collection of photographs, some of which date back to 1865, and an underground lime kiln.

FAKENHAM

Fakenham is a busy and prosperous-looking market town, famous for its National Hunt Racecourse, antique & bric-a-brac markets and auctions, and as a major agricultural centre for the region. Straddling the River Wensum, this attractive country town has a number of fine late-18th and early-19th century brick buildings in and around the Market Place. And it must surely be one of the few towns in England where the former gasworks (still intact) have been turned into a **Museum of Gas & Local History**, housing an impressive historical display of domestic gas appliances of every kind. Fakenham Church also has an unusual feature, a powder room - although the room over the large porch, built in 1497, was used for storing gunpowder rather than cosmetics. Even older than the church is the 700 year-old hunting lodge, built for the Duchy of Lancaster, which is

now part of the Crown Hotel. As an antidote to the idea that Norfolk is unremittingly flat, take the B1105 north out of Fakenham and after about half a mile take the first minor road to the left. This quiet road loops over and around the rolling hills, a 10 mile drive of wonderfully soothing countryside that only ends at Wells-next-the-Sea.

AROUND FAKENHAM

Southeast of Fakenham, off the A1067, **Pensthorpe Waterfowl Park** is home to Europe's best collection of endangered and exotic waterbirds. Over 120 species of waterfowl can be seen here in their natural surroundings, a wonderful avian refuge where you may come across anything from a scarlet ibis to the more familiar oystercatcher, along with avocets and ruff. The spacious walk-through enclosures offer close contact with shy wading birds, and in the Dulverton Aviary elegant spoonbills and bearded tits vie for your attention. There are good facilities for the disabled and children, a Wildlife Brass Rubbing Centre, nature trails through 200

HOLLY LODGE

The Street, Thursford Green,
Norfolk NR21 0AS
Tel/Fax: 01328 878465
e-mail: hollyguestlodge@talk21.com

Holly Lodge dates back to the 18th century and enjoys a splendid rural setting. Set back from the road in one acre of lawns, attractive garden and fruit orchards, leading onto open farmland, this very attractive home has many lovely original features that will be welcomed by discerning guests, who will relish the real luxury offered amid tranquil surroundings.

Adjacent to the house are the three guest cottages, created from the

former stable block which has been delightfully rebuilt, sympathetically restored and refurbished. All are beautifully furnished and decorated, with exposed beams and other charming features. The first cottage has a medieval feel, with a large four-poster bed. The second is more Colonial in style, with furnishings and decor to match, while the third cottage offers a taste of New England. The guests' lounge and dining area are in the main house. The first has flagstone flooring and a lovely inglenook fireplace, and overlooks the rear sun terrace and front orchard. The excellent breakfast includes fresh farm produce.

The area is popular with birdwatchers and walkers as there are many superb walks in the region. Holly Lodge is conveniently located near many places of interest and beautiful north Norfolk coastline and countryside. AA 5 Diamonds and English Tourism Council 5 Diamonds.

acres of the Wensum Valley countryside, a restaurant and a shop.

THURSFORD GREEN
4 miles NE of Fakenham off the A148

About two minutes' walk from Thursford Green stands what is perhaps the most unusual museum in Norfolk, **The Thursford Collection**. George Cushing began this extraordinary collection of steam-powered traction engines, fairground organs and carousels back in 1946 when "one ton of tractor cost £1". Perhaps the most astonishing exhibit is a 1931 Wurlitzer organ whose 1,339 pipes can produce an amazing repertoire of sounds, - horses' hooves, fire engine sirens, claps of thunder, waves crashing on sand, and the toot-toot of an old railway engine are just some of the Wurlitzer's marvellous effects. There are regular live music shows when the Wurlitzer displays its virtuosity and other attractions include a steam-powered Venetian Gondola ride, shops selling a wide variety of goods, many of them locally made, and a tearoom. A mile or so north of the Thursford museum, in the village of Hindringham, Mill Farm Rare Breeds is home to dozens of cattle, sheep, pigs, goats, ponies, poultry and waterfowl which were once commonplace but are now very rare. These intriguing creatures have some 30 acres of lovely countryside to roam around. Children are encouraged to feed the animals and there's also an Adventure Playground, crazy golf course, craft & gift shop, picnic area and tearoom.

GREAT SNORING
5 miles NE of Fakenham off the A148

The names of the twin villages, Great and Little Snoring, are such a perennial source of amusement to visitors it seems almost churlish to explain that they are derived from a Saxon family called Snear. At Great Snoring, the main street rises from a bridge over the River Stiffkey and climbs up to St Mary's Church. Just across from the church,

LITTLE WALSINGHAM
5 miles N of Fakenham on the B1105

Every year, some half a million pilgrims make their way to this little village of just over 500 souls to worship at the **Shrine of Our Lady**

Shrine of Our Lady of Walsingham

of Walsingham. In 1061 the Lady of the Manor of Walsingham, Lady Richeldis de Faverches, had a vision of the Holy Virgin in which she was instructed to build a replica of the Holy House in Nazareth, the house in which the Archangel Gabriel had told Mary that she would be the mother of Christ. Archaeologists have located the original house erected by Lady Richeldis. It was just 13 feet by 23 feet and made of wood, later to be enclosed in stone.

These were the years of the Crusades, and the **Holy House** at Walsingham soon became a major centre of pilgrimage, because it was regarded by the pious as an authentic piece of the Holy Land. Around 1153, an **Augustinian Priory** was established to protect the shrine, now encrusted with jewels, gold and silver, and to provide accommodation for the pilgrims. The Priory is in ruins now but the largest surviving part, a stately Gatehouse on the east side of the High Street is very impressive.

For almost 500 years, Walsingham prospered. Erasmus of Rotterdam visited in 1511 and was critical of the rampant commercialisation of the Shrine with its plethora of bogus relics and religious souvenirs for sale. He was shown a gigantic bone, "the finger-joint of St Peter" no less, and in return for a small piece of translation was presented with a highly aromatic fragment of wood - a sliver of a bench on which the Virgin had once seated herself.

In the same year that Erasmus visited, Henry VIII also made the pilgrimage that all his royal predecessors since Richard I had undertaken. He stayed overnight at the enchanting early-Tudor mansion, **East Barsham Hall**, a glorious medley of mullioned windows, towers, turrets, and a group of 10 chimneys, each one individually carved with an amazing variety of styles. Since the King's visit, the Hall has had a succession of owners over the years, among them a Hapsburg Duke who entertained his neighbours in truly Imperial style before disappearing leaving behind some truly imperial debts, and the pop group the Bee Gees. The Hall is today owned by a London businessman and not open to the public, but it stands for all to see as you enter the village.

After his overnight stay at East Barsham Hall, Henry VIII, like most other pilgrims, went first to the **Slipper Chapel**, a beautiful 14th century building about a mile away in Houghton St Giles. Here he removed his shoes and completed the last stretch on foot. Despite this show of piety, some 25 years later Henry had no hesitation in closing the Priory along with all the other monastic institutions in his realm, seizing its treasures and endowments, and having its image of the Virgin publicly burnt at Chelsea.

Little Walsingham itself is an exceptionally attractive village, set in the midst of parks and woodlands, and with fine medieval and Georgian houses lining its streets. Also of interest is the 16th century octagonal **Clink in Common Place**, used in medieval times as a lock-up for petty offenders; the scanty ruins of Walsingham's **Franciscan Friary** of 1347; and the former **Shire Hall**, which is now a museum.

GREAT WALSINGHAM
5 miles N of Fakenham on the B1388

English place names observe a logic of their own, so Great Walsingham is of course smaller than Little Walsingham. The two villages are very different in atmosphere and appearance, Great Walsingham displaying the typical layout of a rural Norfolk settlement, with attractive cottages set around a green watered by the River Stiffkey, and dominated by a fine 14th century church, **St Peter's**, noted for its superb window tracery, wondrously carved Norman font, and perfectly preserved 15th century carved benches.

WIGHTON
7 miles N of Fakenham, on the B1105

Wighton Post Office must be one of very few in the country where you can buy a postal order and a pint at the same time. This happy state of affairs has come about because the post office desk is located in the bar of the village pub, The Carpenters Arms. The desk is open two days a week and provides all the normal post office services apart from passports and Road Tax licences. This unusual arrangement has been featured on the TV programme *Country File*.

Just outside the village, the Wells & Walsingham Railway trundles its way between Little Walsingham and Wells-next-the-Sea.

TATTERFORD
5 miles SW of Fakenham off the A148 or A1065

This tiny village is well-known to botanists for **Tatterford Common**, an unspoilt tract of rough heathland with tiny ponds, some wild apple trees, and the River Tat running through it to join the River Wensum about a mile away.

About four miles west of Tatterford stands **Houghton Hall**, home of the Marquess of Cholmondely and one of Norfolk's most magnificent buildings. This glorious demi-palace was built in the Palladian style during the 1720s by Sir Robert Walpole, England's first Prime Minister. The Walpoles had been gentlemen of substance here since the 14th century. With his family revenues augmented by the considerable profits Sir Robert extracted from his political office, he was in a position to spend lavishly and ostentatiously on his new house. The first step was to completely destroy the village of Houghton (it spoilt the view), and re-house the villagers a mile away at New Houghton.

Although Sir Robert deliberately cultivated the manner of a bluff, down-to-earth Norfolk squire, the personal decisions he made regarding the design and furnishings of the house reveal a man of deep culture and refined taste. It was he who insisted that the Hall could not be built in homely Norfolk brick, but in the whole of the county there is virtually no stone suitable for construction on this scale. The expensive decision was taken to use the exceptionally durable stone quarried at Aislaby in North Yorkshire, transporting it by sea from Whitby to King's Lynn. More than two and a half centuries later, the Aislaby stone is still flawless, the only sign of its age a slight weathering that has softened its colour to a creamy gold.

To decorate the interior and design the furniture, Sir Robert commissioned the versatile William Kent. Kent was at the peak of his powers - just look at the decoration in the Stone Hall, the exquisite canopied bed in the Green Velvet Bedchamber, and the finely-carved woodwork throughout which made impressive use of the newly-discovered hardwood called mahogany. And then there were the paintings, an incomparable collection of Old Masters personally selected by Sir Robert. Sadly, many of them are now in the Hermitage Museum in St Petersburg, sold by his wastrel grandson to the Empress Catherine of Russia.

This grandson, George, 3rd Earl of Orford, succeeded to the title at the age of 21 and spent the next 40 years dissipating his enormous inheritance. When his uncle Horace (the 4th Earl, but better known as Horace Walpole, novelist, MP and inveterate gossip) succeeded to the title he found "Houghton half a ruin ... the two great staircases exposed to all weathers; every room in the wings rotting with wet; the park half-covered with nettles and weeds; mortgages swallowing the estate, and a debt of above £40,000."

Houghton's decline was arrested when the Hall passed by marriage to the Marquess of Cholmondely, Lord Great Chamberlain, in 1797. But it wasn't until 1913, when George, later the 5th Marquess, moved into the house with his new wife, Sybil Sassoon, that Houghton was fully restored to its former state of grace. The depleted collection of paintings was augmented with fine works by Sir Joshua Reynolds and others from Cholmondely Castle in Cheshire, and the Marchioness introduced new collections of exquisite French furniture and porcelain.

One of the 6th Marquess' interests was military history, and in 1928 he began the astonishing Model Soldiers Collection now on display at Houghton. More than 20,000 perfectly preserved models are deployed in meticulous reconstructions of battles such as Culloden and Waterloo, and in one exhibit, recreating the Grand Review of the British Army in 1895, no fewer than 3,000 figures are on parade.

EAST RAYNHAM
3 miles SW of Fakenham, on the A1065

Raynham Hall is another superb Palladian mansion, designed by Inigo Jones and with

THE COLKIRK CROWN

Crown Road, Colkirk, Fakenham, Norfolk NR21 7AA
Tel: 01328 862172 Fax: 01328 863916

The Colkirk Crown is not to be missed. A pub has stood on this spot for over 300 years, and licensees Pat and Rosemary Whitmore have been resident here for 21 of them, attracting custom with delicious food, their knowledge of wine and most pleasant and convivial atmosphere. Popular with locals and visitors alike, the Lions Club meets at the pub on the first Monday evening of each month. There's a lovely lawned garden fringed with trees and shrubs, and ample car parking. Pat says, 'I always make a point of selling wine by the glass (125ml and 175ml), which means its easier to try more wines than would be possible buying a bottle every time.' Real ales on tap include a changing guest beer. Rosemary creates interesting traditional menus which offer a wide choice for everyone's taste, cooked to perfection and served in the comfortable non-smoking dining area and the bar. The local MG club brings a collection of classic MGs to the car park on the first Tuesday evening of each month.

BURLEIGH HOUSE HOTEL

7 Cliff Terrace, Hunstanton,
Norfolk PE36 6DY
Tel: 01485 533080

Rated 4 Diamonds by the English Tourist Board, **Burleigh House Hotel** is a charming Victorian family-run hotel in an enviable location close to Hunstanton's sea front, garden and town centre, yet still peaceful and quiet.

The guest bedrooms are large and inviting. Some offer sea views and all are en suite. The guests' lounge and separate bar are welcoming and comfortable. Evening meals are available, with an extensive menu of home-cooked and home-prepared favourites.

MARINE HOTEL

St Edmunds Terrace, Hunstanton, Norfolk PE36 5EH
Tel: 01485 533310

Hunstanton's **Marine Hotel** has a friendly atmosphere and occupies a fine and very convenient location in the town, near the Green and overlooking the sea. Handy for shops and all of the town's amenities, this very good hotel has 14 guest bedrooms, most of which offer sea views. Every room is comfortable and welcoming, furnished and decorated to a good standard of comfort and quality. The spacious dining room is well-appointed; it is here that guests take their breakfast. There's also a very good residents' bar open weekdays 11-11 and Sundays midday-10.30. Food is served here from 11 a.m.-9 p.m. A good range of snacks and meals are served here, including traditional favourites, chicken and meat dishes, fish, salads, steaks, sandwiches and more, all expertly prepared and presented. For a real home from home, look no further.

STONECOURT

33 Greave Gate, Hunstanton, Norfolk PE36 6AF
Tel: 01485 533892 Fax: 01485 533088

In the centre of Hunstanton, yet just five or six minutes from the beach, there are two different types of self-catering holiday accommodation worth taking a closer look at. **Stonecourt** is the name of the first. This delightful flat offers three charming bedrooms (two doubles and a twin), cosy lounge and large, well-equipped kitchen with washing machine. All linen provided. The second property, **St Edmunds Cottage**, stands opposite the church and next to Stonecourt. This very large

cottage sleeps two people. Comprising a twin bedroom, shower room, toilets upstairs and down, fully fitted kitchen and laundry room, it is beautifully furnished and decorated. Pets welcome. Owners Elwyn and Eric Price maintain a high standard of comfort in both properties. The atmosphere in both is warm and welcoming. Bed & breakfast accommodation is also available - please phone for details.

magnificent rooms created a century later by William Kent. The house is only open to the public by appointment since it is the private residence of the 7th Marquess of Townshend. It was his 18th century ancestor, the 2nd Viscount (better known as "Turnip" Townshend), who revolutionised English agriculture by promoting the humble turnip as an effective means of reclaiming untended land, for feeding cattle in winter, and along with wheat, barley and clover, as part of the four year rotation of crops that provided a cycle of essential nutrients for the soil. The Townshend family have owned extensive estates in this area for centuries and in St Mary's Church there are some fine monuments to their ancestors, the oldest and most sumptuous of which commemorates Sir Roger, who died in 1493.

THE NORTHWEST COAST

Although the whole of Norfolk lies on a foundation of chalk, 1,000 feet deep in places, it is only in this northwest corner that it lies close enough to the surface to have been used as a building material. Once exposed to the air, the chalk, or "clunch" as it's known, becomes a surprisingly durable material. It was widely used in medieval buildings and can still be found in many barns, farmhouses and cottages in the area. Chalk was also quarried and then burnt to produce lime, prodigious quantities of which were used in building the sublime churches of the Middle Ages.

HUNSTANTON
16 miles N of King's Lynn on the A149

The busy seaside resort of Hunstanton can boast two unique features: one, it has the only cliffs in England made up of colourful levels of red, white and brown strata, and two, it is the only east coast resort that faces west, looking across The Wash to the Lincolnshire coast and the unmistakeable tower of the 272 foot high Boston Stump, (more properly described as the Church of St Botolph).

Hunstanton town is a comparative newcomer, developed in the 1860s by Mr Hamon L'Estrange of nearby Hunstanton Hall to take advantage of the arrival of the railway

Hunstanton Cliffs and Beach

here, and to exploit the natural appeal of its broad, sandy beaches. The centre is well-planned with mock-Tudor houses grouped around a green that falls away to the shore.

Hunstanton's social standing was assured after the Prince of Wales, later Edward VII, came here to recover from typhoid fever. He stayed at the Sandringham Hotel which, sadly, has since been demolished, along with the grand Victorian pier, and the railway. But Hunston, as locals call the town, still has a distinct 19th century charm about it and plenty to entertain visitors.

The huge stretches of sandy beach, framed by those multi-coloured cliffs, are just heaven for children who will also be fascinated by the **Kingdom of the Sea**, on the South Promenade, where an underwater glass tunnel provides a fascinating opportunity to watch the varied and often weird forms of marine life that inhabit Britain's waters. A popular excursion from Hunstanton is the boat trip to Seal Island, a sandbank in The Wash where seals can indeed often be seen sunbathing at low tide.

SEDGEFORD ROAD FARM HOLIDAY COTTAGES

Ringstead, Hunstanton, Norfolk PE36 5JZ
Tel: 01485 525530/525316 Fax: 01485 525321

Located on the outskirts of this unspoilt village and surrounded by beautiful countryside, **Sedgeford Road Farm Holiday Cottages** more than deserve their English Tourist Board rating of 5 Keys, Highly Commended. The Good Holiday Cottage Guide also heaps praise on these two "absolute delights", noting their "beautifully cared for interiors, deep sofas and armchairs, the most appealing pictures and prints we have seen on our travels, attractive lamps, pretty curtains, good fitted carpets, peace and quiet". These two exceptional cottages have been carefully converted from

old farm buildings, beautifully furnished and well equipped with central heating and double glazing. "Tumblers" was formerly the old cart shed, which used to house the old Norfolk "tumbler" carts - hence the name. This two-bedroomed building has been sympathetically converted and retains many original features, such as the exposed beams. The other cottage, named "Pickles Patch" after owner Margaret Greer's beloved cat, has three bedrooms, its own partly-enclosed patio, and lovely views over the countryside. Both cottages, each of which has its own garden furniture, have access to nearly an acre of garden.

THE RINGSTEAD GALLERY

Ringstead, Hunstanton, Norfolk PE36 5JZ
Tel: 01485 525316 Fax: 01485 525321 email: ringstead.gallery@btinternet.com

Margaret Greer, owner of Sedgeford Road Farm, and her husband Don are also partners in the **Ringstead Gallery**, which attracts discerning art lovers from across the country. Don and Margaret opened the gallery some 27 years ago in a lovely old traditional stable building with whitewashed stone walls, an upper level gallery and two display areas on the ground floor. Here visitors will find an excellent choice of fine paintings by such artists as Lawrie Williamson, Jeremy Barlow, Philip Gardner,Patrick Boswell, Godfrey Sayers, Rosemary Cook, Sue Riley, Peter Barker, Neil Cox and many more. Their paintings capture the essence of the beguiling Norfolk landscape of sea, marshes and gently rolling countryside, wildlife and Continental influences.

The gallery also displays an exciting range of striking bronzes and a good selection of limited editions. All the works exhibited, from fine turned wood and oak furniture to sculpture and paintings, bear witness to the high standard of quality maintained by the Greers. Mixed exhibitions throughout the year are interspersed with special one-artist shows. Open: Monday-Saturday 10-5; certain Sundays - please ring for details.

THE WHITE HORSE

40 Kirkgate Street, Holme-next-the-Sea, Norfolk PE36 6LH
Tel: 01485 525512

The White Horse in Holme is a delightful classic English public house offering great food, drink and a relaxing and friendly ambience. Paul and Sue Middleton took over in 1984; this family-run concern had been run by Sue's grandmother, who took over in 1943, then by her parents Albert and Mary Hayter who ran it until 1984. Paul and Sue are now ably assisted by their daughter Stephanie who is their talented chef. They and their attentive staff are friendly and helpful. They have a loyal group of regulars, as well as being popular with visitors, many of whom are returning holiday-makers who come year after year for the unique brand of hospitality found here. Originally a farmhouse, built in the 1600s, it became an alehouse in

1860. The Tap Bar is handsome and welcoming, with a wood/brick bar, quarry tiled floor, low beamed ceiling and horse brasses adorning the walls and bar. The Small Bar is adorned with interesting police memorabilia such as hats, helmets, badges and insignia from police forces all over the world. The

large (no smoking) restaurant is comfort-able and attractive, with a large brick inglenook fireplace. The menu features traditional and inspired dishes from the sea, the "feathered brigade", and chef's grill, with beef, pork and chicken favourites, plus a good selection of vegetarian dishes. The daily fresh fish is just one speciality. Stephanie's steak pie and fish pie are very popular, and deservedly so as they are hearty and delicious. The excellent puddings are well worth leaving room for. In addition there's a daily specials board. Booking is advised for the popular Sunday lunch. Food is served Tuesday to Sunday at lunch; Tuesday to Saturday evening meals. Real ales on tap include Flowers and Adnams; there's also a good range of lagers, wines, spirits and soft drinks. Food and drink can be enjoyed in the comfortable and pristine restaurant itself or in the lawned beer garden. This fine pub is open seven days a week in summer; every session apart from Monday lunchtime November to March.

PILGRIMS REACH RESTAURANT AND FREEHOUSE

High Street, Docking, Norfolk PE31 8NH
Tel: 01485 518383

Pilgrims Reach Restaurant and Freehouse on the edge of the village is certainly worth a pilgrimage for its excellent food, drink, attentive service and hospitality. There's a relaxed atmosphere in this jolly inn, owned and run by James Lee and Sally Mash, enthusiastic hosts who have made this a "must-visit" restaurant for anyone in the area.

Although widely travelled, James was born and bred locally and is delighted that he is now running a successful business in "his own backyard''. The restaurant is housed in a traditional Norfolk building of brick, chalk and flint, parts of which are believed to date back to the 16th century. The interior is adorned with some fascinating local memorabilia: old hand tools, eel picks, the tools of the

shepherd's trade, old implements used by marshmen and thatchers - all relating to a bygone Norfolk when life was lived at a gentler pace. A collection of old photographs of wherries and punts on the Norfolk Broads, and sailing vessels and lifeboats on the Norfolk coast, enhance the strong "local flavour'' of the place.

Flavours of a different kind are in evidence on the quite outstanding menu, in which fish dishes have pride of place - Lowestoft-landed cod fillet in crispy beer batter, for example, or kiln-smoked Scottish salmon fillet roasted with whisky and dill. If mussels are on the menu, only a couple of hours may have elapsed between their being harvested and served. There's a special mussel menu in winter, and a crab menu in summer. If guests prefer meat, poultry or vegetarian dishes, the menu can oblige. There's also a daily specials board of fresh fish and other tempting dishes. The Bar Snacks menu shows the same inventiveness and concern with top-quality ingredients, meticulously prepared.

A great deal of expert knowledge has also shaped the wine list, and the Greene King and Shepherd Neame breweries supply an excellent range of real ales, lagers and spirits. Open: Monday and Wednesday to Friday, midday - 2.30 and 6-11; Saturday midday-3 and 6-11.30; Sunday midday-3 and 7-10.30. Closed Tuesdays.

OLD HUNSTANTON
1 mile N of Hunstanton, off the A149

With its mellow old houses and narrow winding lanes, Old Hunstanton is utterly charming. The sand dunes and creeks provide a perfect habitat for interesting varieties of colourful flora - sea poppies, samphire, marram and sea lavender and more. The glorious sands continue here, and the **Norfolk Coastal Footpath** leads eastwards all the way to Cromer, some 36 miles distant.

RINGSTEAD
3 miles E of Hunstanton off the A149

Another appealing village, with pink and white-washed cottages built in wonderfully decorative Norfolk carrstone. A rare Norman round tower, all that survives of St Peter's Church, stands in the grounds of the former Rectory and adds to the visual charm.

In a region well-provided with excellent nature reserves, the one on **Ringstead Downs** is particularly attractive, and popular with picnickers. The chalky soil of the valley provides a perfect habitat for the plants that thrive here and for the exquisitely marked butterflies they attract.

HOLME NEXT THE SEA
3 miles NE of Hunstanton, off the A149

This otherwise unremarkable village is notable as the northern end of the **Peddar's Way**, the 50-mile pedestrian trail that starts at the Suffolk border near Thetford and, almost arrow-straight for much of its length, slices across northwest Norfolk to Holme with only an occasional deviation to negotiate a necessary ford or bridge. This determinedly straight route was already long-trodden for centuries before the Romans arrived, but they incorporated long stretches of it into their own network of roads. It was from the Latin word "pedester", pedestrian, that the route takes its name. With few gradients of any consequence to negotiate, the Peddar's Way is ideal for the casual walker. At Holme, the Peddar's Way meets with the Norfolk Coastal Footpath, a much more recent creation. Starting at Hunstanton, it closely follows the coastline all the way to Cromer.

Holme-next-the-Sea is of course famous in part as the site of "Sea Henge", a 4,500-year-old Bronze Age tree circle discovered on Holme Beach. This early religious monument was removed by English Heritage for study and preservation to Flag Fen, Peterborough, though after its restoration it is hoped that it will be returned to Holme. For the time being there's a replica - built by Channel 4's *Time Team* - now on display in the village.

DOCKING
9 miles SE of Hunstanton, on the B1454 & B1153

One of the larger inland villages, Docking was at one time called Dry Docking because, perched on a hilltop 300 feet above sea level, it had no water supply of its own. The nearest permanent stream was at Fring, almost three miles away, so in 1760 the villagers began boring for a well. They had to dig some 230 feet down before they finally struck water which was then sold at a farthing (0.1p) per bucket. A pump was installed in 1928, but a mains supply didn't reach Docking until the 1930s.

GREAT BIRCHAM
7 miles SE of Hunstanton off the B1153

A couple of miles south of Docking stands the five storey **Great Bircham Windmill**,

Great Bircham Windmill

one of the few in Norfolk to have found a hill to perch on, and it's still working. If you arrive on a day when there's a stiff breeze blowing, the windmill's great arms will be groaning around; on calm days, content yourself with tea and home-made cakes in the tea room, and take home some bread baked at the Mill's own bakery.

TITCHWELL
7 miles E of Hunstanton, on the A149

Perhaps in keeping with the village's name, the Church of **St Mary** at Titchwell is quite tiny, and very pretty indeed. Its circular, probably Norman, tower is topped by a little "whisker" of a spire, and inside is some fine

KING'S HEAD HOTEL

Great Bircham, King's Lynn, Norfolk PE31 6RJ
Tel: 01485 578265

At the edge of the royal Sandringham estate, **The King's Head Hotel** is a large and welcoming inn with a handsome exterior and a warm and welcoming ambience inside. There are two friendly and comfortable bars, one with an open fire in winter and a central wooden bar, complete with cosy 'snug'. Here can be enjoyed a wide selection of beers, wines and spirits as well as coffee and tea, and lunchtime and evening hot and cold snacks. Owned and personally run by Iris and Isidoro Verrando - Isodoro is a fully experienced hotelier and caterer, having worked in Italy and Monte Carlo, and been here with Iris since 1986 - this welcoming hotel attracts a wide variety of guests with its reputation for warm hospitality and excellent menu of English and Italian dishes. The Lodge Restaurant is very elegant, just the place to enjoy the superb selection of Mediterranean and English specialities, which make use of fresh, mainly local produce. The accommodation comprises five ensuite guest bedrooms, cosy residents' lounge and spacious and attractive garden.

THE JOLLY SAILORS

Main Road, Brancaster Staithe, Norfolk PE31 8BJ
Tel: 01485 210314

The north Norfolk coast is famed for the abundance and variety of the birds to be seen there, and **The Jolly Sailors** at Brancaster Staithe is equally renowned among twitchers for the quality of its food and its warm, cosy atmosphere. The Inn is a famlly-run business, owned by George, Joan and Darren Humprey and Wendy Darrington. The extensive snack and restaurant menus are prepared by head chef, Robert Nolan, who was trained at the Savoy in London. Both menus are served 7 days a week from 10.00 am until late in the evening and breakfast is served until midday.

Fish is, of course, a speciality of the house - the day's fresh catch is listed on the blackboard. All

food from both menus is available throughout the pub and also in the beer garden. Children have their own menu and a play area in the large garden. Not only are children welcome, but so too are dogs and muddy boots! This informal atmosphere, along with the good range of real ales - including Green King IPA, Woodfordes Wherry and several changing guest ales - and an excellent selection of wines, all contribute to the popularity of this exceptionally appealing hostelry.

late 19th century glass. Just to the west of the village is a path leading to **Titchwell Marsh**, a nationally important RSPB reserve comprising some 420 acres of shingle beach, reed beds, freshwater and salt-marsh. These different habitats encourage a wide variety of birds to visit the area throughout the year, and many of them breed on or around the reserve. Brent geese, ringed plovers, marsh harriers, terns, waders and shore larks may all be seen, and two of the three hides available are accessible to wheelchairs.

BRANCASTER STAITHE
9 miles NE of Hunstanton, on the A149

In Roman times a castle was built near Brancaster to try and control the Iceni, Boadicea's turbulent tribe. Nothing of it remains, although a Romano-British cemetery was discovered nearby in 1960. In the 18th century, this delightful village was a port of some standing, hence the "Staithe", or quay, in its name. The waterborne traffic in the harbour is now almost exclusively pleasure craft, although whelks are still dredged from the sea bed, 15 miles out, and

mussels are farmed in the harbour itself.

From the harbour, a short boat trip will take you to Scolt Head Island (National Trust), a three and a half mile sand and shingle bar separated from the mainland by a narrow tidal creek. It was originally much smaller but throughout the centuries deposits of silt and sand have steadily increased its size, and continue to do so. Scolt Head is home to England's largest colony of Sandwich terns who flock here to breed during May, June and July. A Nature Trail leads past the ternery, (closed during the breeding season), and on to a fascinating area where a rich variety of plantlife and wildlife abounds. During the summer, the sea asters, sea lavender and sea pinks put on a colourful display, attracting many different types of moths and butterflies.

BURNHAM MARKET
9 miles E of Hunstanton, on the B1155

There are seven Burnhams in all, strung along the valley of the little River Burn. Burnham Market is the largest of them, its past importance reflected in the wealth of

THE LORD NELSON

Creake Road, Burnham Market,
Norfolk PE31 8EN
Tel: 01328 738321

The Lord Nelson on Creake Road is a relaxed and welcoming public house with a fine traditional atmosphere. Paula and Richard Ayres, who took over in February 2000, are warm, friendly and hospitable hosts born and bred in the area - Paula's from Burnham Overy, Richard's from Stanhoe.

Very much the hub of the community, this wonderful pub is popular with tourists, walkers and

locals. Built during the late 1700s at cottages, it became an inn called the Mermaid during its first hundred years. The name was changed after the Battle of Trafalgar in 1805. The panelled lounge bar is cosy and welcoming, with naval memorabilia adorning the walls. The public bar features caricatures from Punch on the walls. The recently refurbished restaurant has an attractive rustic atmosphere. There's also an adjoining room, sometimes used as a function room, in the converted stables.

The emphasis at this pub is on great food and drink, with several real ales, wine, spirits and other liquid refreshment, and an extensive menu of traditional favourites such as steaks, beef and red wine casserole and wild sea trout. The tempting home-made puddings are definitely worth saving room for. From Easter of 2001 accommodation will be available, with two comfortable ensuite guest bedrooms (both doubles).

FISHES' RESTAURANT

Market Place, Burnham Market,
Norfolk PE31 8HE
Tel: 01328 738588
Fax: 01328 730534

Lying so close to the coast, it's appropriate that Burnham Market should be able to boast one of the best seafood restaurants in the country, **Fishes' Restaurant**. The Victorian-style double frontage with its large windows presents a welcoming face to the world. This superb eatery specialises in fresh local sea food, including shellfish, shrimp from the Wash, lobster (when available) and fish landed on the beach at nearby Holkham Bay. Starters include crab soup, smoked fish paté and Brancaster oysters, as well as interesting non-seafood choices such as a Mediterranean salad with mozzarella, tomato, black olive and basil. The enticing main courses range from grilled halibut with

avocado salsa or Monkfish with fennel and cream sauce to a crustacean plate of lobster, crab, prawns, shrimp and crevettes, or home-baked ham with smoked duck and home-made chutney. The dessert menu features some truly mouth-watering home-made puddings such as lemon and lime cheesecake, blueberry and almond tart and double chocolate mousse. Smaller portions are available for children, and all dishes can be ordered individually. The impressive wine list embraces vintages from both Europe and the New World. Gillian Cape has run this fine establishment for over 25 years, upholding an enviable reputation for fine food, excellent service and outstanding value for money. The interior is charming and comfortable, with cane furnishings, handsome prints and paintings adorning the walls, and a fascinating collection of books. These friendly surroundings make any meal here a relaxed and very enjoyable experience.

It's the perfect place to enjoy a break after a day's sightseeing or exploring Burnham Market's excellent shops, including the two fine book shops and probably the best hat shop in the county. Every other Monday in summer there's an auction held on the village green. Guests who are keen ramblers will find a kindred spirit in Gillian, who has participated in the Mount Everest Base Trek and also travelled on foot through such exotic locations as Laos and Vietnam. The 40-mile long Norfolk Coastal Footpath passes nearby - by far the best way of getting to know this beguiling part of the county.

Georgian buildings surrounding the green, and the two churches that lie at each end of its broad main street, just 600 yards apart. In the opinion of many, Burnham Market has the best collection of small Georgian houses in Norfolk and it's a delight to wander through the yards and alleys that link the town's three east-west streets.

Burnham Market also boasts two excellent book shops and probably the best hat shop in the county. Auctions are held on the village green every other Monday in Summer.

BURNHAM THORPE
11 miles E of Hunstanton off the B1355

From the tower of All Saints' Church, the White Ensign flaps in the breeze; the only pub in the village is the *Lord Nelson*; and the

Sign at Old Rectory

shop next door to it is called the Trafalgar Stores. No prizes for deducing that Burnham Thorpe was the birthplace of Horatio Nelson. His father, the Revd Edmund Nelson was the Rector here for 46 years and Horatio was the sixth of his eleven children.

Parsonage House, where he was born seven weeks premature in 1758, was demolished during his lifetime but the pub, (one of more than 200 hostelries across the country bearing the hero's name), has become a kind of shrine to Nelson's memory, its walls covered with portraits, battle scenes and other marine paintings.

Nelson's Medicine Chest, Burnham Thorpe

There's more Nelson memorabilia in the church, amongst them a crucifix and lectern made with wood from *HMS Victory*; a great chest from the pulpit used by his father; and two flags from *HMS Nelson*. Every year on Trafalgar Day, October 21st, members of the Nelson Society gather at this riverside church for a service in commemoration of the man who had specified in his will that he wanted to be buried in its country graveyard, "unless the King decrees otherwise". George III did indeed decree otherwise and the great hero was interred in St Paul's Cathedral.

Burnham Overy

A little over a mile to the south of Burnham Thorpe stand the picturesque ruins of Creake Abbey (English Heritage, free), an Augustinian monastery founded in 1206. The Abbey's working life came to an abrupt end in 1504 when, within a single week, every one of the monks died of the plague.

HOLKHAM
16 miles E of Hunstanton, on the A149

If the concept of the Grand Tour ever needed any justification, **Holkham Hall** amply provides it. For six years, from 1712 to 1718, young Thomas Coke (pronounced Cook) travelled extensively in Italy, France and Germany, studying and absorbing at first hand the glories of European civilisation. And, wherever possible, buying them. When he returned to England, Coke realised that his family's modest Elizabethan manor could not possibly house the collection of treasures he had amassed. The manor would have to be demolished and a more worthy building erected in its place.

During his travels in Italy, Coke had been deeply impressed by the cool, classical lines favoured by the Renaissance architect, Andrea Palladio. Working with his friend Lord Burlington - another fervent admirer of Palladio, and the architect William Kent, Coke's monumental project slowly took shape. Building began in 1734 but was not completed until 1762, three years after Coke's death.

Green State Bedroom, Holkham Hall

The completed building, its classical balance and restraint emphasised by the pale honey local brick used throughout, has been described as "the ultimate achievement of the English Palladian movement". As you step into the stunning entrance hall, the tone is set for the rest of the house. Modelled on a Roman Temple of Justice, the lofty coved ceiling is supported by 18 huge fluted columns of pink Derbyshire alabaster transported to nearby Wells by river and sea.

Historically, the most important room at Holkham is the Statue Gallery which contains one of the finest collections of classical sculpture still in private ownership. In this sparsely furnished room there is nothing to distract one's attention from the sublime statuary that has survived for millennia, amongst them a bust of Thucydides, (one of the earliest portrayals of man), and a statue of Diana, both of which have been dated to 4 BC.

Each room reveals new treasures: Rubens and Van Dyck in the Saloon (the principal reception room); the Landscape Room with its incomparable collection of paintings by Lorrain, Poussin and other masters; the Brussels tapestries in the State Sitting Room; and, on a more domestic note, the vast, high-ceilinged Kitchen which remained in use until 1939 and still displays the original pots and pans.

Holkham Hall

Astonishingly, the interior of the house remains almost exactly as Thomas Coke planned it, his descendants having respected the integrity of his vision. They concentrated their reforming zeal on improving the enormous estate and it was Coke's great-nephew, Thomas William Coke (1754-1842), in particular who was responsible for the elegant layout of the 3000 acre park we see today. Universally known as "Coke of Norfolk", Thomas was a pioneer of the Agricultural Revolution, best known for introducing the idea of a four-crop rotation. He was also a generous patron of agricultural innovations and the "Sheep Shearings" he inaugurated - gatherings to which several hundred people came to exchange ideas on all aspects of agriculture, were the direct forerunners of the modern agricultural show.

The Thomas Coke who built the house had been created Earl of Leicester in 1744, but as his only son died before him, the title lapsed. However, when his grand-nephew, "Coke of Norfolk", was elevated to the peerage by Queen Victoria in 1837 he adopted the same title. The present Earl, the 7th of the second creation, lives at Holkham in the private apartments known as the Family Wing but still uses the State Rooms when entertaining guests. The Earl continues in the tradition of "Coke of Norfolk" by overseeing the vast estate with its 30 tenant farmers and more than 300 houses: the Countess has established a new tradition by setting up the Holkham Pottery in the former brickworks.

As well as the Pottery and its associated shop, Holkham's other attractions include an 18th century walled garden, a fascinating bygones museum, a garden centre, gift shop and tea room.

WELLS-NEXT-THE-SEA
17 miles E of Hunstanton, on the A149

It's difficult to decide whether Wells is a small town or a large village, but there's no doubt about the appeal of its picturesque quayside, narrow streets and ancient houses. Wells has been a working port since at least the 13th century but over the years the town's full name of Wells-next-the-Sea has become increasingly inapt - its harbour now stands more than a mile from the sea. In 1859, to prevent the harbour silting up altogether, Lord Leicester of Holkham Hall built an Embankment cutting off some 600 acres of marshland. This now provides a pleasant walk down to the sea.

The Embankment gave no protection however against the great floods of 1953 and 1978. On the 11th January, 1978, the sea rose 16ft 1in above high tide, a few inches less than the 16ft 10in recorded on the 31st January, 1953 when the flood-waters lifted a ship on to the quay. A silo on the harbour is marked with these abnormal levels.

Running alongside the Embankment is the **Harbour Railway**, which trundles from the small Museum on the quay to the lifeboat station by the beach. This narrow-gauge

THE CROWN HOTEL
The Buttlands, Wells-next-the-Sea, Norfolk NR23 1FX
Tel: 01328710209 Fax: 01328 711432

Presenting a gracious exterior to the world, **The Crown Hotel** in Wells-next-the-Sea offers guests a taste of traditional elegance. This charming 16th century coaching inn is set amid Norfolk's unspoilt coastal scenery and attracts visitors from all over the world. A listed building dating back to Tudor times, it overlooks the green known as The Buttlands where medieval townsmen practised their archery. Comfortable accommodation and a friendly, attentive staff ensure that any stay here is a most pleasant one. The 12 ensuite guest bedrooms are tastefully furnished and decorated, with full facilities. The two celebrated restaurants use only the freshest local produce to create innovative and traditional dishes. The five chefs have received recognition in major guides and publications for the high standard of their cuisine. In one of the three cosy bars, guests can relax and enjoy a range of real ales, wines, lager or spirits.

railway is operated by the same company as the **Wells & Walsingham Railway** which carries passengers on a particularly lovely ride along the route of the former Great Eastern Railway to Little Walsingham. The four mile journey takes about 25 minutes with stops at Warham St Mary and Wighton. Both the WWR and the Harbour Railway services are seasonal. In a curious change of function, the former GER station at Wells is now home to the well-known Burnham Pottery, the former signal box is now the station, while the old station at Walsingham is now a church!

In addition to being the largest of North Norfolk's ports, Wells is also a popular resort with one of the best beaches in England bordered by the curiously named **Holkham Meals**, a plantation of pines established here in the 1860s to stabilise the dunes.

Binham Abbey

7 Cambridge and East Cambridgeshire

Far removed from the hustle and bustle of modern life, the Fens are like a breath of fresh air. Extending over much of Cambridgeshire from the Wash, these flat, fenland fields contain some of the richest soil in England and the villages such as Soham and small towns like Ely rise out of the landscape on low hills.

Bridge of Sighs, Cambridge

Before the Fens were drained this was a land of mist, marshes and bogs; of small islands, inhabited by independent folk, their livelihood the fish and waterfowl of this eerie, watery place. The region is full of legends of web-footed people, ghosts and witchcraft.

Today's landscape is a result of the ingenuity of humanity, with its constant desire to tame the wilderness and create farmland. This fascinating story spans the centuries, from the earliest Roman and Anglo-Saxon times, when the first embankments and drains were constructed to lessen the frequency of flooding. Throughout the Middle Ages large areas were reclaimed, with much of the work being undertaken by the monasteries. The first straight cut bypassed the Great Ouse, allowing the water to run out to sea quicker. After the Civil War, the **New Bedford River** was cut parallel to the first. These two still provide the basic drainage for much of Fenland.

The significant influence of the Dutch lives on in some of the architecture and place names of the Fens. Over the years it became necessary to pump rainwater from the fields up into the rivers, and, as in the Netherlands, windmills took on the task. They could not always cope with the height of the lift required, but fortunately the steam engine

Kings Mill and River Cam, Great Shelford

came along, to be replaced eventually by the electric pumps that can raise thousands of gallons of water a second to protect the land from the ever-present threat of rain and tide. The Fens offer unlimited opportunities for exploring on foot, by car, bicycle or by boat. Anglers are well catered for, and visitors with an interest in wildllife will be in their element.

Southeastern Cambridgeshire covers the area around the city of Cambridge and is rich in history, with a host of archaeological sites and monuments to visit, as well as many important museums. The area is fairly flat, so it makes for great walking and cycling tours, and offers a surprising variety of landscapes. The Romans planted vines here and to this day the region is among the main producers of British wine.

At the heart of it all is Cambridge itself, one of the leading academic centres in the world and a city which deserves plenty of time to explore - on foot, by bicycle or by the gentler, romantic option of a punt.

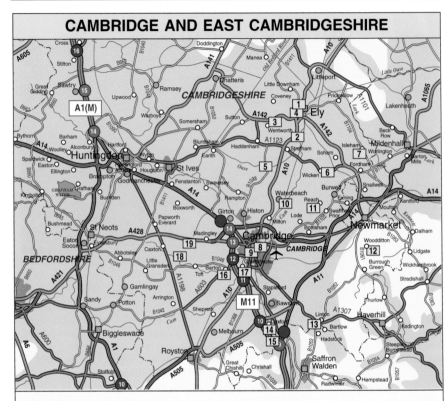

CAMBRIDGE AND EAST CAMBRIDGESHIRE

© MAPS IN MINUTES ™ (1999)

PLACES TO STAY, EAT, DRINK AND SHOP

ELY

Ely is the jewel in the crown of the Fens, in whose history the majestic **Cathedral** and the Fens themselves have played major roles. The Fens' influence is apparent even in the name: Ely was once known as Elge or Elig (eel island) because of the large number of eels which lived in the surrounding fenland. Ely owes its existence to St Etheldreda, Queen of Northumbria, who in 673AD founded a monastery on the 'Isle of Ely', where she remained as abbess until her death in 679. It was not until 1081 that work started on the present Cathedral, and in 1189 this remarkable example of Romanesque architecture was completed. The most outstanding feature in terms of both scale and beauty is the Octagon, built to replace the original Norman tower, which collapsed in 1322.

Alan of Walsingham was the inspired architect of this massive work, which took 30 years to complete and whose framework weighs an estimated 400 tons. Many other notable components include the 14th century

Ely Cathedral

STEEPLEGATE TEA ROOMS AND CRAFTS

16/18 High Street, Ely, Cambridgeshire CB7 4JU
Tel: 01353 664731

Ely's historic Steeple Gate is a timber-framed gateway known as one of the oldest surviving secular buildings in Ely, and was constructed during the Tudor age (circa 1500). Four "tenements" or cottages appear in records of the time as abutting the gateway itself, two to the east and two to the west. The gateway was once the entrance to the burial ground of the parish church of the Holy Cross.

Housed in one of these venerable cottages, **Steeplegate** is a delightful tea room/craft shop. The three levels of this charming establishment comprise a very comfortable traditional English tea room on the first floor overlooking Ely's High Street, the ground floor craft shop, presenting a wonderful mix of crafts, music, candles, jewellery, cards and wood-turned objets d'art, and the cellar with its finely preserved medieval vaulted chamber. Starting at the top, the tea rooms offer a superb selection of coffees, teas, light lunches, savoury snacks and home-made cakes. The atmosphere is homely and welcoming.

The craft shop specialises in locally crafted wood-turned bowls, plates, fruit and other sculpted pieces. Demonstrations of wood-turning are held occasionally. The cellar's vaulted chamber is filled with original paintings and hand-made wooden artefacts for sale.

SPRINGFIELDS

Ely Road, Little Thetford, Ely, Cambridgeshire CB6 3HJ
Tel: 01353 663637 Fax: 01353 663130

Just a mile and a half from Ely city centre, **Springfields** is a delightful property offering bed and breakfast accommodation. Owners Dawn and Derek Bailey are welcoming hosts who have been running this fine B&B since 1983. Built originally in 1928, the house was completely renovated in 1980 to offer a high standard of comfort. Set back from the main road, it is very quiet and restful. Luxurious touches enhance the three en suite guest bedrooms (two doubles and one twin) , which have their own private entrance and so are totally self-contained. The furnishings and decor are tasteful and elegant. The

impressive one-acre garden is very beautiful, with mature trees, roses, orchard and handsome shrubs. Nominated as one of the country's top 20 B&Bs by Which?, and awarded De-Luxe classification by the English Tourist Board, the full English or Continental breakfast at this superior establishment makes use of the freshest ingredients and is served in the gracious dining room. Special dietary requirements are happily catered for. The owners' conscientious service make any stay here a memorable one. Local attractions include swimming, fishing and golf. No smoking.

DESIDERATA

44 Main Street, Wentworth,
Cambridgeshire CB6 3QG
Tel: 01353 776131/0468 827901
e-mail: chips.1@virgin.net

Taking its name from the 17th-century poem found in St Paul's church, Baltimore, and written by an unknown author, **Desiderata** (the name means "heart's desire") is a charming home offering bed and breakfast accommodation.

Convenient for visits to Ely, Cambridge, Wickham Fen, Welney Sanctuary and many of the other sights and attractions of this part of the county, this welcoming establishment has three attractive and comfortable guest bedrooms (one double and two twins). Many visitors return again and again, attesting to owner Margaret Graham's hospitality and the pleasantness of the place. The house is located on a quiet cul de sac here in the peaceful hamlet of Wentworth. A modern, light and airy home built in 1980, all rooms are on the ground floor and accessible to people with disabilities. The house is tastefully furnished and decorated to a very high standard of comfort. All rooms are well equipped, with extras such as hair dryers and ironing facilities. The shared sunken bath is a taste of luxury. The large and bright breakfast room is particularly lovely, with a view through the large patio doors over the half-acre garden. Breakfast - English or Continental - offers a good variety of choice and makes use of the freshest ingredients.

Oliver Cromwell's House, Ely

Lady Chapel, the largest in England, the Prior's Door, the painted nave ceiling and St Ovin's cross, the only piece of Saxon stonework in the building. The Cathedral is set within the walls of the monastery, and many of the ancient buildings still stand as a tribute to the incredible skill and craftsmanship of their designers and builders. Particularly worth visiting among these are the monastic buildings in the College, the Great Hall and Queens Hall. Just beside the Cathedral is the Almonry, in whose 12th century vaulted undercroft visitors can take coffee, lunch or tea - outside in the garden if the weather permits. Two other attractions which should not be missed are the **Brass Rubbing Centre**, where visitors can make their own rubbings from replica brasses, and the **Museum of Stained Glass**. The latter, housed in the south Triforium of the Cathedral, is the only museum of stained glass in the country and contains over 100 original panels from every period, tracing the

complete history of stained glass.

Ely's **Tourist Information Centre** is itself a tourist attraction, since it is housed in a pretty black and white timbered building that was once the home of Oliver Cromwell. It is the only remaining house, apart from Hampton Court, where Oliver Cromwell and his family are known to have lived; parts of it trace back to the 13th century, and its varied history includes periods as a public house and, more recently, a vicarage. The Old Gaol, in Market Street, houses **Ely Museum**, with nine galleries telling the Ely story from the Ice Age to modern times. The tableaux of the condemned and debtors' cells are particularly fascinating and poignant.

Ely is not just the past, and the fine architecture and sense of history blend well with the bustle of the streets and the shops and the riverside. That bustle is at its most bustling on Thursday, when the largest general market in the area is held.

COVENEY
3 miles W of Ely off the A10

A Fenland hamlet on the Bedford Level just above West Fen. Its Church of St Peter-ad-Vincula has several interesting features, including a colourful German screen dating from around 1500 and a painted Danish pulpit. Unusual figures on the bench ends and a fine brass chandelier add to the opulent feel of this atmospheric little church.

CASTLE LODGE HOTEL

50 New Barns Road, Ely, Cambridgeshire CB7 4PW
Tel: 01353 662276 Fax: 01353 666606

The **Castle Lodge Hotel**, as befits its name, has a charming crenellated frontage - built as a "folly" in 1848. This superb hotel has 11 guest bedrooms and a distinguished evening meal menu, with an extensive selection of hearty and delicious traditional English dishes. A warm welcome and comfortable, homely atmosphere awaits all guests. Just 5 minutes' walk from Ely Cathedral, it is suitable for individuals, families and small groups.

SUTTON
6 miles W of Ely off the A142

A very splendid 'pepperpot' tower with octagons, pinnacles and spire tops marks out the grand church of St Andrew. Inside, take time to look at the 15th century font and a fine modern stained-glass window. The reconstruction of the church was largely the work of two Bishops of Ely, whose arms appear on the roof bosses. One of the Bishops was Thomas Arundel, appointed at the age of 21. A mile further west, there's a great family attraction in the **Mepal Outdoor Centre**, an outdoor leisure centre with a children's playpark, an adventure play area and boat hire.

HADDENHAM
5 miles SW of Ely on the A1123

More industrial splendour: **Haddenham Great Mill**, built in 1803 for a certain Daniel

Cockle, is a glorious sight, and one definitely not to be missed. It has four sails and three sets of grinding stones, one of which is working. The mill last worked commercially in 1946 and was restored between 1992 and 1998. Open on the first Sunday of each month and by appointment.

The Church of St Andrew stands on a hillside. Look for the stained-glass window depicting two souls entering Heaven, and the memorial (perhaps the work of Grinling Gibbons) to Christopher Wren's sister Anne Brunsell.

STRETHAM
5 miles S of Ely off A10/A1123

The **Stretham Old Engine**, a fine example of a land drainage steam engine, is housed in a restored, tall-chimneyed brick engine house. Dating from 1831, it is one of 90 steam pumping engines installed throughout the

TWENTY PENCE INN

Wilburton, Cambridgeshire CB6 3PX
Tel: 01954 252254

The Twenty Pence Inn is a delightful pub on the banks of the River Ouse near the Twenty Pence Marina between Wilburton and Cottenham. A real seaside feel can be found here, as there's free mooring for visitors, and the pub, set on the first floor overlooking the river, is approached up a wooden ramp. Real ales, including a guest ale, and traditional meals are among the attractions here. There's also live entertainment every weekend, and delicious Sunday roasts.

THE OLD SCHOOL

48 North Street, Wicken, Ely, Cambridgeshire CB7 5XW
Tel: 01353 720526

As its name suggests, **The Old School** was once the school and headmasters house for the beautiful conservation village of Wicken, home to the oldest nature reserve in the country (circa. 1899), and its recently renovated windmill. The school now offers superior bed and breakfast accommodation, a tea room with delicious home-made fayre and a gift/Bygones shop

stocking lots of unusual items. This charming establishment occupies an extensive building dating back to 1908, set in 3/4 acre of delightful gardens and surrounded by pony paddocks.

Run by Ann and Charles Wight with help from their children Amber and Danny it is a friendly and welcoming place to stay. The accommodation comprises two large ensuite bedrooms (one on the ground floor). There is also a games room with table tennis and pool table. The full English breakfast is highly recommended with special diets catered for. This is the ideal base for touring Cambridge, Ely and Newmarket.

Fens to replace 800 windmills. It is the last to survive, having worked until 1925 and still under restoration. During the great floods of 1919 it really earned its keep by working non-stop for 47 days and nights. This unique insight into Fenland history and industrial archaeology is open to the public on summer weekends and on certain dates the engine and its wooden scoop-wheel are rotated (by electricity, alas!). The adjacent stoker's cottage contains period furniture and photographs of fen drainage down the years.

WICKEN
9 miles S of Ely off the A1123

Owned by the NT, **Wicken Fen** is the oldest nature reserve in the country, 600 acres of undrained fenland, famous for its rich plant, insect and bird life and a delight for both naturalists and ramblers. Features include boardwalk and nature trails, hides and watchtowers, a cottage with 1930s furnishings, a working windpump (the oldest in the country), a visitor centre and a shop. Open daily dawn to dusk. St Lawrence's Church is well worth a visit, small and secluded among trees.In the churchyard are buried Oliver Cromwell and several members of his family. One of Cromwell's many nicknames was Lord of the Fens: he defended the rights of the Fenmen against those who wanted to drain the land without providing adequate compensation.

ISLEHAM
10 miles SE of Ely off the B1104

The remains of a Benedictine priory, with a lovely Norman chapel under the care of English Heritage, are a great draw. Also well worth a visit is the Church of St Andrew, a 14th century cruciform building entered by a very fine lychgate. The 17th century eagle lectern is the original of a similar lectern in Ely Cathedral.

FORDHAM
10 miles SE of Ely off the A142/B1102

A small village on the **Newmarket Cycle Way**. The poet James Withers spent most of his life here and is buried in the churchyard. A stained-glass window in the church is inscribed in his memory.

SNAILWELL
12 miles SE of Ely off the A142

Visit the pretty mainly 14th century Church of St Peter on the banks of the River Snail: 13th century chancel, a hammerbeam and tie beam nave roof, a 600-year old font, pews with poppy heads, two medieval oak screens. The Norman round tower is unusual for Cambridgeshire.

SOHAM
6 miles SE of Ely on the A142 bypass

Do not sail past Soham without stopping to look at (or visit if it is a Sunday or Bank

THE MERRY MONK

30 West Street, Isleham, Ely,
Cambridgeshire CB7 5SB
Tel: 01638 780900

At the western end of the village of Isleham, near Isleham Priory, **The Merry Monk** is a convivial and welcoming public house dating back to the late 1600s. Originally four cottages, this charming Free House has a cosy interior, with its inglenook fireplaces, brightly painted walls and large open area bar. Hop bines adorn the walls and exposed beamwork. Real ales on tap include Flowers IPA and Castle Eden ale. The menu offers far more than the usual pub grub, with a comprehensive and changing selection of Thai, Chinese and Indian dishes, Norfolk-grown meats, vegetarian options and an excellent range of baguettes, salads and bar snacks. Hosts Alan and Susan Goldson and their friendly staff offer excellent service and genuine hospitality to all their guests, which range from locals to visitors to this quiet, relaxed Free House. Open seven days a week. No food Mondays.

KETTLE'S YARD,

University of Cambridge, Castle Street, Cambridge CB3 0AQ
Tel: 01223 352124 Fax: 01223 324377
email: kettles-yard-gen@lists.cam.ac.uk website: www.kettlesyard.co.uk

Kettle's Yard in Cambridge is neither an art gallery nor a museum. It is instead a home which includes a permanent display of 20th-century art in a house maintained just as it was when the Ede family gave it, with the collection, to the University in 1966.

Kettle's Yard House is the result of one man's vision to 'create a living place where works of art could be enjoyed, inherent to the domestic setting, where young people could be at home unhampered by the greater austerity

of the museum or public art gallery'. It was home to Jim Ede, a former curator of the Tate Gallery during the 1920s and 30s, and his wife Helen for 16 years from 1957, when it was created from four derelict cottages. Jim Ede restored and adapted these tiny cottages, and held an open house every afternoon to allow people to view his collection. Here he realised his vision of art being seen as a part of everyday living, alongside natural objects and household items. An extension was added in 1970, designed by the architect Sir Leslie Martin.

The house is now home to the Edes' extensive and historic collection, with works by Ben and Winifred Nicholson, Gaudier-Brzeska, Christopher Wood, David Jones, Alfred Wallis, Henry Moore, Barbara Hepworth, Joan Miro, Brancusi and many other of the most important names in 20th-century

art. Presentations, music concerts and other events take place in the House extension regularly throughout the year. The Kettle' Yard Gallery, adjacent to the House, was added in 1970 and last extended in the early 1990s, presents a changing programme of exhibitions of modern and contemporary art. In addition to this extensive programme, Kettle's Yard organises a variety of events including talks and tours.

This innovative and exciting place repays a visit with its unique setting and relaxed, welcoming atmosphere. Last but not least, Kettle's Yard offers a unique opportunity to entertain friends, potential recruits, business associates or clients within a stimulating atmosphere.

Holiday) **Downfield Windmill**. Built in 1726 as a smock mill, it was destroyed by gales and rebuilt in 1890 as an octagonal tower mill. It still grinds corn and produces a range of flours and breads for sale. St Andrew's Church is a fine example of the Perpendicular style of English Gothic architecture. Very grand and elaborate, it was built on the site of a 7th century cathedral founded by St Felix of Burgundy. The 15th century west tower has an ornate parapet and two medieval porches. Note, too, the chancel with its panelling and stained glass. A plaque in Soham commemorates engine driver Ben Gimbert and fireman James Nightall, who were taking an ammunition train through the town when a wagon caught fire. They uncoupled it and began to haul it into open country. The wagon exploded, killing the fireman and a signalman.

PRICKWILLOW
4 miles E of Ely on the B1382

On the village's main street is the **Prickwillow Drainage Museum**, which houses a unique collection of large engines associated with the drainage of the Fens. The site had been in continuous use as a pumping station since 1831, and apart from the engines there are displays charting the history of Fens drainage, the effects on land levels and the workings of the modern drainage system.

LITTLE DOWNHAM
3 miles N of Ely off the A10

The church of St Leonard shows the change from Norman to Gothic in church building at the turn of the 13th century. The oldest parts are the Norman tower and the elaborately carved south door. Interior treasures include what is probably the largest royal coat of arms in the country. At the other end of the village are the remains (mainly the gatehouse and kitchen) of a 15th century palace built by a Bishop of Ely. The property is in private hands and part of it is an antiques centre.

LITTLEPORT
6 miles N of Ely on the A10

St George's Church, with its very tall 15th century tower, is a notable landmark. Of particular interest are two stained-glass windows depicting St George slaying the dragon. Littleport was the scene of riots in 1861, when labourers from Ely and Littleport, faced with unemployment or low wages, and soaring food prices, attacked houses and people in this area, causing several deaths. Five of the rioters were hanged and buried in a common grave at St Mary's Church. A plaque commemorating the event is attached to a wall at the back of the church.

CAMBRIDGE

There are nearly 30 Cambridges spread around the globe, but this, the original, is the one that the whole world knows as one of the leading university cities. Cambridge was an important town many centuries before the scholars arrived, standing at the point where forest met fen, at the lowest fording point of the river. The Romans took over a site previously settled by an Iron Age Belgic tribe, to be followed in turn by the Saxons and the Normans. Soon after the Norman Conquest William I built a wooden motte and bailey castle and Edward I, a stone replacement: a mound still marks the spot. The town flourished as a market and river trading centre, and in 1209 a group of students fleeing Oxford riots arrived. The first College was **Peterhouse**, founded by the Bishop of Ely in 1284, and in the next century Clare, Pembroke, Gonville & Caius, Trinity Hall and

Kings College Chapel

Trinity College Great Court

Corpus Christi followed. The total is now 31, the latest being **Robinson College**, the gift of self-made millionaire David Robinson. The Colleges represent various architectural styles, the grandest and most beautiful being King's. Robinson has the look of a fortress; its concrete structure covered with a 'skin' of a million and a quarter hand-made red Dorset bricks. The Colleges are all well worth a visit, but places that simply must not be missed include **King's College Chapel** with its breathtaking fan vaulting, glorious stained glass and Rubens' *Adoration of the Magi*; **Pepys Library**, including his diaries, in Magdalene College; and Trinity's wonderful **Great Court**. A trip by punt along the 'Backs' of the Cam brings a unique view of many of the Colleges and passes under six bridges, including the **Bridge of Sighs** (St John's) and the extraordinary wooden **Mathematical Bridge** at Queens'. Cambridge has nurtured more Nobel Prize winners than most countries - 29 from Trinity alone - and the list of celebrated alumni covers every sphere of human endeavour and achievement: Byron, Tennyson, Milton and Wordsworth; Marlowe and Bacon; Samuel Pepys; Charles Darwin; Charles Babbage; Bertrand Russell and Ludwig Wittgenstein; actors Sir Ian McKellen and Sir Derek Jacobi; Lord Burghley and Harold Abrahams who ran for England;

Burgess, Maclean, Philby and Blunt who spied for Russia.

The Colleges apart, Cambridge is packed with interest for the visitor, with a wealth of grand buildings both religious and secular, and some of the country's leading museums, many of them run by the University. The **Fitzwilliam Museum** is renowned for its art collection, which includes works by Titian, Rembrandt, Gainsborough, Hogarth, Turner, Renoir, Picasso and Cezanne, and for its antiquities from Egypt, Greece and Rome.

Kettle's Yard (see page 234) has a permanent display of 20th century art in a house maintained just as it was when the Ede family gave it, with the collection, to the University in 1967. The **Museum of Classical Archaeology** has 500 plaster casts of Greek and Roman statues, and the **University Museum of Archaeology and Anthropology** covers worldwide prehistoric archaeology with special displays relating to Oceania and to the Cambridge area. The **Museum of Technology**, housed in a Victorian sewage pumping station, features an impressive collection of steam, gas and electric pumping engines and examples great and small of local industrial technology. Anyone with an interest in fossils should make tracks for the **Sedgwick Museum of Geology**, while in the same street (Downing) the **Museum of Zoology** offers a comprehensive and

Botanic Gardens

spectacular survey of the animal kingdom. The **Whipple Museum of the History of Science** tells about science through instruments; the **Scott Polar Research Institute** has fascinating, often poignant exhibits relating to Arctic and Antarctic exploration; and the **Botanic Gardens** boast a plant collection that rivals those of Kew Gardens and Edinburgh. The work and life of the people of Cambridge and the surrounding area are the subject of the **Cambridge and County Folk Museum**, housed in a 15th century building that for 300 years was the White Horse Inn. One of the city's greatest treasures is the **University Library**, one of the world's great research libraries with 6 million books, a million maps and 350,000 manuscripts.

Cambridge also has many fine churches, some of them used by the Colleges before they built their own chapels. Among the most notable are **St Andrew the Great** (note the memorial to Captain Cook); **St Andrew the Less**; **St Bene's** (its 11th century tower is the oldest in the county); **St Mary the Great**, a marvellous example of Late Perpendicular Gothic; and **St Peter Castle Hill**. This last is one of the smallest churches in the country with a nave measuring just 25' by 16'. Originally much larger, the church was largely demolished in 1781 and rebuilt in its present diminished state using the old materials, including flint rubble and Roman bricks. The **Church of the Holy Sepulchre**, always known as the Round Church, is one of only four surviving round churches in England.

WATERBEACH
5 miles N of Cambridge off the A10

A sizeable village by the River Cam, with Denny Abbey, Anglesey Abbey and Swaffham Prior windmill all withing easy reach.

RAINBOW VEGETARIAN CAFÉ

9a Kings Parade, Cambridge, Cambridgeshire CB2 1SJ Tel: 01223 321551

The cosy basement of a 17th-century building opposite the gates of Kings College is the delightful 70s-style setting for **Rainbow Vegetarian Café**, the only restaurant in the area serving totally vegetarian, vegan and gluten-free food. Everything is freshly made each day on the premises. A full menu is served all day for those late lunches or early dinners. Owner Sharon Meijland's aim is to provide as much variety as she can for her numerous regular customers, and to introduce non-vegetarians to the huge choice of vegetarian food it is possible to make attractive and interesting. The menu certainly lives up to this aim, with internationally-inspired main courses, soups and puddings. All the wines, beers and ciders are vegan and organic. Open: Monday - Saturday 11.00-23.00 (last orders 22.30). Closed Sundays.

THE WHITE HORSE,

12 Greenside, Waterbeach,
Cambridgeshire CB5 9LT
Tel: 01223 505053 Fax: 01223 505122

Just four miles from Cambridge and near the River Cam, **The White Horse** in Waterbeach is a comfortable, friendly pub. Owners Ian and Donna Wilson are welcoming hosts; they have been in the licensing trade since 1985 and here at The White Horse since 1996. Popular with locals and visitors alike, the pub attracts a mixed clientele, in particular those on boating holidays along the river. Real ales on tap (there's always a choice of three) include Greene King IPA and Ruddles. Bar snacks and full meals are expertly prepared and presented. The menu specialises in Indian and Bangladeshi cuisine in the evenings, as well as a good selection of traditional English fare and changing daily specials, all home-cooked. On Sundays there's a choice of three roasts. Open seven days a week, with food every lunch and evening.

GIRTON
3 miles NW of Cambridge off the A14

The first Cambridge College for women was founded in 1869 in Hitchin, by Emily Davies. It moved here in 1873 to be *'near enough for male lecturers to visit but far enough away to discourage male students from doing the same'*. The problem went away when Girton became a mixed College in 1983.

MILTON
3 miles N of Cambridge off the A10

Milton Country Park offers fine walking and exploring among acres of parkland, lakes and woods. There's a visitor centre, a picnic area and a place serving light refreshments.

RAMPTON
6 miles N of Cambridge off the B1049

A charming village in its own right, with a tree-fringed village green, Rampton is also the site of one of the many archaeological sites in the area. This is **Giant's Hill**, a motte castle with part of an earlier medieval settlement.

LODE
6 miles NE of Cambridge on the b1102

Denny Abbey, easily accessible on the A10, is an English Heritage Grade 1 Abbey with ancient earthworks. On the same site, and run as a joint attraction, is the **Farmland Museum**. The history of Denny runs from the 12th century, when it was a Benedictine monastery. It was later home to the Knights Templar, Franciscan nuns and the Countess of Pembroke, and from the 16th century was a farmhouse. The old farm buildings have been splendidly renovated and converted to tell the story of village life and Cambridgeshire farming up to modern times. The museum is ideal for family outings, with plenty of hands-on activities for children, and a play area, gift shop and weekend tearoom.

Anglesey Abbey dates from 1600 and was built on the site of an Augustinian priory, but the house and the 100-acre garden came together as a unit thanks to the vision of the 1st Lord Fairhaven. The garden, created in its present form from the 1930s, is a wonderful place for a stroll, with wide grassy walks, open lawns, a riverside walk, a working water mill and one of the finest collections of garden statuary in the country. There's also a plant centre, shop and restaurant. In the house itself is Lord Fairhaven's magnificent collection of paintings, sumptuous furnishings, tapestries and clocks.

At nearby **Cottenham**, on the B1049, All Saints Church has an unusual tower of yellow and pink Jacobean brick topped with four pinnacles that look like pineapples. The original tower fell down in a gale and this replacement was partially funded by former US President Calvin Coolidge, one of whose ancestors had been living in the village when the tower fell down.

SWAFFHAM PRIOR
8 miles NE of Cambridge on the b1102.

Swaffham Prior gives double value to the visitor, with two churches in the same churchyard and two fine old windmills. The Churches of St Mary and St Cyriac stand side by side, a remarkable and dramatic sight in the steeply rising churchyard. One of the mills, a restored 1850s tower mill, still produces flour and can be visited by appointment.

Swaffham Prior Windmill

At **Swaffham Bulbeck**, a little way to the south, stands another Church of St Mary, with a 13th century tower and 14th century arcades and chancel. Look for the fascinating carvings on the wooden benches and a 15th century cedarwood chest decorated with biblical scenes.

BURWELL
10 miles NE of Cambridge on the b1102

A village of many attractions with a history going back to Saxon times. **Burwell Museum** reflects many aspects of a village on the edge of the Fens up to the middle of the 20th century. A general store, model farm, local industries and children's toys are among the displays. Next to the museum is the famous Stephens Windmill, built in 1820 and extensively restored. The man who designed parts of King's College Chapel, Reginald Ely, is thought to have been responsible for the beautiful St Mary's Church, which is built of locally quarried clunch stone and is one of the finest examples of the Perpendicular style. Notable internal features include a 15th century font, a medieval wall painting of St

Christopher and roof carvings of elephants, while in the churchyard a gravestone marks the terrible night in 1727 when 78 Burwell folk died in a barn fire while watching a travelling Punch & Judy show. Behind the church are the remains of Burwell Castle, started in the 12th century but never properly completed. The Devil's Dyke runs through Burwell on its path from Reach to Wooddition. This amazing dyke, 30 yards wide, was built, it is thought, to halt Danish invaders.

REACH
8 miles NE of Cambridge off the A4280

The charming village of Reach is home to the oldest fair in England, which celebrated its 800th anniversary on 1st May, 2000.

BOTTISHAM
5 miles E of Cambridge on the A1303

John Betjeman ventured that Bottisham's Holy Trinity Church was "perhaps the best in the county", so time should certainly be made for a visit. Among the many interesting features are the 13th century porch, an 18th

THE DYKE'S END

8 Fair Green, Reach,
Cambridgeshire CB5 0JD
Tel: 01638 743816

The Dyke's End is a pristine and welcoming Free House owned collectively by residents of this handsome village. Tenants Phil and Tessa Vincent extend warm hospitality to all their guests. Attracting visitors from nearby Devil's Dyke - built circa 370 AD - as well as Cambridge and Newmarket, both just eight miles away, the pub has a quiet and relaxed atmosphere. Overlooking the village green, the charming front garden is dotted with picnic tables on the grass. The interior has recently been refurbished, to offer a high standard of comfort. The small, open plan bar has three distinct areas, including a non-smoking dining area. There's also a fine restaurant upstairs. Real ales on tap include Adnams and IPA, as well as changing guest ales; other ways to slake one's thirst include a good range of lagers, wines and spirits, particularly a great selection of malt whiskies. Phil is a qualified chef. The emphasis is on the freshest possible ingredients, the menu featuring traditional English cuisine, with fish a speciality. Locally grown produce and game (in season) are also features of the excellent dishes on offer. When the weather is fine, the lovely rear garden is used for dining and for barbecues.

century monument to Sir Roger Jenyns and some exceptionally fine modern woodwork in Georgian style.

LINTON
10 miles SE of Cambridge on the B1052

The village is best known for its zoo, but visitors will also find many handsome old buildings and the Church of St Mary the Virgin, built mainly in Early English style. A world of wildlife set in 16 acres of spectacular gardens; **Linton Zoo** is a major wildlife breeding centre and part of the inter-zoo breeding programme for endangered species. Collections include wild cats, birds, snakes and insects. For children there is a play area and, in summer, pony rides and a bouncy castle. Chilford Hall vineyard, on the B1052 between Linton and Balsham, comprises 18 acres of vines, with tours and tastings available.

Some two miles further off the A604, **Bartlow Hills** are the site of the largest Roman burial site to be unearthed in Europe.

THE THREE BLACKBIRDS

36 Ditton Green, Woodditton,
Suffolk CB8 9SQ
Tel: 01638 730811
Fax: 01638 730162

"Food with flair!" is the motto at **The Three Blackbirds** in Woodditton. This traditional thatched pub dates back to 1642, and retains the air of a large country cottage, with a large front garden and truly welcoming ambience. Two separate bars lead off the main entrance. The bar to the right leads through to the extensive rear dining area. This has an unusual upstairs room which can be used for private functions. Low beams and open fires add to the charming traditional atmosphere. Seating is primarily at four-person "cubicles" - very discreet and cosy. The village's proximity to Newmarket is reinforced by the many fine paintings and prints of equestrian scenes adorning the walls. Chef/proprietor Paul Lange is widely travelled and brings a wealth of knowledge and experience to creating a superb menu of tempting dishes such as pan-fried swordfish, shank of lamb, duckling, guinea fowl, steak, venison or vegetarian meals. Guests will find the perfect wine to accompany their choice on the extensive wine list. Relaxed and informal, the service is very conscientious and efficient. Interested guests can also purchase a book about Woodditton at the pub, written by the villagers themselves. Anyone who enjoys excellent food and drink amid the supremely comfortable surroundings of a quintessentially English pub will find what they're looking for here.

DOG & DUCK

63 High Street, Linton, Cambridgeshire CB1 6HS
Tel: 01223 891257

The charming thatched **Dog & Duck** in Linton dates back in parts to the 16th century. The River Granta runs through the village, which has a thriving duck population. The long bar has handsome oak beams; outdoors there's a small garden by the riverside. This traditional and very comfortable fine old pub offers a selection of real ales and delicious freshly cooked snacks and meals.

STAPLEFORD
5 miles S of Cambridge off the A1307

More great walking and an abundance of history: parkland with traces of an Iron Age hill fort, picnic area, woodland walks and nature trail. Magog Downs, with the famous Gog Magog Hills, is an open area that is perfect for walking and picnics.

DUXFORD
8 miles S of Cambridge off A505 by J10 of M11

Part of the Imperial War Museum, **Duxford Aviation Museum** is probably the leader in its field in Europe, with an outstanding collection of over 150 historic aircraft from biplanes through Spitfires to supersonic jets. The American Air Museum, where aircraft are suspended as if in flight, is part of this terrific place, which was built on a former RAF and US fighter base. Major air shows take place several times a year, and among the permanent features are a reconstructed wartime operations room, a hands-on exhibition for children and a dramatic land

warfare hall with tanks, military vehicles and artillery. Everyone should take time to see this marvellous show - and it should be much more than a flying visit!

At nearby **Hinxton** is another mill: a 17th century water mill that is grinding once more.

SHEPRETH
8 miles S of Cambridge off A10

A paradise for lovers of nature and gardens and a great starting point for country walks. **Shepreth L Moor Nature Reserve** is an L-shaped area of wet meadowland - now a rarity - that is home to birds and many rare plants. The nearby **Willers Mill Wildlife Park & Fish Farm** is a haven in natural surroundings to a wide variety of animals, which visitors can touch and feed. Around 18th century **Docwra's Manor** is a series of enclosed gardens with multifarious plants that is worth a visit at any time of year. Fowlmere, on the other side of the A10, is another important nature reserve, with hides and trails for the serious watcher.

THE JOHN BARLEYCORN

3 Moorfields Road, Duxford,
Cambridge CB2 4PP
Tel/Fax: 01223 832699

Taking its name from the legendary figure who travelled round the country, sowing seeds as he went, **The John Barleycorn** is a gorgeous thatched pub dating back to 1660. This beauty of this pub is enhanced by the wealth of flowering baskets and pots outside. The interior also lives up to expectations: low beamed ceilings, pew benches, refectory tables with brass nameplates (such as "Poachers' Corner" and "Smugglers' Retreat") and other original features add to the sense of tradition and homeliness of this fine

pub. Old proverbs are painted on the exposed beams, and there's a fascinating list of the pub's landlords - from 1720 to the present - on one wall. Built as a coaching house, it was known as the Coach & Horses up until the mid-19th century. This outstanding pub serves home-cooked food all day seven days a week, to be enjoyed either in the large bar/dining area or in the attractive garden (complete with safe children's play area) to the rear. The pub is proud to serve some of the best-kept ales in the country, and enjoys an excellent reputation for its food. There are always five real ales on tap, and a changing menu offering delicious lunchtime (midday - 5 p.m.) and supper (5 - 10 p.m.) dishes such as Irish stew, beef and Stilton pie, salmon steak, rack of ribs, grills, sandwiches, salads and much more, all expertly prepared.

THE ICKLETON LION

9 Abbey Street, Ickleton, Cambridgeshire CB10 1SS
Tel/Fax: 01799 530269

The Ickleton Lion is run by Doug and Paula Bollen. Doug is originally from North Yorkshire, where he trained as a master chef, while Paula is a native East Anglian. They have over 16 years' experience in the licensing trade, and it shows in their expert hospitality and service. A "destination" pub for its food, it is very popular with locals and visitors alike. The building is thought to date back to the 1700s, and the grounds include an enclosed lawned garden, safe children's play area and barbecue/picnic area. The interior has sanded pine floors and beamed uprights. The open log fire and abundance of fresh flowers add to the cosy and welcoming ambience. There are two bar areas, one of which, known

as "The Low Bar", is a traditional intimate snug. Five real ales are available, including changing guest ales. In the separate dining room, the menu boasts traditional English fare expertly prepared and presented. There's a good selection of starters, main courses and mouth-watering desserts, all home made and using the freshest local ingredients. Fridays offer fresh fish dishes. People come from far and wide for the Sunday roast, and there are also special hog roast days accompanied by family entertainments. Open seven days a week; food available every day.

WHITE HORSE

118 High Street, Barton, Cambridgeshire CB3 7BG
Tel: 01223 262327

On the main street of the village, just half a mile from Junction 12 of the M11, the 17th-century **White Horse** attracts both local and passing trade with its winning combination of warm welcome, old-world charm, great hospitality and good food. The first is offered by genial hosts Richard and Lyn Ellis and their children Steven and Joanne. The second is provided in abundance by ancient wooden beams, country furniture, tasteful decor and a log fire blazing in an inglenook hearth adorned with horse brasses; the third by the delightful secluded patio garden, safe play area, extensive restaurant and two ensuite double guest bedrooms. The fourth is the responsibility of chef James, whose three menus cater for most tastes and appetites. The bar menu, which ranges from sandwiches to hot dishes such as chicken curry, operates all day seven days a week, supplemented Monday to Saturday by daily specials. The restaurant menu, available in the evening, extends the choice still further, and on Sunday the carvery runs from midday until 3 p.m. All food is freshly prepared. Real ales on tap include Everards Tiger Best Bitter, Greene King IPA and Abbot Ale. There are also regular guest ales.

GREAT CHISHILL
12 miles S of Cambridge on the B1039

More great walking and an abundance of history: parkland with traces of an Iron Age hill fort, picnic area, woodland walks and nature trail. Magog Downs, with the famous Gog Magog Hills, is an open area that is perfect for walking and picnics.

GRANTCHESTER
2 miles SW of Cambridge off the A603

A pleasant walk by the Cam, or a punt on it, brings visitors from the bustle of Cambridge to the famous village of Grantchester, where Rupert Brooke lived and Byron swam. The walk passes through **Paradise Nature Reserve**.

"Stands the church clock at ten to three
And is there honey still for tea?"

The Orchard, with its Brooke connections, is known the world over. Brooke spent two happy years in Grantchester, and immortalised afternoon tea in The Orchard in a poem he wrote while homesick in Berlin. Time should also be allowed for a look at the Church of St Andrew and St Mary, in which the remains of a Norman church have been incorporated into the 1870s main structure.

BARTON
3 miles SW of Cambridge off the A603

Looking south from this pleasant village, you can see the impressive array of radio

telescopes that are part of the University's Mullard Radio Astronomy Observatory.

ARRINGTON
11 miles SW of Cambridge off the A603

18th century **Wimpole Hall**, owned by the National Trust, is probably the most spectacular country mansion in the whole county. The lovely interiors are the work of several celebrated architects, and there's a fine collection of furniture and pictures. The magnificent formally laid-out grounds include a Victorian parterre, a rose garden

Chapel in the Hall, Wimpole

and a walled garden. Landscaped **Wimpole Park**, with hills, woodland, lakes and a Chinese bridge, provides miles of wonderful walking and is perfect for anything from a gentle stroll to a strenuous hike. A brilliant

---

THE BLUE BALL INN

57 Broadway, Grantchester, Cambridgeshire CB3 9NQ
Tel: 01223 840679

The Blue Ball Inn, the oldest licensed premises in Grantchester, was named after a balloon flight that took place in 1785. The present building is about 100 years old, and behind the whitewashed facade and the slate roof are wooden floors, Victorian tables and an upright piano whose ivories anyone is welcome to tinkle. A log fire keeps the bars cosy in winter, and the small sheltered garden is popular when the sun shines. Landlord John Roos, in the trade all his working life, was a customer for 22 years before buying the inn in May 1997. His customers are a complete cross-section of the local community, who enjoy the excellent Greene King real ales on offer, and there's always someone to talk to at this friendliest of places. Karolin Rejniak does all the cooking, producing excellent meals lunchtime and evening from Tuesday to Sunday. The Sunday roasts are a speciality. Pub games here include shove ha'penny, "Shut the Box" and "Ringing the Bull". The inn also has three letting bedrooms.

attraction for all the family is **Wimpole Home Farm**, a working farm that is the largest rare breeds centre in East Anglia. The animals include Bagot goats, Tamworth pigs, Soay sheep and Longhorn cattle, and there's also a pets corner and horse-drawn wagon ride. Children can spend hours with the animals or in the adventure playground.

CAXTON
6 miles W of Cambridge off the A12198/A428

Caxton is home to Britain's oldest surviving postmill, and at nearby **Little Gransden** another venerable mill has been restored. A scheduled ancient monument, it dates from the early 17th century and was worked into the early years of this century.

MADINGLEY
4 miles W of Cambridge on the A428

The **American Cemetery** is one of the loveliest, most peaceful and most moving places in the region, a place of pilgrimage for the families of the American servicemen who operated from the many wartime bases in the county. The cemetery commemorates 3,800 dead and 5,000 missing in action in the Second World War.

Duke of Wellington

Alms Hill, Bourn, Cambridgeshire CB3 7SH
Tel/Fax: 01954 719364

The Duke of Wellington in Bourn is a welcoming and very attractive public house offering "the finest foods from around the globe". This handsome pub was built at the end of the 19th century; the restaurant to the rear was built in 1983. Among the many enticing features are the large open-plan interior, lawned garden area and relaxed and comfortable ambience. There are always three real ales available at this Free House, as well as an excellent selection of wines, lagers and spirits. The menu offers lunch and evening meals featuring traditional English as well as Thai and Italian dishes, all freshly prepared on the premises. These three-course meals are hearty and delicious, as is the excellent Sunday lunch. Owner Alex Williams is locally born and bred; both he and his wife Lynn are qualified and experienced chefs, and offer all their guests a warm welcome.

The Poplars

12 East Drive, Highfields Caldecote,
Cambridge CB3 7NZ
Tel/Fax: 01954 210396

The Poplars is located half a mile along a private road here in Highfields Caldecote. A secluded, quiet and relaxing place to stay, there is a large lawned garden to the front fringed with the trees that give it its name. There are two wonderful en suite guest bedrooms - including a family room - both furnished and decorated to the highest standard. The breakfast room is warm and welcoming; here, guests choose from an extensive breakfast menu. Evening meals are also available by arrangement. Owners Brenda and Paul Phillips are gracious and friendly hosts. Among their several pets is "Zak", a British miniature horse whom they proudly "show" and who was all-Ireland Champion 1998. This is the kind of B&B where guests and hosts join together for a chat and a drink. No smoking. Pets and children welcome. Disabled facilities. For a real taste of peaceful country life amid charming surroundings, look no further.

The old county of Huntingdonshire is the heartland of the rural heritage of Cambridgeshire, and the home of Oliver Cromwell beckons with a wealth of history and pleasing landscapes. Many motorists follow the Cromwell Trail, which guides tourists around the legacy of buildings and places associated with the great man in the area. The natural start of the Trail is Huntingdon itself, where he was born the son of a country gentleman, and other main stopping places will be covered in this chapter.

Burghley House, Stamford

The **Ouse Valley Way** (26 miles) follows the course of the Great Ouse through pretty villages and a variety of natural attractions. A gentle cruise along this area can fill a lazy day to perfection, but for those who prefer something more energetic on the water there are excellent, versatile facilities at Grafham Water.

The Nene-Ouse Navigation Link, part of the Fenland Waterway, provides the opportunity for a relaxed look at a lovely part of the region. It travels from Stanground Lock near Peterborough to a lock at the small village of Salters Lode in the east, and the 28-mile journey passes through several Fenland towns and a rich variety of wildlife habitats.

View to Riverside, Wansford

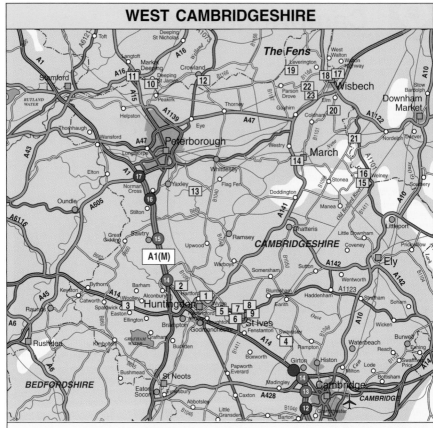

WEST CAMBRIDGESHIRE

© MAPS IN MINUTES ™ (1999)

PLACES TO STAY, EAT, DRINK AND SHOP

HUNTINGDON

The former county town of Huntingdonshire is an ancient town first settled to any extent by the Romans. It boasts many grand Georgian buildings, including the handsome three-storeyed Town Hall.

Oliver Cromwell was born in Huntingdon in 1599 and attended Huntingdon Grammar School. The schoolhouse was originally part of the Hospital of St John the Baptist, fuonded in the reign of Henry II by David, Earl of Huntingdon. Samuel Pepys was also a pupil here. Cromwell was MP for Huntingdon in the Parliament of 1629, was made a JP in 1630 and moved to St Ives in the following year. Rising to power as an extremely able military commander in the Civil War, he raised troops from the region and made his headquarters in the Falcon Inn. Appointed Lord Protector in 1653, Cromwell was never proclaimed King, though he ran the country until his death in 1658. The school he attended is now the **Cromwell Museum**, located on Huntingdon High Street, housing the only public collection relating specifically to him, with exhibits that reflect many aspects of his political, social and religious life. The museum's exhibits include an extensive collection of Cromwell family portraits and personal objects, among them a hat and a seal, contemporary coins and medals, and an impressive Florentine cabinet - the gift of the Grand Duke of Tuscany - and a surgeon's chest made by Kolb of Augsburg. This fine collection helps visitors interpret the life and legacy of this remarkable man.

All Saints Church, opposite the Cromwell Museum, displays many architectural styles, from medieval to Victorian. One of the two surviving parish churches of Huntingdon, All Saints was considered to be the church of the Hinchingbrooke part of the Cromwell family, though no memorials survive to attest to this. The Cromwell family burial vault is contained within the church, however, and it is here that Oliver's father Robert and his grandfather Sir Henry are buried. The church has a fine chancel roof, a very lovely organ chamber and a truly impressive stained glass window.

Huntingdon's other church, **St Mary's**, dates from Norman times but was almost completely rebuilt in the 1400s. It boasts a fine Perpendicular west tower, which partially collapsed in 1607. The damage was extensive, and the tower was not completely repaired until 1621. Oliver Cromwell's father Robert contributed to the cost of the repairs, as recorded on the stone plaque fixed to the east wall on the nave, north of the chancel arch.

Cowper House (No 29 High Street) has an impressive early 18th century frontage. A plaque commemorates the fact that the poet William Cowper lived here between 1765 and 1767.

Among Huntingdon's many fine former coaching inns is **The George Hotel**. Although badly damaged by fire in 1865, the north and west wings of the 17th century courtyard remain intact, as does its very rare wooden gallery. The inn was one of the most famous of all the posting houses on the old Great North Run. It is reputed that Dick Turpin used one of the rooms here. The medieval courtyard, gallery and open staircase are the scene of annual productions of Shakespeare.

Along the south side of the Market Square, the **Falcon Inn** dates back in parts to the 1500s. Oliver Cromwell is said to have used this as his headquarters during the Civil War.

About half a mile southwest of town stands **Hinchingbrooke House**, which today is a school but which has its origins in the Middle Ages, when it was a nunnery. It was given to the Cromwell family by Henry VIII in 1538, though ghostly nuns are said to still haunt the building. Converted by the Cromwell family in the 16th century and later extended by the Earls of Sandwich, today's visitors can see examples of every period of English architecture from the 12th to early 20th century. King James I was a regular visitor, and Oliver Cromwell spend part of his childhood here. The 1st Earl of Sandwich was a central figure in the Civil War and subsequent Restoration, while the 4th Earl (inventor of the snack named after him) was one of the most flamboyant politicians of the 18th century. The remains of the Benedictine nunnery can still be seen. The House is open for guided tours, including lovely cream teas served in the Tudor kitchens.

Hinchingbrooke Country Park covers 180 acres of grassy meadows, mature woodland, ponds and lakes. There is a wide variety of wildlife including woodpeckers, herons, kestrels, butterflies and foxes. The network of paths makes exploring the park easy, and battery-powered wheelchairs are provided for less able visitors. The Visitors Centre serves refreshments at peak times.

Half a mile north, **Spring Common** offers another chance to enjoy some Cambridgeshire countryside. Covering 13 acres, its name comes from the natural spring which runs constantly and has long been a gathering place. The town developed around rather than within this area of rural tranquillity, which boasts a range of diverse habitats including marsh, grassland, scrub and streams. Plant life abounds, providing food and shelter for a variety of animals, amphibians, birds and invertebrates.

All Saints, Huntingdon

AROUND HUNTINGDON

WARBOYS
7 miles NE of Huntingdon off the B1040

An interesting walk to Ramsey takes in a wealth of history and pretty scenery. St Mary Magdalene's Church has a tall, very splendid tower.

RAMSEY
9 miles NE of Huntingdon on the B1040

A pleasant market town with a broad main street down which a river once ran. The medieval Ramsey Abbey was founded in 969 by Earl Ailwyn as a Benedictine monastery. The Abbey became one of the most important in England in the 12th and 13th centuries, and as it prospered so did Ramsey, so that by the 13th century it had become a town with a weekly market and an annual three-day festival at the time of the feast of St Benedict. After the Dissolution of the Monasteries in 1539, the Abbey and its lands were sold to Sir Richard Williams, great-grandfather of Oliver Cromwell. Most of the buildings were then demolished, the stones being used to build Caius, Kings and Trinity Colleges at Cambridge, the towers of Ramsey, Godmanchester and Holywell churches, the gate at Hinchingbrooke House and several local properties. In 1938 the house was converted for use as a school, which it remains to this day. To the northwest are the ruins of the once magnificent stone gatehouse of the late 15th century - only the porter's lodge remains, but inside can be seen an unusual large carved effigy made of Purbeck marble and dating back to the 14th century. It is said to represent Earl Ailwyn, founder of the Abbey. The gatehouse, now in the care of the National Trust, can be visited daily from April to October.

The church of **St Thomas a Becket of Canterbury** forms an impressive vista at the end of the High Street. Dating back to about 1180, it is thought to have been built as a hospital or guesthouse for the Abbey. It was converted to a church to accommodate the many pilgrims who flocked to Ramsey in the 13th century. The church has what is reputed to be the finest nave in Huntingdonshire, dating back to the 12th century and consisting of seven bays. The church's other treasure is a 15th century carved oak lectern, thought to have come from the Abbey.

Most of **Ramsey Rural Museum** is housed in an 18th century farm building and several barns set in open countryside. Among the many fascinating things to see are a Victorian home and school; a village store; and restored farm equipment, machinery, carts and wagons. The wealth of traditional implements used by local craftsmen such as the farrier, wheelwright, thatcher, dairyman, animal husbandman and cobbler offer an insight into bygone days.

The unusual Ramsey War Memorial is a listed Grade II memorial consisting of a fine bronze statue of St George slaying the dragon atop a tall, octagonal pillar crafted of Portland stone.

UPWOOD
8 miles NE of Huntingdon off the B1040

A pleasant, scattered village in a very calm and picturesque part of the world. **Woodwalton Fen** nature reserve is a couple of minutes to the west.

HARTFORD
½ mile N of Huntington off the B1514

At just half a mile from Hartford Marina, this lovely village offers plenty of excellent riverside walks.

HARTFORD COTTAGE GUEST HOUSE

1 Longstaff Way, Hartford, Huntingdon, Cambridgeshire PE29 1XT
Tel/Fax: 01480 454116

Over 100 years old, **Hartford Cottage Guest House** is a delightful brickbuilt house offering superior bed and breakfast accommodation. Each of the six guest bedrooms (three doubles, two twins, one family room with one double and one single bed) offers full facilities, and is comfortably furnished and tastefully decorated. Two rooms overlook the garden. The entire house is open to guests, who will appreciate the attractive guests' lounge and lovely dining room. Dietary or special needs are happily catered for at breakfast, which is delicious and filling. The extensive mature gardens offer interest on three gentle levels. Guests are welcome to wander around and enjoy the trees, shrubs and flowering plants. And at just half a mile from Hartford Marina, there are plenty of excellent riverside walks, beginning just 150 yards from the house. The house is also a wonderful base for exploring Huntingdon, St Ives, and the many other attractions in the region. Open all year round.

THE THREE HORSESHOES

Ermine Street, Great Stukeley, Huntingdon, Cambridgeshire PE28 5AH
Tel: 01480 453583 Fax: 01480 411991

The Three Horseshoes in Great Stukeley is a welcoming and comfortable pub with a friendly ambience. With a large front lawn and paved area dotted with picnic tables, it makes an ideal place to stop for a

relaxing drink in fine weather, while the interior is just as welcoming, with its comfortable seating and tasteful decor. There is an extensive lounge/bar area, separate back bar and no-smoking restaurant area. Real ales available at this Free House include Websters bitter and Theakstons mild, as well as changing guest ales. The menu boasts a range of tempting home-made pies and many other delicious options. Food is available at lunch and evenings seven days a week. The caravan site to the rear has room for 30 tourers, and is complete with shower/toilet block. Owners Gary and Christine and their helpful staff offer a high standard of service.

SAWTRY
8 miles NW of Huntingdon on the A1

The main point of interest has no point! All Saints Church, built in 1880, lacks tower and steeple, and is topped by a bellcote. Inside are marvellous brasses and pieces from ancient Sawtry Abbey. Just south of Sawtry, Aversley Wood is a conservation area with abundant birdlife and plants.

GREAT GIDDING
10 miles NW of Huntingdon off the B660

Stained-glass windows are a notable feature of St Michael's Church in the largest of the three Giddings. A fire ravaged the village in the 1860s and the church was one of the few buildings to survive. The church is the atmospheric setting for concerts and plays.

STILTON
12 miles NW of Huntingdon off A1

An interesting high street with many fine buildings and a good choice for the hungry or thirsty visitor, as it has been since the heyday of horse-drawn travel. Journeys were a little more dangerous then, and Dick Turpin is said to have hidden at the Bell Inn. The famous cheese is still produced and is sold in Stilton.

ALCONBURY
3 miles NW of Huntingdon off the A1

Fenland walks can be interspersed with pauses at the local inns and a look at the Church of St Peter and St Paul, whose steeple and chancel are particularly noteworthy. This long village has a large green, an ancient village pump and a 15th century bridge crossing the brook that runs through Alconbury.

BARHAM
6 miles W of Huntingdon off the A1/A14

This delightful hamlet boasts 12 houses, 30 people and an ancient church with box pews, surrounded by undulating farmland. Nearby attractions include angling and sailing on Grafham Water, Go-karting at Kimbolton and National Hunt racing at Huntingdon.

CHESTNUT VIEW

8/10 High Street, Spaldwick, Huntingdon, Cambridgeshire PE28 0TD
Tel: 01480 890216 Fax: 01480 891889
email: GrahameGreyHorse@aol.com

Chestnut View is a charming and pristine whitewashed house dating back to 1650. Originally three separate cottages, this homely and traditional bed and breakfast offers one ground floor twin room and two rooms on the first floor (one family room, one twin). The bedrooms have exposed oak beams and other traditional features. They are located in a self-contained building (the former barn) with its own access.

The rear garden is secluded and peaceful, fringed with trees surrounding the attractive patio and lawn. Guests are welcome to make themselves at home here, just as they are throughout the rest of this handsome and comfortable home. Breakfast is served in the main house. Any special dietary requirements are happily catered for. Evening meals by prior arrangement. A baby-sitting service is also available. Owner Joyce Leach is an accomplished cook and a welcoming host. All guests will enjoy a very pleasant and memorable stay here at this delightful B&B.

WOOLLEY
5 miles W of Huntingdon off the A1/A14

This quiet and secluded hamlet attracts a broad spectrum of visitors including anglers, golfers, walkers and riders, drawn by its lush and picturesque beauty and rural tranquillity.

ELLINGTON
4 miles W of Huntingdon off the A14

A quiet village just south of the A14 and about a mile north of **Grafham Water**. Both Cromwell and Pepys visited, having relatives living in the village, and it was in Ellington that Pepys' sister Paulina found a husband, much to the relief of the diarist, who had written: *"We must find her one, for she grows old and ugly"*. All Saints Church is magnificent, like so many in the area, and among many fine features are the 15th century oak roof and the rich carvings in the nave and the aisles. The church and its tower were built independently.

EASTON
5 miles W of Huntingdon off the A14

Picturesque cottages and ancient farmhouses are secondary attractions to the Church of St Peter, most of which, including the graceful spire, dates from the 14th century.

SPALDWICK
6 miles W of Huntingdon off the A14

A sizable village that was once the site of the Bishop of Lincoln's manor house. The grand Church of St James dates from the 12th century and has seen restoration in most centuries including the 20th, when the spire had to be partly rebuilt after being struck by lightning.

The area north and west of Huntingdon is a very agreeable one for walking, with pretty villages and interesting churches.

CATWORTH
8 miles W of Huntingdon off the A14

Another charming village, voted Best Kept Village in Cambridgeshire in 1998, and well worth exploring.

BYTHORN
12 miles W of Huntingdon off the A14

Bythorn boasts picturesque cottages, good walking and the parish church of St Lawrence, where elements from the 12th to the 17th centuries are successfully combined.

KEYSTON
12 miles W of Huntingdon off the A14

A delightful village with a pedigree that can be traced back to the days of the Vikings. Major attractions both sacred and secular: the Church of St John the Baptist is impressive in its almost cathedral-like proportions, with one of the most magnificent spires in the whole county; the Pheasant is one of the country's best and best-known pub-restaurants.

BRAMPTON
2 miles SW of Huntingdon off the A1

Brampton is where Huntingdon racecourse is situated. An average of 18 meetings (all jumping) are scheduled every year, including Bank Holiday fixtures (extra-special deals for families). In November, when the Grade 2 Peterborough Chase is the feature race. Brampton's less speculative attractions include the 13th century Church of St Mary, and Pepys House, the home of Samuel's uncle. This person was a cousin of Lord Sandwich, who got Samuel his job at the Admiralty.

GRAFHAM
5 miles SW of Huntingdon on the B661

Created in the mid-1960s as a reservoir, **Grafham Water** offers a wide range of outdoor activities for visitors of all ages, with 1,500 acres of beautiful countryside, including the lake itself. A ten-mile perimeter track is great for jogging or cycling, and there's excellent sailing, windsurfing and fly fishing. The area is a Site of Special Scientific Interest, and an ample nature reserve at the western edge is run jointly by Anglian Water and the Wildlife Trust. There are nature trails, information boards, a wildlife garden and a dragonfly pond. Many species of waterfowl stay here at various times of the year, and bird-watchers have the use of six hides, three of them accessible by wheelchair. An exhibition centre has displays and video presentations of the reservoir's history, a gift shop and a café.

KIMBOLTON
8 miles SW of Huntingdon on the B645

History aplenty here, and a lengthy pause is in order to look at all the interesting buildings. St Andrew's Church would head the list were it not for **Kimbolton Castle**, which along with its gatehouse dominates the village. Parts of the original Tudor building are still to be seen, but the appearance of the castle today owes much to the major remodelling carried out by Vanbrugh and Nicholas Hawksmoor in the first decade of the 18th century. The gatehouse was added by Robert Adam in 1764. Henry VIII's first wife Catherine of Aragon spent the last 18 months of her life imprisoned here, where she died in 1536. The castle is now a school, but can be visited on certain days in the summer (don't miss the Pellegrini murals).

BUCKDEN
4 miles SW of Huntingdon on the A1

This historic village was an important coaching stop on the old Great North Road. It is known particularly as the site of Buckden Towers, the great palace built for the Bishops of Lincoln. In the splendid grounds are the 15th century gatehouse and the tower where Henry VIII imprisoned his first wife, Catherine of Aragon, in 1533.

ST NEOTS
10 miles SE of Huntingdon off the A1

St Neots dates back to the founding of a Saxon Priory, built on the outskirts of Eynesbury, in 974. Partially destroyed by the Danes in 1010, it was re-established as a Benedicting Priory in about 1081 by St Anselm, Abbot of Bec and later Archbishop of Canterbury. For the next two centuries the Priory flourished. Charters were granted by Henry I to hold fairs and markets. The first bridge over the Great Ouse, comprising 73 timber arches, was built in 1180. The name of the town comes from the Cornish saint whose remains were interred in the Priory some time before the Norman

Conquest. With the Dissolution of the Monasteries, the Priory was demolished. In the early 17th century the old bridge was replaced by a stone one. This was then the site of a battle between the Royalists and Roundheads in 1648 - an event sometimes re-enacted by Sealed Knot societies, as on the 350th anniversary in July 1998.

St Neots repays a visit on foot, since there are many interesting sites and old buildings tucked away. The famous Market Square is one of the largest and most ancient in the country. A market has been held here every Thursday since the 12th century. The magnificent parish church of St Mary the Virgin is a very fine edifice, known locally as the Cathedral of Huntingdonshire. It is an outstanding example of Late Medieval Architecture. The gracious interior complements the 130 foot Somerset-style tower, with a finely carved oak alter, excellent Victorian stained glass and a Holdich organ, built in 1855.

St Neots Museum - opened in 1995 - tells the story of the town and the surrounding area. Housed in the former magistrates court and police station, it still has the original cells. Eye-catching displays trace local history from prehistoric times to the present day. Open Wednesday to Saturday.

Less than three miles north of St Neots at **Little Paxton** is **Paxton Nature Reserve**. Created alongside gravel workings, the Reserve attracts thousands of water birds for visitors to observe from hides. The wealth of wildlife means that the area is a SSSI (Site of Special Scientific Interest) and ensures a

Riverside Walk, St Neots

plethora of colour and activity all year round. The site also features nature trails and a visitor centre. It has thousands of visiting waterfowl, including one of the largest colonies of cormorants, and is particularly noted for its wintering wildfowl, nightingales in late spring and kingfishers. There are about four miles of walks, some suitable for wheelchairs. Spring and summer also bring a feast of wildflowers, butterflies and dragonflies.

Just north again is the Saxon **Minster** at Great Paxton.

EYNESBURY
1 mile S of St Neots on the A428

Eynesbury is actually part of St Neots, with only a little stream separating the two. Note the 12th century Church of St Mary with its Norman tower. Rebuilt in the Early English period, it retains some well preserved locally sculpted 14th century oak benches. History has touched this quiet and lovely village from time to time: it was the home of the famous giant James Toller, who is buried in the middle aisle of the church in 1818. Only 21 when he died, he measured some 8 feet tall - it is said he was buried here to escape the attentions of body snatchers, whose activities were widespread at the time. Eynesbury was also the birthplace of the Miles' Quads, the first ever surviving quadruplets in Britain.

BUSHMEAD
6 miles W of St Neots off the B660

The remains of Bushmead Abbey, once a thriving Augustinian community, are well worth a detour. The garden setting is delightful, and the surviving bits include some interesting stained glass.

GODMANCHESTER
2 miles SW of Huntingdon off the A1

Godmanchester is linked to Huntingdon by a 14th century bridge across the Ouse. It was a Roman settlement and one that continued in importance down the years, as the number of handsome buildings testifies. One such is **Island Hall**, a mid-18th century mansion built for John Jackson, the Receiver General for Huntingdon; it contains many interesting artefacts. This family home has lovely Georgian rooms, with fine period detail and

fascinating possessions relating to the owners' ancestors since their first occupation of the house in 1800. The tranquil riverside setting and formal gardens add to the peace and splendour - the house takes its name from the ornamental island that forms part of the grounds. Octavia Hill was sometimes a guest, and wrote effusively to her sister that Island Hall was "the loveliest, dearest old house, I never was in such a one before."

Wood Green Animal Shelter at Kings Bush Farm, Godmanchester is a purpose-built, 50 acre centre open to the public all year round. Cats, dogs, horses, donkeys, farm animals, guinea pigs, rabbits, llamas, wildfowl and pot-bellied pigs are among the many animals for visitors to see, and there is a specially adapted nature trail and restaurant.

St Mary's Church is Perpendicular in style, though not totally in age, as the tower is a 17th century replacement of the 13th century original. A footpath leads from the famous Chinese Bridge (1827) to **Port Holme Meadow**, at 225 acres one of the largest in England and the site of Roman remains. It is a Site of Special Scientific Interest, with a huge diversity of botanical and bird species. Huntingdon racecourse was once situated here, and it was a training airfield during the First World War. Another site of considerable natural activity is Godmanchester Pits, accessed along the Ouse Valley Way and home to a great diversity of flora and fauna.

PAPWORTH EVERARD
6 miles S of Huntingdon on the A1198

One of the most recent of the region's churches, St Peter's dates mainly from the mid-19th century. Neighbouring **Papworth St Agnes** has an older church in St John's, though parts of that, too, are Victorian. Just up the road at **Hilton** is the famous **Hilton Turf Maze**, cut in 1660 to a popular medieval design.

BOXWORTH
7 miles SE of Huntingdon off the A14

A village almost equidistant from Huntingdon and Cambridge, and a pleasant base for touring the area. The Church of St Peter is unusual in being constructed of pebble rubble. A mile south of Boxworth is **Overhall Grove**, one of the largest elm

THE WHITE HORSE INN

1 Market Street, Swavesey,
Cambridgeshire CB4 5QG
Tel: 01954 232470

Having seen service as an auction house, a public health office and a meeting place for various societies in its 480-year history, **The White Horse Inn** in Swavesey continues to play many parts. First and foremost, of course, it's a friendly village pub, run by Pat and Will Wright, who have a strong interest in real ales and fine malt whiskeys. Guest ales are always featured. Bar lunches are served mondays to saturdays, sunday roast dinners, including a vegetarian option, and senior citizen specials on tuesdays. Evening meals are available monday through saturday. The bars are warm and welcoming, with open log fires and exposed oak beams. The public bar has bar billiards and darts, and there's a separate pool room and a function room. Old photographs of the village share wall space with prints and drawings of Cambridge colleges. The White Horse is the headquarters of the Cambridge motorcycle scrambling club and of the MG owners club (also one of the increasingly few sources of spare parts for old MGs) and other groups to meet here include wildlife conservationists and the local PTA. Various charities benefit from events organised here, the most notable event being the annual barrel-rolling contest which the publicans revived in 1997.

THE THREE JOLLY BUTCHERS

Huntingdon Road, Wyton, Cambridgeshire PE28 2AD
Tel: 01480 463228 Fax: 01480 463726

The Three Jolly Butchers pub occupies one of the most attractive buildings in the village of Wyton. The date '1622' is clearly visible on its central chimney, and it is believed to have begun life as a yeoman farmer's house. Run by sisters Sarah Bell and Kathryne Cookson, it is a popular, friendly and very hospitable pub. The heavily beamed ceilings, upright timbers and wide inglenook fire add to the traditional and cosy ambience of the place. Out back there's a large and very beautiful garden, stretching

down to the riverside. Real ales on tap at this Free House include Worthingtons, Bass, and Warsteiner lager.

The extensive menu offers a truly superb range of delicious and nutritious dishes, from traditional English fare to more innovative options. All meals are created using the freshest produce, and all are freshly prepared and cooked. Tempting dishes include home-made steak and kidney pie, fish specialities and an impressive variety of sandwiches, snacks and main courses, guaranteed to satisfy every palate.

woods in the country and home to a variety of wildlife.

THE GREAT OUSE VALLEY

HEMINGFORD ABBOTS
3 miles SE of Huntingdon off the A14

Once part of the Ramsey Abbey Estate, Hemingford Abbots is set around the 13th century Church of St Margaret, along the banks of the Great Ouse. Opportunities for angling and boating facilities, including rowing boats for hire, swimming, country walks, golf and a recreation centre are all within a couple of miles. The village hosts a flower festival every two years.

Just to the east is **Hemingford Grey**, with its church on the banks of the Ouse. The manor at Hemingford Grey is reputedly the oldest continuously inhabited house in England, built around 1130, and visits (by appointment only) will reveal all the treasures in the house and garden.

FENSTANTON
7 miles SE of Huntingdon off the A14 bypass

Capability Brown was Lord of the Manor from 1768, and he, his wife and his son are buried in the medieval church. See also the 17th century manor house and the red brick Clock Tower.

SWAVESEY
10 miles SE of Huntingdon off the A14

Look for the large 14th century church and the windmill a little way west, on the way to Fen Drayton, whose church is built of pebble rubble.

WYTON
2 miles E of Huntington off the A1123

Wyton is mentioned in the Domesday Book, and is thought to have been founded in the 8th century. It is a popular tourist destination thanks to its proximity to Houghton Mill (see panel below) and opportunities for riverside walks, as well as its charming thatched buildings and shops.

HOUGHTON MILL

Houghton, Huntingdon,
Cambridgeshire PE28 2AZ
Tel: 01480 301494 Fax: 01480 469641
website: www.nationaltrust.org.uk/
  houghtonmill

The National Trust-owned **Houghton Mill** deserves its reputation as a popular tourist attraction. There has been a mill on this site for some 1,000 years. The present mill dates from the 18th century. This impressive five-story brick and clapboard structure stands on a tributary of the River Ouse midway between Huntingdon and St Ives.

The mill is one of the last and the most complete to survive in the area. As such it is the most important of the very few remaining mills. It has recently had its wheel restored, as part of a 1.2 million pound restoration project and is fully operational. This has provided improved facilities for visitors. Open days during the summer months offer visitors the chance to see the mill in action, and to appreciate the different forms of sustainable energy - a water turbine which generates electricity for the site and for other NT properties, and the waterwheel at work to produce stoneground flour. Milling takes place on Sundays and Bank Holiday Mondays, and the site also contains an art gallery, miniature millstones to turn by hand, and a tea room. In addition, the area to the north of the mill is an unusual survival of undeveloped Ouse riverbank, which the Trust intends to protect for its ecological interest and landscape value as an appropriate setting for this fine mill.

Restaurant Molise

22 Bridge Street, St Ives, Huntingdon,
Cambridgeshire PE27 5EG
Tel: 01480 496378 Fax 01480 464898

Restaurant Molise is the genuine article - a fine Italian restaurant run by Pasquale Adamante, Luigi Dirita and Angelo Bucciero along traditional Mediterranean lines: family run, with excellent food and drink. Popular and friendly, this superb establishment enjoys an enviable reputation for quality and service. Occupying a listed building near the quay in the centre of St Ives, it is small and intimate, tastefully furnished and decorated with understated style. Personal and attentive service is just one of the hallmarks of this impressive restaurant. Linen tablecloths and sparkling glassware set the tone for a truly memorable meal.

All food on the extensive menu is freshly prepared and cooked. The menu offers a range of tempting dishes, from pasta (freshly made by Pasquale's mother, Rosa) and risottos to steak, veal, poultry, seafood, and fresh fish in season, all expertly prepared and presented. Open: Monday to Friday for lunch (midday - 1.30), Monday to Thursday evening (6.30-10) and Friday and Saturday evening (6.30-10.30). For a mouth-watering treat amid warm and very congenial surroundings, look no further.

The White Hart Inn

The Sheep Market, St Ives, Huntingdon, Cambridgeshire PE27 5AH

Tel: 01480 463275

The White Hart Inn in St Ives is located just opposite the popular town square, host to a weekday market. Owners Terry and Ann Richardson are friendly and welcoming hosts. They and their able staff offer a high standard of service and efficiency. Popular with locals and visitors alike, this traditional inn is a cut above the rest. Apart from a superb range of real ales (including London Pride, Tetley and Greene King IPA), wines and spirits,
there is a fine menu of favourites such as home-made steak and kidney pie, roasts, burgers, curry, chili, barbecued chicken or ribs, pasta dishes, seafood and a selection of daily specials, all freshly prepared and cooked.

The interior of this fine establishment - which dates back to the 1700s - is very comfortable, with panelled walls and upholstered banquette seating overlooking the town square. The lounge features photographs of St Ives in the 1930s. Food is served every lunchtime, and evening Monday - Saturday. The inn is open from 11 a.m. to 11 p.m. Monday - Saturday, and until 10.30 p.m. on Sundays.

HOUGHTON
5 miles E of Huntingdon on the A1123

Houghton Meadows is a Site of Special Scientific Interest with an abundance of hay meadow species. One of the most popular walks in the whole area links Houghton with St Ives.

ST IVES
6 miles E of Huntingdon off the A1123

An ancient town on the banks of the Great Ouse which once held a huge annual fair and is named after St Ivo, said to be a Persian bishop who came here in the Dark Ages to spread a little light. In the Middle Ages, kings bought cloth for their households at great wool fairs and markets, and a market is still held every Monday. The Bank Holiday Monday markets are particularly lively affairs, and the Michaelmas fair fills the town centre for three days. Seagoing barges once navigated up to the famous six-arched bridge that was built in the 15th century and has a most unusual two-storey chapel in its middle. Oliver Cromwell lived in St Ives in the 1630s and the statue of him on Market Hill, with its splendid hat, is one of the most familiar landmarks. It was made in bronze, with a Portland stone base, and was erected in 1901. It was originally designed for Huntingdon, but they wouldn't accept it!

The beautiful parish church in its churchyard beside the river is well worth a visit. The quayside provides a tranquil mooring for holidaymakers and there are wonderful walks by the riverside.

Clive Sinclair developed his tiny TVs and pocket calculators in the town, and a famous son of St Ives was the great Victorian rower John Goldie, whose name is remembered each year by the second Cambridge boat in the Boat Race.

The **Norris Museum**, in a delightful setting by the river, tells the story of Huntingdonshire for the past 175 million years or so, with anything from fossils, mammoth tusks and models of the great historic reptiles through flint tools, Roman artefacts and Civil War armour to lace-making and ice-skating displays, and

St Ives Bridge and River Ouse

THE AVIATOR

Ramsey Road, St Ives, Huntingdon,
Cambridgeshire PE27 5BZ
Tel/Fax: 01480 464417

The Aviator pub in Ramsey Road, St Ives, takes its name from the pub's long association with the RAF. Pictures of aeroplanes adorn the walls, and there are two actual propellers (from a Spitfire and Wellington) on display. Occupying a site next to the village church, just 100 yards from the moorings on the River Ouse, it was built in 1647 and is a traditional pub in the best sense of the word. Leaded windows, oak beams and timber uprights and the open fire enhance the cosy and welcoming ambience. CAMRA-registered, this fine pub offers at least three real ales, which change regularly to feature the best in the country. The food is all home-cooked using the freshest local ingredients. Tuesday night is Steak Night, and there are special rates for diners between 5 and 7 p.m. Tuesday to Friday. The pub's special themed suppers have proved very popular; booking is advised. For a truly relaxing drink or meal in comfortable, welcoming surroundings, look no further.

contemporary works of art. A truly fascinating place that is open throughout the year, admission free. Exhibitions include a life-size replica of a 160 million year old Ichthyosaur. There are remains of Mammoths from the Ice Ages, tools and pottery from the Stone Age to Roman times and relics from the medieval castles and abbeys. Also on show are toys and models made by prisoners of the Napoleonic Wars.

> *"As I was going to St Ives I met a man*
> *with seven wives.*
> *Each wife had seven sacks, each sack*
> *had seven cats, each cat had seven kits.*
> *Kits, cats, sacks and wives, how many*
> *were going to St Ives?"*

- None, of course, but today's visitors are certain to have a good time while they are here.

Just outside St Ives are **Wilthorn Meadow**, a Site of Natural History Interest where Canada geese are often to be seen, and Holt Island Nature Reserve, where high-quality willow is being grown to re-introduce the traditional craft of basket-making. Spot the butterflies, dragonflies and kingfishers.

BLUNTISHAM
3 miles NE of St Ives on the A1123

An impressive church here, with a unique 14th century chancel that ends in three sides. The father of Dorothy L Sayers was once the rector, and Dorothy once lived in the large Georgian rectory on the main road.

EARITH
4 miles E of St Ives on the A1123

The **Ouse Washes**, a special protection area, runs northeast from the village to Earith Pits, a well-known habitat for birds and crawling creatures; some of the pits are used for fishing. The Washes are a wetland of major international importance supporting such birds as ruffs, Bewick and Whooper swans, and hen harriers. The average bird population is around 20,000. Some of the meadows flood in winter, and ice-skating is popular when the temperature really drops. There's a great tradition of ice skating in the Fens, and the Fenmen were the national champions until the 1930s.

SOMERSHAM
4 miles NE of St Ives on the B1040/B1060

The **Raptor Foundation** is found here, a major attraction, where owls and other birds of prey find refuge. There are regular flying displays and falconry displays. Somersham once had a palace for the Bishops of Ely, and its splendid Church of St John would have done them proud.

PETERBOROUGH

The second city of Cambridgeshire has a long and interesting history that traces back to the Bronze Age, as can be seen in the archaeological site at Flag Fen. Although a cathedral city, it is also a New Town (designated in 1967), so modern development and expansion have vastly increased its facilities while retaining the quality of its historic heart. Its crowning glory is, of course, the Romanesque **Cathedral**, built in the 12th and 13th centuries on a site that had seen Christian

Peterborough Cathedral

Lock on the River Nene

worship since 655AD. Henry VIII made the church a cathedral, and his first queen, Catherine of Aragon, is buried here, as for a while was Mary Queen of Scots after her execution at Fotheringay. Features to note are the huge (85 foot) arches of the West Front, the unique painted wooden nave ceiling, some exquisite late-15th century fan vaulting, and the tomb of Catherine. Though the best known of the city's landmarks, the Cathedral is by no means the only one. The **Peterborough Museum and Art Gallery** covers all aspects of the history of Peterborough from the Jurassic period to Victorian times..

There are twin attractions for railway enthusiasts in the shape of **Railworld**, a hands-on exhibition dealing with modern rail travel, and the wonderful **Nene Valley Railway**, which operates 15-mile steam-hauled trips between Peterborough and its

Ferry Meadows and River Nene

HQ and museum at Wansford. Thomas the Tank Engine, which used to work at a local sugar beet factory, is the children's favourite, but there are many other locomotives from the British Railways days, including "Brittania" (away in 1999 for a major refit) and a Bulleid Battle of Britain Pacific. A feature on the main railway line at Peterborough is the historic Iron Bridge, part of the old Great Northern Railway and still virtually as built by Lewis Cubitt in 1852.

Just outside the city, by the river Nene, is **Thorpe Meadows Sculpture Park**, one of several open spaces in and around the city with absorbing collections of modern sculpture.

AROUND PETERBOROUGH

LONGTHORPE
2 miles W of Peterborough off the A47

Longthorpe Tower, part of a fortified manor house, is graced by some of the very finest 14th century domestic wall paintings in Europe, featuring scenes both sacred and secular: the Nativity, the Wheel of Life, King David, the Labours of the Months. The paintings were discovered during renovations after the Second World War.

ELTON
6 miles W of Peterborough on the B671

A village on the river Nene, with stone-built houses and thatched roofs. **Elton Hall** is a mixture of styles, with a 15th century tower and chapel, and a major Gothic influence. The grandeur is slightly deceptive, as some of the battlements and turrets were built of wood to save money. The hall's sumptuous rooms are filled with art treasures (Gainsborough, Reynolds, Constable) and the library has wonderful collection of books.

THORNHAUGH
8 miles W of Peterborough off the A1/A47

Hidden away in a quiet valley is **Sacrewell Farm and Country Centre**, whose centrepiece is a working watermill. All kinds of farming equipment are on display, and there's a collection of farm animals, along with gardens, nature and general interest trails, play areas, a gift shop and a restaurant serving light refreshments.

PEAKIRK
7 miles N of Peterborough off the A15

A charming little village, somewhat off the beaten track, with two important attractions. In the wetland to the east of the village are

CROWN & ANCHOR

60 Bridge Street, Deeping St James,
Cambridge PE6 8HA
Tel: 01778 342360

The **Crown & Anchor** in Deeping St James is a traditional public house in the best sense. A typically English country pub, it has exposed beamwork, a stone bar and fireplace and a cosy ambience. Owner Sue Goodman has been in the licenced trade in East Anglia for 16 years, and brings the wealth of her experience to bear on providing excellent service and hospitality. She runs the pub on her own, and makes a point of creating an atmosphere welcoming to men and women alike. Her efficient staff are helpful and friendly. She's also a qualified caterer, as reflected in the fine range of bar snacks on offer. Popular with locals and regulars alike, this welcoming establishment is pleasantly situated opposite the village river and footbridge. Real ales include John Smith Cask and changing guest ales. Open seven days a week and all day at weekends. Accommodation is also available on request.

ROSE GARDEN TEA ROOMS

102 Church Street, Market Deeping, Peterborough, Cambridgeshire PE6 8AL
Tel/Fax: 01778 344719

Rose Garden Tearooms and Bed and Breakfast is a wonderful and charming traditional establishment occupying a Grade II listed building. Originally a blacksmith's dating back to the 1700s, it has served as the village greengrocer's before becoming a tea room in the 1960s. Honeysuckle climbs the garden walls. The rear paved courtyard has tables where guests can enjoy their delicious repast in the sunshine. The interior has exposed beams and other traditional features. Homely and cosy, the menu boasts a range of tempting home-made cakes and pastries.

The dining room is furnished and decorated like a front room, adding to the hospitable and welcoming ambience. Not just open for tea-time, breakfast and lunch are served Tuesday-Sunday all year round, for dishes such as roasts, pies, baguettes and more. And plans are afoot to extend the tea room's hours to serve evening meals (7-11 p.m.) Thursday-Saturday beginning in February 2001. The superior bed and breakfast accommodation comprises one twin and one double guest bedroom, each very comfortable and pleasant. The double room is ensuite, while the twin has a private bath. Guests are welcome to enjoy the lovely garden. Owners Sandra and Peter Hoyland are amiable hosts. Please note that All parts of the B&B are non-smoking.

the **Peakirk Waterfowl Gardens**, 20 acres of gardens and waterways that are home to hundreds of birds from all over the world. The village church is of Norman origin and is the only one in the country dedicated to St Pega, the remains of whose hermit cell can still be seen.

CROWLAND
10 miles NE of Peterborough off the A1073

It is hard to imagine that this whole area was once entirely wetland and marshland, dotted with inhospitable islands. Crowland was one such island, then known as Croyland, and on it was established a small church and hermitage back in the 7th century, which was later to become one of the nation's most important monasteries. The town's impressive parish church was just part of the great edifice which once stood on the site. A wonderful exhibition can be found in the Abbey at Crowland, open all year round. The remains cover a third of the Abbey's original extent.

Crowland's second gem is the unique Trinity Bridge - set in the centre of town on dry land! Built in the 14th century, it has three arches built over one over-arching structure. Before the draining of the Fens, this bridge crossed the point where the River Welland divided into two streams.

THORNEY
8 miles E of Peterborough on the A47

Thorney Abbey, the church of St Mary and St Botolph, is the dominating presence even though what now stands is but a small part of what was once one of the greatest of the Benedictine Abbeys. Gravestones in the churchyard are evidence of a Huguenot colony settling here after fleeing from France in the wake of the St Bartholomew's Day massacre of 1572. The **Thorney Heritage Museum** is a small, independently run museum of great fascination, describing the development of the village from a Saxon monastery, via Benedictine Abbey to a model village built in the 19th century by the Dukes of Bedford. The main innovation was a 10,000 gallon water tank that supplied the whole village; other villages had to use unfiltered river water.

Ye Olde Bridge Inn

The Common, Crowland, Peterborough, Cambridgeshire PE6 0HJ
Tel: 01733 210567 Fax: 01773 210452
email: yeolde_bridgeinn@yahoo.co.uk

Half a mile north of Crowland, **Ye Olde Bridge Inn** is, as its name suggests, is located just off the road near a bridge crossing the River Welland. Dating back some 150 years, the handsome exterior is whitewashed, with new leaded windows and an attractive patio garden to the rear. Inside, traditional low beams and brassware add to the homely and comfortable ambience and old-world feel. this welcoming pub serves a range of real ales including Abbott, Speckled Hen and Tetleys. There's also a good selection of lagers, wines and spirits. The home-cooked meals available offer a tempting range of traditional and more innovative favourites, together with a choice of changing daily specials, all

freshly prepared and expertly presented. In addition to the delicious steaks, chicken and fish dishes, specialities include venison, ostrich, trout and paella. Open: Monday to Thursday 11-3 and 5-1; Friday to Sunday 11-11. Booking advised for Friday-Sunday. The friendly and efficient staff provide a high standard of service. Beginning in 2001 there will be a caravan site adjacent to the pub. Golf enthusiasts will be happy to learn that the inn is handy for Thorney, Spalding and Gedney Hall courses.

THE PLOUGH

Milk and Water Drove, Ramsey Road, Farcet Fen, Peterborough, Cambridgeshire PE7 3DR
Tel: 01733 844307 Fax: 01733 844078

The Plough in Farcet Fen is an excellent pub and restaurant boasting a fine menu, a great selection of real ales and a wonderful atmosphere. Owner Colin Harrison is a master chef who has travelled widely throughout the

world. Originally from Lincolnshire, he took over at the Plough in 1997. He is a talented chef with expertise in a wide spectrum of different cuisines. He is also a friendly and very amiable host. His enthusiasm is infectious, enlivening the atmosphere of this relaxing and welcoming inn.

A traditional ale house dating back to the 1740s, when it served the local farming community. The local community remains loyal, but has been joined by a mixed clientele from near and far, including holidaymakers and tourists, all to enjoy the comfortable ambience. The interior boasts a small, cosy snug and two larger areas where guests can dine. The walls are adorned with old agricultural implements and a selection of china plates. Exposed black beams and brassware add to the traditional feel of this superior inn.

The extensive lawned garden to the rear is set out with picnic tables, overlooking the surrounding countryside. It makes the perfect place to enjoy a relaxing drink or meal when the weather is fine. At

any one time there are six real ales on tap in this Free House, which has won a CAMRA gold award. In addition there is a good range of lagers, wines and spirits.

The menu boasts an impressive variety of home-cooked dishes, from soups and starters such as spare ribs or home-made paté to tempting meals featuring lamb, duck, chicken, fish, steak or vegetables, all expertly prepared and presented. The desserts are definitely worth leaving room for. Snacks are available Monday to Thursday 5.30 to 8.30 p.m., Saturdays 12 to 2 p.m., and Sundays 4 to 8 p.m. Evening meals are served Monday to Thursday 5.30 to 7 p.m.; a la carte from 7 to 8.30 p.m., Friday and Saturday 6 to 9.30 p.m. For a pleasant and memorable meal in comfortable surroundings, look no further.

WHITTLESEY
5 miles E of Peterborough off the A605

The market town of Whittlesey lies close to the western edge of the Fens and is part of one of the last tracts to be drained. Brick-making was a local speciality, and 180' brick chimneys stand as a reminder of a flourishing industry. The **Church of St Andrews** is mainly 14th century, with a 16th century tower, and the chancel, chancel chapels and naves still have their original roofs. A walk round this charming town reveals an interesting variety of buildings: brick, of course, and also some stone, thatch on timber frames, and rare thatched mud boundary walls. A highlight of Whittlesey's year is the **Straw Bear procession** that is part of the four-day January festival. A man clad in a suit of straw dances and prances through the streets, calling at houses and pubs to entertain the townspeople. The origins are obscure: perhaps it stems from pagan times when corn gods were invoked to produce a good harvest; perhaps it is linked with the wicker idols used by the Druids; perhaps it derives from the performing bears which toured the villages until the 17th century. What is certain is that at the end of the jollities the straw suit is ceremoniously burnt. Whittlesey is the birthplace of the writer L P Hartley (*The Go-Between*) and the soldier Sir Harry Smith, hero of many 19th century Indian campaigns. He died in 1860, and the south chapel off St Mary's Church (note the beautiful spire) was restored and named after him.

FLAG FEN
6 miles E of Peterborough
signposted from the A47 and A1139

Flag Fen Bronze Age Excavations comprise massive 3,000-year-old timbers that were part of a major settlement and

Flag Fen

have been preserved in peaty mud; a Roman road with its original surface; re-creations of a Bronze Age settlement; a museum of artefacts; rare breed animals; and a visitor centre with a shop and restaurants. Ongoing excavations, open to the public, make this one of the most important and exciting sites of its kind.

MARCH
14 miles E of Peterborough off the A141

March once occupied the second largest 'island' in the great level of Fens, and as the land was drained the town grew as a trading and religious centre, and in more recent times as a market town and major railway hub. **March and District Museum**, in the High Street, tells the story of the people and

Riverside Walk, March

WOODPECKER COTTAGE

20 Kingswood Road, March,
Cambridgeshire PE15 9RT
Tel: 01354 660188 Fax: 01354 655866
email:johnliz.spencer@talk21.com

For peaceful and quiet accommodation in luxury and yet within easy reach of Cambridge, the Norfolk coast and the many attractions of the area, **Woodpecker Cottage** offers an ideal base. A spacious and impressive modern home situated at the end of a quiet cul-de-sac, the immaculate interior is beautifully furnished and decorated.

There are three comfortable and welcoming guest bedrooms (one double, one twin, one single). The open views over meadows and grazing pastures are truly lovely. The large and attractive rear garden has been tastefully landscaped to include a manicured lawn, fountain and well-stocked fish pond, amid some lovely flowering plants. The patio is the perfect place to relax. Just a 10-minute walk from the busy market town of March with walks along the river bank, it is a true rural idyll. Liz and John Spencer are amiable and helpful hosts who make every effort to ensure that guests have a pleasant and memorable stay. They have the knack of making all their guests feel right at home.

THE WILDFOWL & WETLANDS TRUST

Hundred Foot Bank, Welney, Wisbech, Cambridgeshire PE14 9TN
Tel/Fax: 01353 860711
email: welney@wwt.org.uk website: wwt.org.uk

The **Wildfowl & Wetland Trust Welney** is a wetland paradise of international importance with something to offer whatever the season. In winter, enjoy the magic of hundreds of Whooper and Bewick's Swans accompanied by flocks of thousands of ducks. During the day, carpets of Wigeon graze this precious wetland, while flocks of Pintail, Teal, Gadwall and Shoveler dabble in the pools and

lagoons. Late afternoon is a special time as flocks of swans flight-in to claim their night roosting sites. Summer brings an atmosphere of peace and tranquillity broken only by the piping calls of waders, drumming Snipe and the chatter of warblers. Lush meadows are bordered by a dazzling display of Purple Loosestrife, Great Willowherb and Marsh Woundwort. Visitors can stroll along the boardwalks through rustling reedbeds, and spend a while pond-dipping for water beasts. The Visitor Centre houses displays, educational facilities and a well-stocked gift shop. The Wigeon Tearoom offers a tempting variety of hot and cold food. WWT Welney also runs a packed programme of special events for visitors to enjoy throughout the year.

the history of March and the surrounding area, and includes a working forge and a reconstruction of a turn-of-the-century home. St Wendreda's uniquely dedicated church, at Town End, is notable for its magnificent timber roof, a double hammerbeam with 120 carved angels, a fine font and some impressive gargoyles. John Betjeman declared the church to be 'worth cycling 40 miles into a headwind to see'.

The **Nene-Ouse Navigation Link** runs through the town, affording many attractive riverside walks, and just outside the town, off the B1099, is **Dunhams Wood**, four acres of woodland set among the fens. The site contains an enormous variety of trees, along with sculptures and a miniature railway. Also on the outskirts, signposted from the A141 and B1101, is **Stagsholt Farm Park and Stud**, home to many horses (including the superb Suffolk Punch) and housing a fascinating array of farming and rural bygones.

STONEA
3 miles SE of March off the B1098

Stonea Camp is the lowest 'hill' fort in Britain, built in the Iron Age and unsuccessful against the Romans. It is a scheduled ancient monument whose banks and ditches were restored after excavations in 1991. The site is also an increasingly important habitat for wildlife.

CHATTERIS
8 miles S of March off the A141

A friendly little market town with a museum whose scope is being increased by a move into modern town-centre premises. While work is ongoing, a series of temporary exhibitions will be on show pending the creation of five permanent galleries. The Church of St Peter and St Paul has some 14th century features but is mostly more modern in appearance, having been substantially restored in 1909.

WISBECH

One of the largest of the Fenland towns, a port in medieval times and still enjoying shipping trade with Europe. Somewhere along the navigable channel to the sea King John lost his jewels. Wisbech is at the centre of a thriving agricultural region and the 18th century in particular saw the building of rows of handsome houses, notably in North Brink and South Brink, which face each other across the river. The finest of all the properties is undoubtedly **Peckover House**, built in 1722 and bought at the end of the 18th century by Jonathan Peckover, a member of the Quaker banking family. The family gave the building to the National Trust in 1948. Behind its elegant facade are splendid panelled rooms, Georgian fireplaces with richly carved overmantels, and ornate

THE LAMB & FLAG, MAISON DE LA CHIEN

Main Street, Welney, Cambridgeshire PE14 9RB
Tel: 01354 610242

The Lamb & Flag in Welney is a charming and gracious public house here on the Norfolk/Cambridgeshire border. Thought to be some 300 years old, as its lengthy exterior tells us it was originally a row of traditional cottages. Boasting an impressive Boston creeper covered exterior, this superior pub offers an excellent range of real ales.

The low beamed ceilings and open log fires enhance the cosy, welcoming ambience. Tastefully furnished and decorated throughout, this makes a relaxing place to enjoy the range of drinks and traditional meals, expertly cooked, prepared and presented. Open all day every day, meals are available at every session apart from Sunday evenings. There are also four attractive and comfortable guest bedrooms (two doubles, one twin and one family room), and a full hearty English breakfast. Children are made very welcome and there is a large beer garden as well as ample car parking facilities.

ELGOOD'S BREWERY & GARDENS

North Brink, Wisbech,
Cambridgeshire PE12 1LN
Tel: 01945 583160
Fax: 01945 587711

Elgood's Brewery is a 200-year-old classic Georgian brewery situated on the bank of the River Nene. This friendly and relaxing place is set amid true rural splendour.

The brewery was established in 1795, and was one of the first in this style to be built outside London. It is a lively and welcoming establishment, the perfect setting in which to savour a pint of one of their famous award-winning ales, enjoy a range of delicious snacks and home-made cakes in the cafe, or stroll around the gardens. Visitors can also enjoy observing traditional brewing methods, which use original open copper vessels - and can then sample a selection of real ales.

Famous locally and further afield for its welcoming hospitality and classic ales, Elgood's is not just for real ale enthusiasts - though there's plenty here to delight them as well. Behind the brewery is a four-acre garden with 150-year-old specimen trees, herbaceous borders, a lake, rockery, water features, exotics house, rose and herb gardens, and boasting many original Georgian and Victorian features. Beyond the walled gardens, there are lawns leading to the Millennium Maze, planted in the winter of 1992/93 - photographs of its progress are in the Visitors' Centre. The resident team of gardeners are happy to answer any questions. There is no 'formal route' to follow; visitors are welcome to roam at will, enjoying this marvellous garden, as have the Elgoods for many years.

This family-owned business is still run by the Elgoods: Nigel, his wife Anne and their three daughters. Belinda Sutton and Jennifer Everall are responsible for the Brewery and Claire Simpson,

who is qualified in garden design, has re-landscaped and planted the garden. Other amenities and attractions to delight the visitor include the café and licensed bar, gift and plant shop. The staff are helpful and friendly; in the garden shop they are happy to offer advice. Gardens open: May to September, Wednesday to Friday, Sundays and Bank Holiday Mondays 1-5 p.m.; brewery tours Wednesday to Friday 2 p.m. Please phone for more details.

Georgian Crescent, Wisbech

plaster decorations. At the back of the house is a beautiful walled garden with summerhouses and an orangery.

No 1 South Brink is the birthplace of Octavia Hill (1838-1912), co-founder of the National Trust and a tireless worker for the cause of the poor, particularly in the sphere of housing. The house is now the **Octavia Hill Museum** with displays and exhibits commemorating her work. More Georgian splendour is evident in the area where the Norman castle stood. The castle was replaced by a bishop's palace in 1478 and in the 17th century by a mansion built for Cromwell's Secretary of State John Thurloe. Local builder Joseph Medworth built the present Regency villa in 1816, and of the Thurloe mansion only the gate piers remain. The **Wisbech and Fenland Museum** is one of the oldest purpose-built museums in the country, and in charming

Victorian surroundings visitors can view displays of porcelain, coins, rare rocks, Egyptian tomb treasures and several items of national importance, including the manuscript of Charles Dickens' *Great Expectations*, Napoleon's Sèvres breakfast set captured at Waterloo, and an ivory chess set that belonged to Louis XIV.

Wisbech is the stage for East Anglia's premier church **flower festival**, with flowers in four churches, strawberry teas, crafts, bric-a-brac, plants and a parade of floats. The event takes place at the beginning of July. The most important of the churches is the Church of St Peter and St Paul, with two naves under one roof, and an independent tower with a peal of ten bells. Note the royal arms of James I and the 17th century wall monuments in the chancel. Other sights to

Museum Square, Wisbech

see in Wisbech include Elgoods Brewery on North Brink and the impressive 68' limestone memorial to Thomas Clarkson, one of the

WISBECH WHOLEFOODS

8 North Street, Old Market, Wisbech, Cambridgeshire PE13 1NP
Tel: 01945 464468

The charming **Wisbech Wholefoods** has been providing a healthy alternative since 1985. Occupying a handsome Georgian property in Wisbech's Old Market, this small and intimate shop offers a wonderful variety of organic foods and wines, beers and ciders, including home-baked breads, nuts, cereals, pasta, pulses, and dried and fresh fruits, as well as a selection of Bach Flower Remedies, homeopathic medicines and aromatherapy products. Accommodation is also available in the two guest bedrooms.

MAISON DE LA CHIEN

35 Churchill Road, Gorefield, nr Wisbech,
Cambridgeshire PE13 4NA
Tel/Fax: 01945 870789 Mobile: 07790 575219
e-mail: hols-maisonchien@faxvia.net

In 1997 Lilian and Don Barnard decided to start offering superior bed and breakfast accommodation from their lovely brickbuilt home, **Maison de la Chien**, in the handsome village of Gorefield, just a short drive from Wisbech. Friendly and welcoming hosts, they gave their charming establishment its name in honour of their two friendly Yorkshire terriers, 'Buttons' and 'Candy'. There are two cosy guest bedrooms (one double, one twin). The spacious twin room overlooks the garden. Tastefully furnished and decorated, they come equipped with books, television and videos. Lilian bakes her own bread and makes her own jams and preserves. Local produce and organic ingredients are used wherever possible. Evening meals by arrangement - all diets are catered for; free packed lunches. Handy for Peckover House and the many sights and attractions in this part of Cambridgeshire, it makes an ideal and most comfortable base. No smoking.

THE CHEQUERS INN

2 March Road, Friday Bridge, Wisbech,
Cambridgeshire PE14 0HF
Tel: 01945 860059

The Chequers Inn is a handsome and welcoming pub occupying a distinguished Grade II Listed building. A bill of sale on the pub wall shows that back in 1843 the establishment - then an inn and blacksmiths - was sold for the princely sum of £163. Situated on the village square, there is a large garden with children's area to the rear. The interior is simply lovely, with traditional oak beams, a quarry tiled floor, brick bar and open fire. The separate dining room overlooks the square. Popular with locals and with visitors to the Fens and the region's many other attractions, this fine pub offers a range of real ales including the local Elgoods brews, together with a good variety of lagers, wines and spirits. Delicious meals and snacks are also available. Open seven days a week, this charming inn also boasts cosy and comfortable accommodation in two tasteful double bedrooms.

THE RED HART INN

Main Road, Three Holes, Wisbech,
Cambridgeshire PE14 9JR
Tel: 01945 773328
e-mail: judydaveflather@lineone.net

Originally a cafe, rebuilt and restored as a pub in 1934, **The Red Hart Inn** is a handsome, extensive and very welcoming place to stop and enjoy a quiet, relaxing drink or meal. This traditional inn boasts a public bar with open fire, old photographs and agricultural/fishing implements adorning the walls and classic games such as darts and board games. The loung bar has a collection of famous faces over the bar - guests enjoy a game of 'guess who' as they try to identify the stars in the photographs. Real ales on tap include Elgoods, together with a good range of lagers, wines and spirits. The home-cooked food is excellent, with everything from bar snacks to delicious beef, chicken, seafood and vegetarian dishes, all freshly prepared and cooked to order. On Friday and Saturday evenings and Sunday lunchtimes, the tempting carvery is a popular choice. This fine pub also offers five very comfortable guest bedrooms - a family room (sleeps four), three doubles and a single.

earliest leaders of the movement to abolish slavery. The monument was designed by Sir Giles Gilbert Scott in Gothic style.

AROUND WISBECH

WEST WALTON AND WALTON HIGHWAY
3 miles NE of Wisbech off the A47/B198

Several attractions here, notably the Church of St Mary the Virgin with its magnificent 13th century detached tower that dominates the landscape. West Walton is home to the **Fenland and West Norfolk Aviation Museum**, whose exhibits include Rolls-Royce Merlin engines, a Lightning jet, a Vampire and a Jumbo jet cockpit simulator. The museum is open weekends in the summer.

LEVERINGTON
1 mile NW of Wisbech off the A1101

The tower and spire of the Church of St Leonard date from the 13th and 14th centuries. The most exceptional feature of an exceptionally interesting church is the 15th century stained-glass Jesse window in the north aisle. There are many fine memorials in the churchyard. Oliver Goldsmith wrote *She Stoops to Conquer* while staying in Leverington.

PARSON DROVE
6 miles W of Wisbech on the B1187

Parson Drove is a Fenland village which Samuel Pepys visited in 1663. He stayed at the village's **Swan Inn** and mentions it in his diaries. It was a centre of the woad industry until 1914, when the last remaining woad mill was established. Parson Drove is most

---

RAILWAY & IVYWOOD CARRIAGES

Mandalay, Station Road, Wisbech St Mary, Wisbech, Cambridgeshire PE13 4RY
Tel: 01945 410680

In quiet fields on the outskirts of Wisbech St Mary, **Railway & Ivywood Carriages** present a unique opportunity for those looking for a place to stay. As their name suggests, these properties are in fact two converted Victorian railway carriages, fitted and decorated to offer very comfortable and charming accommodation. The site also has a lovely Edwardian farmhouse. These self-catering properties are just the thing for rail buffs or anyone who wants a taste of gracious
living from a bygone age. Both carriages offer kitchen/diner, lounge and full bathroom. The Railway Carriage has a double bedroom (there's also a folding single bed) and is set in its own private garden, leading to orchards. Ivywood Carriage also has its own garden and patio area, as well as two double bedrooms (and spare single folding bed). Woodlands farmhouse is situated in a quiet country lane. It boasts two double bedrooms and a single, large dining room, full bathroom and kitchen. All linen provided. Open all year round.

COMMON RIGHT BARNS

Plash Drove, Tholomas Drove, Wisbech St Mary,
Cambridgeshire PE13 4SP
Tel/Fax: 01945 410424

For those seeking self-catering accommodation in renovated farm buildings, **Common Right Barns** is the place to look. Signed from the A47 between Peterborough and Wisbech at Guyhirn, there are two properties - The Barn, which sleeps up to four people, and The Stable, for two persons - offering comfortable and pleasant accommodation in the heart of rural Fenland. Home-cooked breakfast and dinner are available. Wheelchair friendly.

certainly not the *"heathen place"* once described by Pepys!

The Parson Drove Visitors Centre is set in the old Victorian lock-up on the village green, a building with an unusual 170-year history. Photographs and documents trace the story of this lovely Fens village.

List of Tourist Information Centres

CAMBRIDGESHIRE

CAMBRIDGE

Wheeler Street, Cambridge CB2 3QB

Tel: 01223 322640

ELY

Oliver Cromwell's House,
29 St Mary's Street, Ely CB7 4HF

Tel: 01353 662062 Fax: 01353 668518

e-mail: elytic@compuserve.co.uk

HUNTINGDON

The Library, Princes Street,
Huntingdon PE29 3PH

Tel: 01480 388588 Fax: 01482 388591

PETERBOROUGH

3 Minster Precincts,
Peterborough PE1 1XS

Tel: 01733 452336 Fax: 01733 452353

WISBECH

2-3 Bridge Street, Wisbech PE13 1EW

Tel: 01945 583263 Fax: 01945 463078

ESSEX

BRAINTREE

Town Hall Centre, Market Square,
Braintree CM7 3YG

Tel: 01376 550066 Fax: 01376 344345

BRENTWOOD

Pepperell House, 44 High Street,
Brentwood CM14 4AJ

Tel: 01277 200300 Fax: 01277 202375

CHELMSFORD

County Hall, Market Road,
Chelmsford CM1 1GG

Tel: 01245 283400 Fax: 01245 430705

CLACTON-ON-SEA

23 Pier Avenue,
Clacton-on-Sea CO15 1QD

Tel: 01255 423400 Fax: 01255 430906

COLCHESTER

Visitor Information Centre,
1 Queen Street, Colchester CO1 2PJ

Tel: 01206 282920 Fax: 01206 282924

HARWICH

Essex County Council, Iconfield Park,
Parkeston, Harwich CO12 4EN

Tel: 01255 506139   Fax: 01255 240570

MALDON

Coach Lane, Maldon CM9 4UH

Tel: 01621 856503 Fax: 01621 875873

SAFFRON WALDEN

1 Market Place, Market Square,
Saffron Walden CB10 1HR

Tel: 01799 510444 Fax: 01799 510445

SOUTHEND-ON-SEA

19 High Street,
Southend-on-Sea SS1 1JE

Tel: 01702 215120 Fax: 01702 431449

THURROCK

Granada Motorway Services,
M25 West Thurrock, Grays RM16 3BG

Tel: 01708 863733 Fax: 01708 862440

WALTHAM ABBEY

4 Highbridge Street,
Waltham Abbey EN9 1DG

Tel: 01992 652295 Fax: 01992 652295

NORFOLK

AYLSHAM

Bure Valley Railway Station,
Norwich Road, Aylsham NR11 6BW

Tel: 01263 733903 Fax: 01263 733814

CROMER

Cromer Bus Station, Prince of Wales
Road, Cromer NR27 9HS

Tel: 01263 512497 Fax: 01263 513613

DISS

The Meresmouth, Mere Street,
Diss IP22 3AG

Tel: 01379 650523 Fax: 01379 650838

FAKENHAM

Fakenham Connect, Oak Street,
Fakenham NR21 9DY

Tel: 01328 850102 Fax: 01328 850103

GREAT YARMOUTH

Town Hall, Great Yarmouth NR3 2PX

Tel: 01493 846345 Fax: 01493 846221

HOVETON

Station Road, Hoveton NR12 8UR

Tel/Fax: 01603 782281

HUNSTANTON

Town Hall, The Green,
Hunstanton PE36 6BQ

Tel: 01485 532610 Fax: 01485 533972

KING'S LYNN

Custom House, Purfleet Quay,
King's Lynn PE30 1HP

Tel: 01553 819440 Fax: 01553 819441

MUNDESLEY

2 Station Road, Mundesley NR11 8JH

Tel: 01263 721070 Fax: 01263 722796

NORWICH

The Guildhall, Gaol Hill,
Norwich NR2 1NF

Tel: 01603 666071 Fax: 01603 765389

SHERINGHAM

Station Approach,
Sheringham NR26 8RA

Tel: 01263 824329

WALSINGHAM

Common Place,
Little Walsingham NR22 6BP

Tel: 01328 820510

WELLS-NEXT-THE-SEA

Staithe Street,
Wells-next-the-Sea NR23 1AN

Tel: 01328 710885

SUFFOLK

ALDEBURGH

152 High Street, Aldeburgh IP15 5AQ

Tel/Fax: 01728 453637

BECCLES

The Ouay, Fen Lane, Beccles NR34 9BH

Tel/Fax: 01502 713196

BURY ST EDMUNDS

6 Angel Hill,
Bury St Edmunds IP33 1UZ.

Tel: 01284 764667 Fax: 01284 757084

FELIXSTOWE

Sea Front, Felixstowe IP11 2AE

Tel: 01394 276770 Fax: 01394 277456

IPSWICH

St Stephen's Church, St Stephen's Lane,
Ipswich IP1 1DP

Tel: 01473 258070 Fax: 01473 432017

LAVENHAM

Lady Street, Market Place,
Lavenham CO10 9RA

Tel: 01787 248207

LOWESTOFT

The East Point Pavilion, Royal Plain,
Lowestoft NR33 OAP

Tel: 01502 533600 Fax: 01502 539023

NEWMARKET

Palace House Mansion, Palace Street,
Newmarket CB8 8EP

Tel: 01638 667200 Fax: 01638 660394

SOUTHWOLD

69 The High Street,
Southwold IP18 6DS

Tel: 01502 724729 Fax: 01502 722978

STOWMARKET, MID-SUFFOLK

Wilkes Way, Stowmarket IP14 1DE

Tel: 01449 676800 Fax: 01449 614691

SUDBURY

Town Hall, Market Hill,
Sudbury CO10 1TL

Tel: 01787 881320

WOODBRIDGE TIC

Station Buildings,
Woodbridge IP12 4AJ

Tel: 01394 382240 Fax: 01394 386337

Index of Towns, Villages and Places of Interest

List of Advertisers

Hidden Places Order Form

To order any of our publications just fill in the payment details below and complete the order form *overleaf*. For orders of less than 4 copies please add £1 per book for postage and packing. Orders over 4 copies are P & P free.

Please Complete Either:

I enclose a cheque for £ [   ] made payable to Travel Publishing Ltd

Or:

Card No: [   ]

Expiry Date: [   ]

Signature: [   ]

NAME: [   ]

ADDRESS: [   ]

POSTCODE: [   ]

TEL NO: [   ]

Please either send or telephone your order to:

Travel Publishing Ltd   Tel : 0118 981 7777
7a Apollo House   Fax: 0118 982 0077
Calleva Park
Aldermaston
Berks, RG7 8TN

	PRICE	QUANTITY	VALUE
Hidden Places Regional Titles			
Cambs & Lincolnshire	£7.99	....	....
Chilterns	£8.99	....	....
Cornwall	£8.99	....	....
Derbyshire	£7.99	....	....
Devon	£8.99	....	....
Dorset, Hants & Isle of Wight	£8.99	....	....
East Anglia	£8.99	....	....
Gloucestershire & Wiltshire	£7.99	....	....
Heart of England	£7.99	....	....
Hereford, Worcs & Shropshire	£7.99	....	....
Highlands & Islands	£7.99	....	....
Kent	£8.99	....	....
Lake District & Cumbria	£7.99	....	....
Lancashire & Cheshire	£8.99	....	....
Lincolnshire	£8.99	....	....
Northumberland & Durham	£8.99	....	....
Somerset	£7.99	....	....
Sussex	£7.99	....	....
Thames Valley	£7.99	....	....
Yorkshire	£7.99	....	....
Hidden Places National Titles			
England	£9.99	....	....
Ireland	£9.99	....	....
Scotland	£9.99	....	....
Wales	£11.99	....	....
Hidden Inns Titles			
West Country	£5.99	....	....
South East	£5.99	....	....
South	£5.99	....	....
South and Central Scotland	£5.99	....	....
Wales	£5.99	....	....

*For orders of less than 4 copies please add £1 per book for
postage & packing. Orders over 4 copies P & P free.*

Hidden Places Reader Reaction

The *Hidden Inns* research team would like to receive reader's comments on any visitor attractions or places reviewed in the book and also recommendations for suitable entries to be included in the next edition. This will help ensure that the *Hidden Inns* series continues to provide its readers with useful information on the more interesting, unusual or unique features of each attraction or place ensuring that their stay in the local area is an enjoyable and stimulating experience.

To provide your comments or recommendations would you please complete the forms below and overleaf as indicated and send to:

The Research Department, Travel Publishing Ltd,
7a Apollo House, Calleva Park, Aldermaston, Reading, RG7 8TN.

Your Name:

Your Address:

Your Telephone Number:

Please tick as appropriate: Comments ☐ Recommendation ☐

Name of *"Hidden Place"*:

Address:

Telephone Number:

Name of Contact:

Hidden Places Reader Reaction

Comment or Reason for Recommendation:

....

....

....

....

....

....

....

....

....

....

....

....

Hidden Places Reader Reaction

The *Hidden Inns* research team would like to receive reader's comments on any visitor attractions or places reviewed in the book and also recommendations for suitable entries to be included in the next edition. This will help ensure that the *Hidden Inns* series continues to provide its readers with useful information on the more interesting, unusual or unique features of each attraction or place ensuring that their stay in the local area is an enjoyable and stimulating experience.

To provide your comments or recommendations would you please complete the forms below and overleaf as indicated and send to:

The Research Department, Travel Publishing Ltd,
7a Apollo House, Calleva Park, Aldermaston, Reading, RG7 8TN.

Your Name:

Your Address:

Your Telephone Number:

Please tick as appropriate: Comments ☐   Recommendation ☐

Name of *"Hidden Place"*:

Address:

Telephone Number:

Name of Contact:

Hidden Places Reader Reaction

Comment or Reason for Recommendation:

....

....

....

....

....

....

....

....

....

....

....

....